HISTORICAL DICTIONARIES
OF LITERATURE AND THE ARTS
Jon Woronoff, Series Editor

1. Science Fiction Literature, by Brian Stableford, 2004.
2. Horror Literature, by John Clute, 2005.
3. American Radio Soap Operas, by Jim Cox, 2005.
4. Japanese Traditional Theatre, by Samuel L. Leiter, 2006.
5. Fantasy Literature, by Brian Stableford, 2005.
6. Australian and New Zealand Cinema, by Albert Moran and Errol Vieth, 2006.
7. African-American Television, by Kathleen Fearn-Banks, 2006.
8. Lesbian Literature, by Meredith Miller, 2006.
9. Scandinavian Literature and Theater, by Jan Sjåvik, 2006.
10. Sacred Music, by Joseph P. Swain, 2006.

Historical Dictionary of Scandinavian Literature and Theater

Jan Sjåvik

Historical Dictionaries of Literature and the Arts, No. 9

The Scarecrow Press, Inc.
Lanham, Maryland • Toronto • Oxford
2006

SCARECROW PRESS, INC.

Published in the United States of America
by Scarecrow Press, Inc.
A wholly owned subsidiary of
The Rowman & Littlefield Publishing Group, Inc.
4501 Forbes Boulevard, Suite 200, Lanham, Maryland 20706
www.scarecrowpress.com

PO Box 317
Oxford
OX2 9RU, UK

Copyright © 2006 by Jan Sjåvik

All rights reserved. No part of this publication may be reproduced, stored in a retrieval system, or transmitted in any form or by any means, electronic, mechanical, photocopying, recording, or otherwise, without the prior permission of the publisher.

British Library Cataloguing in Publication Information Available

Library of Congress Cataloging-in-Publication Data

Sjåvik, Jan.
 Historical dictionary of Scandinavian literature and theater / Jan Sjåvik.
   p. cm. — (Historical dicationaries of literature and the arts ; no. 9)
 Includes bibliographical references.
 ISBN-13: 978-0-8108-5563-2 (alk. paper)
 ISBN-10: 0-8108-5563-1 (alk. paper)
   1. Scandinavian literature—Bio-bibliography—Dictionaries. 2. Authors, Scandinavian—Biography—Dictionaries. I. Title. II. Series.
PT7017.S53 2006
839'.50903—dc22
[B]   2006042261

∞ ™ The paper used in this publication meets the minimum requirements of American National Standard for Information Sciences—Permanence of Paper for Printed Library Materials, ANSI/NISO Z39.48-1992.
Manufactured in the United States of America.

Contents

Editor's Foreword *(Jon Woronoff)*	vii
Acknowledgments	ix
Reader's Note	xi
Chronology	xiii
Introduction	xxv
THE DICTIONARY	1
Bibliography	297
General Scandinavian Literary History and Criticism	300
Denmark	301
Finland	317
Iceland	324
Norway	327
Sweden	340
About the Author	361

Foreword

Although Scandinavia is a fairly small region, its literature is amazingly varied and rich. It includes the national literatures of Denmark, Norway, Sweden, Finland, and Iceland, as well as some rather amazing regional variations. It stretches over time from the Old Norse sagas to the present day, passing through all major literary currents, including romanticism, realism, naturalism, expressionism, modernism, and postmodernism, not to forget feminism. The themes are the greater and lesser ones that concern us all, from nationalism and war, to the meaning of life, political and economic cooperation and exploitation, and love and marriage. This work was generated by numerous Scandinavian authors who are poorly known, if at all, outside of their respective country or region, but also others who have been translated widely and have entered world literature, such as Henrik Ibsen, August Strindberg, Isak Dinesen, Søren Kierkegaard, and Hans Christian Andersen. This literature consists of poetry and novels, short stories and fairy tales, essays and criticism, indeed, all the genres, and most impressively drama. This is consequently a literature that deserves to be known and studied.

But that is not so easy, considering that more than half a dozen languages and dialects are involved, and the portion that has been translated, while considerable, does not quite cover the whole field. So it is particularly helpful to have a book like this *Historical Dictionary of Scandinavian Literature and Theater*. It is a guide to the literature, in its variety and richness, with several hundred entries on specific authors (some well known, others worthy of being better known) which introduce both the author and the oeuvre. Other entries deal with specific periods and currents, themes and groups, favored topics and prizes. The introduction provides the broad historical background, while the chronology places writers and works in their historical setting. The bibliography, uncommonly important for a literature that is less studied than some, is also unusually complete and comprehensive.

This volume was written by Jan Sjåvik, an associate professor of Scandinavian studies at the University of Washington in Seattle, where he has been on the faculty since 1978. He has written numerous articles on Scandinavian writers as well as two books. As should be obvious from the contents, he has also regularly reviewed books and written entries on specific authors for other reference works. This book goes considerably further, including the whole range, and could not have been achieved without a long career devoted to the subject. Although his own background is Norwegian, Sjåvik is hardly parochial, and his presentation of the variety and richness of the field is amply evident.

Jon Woronoff
Series Editor

Acknowledgments

I thank my colleagues at the Department of Scandinavian Studies, University of Washington, for their interest in and support of this project, especially Lotta Gavel Adams, Andy Nestingen, and Marianne Stecher-Hansen. I am also grateful to our department's research assistant, Mia Spangenberg, for her help with the Finnish material.

Reader's Note

The entries in the dictionary appear alphabetically according to the order of the 26 letters used in English and not as it is done in the Scandinavian languages. Consequently, *ä*, *æ*, and *å* are treated as if they were *a*; *ö* and *ø* are treated the same as *o*, and so forth. When a term has an entry of its own in the dictionary, the term appears in **boldface** the first time it is mentioned in an entry other than its own.

Scandinavian-language titles are followed by parentheses that contain the year of publication as well as the title in English translation. The notation tr. before the title in English signifies that the book has been published in English translation with that title. Otherwise the translations of titles are my own. However, some titles in Finnish have been translated with the aid of George Schoolfield, ed., *A History of Finland's Literature*, and Virpi Zuck, ed., *Dictionary of Scandinavian Literature*, as well as with the assistance of my colleague Andrew K. Nestingen.

Chronology

400 The approximate time of the Migration Period. The approximate beginning time for the use of runic letters.
950 Approximately the middle of the life of Icelandic poet Egil Skallagrímsson.
1178 The birth of Icelandic historian Snorri Sturluson.
1323 Finland becomes a province under Sweden.
1349 The Black Death arrives in Bergen, Norway.
1397 The beginning of the Kalmar Union.
1524 The New Testament is translated into Danish.
1526 The New Testament is translated into Swedish.
1618 Thirty Years War begins.
1672 Thomas Kingo, Danish poet, publishes *Kroneborgs korte Beskrivelse*.
1685 Leonora Christina, Danish writer, is released from prison, after which she completes *Jammers Minde*.
1722 Ludvig Holberg publishes *Jeppe paa Bierget*, one of a long series of Danish comedies.
1732 Olof von Dalin begins publication of Swedish periodical *Then Swänska Argus*.
1739 Norwegian poet Petter Dass's long, descriptive *Nordlands trompet* is published, 32 years after his death.
1744 Hedvig Charlotta Nordenflycht, Swedish poet, publishes *Qvinligt Tankespel af en Herdinna i Norden*.
1758 Swedish philosopher Emanuel Swedenborg publishes *De coelo et de inferno* (*Heaven and Hell*).
1772 Johan Herman Wessel, Norwegian writer, publishes his satirical drama *Kierlighed uden Strømper*.
1774 Danish writer Johannes Ewald publishes the drama *Balders Død*, an early example of the literary use of Old Norse material.

1786 **19 January**: The opera *Gustaf Wasa* premieres, written by Swedish king Gustaf III in collaboration with Johan Henric Kellgren.
1790 Carl Michael Bellman, Swedish poet, publishes *Fredmans epistlar*.
1803 Danish writer Adam Oehlenschläger publishes *Digte*, which includes the poem "Guldhornene," a central text in Scandinavian national romanticism.
1809 Sweden cedes Finland to Russia. Danish poet and theologian N. F. S. Grundtvig publishes *Optrin af Kiempelivets Undergang i Nord*.
1814 **17 May**: The Norwegian constitution is signed at Eidsvoll. Norway is ceded by Denmark to Sweden.
1819 Swedish poet Anna Maria Lenngren's *Skaldeförsök* is published, two years after her death. Maurits Hansen publishes his short story "Luren," an early national romantic prose text in Norway.
1821 Erik Johan Stagnelius, Swedish poet, publishes *Liljor i Saron*.
1824 Danish writer Steen Steensen Blicher publishes *Brudstykker af en Landsbydegns Dagbog*. Poul Martin Møller, Danish writer, publishes *En dansk Students Eventyr*. Per Daniel Amadeus Atterbom, Swedish writer, publishes *Lycksalighetens ö*.
1825 Johan Ludvig Heiberg, Danish writer, publishes the first of several vaudevilles, *Kong Salomon og Jørgen Hattemager*.
1828 Danish short story writer Thomasine Gyllembourg publishes *En Hverdags-Historie*. Christian Winther, Danish writer, publishes *Digte*.
1830 Henrik Wergeland, Norwegian writer, publishes his epic poem *Skabelsen, Mennesket og Messias*.
1834 Norwegian poet Johan Sebastian Welhaven publishes *Norges Dæmring*, a cycle of sonnets.
1835 Elias Lönnrot, Finnish folklorist-philologist, publishes the old *Kalevala*. Danish writer Hans Christian Andersen publishes the novel *Improvisatoren* and his first children's story collection *Eventyr, fortalte for Børn*. Icelandic writer Jónas Hallgrímsson and three of his friends found the annual *Fjölnir*.
1837 Erik Gustaf Geijer, Swedish poet, publishes *Den blå boken*.
1839 Swedish writer Carl Jonas Love Almqvist publishes the novel

Det går an, which argues in favor of women's rights and is an early example of realist literature in Scandinavia.
1841 Swedish poet Esaias Tegnér publishes *Kronbruden*.
1842 Danish writer Frederik Paludan-Müller publishes the first part of the epic *Adam Homo*.
1843 Søren Kierkegaard, Danish philosopher, publishes *Enten-Eller* under the pseudonym Victor Eremita.
1844 Johan Ludvig Runeberg, Finland-Swedish writer, publishes *Kung Fjalar*.
1845 Danish writer Meïr Goldschmidt publishes *En Jøde*.
1850 Danish novelist Mathilde Fibiger publishes *Clara Raphael: Tolv Breve*, a milestone in Scandinavian women's literature.
1853 Zacharias Topelius, Finland-Swedish writer, publishes the first volume of *Fältskärns berättelser*. Swedish writer Fredrika Bremer publishes *Hemmen i nya världen*, drawing on a visit to the United States.
1854 Camilla Collett publishes the first part of *Amtmandens Døttre*, Norway's first novel to deal with women's issues.
1857 Danish novelist Hans Egede Schack publishes *Phantasterne*. Norwegian writer Bjørnstjerne Bjørnson publishes *Synnøve Solbakken*, the first of a series of prose narratives characterized by their use of everyday speech.
1859 Viktor Rydberg, Swedish writer, publishes *Den siste atenaren*.
1861 Norwegian writer Aasmund Olafsson Vinje publishes *Ferdaminni fraa Sumaren 1860*.
1863 Ivar Aasen publishes *Symra*, a collection in which he uses his newly created form of written Norwegian, *Landsmaal*, later known as *nynorsk*.
1867 Henrik Ibsen publishes *Peer Gynt*, Norway's national drama.
1870 Aleksis Kivi publishes the first novel written in Finnish, *Seitsemän veljestä*.
1871 **3 November**: Georg Brandes holds his first lecture at the University of Copenhagen, in which he calls for literature to debate current issues.
1872 Swedish dramatist August Strindberg publishes the prose version of *Mäster Olof*.
1880 Danish writer Herman Bang publishes *Haabløse Slægter*, a novel about a family's decline. Danish writer Jens Peter Jacob-

sen publishes *Niels Lyhne*. Norwegian writer Alexander Kielland publishes *Garman og Worse*.

1883 Karl August Tavaststjerna, Finland-Swedish writer, publishes *För morgonbris*. Norwegian writer Jonas Lie publishes *Familjen paa Gilje*, a novel critical of the upbringing of women.

1885 Finnish writer Juhani Aho publishes *Papin tytär*. Swedish writer Victoria Benedictsson publishes *Pengar*. Norwegian writer Amalie Skram publishes *Constance Ring*, one of the most typical examples of naturalism in Scandinavian literature.

1889 Verner von Heidenstam, Swedish writer, publishes both the essay *Renässans*, a brief against the naturalists, and the novel *Endymion*.

1890 Swedish writers Oscar Levertin and Verner von Heidenstam publish the satirical essay "Pepitas bröllop." Norwegian writer Knut Hamsun publishes his groundbreaking psychological novel *Sult*, one of the foundational texts of modernism.

1891 Gustaf Fröding, Swedish poet, publishes *Gitarr och dragharmonika*. Swedish novelist Selma Lagerlöf publishes *Gösta Berlings saga*, a psychological novel of cultural change. Arne Garborg publishes *Trætte Mænd*, one of the first novels to depart from naturalist aesthetics in Norway.

1894 Danish writer Johannes Jørgensen publishes *Bekendelse*, an example of the concern about religion found in the 1890s.

1895 Minna Canth, Finnish writer, publishes *Anna-Liisa*.

1897 Einar Benediktsson, Icelandic writer, publishes *Sögur og kvæði*.

1898 Henrik Pontoppidan, Danish writer, publishes the first volume of *Lykke-Per*. Swedish poet Erik Axel Karlfeldt publishes *Fridolins visor och andra dikter*.

1900 Danish writer Johannes V. Jensen publishes *Kongens Fald*.

1903 Danish writer Thit Jensen publishes *To Søstre*.

1904 Finnish writer Joel Lehtonen publishes *Paholaisen viulu*.

1905 The union between Norway and Sweden ends. Finnish writer Eino Leino publishes *Päivä Helsingissä*. Swedish writer Hjalmar Söderberg publishes *Doktor Glas*, an example of Scandinavian decadent literature.

1906 Martin Andersen Nexø, Danish writer, publishes the first volume of his epic novel *Pelle Erobreren*. Swedish writer Vilhelm Ekelund publishes *Havets stjärna*.

1908 Swedish writer Elin Wägner publishes *Norrtullsligan: Elisabeths krönika*.
1910 Danish writer Karin Michaëlis publishes *Den farlige Alder*.
1912 Marie Bregendahl, Danish writer, publishes *En Dødsnat*. Icelandic writer Gunnar Gunnarsson publishes the first volume of his novel series *Borgslægtens Historie*.
1916 Finland-Swedish poet Edith Södergran publishes *Dikter*, a collection in which free verse is used. Swedish writer Pär Lagerkvist publishes *Ångest*, a collection of early modernist poetry.
1917 Agnes Henningsen, Danish writer, publishes *Den store Kærlighed*.
1918 Runar Schildt, Finland-Swedish writer, publishes *Perdita och andra noveller*, which includes "Den svagare."
1919 Finnish writer Frans Emil Sillanpää publishes *Hurskas kurjuus*. Swedish writer Hjalmar Bergman publishes *Markurells i Wadköping*. Hagar Olsson, Finland-Swedish critic and writer, publishes *Kvinnan och nåden*.
1920 Norwegian writer Sigrid Undset inaugurates her medieval trilogy *Kristin Lavransdatter* with the publication of *Kransen*.
1921 Icelandic writer Guðmundur Gíslason Hagalín publishes *Blindsker*.
1922 Agnes von Krusenstjerna, Swedish novelist, publishes *Tony växer upp*.
1923 Johan Falkberget, Norwegian novelist, publishes his Christian-existentialist *Den fjerde nattevakt*.
1924 Ilmari Kianto publishes *Ryysyrannan Jooseppi*, a novel about backwoods Finnish farmers. Ole E. Rølvaag publishes *I de dage*, the first part of a tetralogy depicting Norwegian settlers on the American frontier in the 1870s.
1925 Sophus Claussen publishes *Heroica*, which contains "Atomernes Oprør," one of Denmark's canonical modernist poems. Rabbe Enckell, Finland-Swedish writer, publishes *Flöjtblåsarlycka*.
1926 Norwegian writer Cora Sandel publishes *Alberte og Jakob*, the first volume in a modernist trilogy about a young woman's artistic development.
1927 Halldór Laxness, Icelandic writer, publishes *Vefarinn mikli frá Kasmír*.

1928 Finnish writer Aino Kallas publishes *Sudenmorsian*. Hans Kirk publishes *Fiskerne*, an early Danish collective novel with a strong Marxist and Freudian slant. Artur Lundkvist, Swedish writer, publishes *Glöd*.

1929 Norwegian writer Olav Duun publishes *Medmenneske*, the first volume in a trilogy about the nature of evil.

1930 Tom Kristensen publishes *Hærværk*, one of Denmark's great modernist novels.

1931 Knud Sønderby, Danish writer, publishes *Midt i en Jazztid*.

1932 Danish playwright Kaj Munk publishes *Ordet*. Jacob Paludan, Danish writer, publishes the first volume of *Jørgen Stein*. Swedish writer Gunnar Ekelöf publishes *Sent på jorden*. Swedish writer Harry Martinson publishes *Resor utan mål*.

1933 Ivar Lo-Johansson publishes *Godnatt, jord*, a collective novel about poor farm workers in Sweden. Moa Martinson publishes *Kvinnor och äppelträd*, one of the central texts in Swedish literature by women. Aksel Sandemose, Norwegian writer, publishes his psychological novel *En flyktning krysser sitt spor*.

1934 Karen Blixen, Danish writer, publishes *Seven Gothic Tales*. Snorri Hjartarson publishes *Høit flyver ravnen*, a novel about an Icelandic artist living in Norway. Steinn Steinarr, Icelandic poet, publishes *Rauður loginn brann*.

1935 Danish writer Kjeld Abell publishes *Melodien der blev væk*. Swedish writer Jan Fridegård publishes *Jag, Lars Hård*.

1938 Hans Scherfig, Danish novelist, publishes *Den forsvundne Fuldmegtig*.

1939 Jørgen-Frantz Jacobsen, Faroese and Danish writer, publishes *Barbara*.

1940 **9 April**: Germany attacks Denmark and Norway. Swedish writer Karin Boye publishes *Kallocain*, a dystopian novel about the dangers of totalitarianism.

1941 Danish writer Tove Ditlevsen publishes *Man gjorde et Barn Fortræd*.

1942 Erik Lindegren, Swedish modernist poet, publishes *Mannen utan väg*.

1943 Swedish writer Lars Ahlin publishes *Tåbb med manifestet*.

1944 Swedish writer Vilhelm Moberg publishes *Soldat med brutet gevär*.

1945 **8 May**: World War II ends in Denmark and Norway. Finnish writer Mika Waltari publishes *Sinuhe, egyptiläinen*. Astrid Lindgren, Swedish writer of children's books, publishes *Pippi Långstrump*, the first book in a long series about Pippi and her friends.
1946 Swedish writer Stig Dagerman publishes *De dömdas ö*. Finland-Swedish writer Bo Carpelan publishes *Som en dunkel värme*.
1947 Finland-Swedish writer Walentin Chorell publishes *Jörgen Hemmelinks stora augusti*. Sigurd Hoel publishes *Møte ved milepelen*, a novel about life in Norway during World War II.
1948 Danish writer Frank Jæger publishes *Dydige Digte*. Swedish writer Willy Kyrklund publishes *Ångvälten och andra noveller*.
1949 Tove Jansson, Finland-Swedish writer, publishes her first Moomin novel, *Trollkarlens hatt*. Danish writer H. C. Branner publishes *Rytteren*. Swedish novelist Eyvind Johnson publishes *Drömmar om rosor och eld*. Vilhelm Moberg publishes *Utvandrarna*, the first volume in a series of novels about the emigration from Sweden to America.
1950 Danish writer Martin A. Hansen publishes *Løgneren*. Faroese and Danish writer William Heinesen publishes *De fortabte spillemænd*. Swedish writer Ulla Isaksson publishes *Ytterst i havet*.
1951 Swedish novelist Per Anders Fågelström publishes *Sommaren med Monika*. Swedish writer Birgitta Trotzig publishes *Ur de älskandes liv*. Icelandic writer Jökull Jakobsson publishes *Tæmdur bikar*.
1953 Danish writer Villy Sørensen publishes *Sære historier*.
1954 Finnish writer Väinö Linna publishes the pacifist novel *Tuntematon Sotilas*.
1955 Sara Lidman, Swedish writer and political activist, publishes *Hjortronlandet*. Finnish novelist Eeva Joenpelto publishes *Neito kulkee vetten päällä*. Norwegian writer Johan Borgen publishes *Lillelord*, the first volume in a trilogy that portrays the decline in the old patrician culture following World War I.
1956 Finnish writer Eeva-Liisa Manner publishes *Tämä matka*. Agnar Mykle publishes *Sangen om den røde rubin*, which leads to a Norwegian debate about obscenity in literature.
1957 Danish writer Peter Seeberg publishes *Fugls føde*. Danish nov-

elist Tage Skou-Hansen publishes *De nøgne træer*. Icelandic writer Thor Vilhjálmson publishes *Andlit í spegli dropans*.

1958 Lars Huldén, Finland-Swedish writer, publishes the poetry collection *Dräpa näcken*. Danish writer Leif Panduro publishes *Rend mig i traditionerne*. Danish writer Klaus Rifbjerg publishes *Den kroniske uskyld*. Swedish writer Lars Forsell publishes *Snurra min jord och andra visor*. Swedish poet Tomas Tranströmer publishes *Hemligheter på vägen*.

1960 Swedish writer Lars Gustafsson publishes *Bröderna: En allegorisk berättelse*.

1961 Maria Gripe, Swedish writer of children's books, begins her series of novels about Hugo and Josephine with *Josefin*. Alfred Hauge publishes *Hundevakt*, the first volume in his Cleng Peerson trilogy, which portrays the earliest organized emigration from Norway to America.

1962 Thorkild Hansen, Danish writer, publishes *Det lykkelige Arabien: En dansk ekspedtion 1761–67*. Swedish writer Per Olof Sundman publishes *Expeditionen*.

1963 Per Højholt, Danish writer, publishes *Poetens hoved*. Lars Gyllensten, Swedish writer, publishes *Kains memoarer*. Jan Myrdal, Swedish writer, publishes *Rapport från kinesisk by*, an important early manifestation of documentarism in Scandinavian literature. Finland-Swedish novelist Christer Kihlman publishes *Den blå modern*. Norwegian writer Tarjei Vesaas publishes *Isslottet*.

1964 Danish writer Elsa Gress publishes *Det uopdagede køn*. Swedish writer Lars Norén publishes *De verbala resterna av en bildprakt som förgår*.

1965 Benny Andersen, Danish writer, publishes *Puderne*. Swedish poet Göran Sonnevi publishes *Ingrepp-modeller*, which includes "Om kriget i Vietnam."

1966 Swedish writer Göran Tunström publishes *De andra de til hälften synliga*. Norwegian writer Jens Bjørneboe publishes *Frihetens øyeblikk*, the first novel in a trilogy that presents the history of cruelty in European life. Norwegian writer Bjørg Vik publishes the short story collection *Nødrop fra en myk sofa*.

1968 Per Olov Enquist, Swedish writer, publishes *Legonärerna*. Sara

Lidman, Swedish writer and political activist, publishes *Gruva*, one of the central documentary novels in Swedish literature.

1969 Icelandic writer Svava Jakobsdóttir publishes *Leigjandinn*. Danish writer Inger Christensen publishes *Det*. Danish writer and filmmaker Henrik Stangerup publishes *Slangen i brystet*. Sven Delblanc, Swedish writer, publishes *Åsnebrygga*. Theodor Kallifatides, Swedish writer, publishes *Minnet i exil*.

1971 Dag Solstad, Norwegian writer, publishes *Arild Asnes, 1970*, a novel about commitment to Marxist-Leninism.

1972 Svend Åge Madsen, Danish writer, publishes *Dage med Diam eller livet om natten*. Tor Obrestad publishes *Sauda! Streik!*, a Norwegian Marxist-Leninist documentary novel.

1973 Danish writer Christian Kampmann publishes *Visse hensyn*.

1974 Finnish novelist Eeva Joenpelto publishes *Vetää kaikista ovista*. Danish writer Thorkild Bjørnvig publishes *Pagten*, which tells about his relationship with the writer Karen Blixen. Norwegian writer Knut Faldbakken publishes *Uår: Aftenlandet*, the first one of two novels about an ecological catastrophe. Edvard Hoem publishes his novel *Kjærleikens ferjereiser*, one of the first examples of metafiction in modern Norwegian literature.

1975 Finland-Swedish novelist Märta Tikkanen publishes *Män kan inte våldtas*, a powerful intervention into the debate about sex roles.

1976 Kristina Lugn, Swedish writer and critic, publishes *Till min man, om han kunde läsa*.

1977 Danish writer Henrik Nordbrandt publishes *Guds hus*. Norwegian novelist Gerd Brantenberg publishes *Egalias døtre*, a feminist satire. Kjartan Fløgstad publishes *Dalen Portland*, one of Norway's first postmodernist novels.

1978 Danish writer Suzanne Brøgger publishes *Crème Fraiche: En føljeton*. Danish writer Dorrit Willumsen publishes *Hvis det virkelig var en film*. Swedish writer Katarina Frostenson publishes *I mellan*. Märta Tikkanen, Finland-Swedish novelist, publishes *Århunradets kärlekssaga*.

1980 Per Christian Jersild, Swedish writer, publishes *En levande själ*.

1981 Pia Tafdrup, Danish writer, publishes *Når det går hul på en engel*. Jonas Gardell, Swedish stand-up comic, writer, and filmmaker, publishes *Den tigande talar/4937*.

1982 Swedish writer Torgny Lindgren publishes *Ormens väg på hälleberget*.
1983 Finnish writer Leena Krohn publishes *Donna Quijote ja muita kaupunkilaisia*. Finland-Swedish writer Solveig von Schoultz publishes *Kolteckning, ofullbordad*. Icelandic writer Einar Kárason publishes *Þar sem djöflaeyjan rís*. Espen Haavardsholm publishes *Store fri*, a novel about life among Norwegian cultural radicals in the 1950s.
1984 Agneta Pleijel, Swedish writer, publishes *Ögon ur en dröm*.
1985 Sámi poet Nils-Aslak Valkeapää publishes *Ruoktu váimmus*. Danish writer Hanne Marie Svendsen publishes *Guldkuglen: Fortælling om en ø*.
1986 Thor Vilhjálmson, Icelandic writer, publishes *Grámosinn glóir*.
1990 Norwegian novelist Erik Fosnes Hansen publishes *Salme ved reisens slutt*, the setting of which is the *Titanic*.
1991 Norwegian writer Jostein Gaarder publishes *Sofies verden*, his blockbuster novel about the history of philosophy.
1992 Peter Høeg, Danish writer, publishes *Frøken Smillas fornemmelse for sne*.
1993 Carina Burman, Swedish literary scholar and novelist, publishes *Min salig bror Jean Hendrich*. Swedish novelist Kerstin Ekman publishes *Händelser vid vatten*. Norwegian writer Jan Kjærstad publishes *Forføreren*, the first volume in a fictional postmodernist biography of his character Jonas Wergeland.
1994 Monika Fagerholm, Finland-Swedish writer, publishes *Underbara kvinnor vid vatten*.
1996 Finland-Swedish writer Kjell Westö publishes the postmodernist novel *Drakarna över Helsingfors*. Norwegian writer Nikolaj Frobenius publishes *Latours katalog*, a novel about the Marquis de Sade's valet. Norwegian novelist Erlend Loe publishes *Naiv. Super*. Danish writer Peter Høeg publishes *Kvinden og aben*.
1998 Norwegian writer Jon Fosse publishes *Natta syng sine songar*. Norwegian writer Cecilie Løveid publishes the drama *Østerrike*. Norwegian writer Kjartan Fløgstad publishes his magic realist novel *Kron og mynt*. Swedish writer Göran Tunström publishes *Berömda män som varit i Sunne*.
1999 Per Olov Enquist, Swedish writer, publishes the historical novel *Livläkarens besök*.

2000 Norwegian writer Knut Faldbakken publishes *Frøken Snehvit*. Danish writer Dorrit Willumsen publishes *Koras stemme*.

2001 Ib Michael, Danish writer, publishes his magic realist novel *Kejserens atlas*. Lars Saabye Christensen, Norwegian writer, publishes *Halvbroren*. Icelandic writer Einar Karason publishes *Óvinafagnaður*.

2002 Norwegian writer Dag Solstad publishes *16.07.41*, a postmodernist autobiographical novel. Danish writer Pia Tafdrup publishes *Hvalerne i Paris*.

2003 Herbjørg Wassmo, Norwegian writer, publishes *Flukten fra Frank*. Gerd Brantenberg, Norwegian novelist, publishes *Landssvikersken*. Swedish writer Lars Gustafsson publishes *Dekanen*, which combines elements of the mystery story with philosophy. Swedish writer Per Christian Jersild publishes *De ondas kloster*.

2004 Danish writer Kirsten Thorup publishes *Ingenmandsland*. Norwegian novelist Hanne Ørstavik publishes *Presten*, about the treatment of the Sámi population in northern Norway. Finland-Swedish writer Monika Fagerholm publishes *Den amerikanska flickan*. Finnish writer Leena Krohn publishes *Unelmakuolema*. Danish writer Svend Åge Madsen publishes *Levemåder*.

2005 Danish writer Ib Michael publishes *Grill*, in which he criticizes the American involvement in Iraq. Swedish writer Torgny Lindgren publishes *Dorés bibel*.

Introduction

DEFINITION OF THE TERM "SCANDINAVIA"

The etymology of the word *Scandinavia* refers to the treacherous sandbanks in the passage between present-day Denmark and Sweden. In the Scandinavian countries the term is applied exclusively to Denmark, Norway, and Sweden, the national languages of which are mutually intelligible to the point that readers of one language can somewhat easily read the other two, and speakers of the three languages usually communicate orally by speaking their respective tongues to speakers of the other two languages. Finland, in which there is a culturally significant Swedish-speaking minority as well as the majority Finns, was a part of Sweden up to the year 1809 but is usually not included as part of Scandinavia. One reason for this exclusion is that Finnish is unrelated to Danish, Norwegian, and Swedish. Together with Estonian and, more distantly, Hungarian, Finnish belongs to the Finno-Ugric language group. Icelandic is closely related to the three major Scandinavian languages, as Iceland was populated mostly by Norwegians during the Viking era, but while there are significant similarities between modern written Icelandic and the written language of continental Scandinavia during the High Middle Ages, neither spoken nor written modern Icelandic is intelligible to users of modern Danish, Norwegian, or Swedish. Iceland was ruled by Denmark until 1944, and during the colonial period educated Icelanders were expected to also know Danish.

In the English-speaking world, on the other hand, it is common to include Finland and Iceland in the term *Scandinavia*, and the *Historical Dictionary of Scandinavian Literature and Theater* follows this practice. Scandinavians use the term *Norden* to designate all five countries, and that term, as well as the adjective *Nordic*, is increasingly being used in English.

ANCIENT AND MEDIEVAL SCANDINAVIA

During the Migration Period (ca. 400) various Germanic tribes moved north into Scandinavia and mixed with the indigenous population. Local kingdoms and earldoms arose, and gradually larger and more powerful political units emerged. By the beginning of the Viking Age it makes sense to talk about Denmark, Norway, and Sweden as separate countries, but Scandinavia was largely one cultural area throughout which the same language was spoken. Finns and Sámi reindeer herders did not speak this language and had a different culture, but as Thomas A. DuBois has shown, there was considerable cultural contact between speakers of Ancient Scandinavian on the one hand, and Finns and Sámis on the other.[1]

The literature of this early period was mostly orally transmitted and consisted of both alliterative poetry and prose narratives. Although fragments of such poetry have been preserved in runic inscriptions (the term "runes" refers to an alphabet with letters that were designed to be easily cut into stone or wood), most of this body of poetry is preserved in manuscripts that originated in 13th-century Iceland, and Icelandic sagas from the same period seem to reflect the existence of an ancient oral prose tradition. It was the coming of Christianity that caused this flowering of an indigenous literature to come about, for missionary monks and priests brought with them both the writing technology and the alphabet that enabled large-scale creation of texts. The result of the Christianization of Scandinavia was thus not only that the older pagan belief system more or less disappeared, but that knowledge of ancient times could be preserved through the work of such literary figures as Snorri Sturluson, the great medieval Icelandic historian.

Scandinavia was, of course, located on the margins of the medieval civilized world, and its isolation became even more pronounced after the ravages of the Black Death. First noticed in Bergen, Norway, in 1349, this plague spread across Scandinavia and destroyed roughly half of the population. The consequences for cultural, economic, and political life were enormous, and it is no exaggeration to say that, intellectually speaking, darkness reigned in Scandinavia for an extended period of time. What literary and intellectual culture remained was associated mostly with the church, which used Latin as its medium of communication and did not encourage literacy among the common people.

THE REFORMATION, THE RENAISSANCE, AND THE ENLIGHTENMENT

The use of Latin as a medium of writing changed with the coming of the Lutheran Reformation. In Lutheranism the individual's relationship with God is paramount, and reading sacred scripture is a primary means by which that relationship can be developed. The New Testament was translated into Danish as early as 1524, and into Swedish by 1526. The entire Bible was available in Danish by 1550, and in Swedish by 1541. The Danish Bible translation was also used in Norway, which had become united with Denmark in 1397. Many Lutheran ministers studied abroad and brought intellectual impulses back to Scandinavia. Thus such general European phenomena as the Renaissance and humanism came to play a role in Scandinavia as well, where there was a resurgence in interest in the literature of the Old Norse period as well as a strong interest in providing topographical descriptions, a mapping of Scandinavia in words, so to speak.

Another watershed in the literary development of Scandinavia is the Thirty Years War (1618–1648), in which Sweden became a European great power and the united Denmark and Norway became more closely connected with the rest of Europe. Such Scandinavian Baroque literary figures as the Dane Thomas Kingo (1634–1703) and the Norwegian Petter Dass (1647–1707) wrote within a general European aesthetic framework of codes and norms. By the time of the great Enlightenment figures Ludvig Holberg (1684–1754) and Olof von Dalin (1708–1763), there were established conduits of artistic and literary communication between Scandinavia and the rest of Europe. Holberg, for example, traveled widely in Holland, England, France, and Italy.

Most of the time, the cultural and literary impulses traveled north, rather than from Scandinavia to Europe. French neoclassicism, for example, manifested itself strongly both at the court of King Gustav III of Sweden and generally in Swedish literature at the time. The songs of the Swedish poet Carl Michael Bellman (1740–1795) are simply unthinkable without the influence of French culture in Stockholm. In Copenhagen, on the contrary, neoclassicism can be observed as the butt of Johan Herman Wessel's jokes in the comedy *Kierlighed uden Strømper* (1772; Love without Stockings).

NATIONAL ROMANTICISM

The northward migration of ideas is even more clearly visible during the period in literary and intellectual history that is referred to as romanticism. In France, Charles-Louis de Secondat Montesquieu (1689–1755) had emphasized the significance of geographic location and climate to the development of a nation's culture. Jean-Jacques Rousseau (1712–1778) had spoken in favor of the particular, nature, and the emotions as opposed to reason, culture, and the general. Already in the first half of the 18th century, the Swiss Albrecht von Haller had extolled the beauty of unspoiled nature in *Die Alpen* (1729), and the Scot James Macpherson called attention to the poetry of the past in his work *Fragments of Ancient Poetry* (1760–1765), which features his character Ossian. Edward Young's *Conjectures on Original Composition* (1759) elevated the individual genius above any system of rules for what constitutes proper literature.

These are but some of the literary figures who pointed the way toward the complex of ideas and attitudes that were comprised within romanticism. Its philosophical ideas, shaped partly by the ideas of the German philosophers Johann Gottlieb Fichte (1762–1814) and Friedrich Schelling (1775–1854), emphasized the unity of the object and human perception as well as the unity of spirit and nature. God, the highest manifestation of spirit, could thus be found in nature, and the romantic genius was thought to be able to apprehend the divine and thus have a prophetic function. Johann Gottfried von Herder (1744–1803) emphasized both the role of the nation and of language and the connection to the divine spirit that could be found in the natural world.

Starting with the Danish writer Adam Oehlenschläger (1779–1850), Scandinavian artists and intellectuals were profoundly influenced by the ideas of romanticism. While the strictly philosophical side of the movement was of some significance, its nationalistic aspects became paramount in Scandinavia. Oehlenschläger's poem "Guldhornene" (1802; The Golden Horns), for example, features a young man who finds a golden horn with a runic inscription on it while plowing his field. This young man is referred to as the son of nature who has been chosen by nature's indwelling spirit to make the discovery. Without conventional learning, he is unspoiled by civilization and thus worthy of his calling. Many of the characteristics of the variant of the romantic movement that became known as national romanticism can be observed in this example: the scene of action is nature as opposed to culture; the main actor is an unlearned youth, a young man of the people; the central object is of great value, symbolized by its being made of gold and further symbolizing the value of the subject that is being discussed in the poem; the activity of plowing lays stress on the connection between the nation and its soil; writing, as an expression of the true spirit of the people, is present; the main object, including the writing on it, is of ancient origin, thus emphasizing the continuity of the nation over time.

Another characteristic example of the literature of national romanticism is a short story by the Norwegian writer Maurits Hansen (1794–1842) entitled "Luren" (1819; The Shepherd's Horn), in which the narrator tells about a visit to a Norwegian farm family in the interior of the country. The farmer, who bears the name of the Old Norse god Thor, is said to be a direct descendant of the ancient king Harald Finehair, and his daughter Ragnhild is named for king Harald's mother. Special mention is made of Thor's powerful and expressive dialect, the traditional dress of the members of the family, and their food ways. As in Oehlenschläger's poem, there is an emphasis on the continuity between the present and the nation's past, the connection between the people and the soil, and the role of language. But some elements of the story may indicate Hansen was aware that the ideal national-romantic scene he painted was, at least to some extent, a rhetorical construction.[2]

In Iceland, the poetry of Jónas Hallgrímsson (1807–1845) emphasized the past of the nation and the significance of its language. Esaias Tegnér (1782–1846) and Per Daniel Amadeus Atterbom (1790–1855) exemplify the national romanticism movement in Sweden, where Auroraförbundet (The Aurora Society), which published the journal *Phosphorus*, was an important voice for romanticism. Tegnér's *Frithiofs saga* (1825; tr. 1833) expands a brief Old Norse story into a Swedish national epic of 24 songs. In Finland, the later stage of national romanticism is seen in the folklore collections of Elias Lönnrot (1802–1884) and the work of Johan Ludvig Runeberg (1804–1877), particularly his play *Kung Fjalar* (1844; tr. *King Fjalar*, 1904), a classic example of the movement's antiquarian side.

The most enduring significance of national romanticism is its attitude toward the oral literature of the people. The enthusiasm that educated people felt for the past and the descendants of the glorious men and women of old resulted in an effort to collect ballads, folktales, and legends and then to identify their origins and most ancient forms. Next, the folklore materials thus collected and analyzed began to influence the works of educated writers. In its subject matter and language, the work of Danish short story writer and poet Steen Steensen Blicher (1782–1848), for example, shows the influence of folk literature. Based on the dialects spoken in Norway, the self-taught linguist Ivar Aasen (1813–1896) single-handedly created Landsmaal (country language), a separate written form of Norwegian that provided an alternative to the Danish-influenced form that was the standard at the time. But the work of the national romantics was also treated with a heavy dose of irony and satire, as in the play *Peer Gynt* (1867; tr. 1892) by Henrik Ibsen (1828–1906), in which the eponymous protagonist has both pleasant and frightening interactions with folklore creatures. But that very same Ibsen also wrote plays which used material from history and folklore without indulging in irony.

REALISM AND NATURALISM

When a current literary movement begins to be treated ironically, it usually means that a new set of literary ideas are in the ascendancy. The successor to national romanticism was realism, which also came from outside Scandinavia, particularly France, where two of its greatest practitioners were the writers Gustave Flaubert (1821–1880), best known for his novel *Madame Bovary* (1857), and Honoré de Balzac (1799–1850). The term *realism* in literary studies denotes a style that tries to describe life as it is, without idealization or subjectivity. In the present context, however, it also refers to Scandinavian prose and drama written from around 1840 through the 1880s, but particularly in the 1870s. Only a few works from the 1840s can confidently be termed realistic. The best early example of realism in Scandinavian literature is arguably the novel *Det går an* (1839; tr. *Sara Videbeck*, 1919; *Why Not?* 1994) by the Swedish writer Carl Jonas Love Almqvist (1793–1866), which anticipates one of the favorite subjects of the realists, namely, the position of women in the family and in society. But the pseudonymous writings of the Danish philosopher-writer Søren Kierkegaard (1813–1855) may also be considered an example of realist concerns, inasmuch as they are written in conscious opposition to the ideas of the German romantics. Such a story of deceit and manipulation as "Forførerens Dagbog" (1843; The Seducer's Diary), the largest section in the first part of Kierkegaard's *Enten-Eller* (1843; tr. *Either/Or*, 1944), certainly shares many of the features of realist literature from the later decades.

The realist movement manifested itself in a couple of different ways in Norwegian literature of the 1850s. Stylistically and narratologically, the peasant stories of Bjørnstjerne Bjørnson (1832–1910) anticipate the prose writings of the 1870s in Norway. In her seminal novel *Amtmandens Døttre* (1854–1855; tr. *The District Governor's Daughters*, 1992), Camilla Collett (1813–1895) wrote about the marital fate of several sisters. Although her narrative technique—her story is replete with letters, diary entries, and direct statements aimed at the reader—is fairly traditional, both her subject and the indignation with which it is treated were harbingers of what was to come a little more than a decade later.

Realism coexisted with late romantic idealism in Scandinavian literature throughout the 1840s, 1850s, and 1860s, but an event in 1871 marks its complete triumph on the Scandinavian Parnassus. This event, after which any other literary style was clearly passé, was the first in a serious of lectures given by the Danish critic Georg Brandes (1842–1927), in which he called for a literary practice that would use literature to debate modern problems and issues. It is no exaggeration to say that just about every progressive writer in Scandinavia fell into line. In Denmark, Jens Peter Jacobsen produced two realist novels that adhered to the new program: *Fru Marie Grubbe* (1876; tr. *Marie Grubbe*, 1917) and *Niels Lyhne* (1880; tr. 1919, 1990). Swedish writer August Strindberg (1849–1912) wrote a great novel, *Röda rummet* (1879; tr. *The Red Room*, 1967), which offers a panoramic view of life among artists, intellectuals, and government employees in Stockholm.

Brandes's influence was at least as great in Norwegian literature. Many of Ibsen's plays from the 1870s and early 1880s come to mind, for example, *Samfundets støtter* (1877; tr. *The Pillars of Society*, 1888), *Et dukkehjem* (1879; tr. *A Doll's House*, 1880), *Gengangere* (1881; *Ghosts*, 1885), and *En folkefiende* (1882; tr. *An Enemy of the People*, 1888), all of which deal with such favorite realist topics as corruption, the role of women, and outmoded ideas. Bjørnstjerne Bjørnson vigorously advocated for Brandes's view of the purpose of literature and practiced it in such plays as *En fallit* (1875; tr. *The Bankrupt*, 1914), *Redaktøren* (1875; tr. *The Editor*, 1914), and *Kongen* (1877; tr. *The King*, 1914). The novelist Jonas Lie wrote *Tremasteren "Fremtiden"* (1872; tr. *The Barque "Future,"* 1879), which is considered Norway's first novel about business affairs, and later *Familjen paa Gilje* (1883; tr. *The Family at Gilje*, 1920), which has the 1840s as its setting and which debates the right of women to choose their own paths through life. Specifically encouraged by Brandes, Lie's colleague Alexander Kielland (1849–1906) wrote a satirical novel, *Garman og Worse* (1880; tr. *Garman and Worse*, 1885), which castigated the rich for their treatment of the poor.

The Scandinavian realists wanted to debate social issues not only for aesthetic reasons, but in order to bring about social change. The women's question is a good example. Women had no right to vote, could not hold political office, and were not entitled to control their own property. They had no access to higher education and were expected to spend their lives as wives and mothers. If they did not marry, they could usually look forward to a difficult old age in the home of a brother or sister. Most of the reforms that improved the lives and economic situation of women were first advocated by writers of novels, short stories, and plays.

Implicit in the realist literary program was the sense that such advocacy was efficacious. When realism turns toward naturalism, however, such optimism largely disappears. While still critical of society, the naturalists had little hope of reforming it. Influenced by the ideas of the French critic Charles-Augustin Sainte-Beuve (1804–1869), the novelist Émile Zola (1840–1902), particularly as expressed in his book *Le roman experimental* (1880), and natural science as practiced by Charles Darwin (1809–1892), the naturalists adhered to the doctrine of determinism, according to which human beings have no real agency but act according to their biological inheritance and the influence of their social milieu. Truth was to be found in nature rather than, as for the romantics, in some kind of transcendental reality, and the task of the naturalist writer was to imitate the scientist as far as possible. What would a certain literary character logically do, based on his or her biological and social background as well as his or her current environment? By setting up a kind of controlled experiment in their works, the naturalists attempted to create scientific truth through literature.

These theoretical concerns had certain consequences for both the style of the naturalist literary work and the author's choice of subject matter. The story would be told in great detail, almost approaching that of a lab report, as in a short story by the Norwegian writer Amalie Skram (1846–1905) entitled "Karens jul" (1885; Karen's Christmas), in which an unwed teenage mother and her baby freeze to death in Christiania (now Oslo) a couple of days before Christmas. Skram is extremely generous in her description of the scene of the action. She gives, for example, the exact dimensions and floor plan of a small shack in which Karen has sought shelter, and even informs the reader about what kind of metal is used for the hook that holds the door closed. Her male colleague Arne Garborg (1851–1924) similarly offers numerous details in his naturalist works, for example, the novel *Hjaa ho Mor* (1890; Living with Mama), which is partly based on the life of his wife Hulda. The story of the development of a young girl named Fanny, *Hjaa ho Mor* seemingly tells about every detail of every stage in Fanny's development.

Naturalists examined the sexual roles of men and women to show that men were biologically unable to control their sexual urges and to argue that women would make essentially the same choices as men if unrestrained by social norms, particularly by the teachings of Christianity. In his novel *Mannfolk* (1886; Men), for example, Arne Garborg created a large number of male and female characters that illustrated these points. In Strindberg's play *Fröken Julie* (1888; tr. *Miss Julie*, 1912), both of the major characters, Julie and Jean, are powerless when faced with a combination of temptation and opportunity. The naturalists further argued that the daughters of the middle class were raised to become sexually dysfunctional, thus more or less compelling their future husbands to seek the company of prostitutes. Naturalist writers also frequently showed that young women who had to work for a living could not earn enough to support themselves as servants or by working in a store, and therefore were forced to prostitute themselves.

Illness was another focus of the naturalists. Ibsen's play *Gengangere* (1881; tr. *Ghosts*, 1885), for example, deals with syphilis. Crime was also a topic, as in Jonas Lie's novel *Livsslaven* (1883; tr. *One of Life's Slaves*, 1895). A determinist view would argue against holding people morally and legally responsible for actions over which they have no control. From the perspective of determinism, for example, Nora's forgery in

Ibsen's play *Et dukkehjem* (1879; tr. *A Doll's House*, 1880) should not be laid to her charge, as she is possibly unable to do anything else, given her situation in life, her biological inheritance, and the way she has been brought up.

NEOROMANTICISM

Scandinavian literature in the 1870s and 1880s can be summed up with the two words "objectivity" and "society." Around 1890 the pendulum swung back toward a greater concern with the individual and with human consciousness. The philosophy of Friedrich Nietzsche (1844–1900) was a contributing factor, but so was French Symbolist poetry. The trend toward individual psychology can be found in both established writers and new talents. One of the most Nietzschean novels of the time is, for example, Strindberg's *I havsbandet* (1890; tr. *By the Open Sea*, 1913 and 1984), in which the mental state of the superman Borg is carefully chronicled. In Norway, Garborg's novel *Trætte Mænd* (1891; tr. *Weary Men*, 1999) attracted a great deal of attention not only because its form was that of a modified diary novel, but also because it carefully articulated the difference between the scientific worldview of the 1880s, represented by the character Georg Jonathan, and the religious striving of its narrator-protagonist, Gabriel Gram. But the most clear-cut example of the new subjectivist literature was surely the novel *Sult* (1890; tr. *Hunger*, 1899), by the young Norwegian writer Knut Hamsun (1859–1952). Set in Christiania, it tells about its narrator's experimentation with his own mind, as he periodically starves himself so as to observe the effects of hunger. In drama, the female psyche was probed by Ibsen in the plays *Fruen fra havet* (1888; tr. *The Lady from the Sea*, 1890) and *Hedda Gabler* (1890; tr. 1891), while the male mind was similarly examined in *Bygmester Solness* (1892; *The Master Builder*, 1893).

One of the major themes in the literature of the 1890s, also known as the fin-de-siècle or the decadent period, is that of decay and degeneration. In Strindberg's *Fröken Julie*, for example, Julie is the last surviving person in her family line and slits her throat at the end of the play. Ibsen's Hedda Gabler, an only child with no family mentioned, similarly shoots herself. Already in the novel *Haabløse Slægter* (1880;

Hopeless Generations) by the Danish novelist Herman Bang (1857–1912), the theme of the decaying family had been prominently featured, with the problem in question being inherited mental illness. Moral degeneration is given a prominent place in the novel *Doktor Glas* (1905; tr. *Doctor Glas*, 1970) by the Swedish writer Hjalmar Söderberg (1869–1941), in which a physician murders a local clergyman because he finds him aesthetically repulsive. But not all literature of the turn of the century is bleak and depressing. The novel *Gösta Berlings saga* (1891; tr. *The Story of Gösta Berling*, 1898), written by the great Swedish story-teller Selma Lagerlöf (1858–1941), offers probing psychological portraits of its characters, while the theme of cultural change—some might say decay—is presented against a background of fable and myth, the result being that Lagerlöf's book is both highly entertaining and a great antidote to cultural pessimism. Life is cyclical, Lagerlöf seems to say, and positive change is always just around the corner.

THE FIRST HALF OF THE 20TH CENTURY

Scandinavian literature in the first half of the 20th century is marked by two names—Karl Marx (1818–1883) and Sigmund Freud (1856–1939)—and two world events: the two world wars. While the Scandinavian countries were neutral during World War I, the war caused tremendous social and economic change as it brought large profits to people who previously had had little economic power, while some families with long-standing wealth were comparatively disadvantaged. The change in the traditional Scandinavian class structure can be observed in the two-volume family saga *Jørgen Stein* (1932–1933; tr. 1966), by the Danish writer Jacob Paludan (1896–1975); the narrative covers the history of the Stein family, starting before World War I and ending around 1930. A similar social and economic dynamic is present in the novel *Lillelord* (1955; tr. 1982) by the Norwegian novelist Johan Borgen (1902–1979), the first volume of a trilogy that concludes during World War II. Wartime profiteering—the industry is shipping and the location of the action is Bergen, Norway—is the theme of the play *Vår ære og vår makt* (1935, tr. *Our Power and Our Glory*, 1971) by the Norwegian poet and dramatist Nordahl Grieg (1902–1943).

The political situation in Scandinavia was strongly affected by the Bolshevik Revolution of 1917, however, and first and foremost in Finland, which seized the opportunity to declare itself independent of Russia. But the labor movements in the other Scandinavian countries were heartened by the changes seen in Russia, until the abuses of the new Soviet state could no longer be ignored, as when the Stalinist purges and the Moscow trials of the 1930s become known in the West. The Finnish civil war of 1918 left its mark on Finnish literature, but it did not much affect other Scandinavian writers.

Marxism left its mark on Scandinavian literature in the interwar period, generally in conjunction with Freudianism. Many progressive writers developed a Freudian anthropology and a Marxian sociology. Hans Kirk (1898–1962) is the most obvious example in Danish literature. In his novel *Fiskerne* (1928; tr. *The Fishermen*, 1999), a collective novel set in Jutland, Kirk tells the story of a group of fishermen and their families who relocate from a harsh coastal area to Limfjorden, a relatively sheltered district. Devout Christians of the Danish Inner Mission type, the parental generation watches as their children adopt less restrictive moral views that seem more appropriate to them in their less challenging surroundings. Economic relations are analyzed according to the theories of Marx, including his labor theory of value, while spirituality, in a very Freudian way, is understood as sublimated sexuality.

The Danish and Norwegian novelist Aksel Sandemose (1899–1965) is another writer in the interwar period who pursued the relationship between the individual and society. In the novel *En flyktning krysser sitt spor* (1933; tr. *A Fugitive Crosses His Tracks*, 1936), Sandemose looks to the childhood of his protagonist and his relationship to his local community for the causes of later action. The Norwegian novelist Sigurd Hoel (1890–1960) likewise pursues Marxian and Freudian themes in several novels from the late 1920s and the 1930s, most prominently in the autobiographical novel *Veien til verdens ende* (1933; The Road to the End of the World), which draws on his childhood memories. Swedish literature in the 1930s has a number of new writers who came from proletarian backgrounds, and who told about the abuses of the working class from a strongly socialist perspective.

The decade of the 1930s was also the time when modernism made its definitive breakthrough in Scandinavian literature. While such poets as the Finland-Swedish writers Edith Södergran (1892–1923) and

Elmer Diktonius (1896–1961) had presented modernist poetry in Scandinavia quite early, the Swede Pär Lagerkvist (1891–1974) wrote both modernist poetry and prose and became one of modernism's great champions in Scandinavian literature. Modernism is difficult to define, but Susan Brantley has offered a sensible tripartite criterion. First, she asks, does the text represent "a new way of thinking about the world"? Second, is the text "characterized by a system of formal innovations and tendencies"? Third, does the text appear during a specified period of time?[3] Modernist poetry became increasingly significant in Scandinavian literature both before and after World War II. A number of modernist prose writers were also active, in addition to Lagerkvist. The Dane Tom Kristensen (1893–1974) published his important modernist novel *Hærværk* (1930; tr. *Havoc*, 1968). The Norwegian Cora Sandel (1880–1974) published her Alberte trilogy, consisting of *Alberte og Jakob* (1926; tr. *Alberta and Jacob*, 1962), *Alberte og friheten* (1931; tr. *Alberta and Freedom*, 1963), and *Bare Alberte* (1939; tr. *Alberta Alone*, 1965). The trilogy tells about the childhood, youth, and early womanhood of the title character, who goes from northern Norway to Paris to study art and ends up becoming a writer. Other modernists of the interwar period are the Finland-Swedish novelist Hagar Olsson (1893–1978) and the Swede Moa Martinson (1890–1964).[4]

World War II left a strong imprint on Scandinavian literature. Denmark and Norway were both attacked by Germany on 9 April 1940 and remained occupied until 8 May 1945. Iceland was used by British and American troops. Sweden managed to remain neutral, and both Danish and Norwegian resistance fighters fled there when the German occupants got too close for comfort. Finland suffered yet another divisive war.

Literary life was severely curtailed during the war, especially in the occupied countries. After World War II many Scandinavian writers attempted to come to terms with the phenomenon of Nazism as well as with the war itself. In Sweden Lagerkvist published his novel *Dvärgen* (1944; tr. *The Dwarf*, 1945), a study in evil set in Renaissance Italy, but which is a thinly veiled exploration of the Nazi personality. Another Swede, Eyvind Johnson (1900–1976), explored the problem of evil in his novel *Drömmar om rosor och eld* (1949; tr. *Dreams of Roses and Fire*, 1984), which is set in 17th-century France under Cardinal Richelieu. The Norwegian novelist and playwright Jens Bjørneboe (1920–

1976) confronted a similar theme in *Før hanen galer* (1952; Before the Cock Crows), which deals with the medical experiments performed by Nazi doctors on concentration camp prisoners. In the novel *Under en hårdere himmel* (1957; Under a Harder Sky), Bjørneboe criticizes Norway's treatment of Nazi wartime collaborators at the close of the war. The play *Fugleelskerne* (1966; tr. *The Bird Lovers*, 1993) is set in an Italian village and dramatizes a confrontation between some former German occupants and the town's population 20 years after the end of the war. Sigurd Hoel dealt with the war and probed the causes of Nazism in his novel *Møte ved milepelen* (1947; tr. *Meeting at the Milestone*, 1951), one of Norway's finest novels about the trauma of occupation and the tragedy of collaboration with the enemy.

THE LATE 20TH AND EARLY 21ST CENTURIES

Scandinavian literature after World War II reflects the political realities of the Cold War era. Denmark, Iceland, and Norway all joined the North Atlantic Treaty Organization (NATO), while Sweden maintained its prewar neutrality and Finland lived in constant awareness of its neighbor to the east. The atomic bomb cast a dark shadow over people's lives, and the fear of nuclear war is reflected by, for example, the novel *Atómstöðin* (1948; tr. *The Atom Station*, 1961), by the Icelandic writer Halldór Laxness (1902–1998). The existentialism of Jean-Paul Sartre (1905–1980) and Albert Camus (1913–1960) also had a strong impact on Scandinavian literature, as exemplified by the novel *Rytteren* (1949; tr. *The Riding Master*, 1951), in which the Dane H. C. Branner (1903–1966) allows freedom and goodness to triumph over the urge to control others, as well as in the novel *Løgneren* (1950; tr. *The Liar*, 1954) by Branner's countryman Martin A. Hansen (1909–1955).

Many writers in Denmark, Iceland, and Norway opposed the decisions by their respective governments to join NATO, as the rivalry between the Soviet Union and the United States was not seen in black and white terms. Sweden, which chose the so-called third way with regard to the conflict between the superpowers, also led the way in the Scandinavian protest against the American involvement in Vietnam. One of the most vocal opponents of the Vietnam War in Scandinavia was the

Swedish poet Göran Sonnevi (1939–), who became known throughout Scandinavia in 1965 when he published his poem "Om kriget i Vietnam" ("About the War in Vietnam"). Another early Swedish opponent of the war was Sara Lidman (1923–).

Opposition to the Vietnam War became a rallying cry for a large number of Scandinavians on the left, including many writers. Some of these writers were committed Marxist-Leninists who looked to the China of Mao Zedong for inspiration; some of them also admired Enver Hoxa's Albania. Believing that their historical mission was to awaken the Scandinavian working class and actualize its revolutionary potential, they wrote books with that specific aim, often with a strong focus on political issues of interest to workers. Much of this literature is written in a style called documentarism, meaning that a lot of factual information is built into the story and that sometimes actual documents are used. This literary technique was pioneered by such Swedish writers as Sara Lidman, whose novel *Gruva* (1968; The Mine) contains interviews with mine workers, and Per Olov Enquist (1935–), who has written several important documentary novels, among them *Legonärerna* (1968; tr. *The Legionnaires*, 1973), which tells the story of a group of soldiers from the Baltic states who were forcibly repatriated at the end of World War II.

One of the more typical Norwegian literary efforts on behalf of Marxist-Leninism is the documentary novel *Sauda! Streik!* (1972; Sauda! Strike!) by Tor Obrestad (1938–), which tells the story of a strike in an industrial community in western Norway. The novel *Historiens kraftlinjer* (1975; The Power Lines of History) by Espen Haavardsholm (1945–) offers Albania as an example of an ideal society. Of greater interest is a novel by Dag Solstad (1941–) entitled *Arild Asnes, 1970* (1971), in which the author, in semi-religious language, describes his transition from a middle-class writer to a committed socialist.

Danish writers were generally less extreme than their Swedish and Norwegian colleagues. A case in point is Villy Sørensen (1929–2001), who in his essay collections *Den gyldne middelvej* (1979; The Golden Mean) and *Demokratiet og kunsten* (1988; Democracy and Art) argued that human life can best flourish at some distance from both radical socialism and dogmatic capitalism, a standpoint he had consistently advocated throughout the 1960s and 1970s.

With the end of the Vietnam War and the decline of Albania and

China as political ideals, there was a reduction in both the revolutionary fervor and the anti-Americanism of Scandinavian leftist writers. One of the major strands in Scandinavian literature in the 1980s and 1990s is a strong interest in the lives of ordinary men and women, exemplified by the Swede Kerstin Ekman (1933–), who in her novel *Händelser vid vatten* (1993; tr. *Blackwater*, 1997) and the trilogy *Vargskinnet* (1999–2003; The Wolf Hide) has given literary life to a central Swedish community near the border of Norway. Existential questions were still of great interest, and erstwhile Marxist-Leninists found it necessary to confess to and reflect upon their past follies, or at least slightly misplaced commitments. Obrestad does so in the novel *Ein gong må du seie adjø* (1981; Someday You Must Say Good-Bye), and Solstad explains his past, with a vengeance, in the two novels *Gymnaslærer Pedersens beretning om den store politiske vekkelsen som har hjemsøkt vårt land* (1982; High School Teacher Pedersen's Account of the Great Political Revival That Has Visited Our Country) and *Roman 1987* (1987; Novel 1987).

The most interesting trend in recent and contemporary Scandinavian literature, however, is what may loosely be termed postmodernism. Sometimes used so as to include metafiction, fabulation, and literary self-reference, postmodernism is a manifestation of a broader tendency toward anti-realism. Unencumbered by the dreams of dialectical harmony, postmodernism celebrates the contradictions of existence and mixes old and new, high and low forms of literary expression. The mystery story, a "low" genre, for example, is mixed with more traditional "high" narrative in the aforementioned Kerstin Ekman's *Händelser vid vatten*. A similar mixture can be found in some of the work of the Finland-Swedish novelist Kjell Westö (1961–), whose books *Drakarna över Helsingfors* (1996; Kites Above Helsinki) and *Lang* (2002) exemplify some of the literary techniques of postmodernism and its focus on cultural analysis. Similar techniques are found in the work of the Danish novelists Peter Høeg (1957–) and Ib Michael (1945–). Høeg's novels *Frøken Smillas fornemmelse for sne* (1992; tr. *Smilla's Sense of Snow*, 1993), which contains elements of the thriller, and *Kvinden og aben* (1996; tr. *The Woman and the Ape*, 1996), in which the wife of a scientist falls in love with an intelligent ape, may be characterized as postmodern or instances of magic realism. Michael's novel *Kejserens atlas* (2001; The Emperor's Atlas) can fruitfully be regarded as a magic realist text.

Kjartan Fløgstad (1944–) and Jan Kjærstad (1953–) exemplify postmodernism in Norway. Fløgstad has written a long series of novels in which anti-realist techniques figure prominently, starting with *Dalen Portland* (1977; tr. *Dollar Road*, 1989), while Kjærstad's novel *Forføreren* (1993; tr. *The Seducer*, 2003) is the first volume in a trilogy about a television personality. As Scandinavian literature has crossed the threshold into the new millennium, its future seems bright indeed.

NOTES

1. Thomas A. DuBois, *Nordic Religions in the Viking Age* (Philadelphia: University of Pennsylvania Press, 1999), 9–28 and passim.

2. See Jan Sjåvik, *Reading for the Truth: Rhetorical Constructions in Norwegian Fiction* (Christchurch, New Zealand: Cybereditions, 2004), 38–48.

3. Susan C. Brantly, *Understanding Isak Dinesen* (Columbia: University of South Carolina Press, 2002), 305.

4. An excellent discussion of modernism in Scandinavia can be found in Ellen Rees, *On the Margins: Nordic Women Modernists of the 1930s* (Norwich, U.K.: Norvik Press, 2005).

The Dictionary

– A –

AAKJÆR, JEPPE (1866–1930). A Danish novelist, short story writer, and poet, Aakjær hailed from western Jutland and retained a lifelong love for his home district. While living in Copenhagen in his youth, he acquired leftist social views, arguing against the power of the Danish state church and in favor of improving the conditions of life for rural laborers. The autobiographical narrative *Bondens Søn* (1899; The Farmer's Son) describes his loss of faith. Aakjær's novel *Vredens Børn* (1904; The Children of Wrath) is an impassioned plea in favor of improving the conditions of the farm day laborers; it is also a realistic description of their living conditions.

Much of the inspiration for Aakjær's work came from his love of traditional rural Danish life. He viewed capitalism, including the capitalization of the farmland, as a threat to traditional values. He was also concerned about industrialization, which pulled people away from the rural areas to the urban centers. Aakjær belongs to a tradition in Scandinavian literature that is sometimes referred to as **heimstaddiktning**, a term that denotes both literary regionalism and a special attachment to one's home, which flourished during the first few decades of the 20th century. Aakjær's novel *Arbeidets Glæde* (1914; The Joy of Work) expresses his love for the cyclical life on the farm.

Aakjær's love of Jutland also inspires his poetry, which is often eminently singable and has become an important part of the Danish cultural heritage. Two of his most important poetry collections are *Fri Felt* (1905; Free Field) and *Rugens Sange* (1906; The Songs of the Rye). Aakjær's short stories also deal with local themes and often have a strong admixture of the local Jutland dialect.

AASEN, IVAR (1813–1896). A Norwegian poet, dramatist, and linguist, Aasen grew up on a small farm on the coast of western Norway. He became a self-taught linguist and dialectologist and devoted his life to studying the lexicon and grammar of Norwegian dialects. Paying special attention to their relationship with the language of Viking Age Scandinavia, he published a grammar in 1848 and a dictionary in 1850. Steeped in the ideology of **national romanticism**, he was nevertheless no dreamer but a diligent promoter of the idea that Norway's written language, which after 400 years of political union with Denmark was strongly colored by Danish, ought to be replaced by a written norm that was founded on Norway's many different popular dialects. To this end, Aasen singlehandedly created a written form of Norwegian called **Landsmaal** (country language) that he then employed as a medium for both poetry and prose. Perhaps predictably, his poetry is heavily colored by the conventions of Old Norse poetry and shows his fondness for both ancient-sounding vocabulary and grammatical features that had become extinct in most forms of Norwegian even in Aasen's own day. His best-known literary works are the play *Ervingen* (1855; The Heir) and the poetry collection *Symra* (1863; The Anemone). While not among Scandinavia's greatest literary works of literature, both are considered classics in Norwegian literature written in **nynorsk** (New Norwegian), a less old-fashioned norm that succeeded Aasen's Landsmaal as an alternative to standard written Norwegian.

ABELL, KJELD (1901–1961). A Danish dramatist and novelist, Abell had his origins in the middle class, toward which he had a critical attitude throughout his life. He first got a degree in political science, after which he traveled to Paris and London in order to study **theater**. Back in Denmark he gained additional experience by working as a scenographer.

Abell's first play, *Melodien der blev væk* (1935; tr. *The Melody That Got Lost*, 1939), takes a critical look at Danish middle-class life in the 1930s, introducing a character named Larsen, who has since become the archetype of the low-level white-collar worker in Denmark and Norway. In the play *Eva aftjener sin Barnepligt* (1936; Eve Does National Service as a Child) Abell's satirical critique of the ways of the middle class is continued, and this time with special focus on its child-rearing practices. The drama *Anna Sophie Hedvig* (1939; tr. 1944) takes the middle class to task for not being sufficiently aware of the threat of Nazism; it also expresses Abell's sympathy with the anti-Franco Spanish freedom fighters.

During World **War** II Abell wrote the play *Dronningen gaar igen* (1943, but published 1955; tr. *The Queen on Tour*, 1955), which contained a hidden call to resistance against the Germans. After the war Danish **critics** exaggerated his **Marxist** leanings, and he never regained his prewar position in Danish cultural life. His last play, *Skriget* (1961; The Cry), castigates the middle class for its passivity in the face of the authoritarianism of the right during the Cold War. Abell also wrote the novel *De tre fra Minikoi* (1957; tr. *Three from Minikoi*, 1960), which was based on his two visits to the People's Republic of China.

AHLIN, LARS (1915–1997). A Swedish novelist, short story writer, dramatist, and essayist, Ahlin differs from most of his literary contemporaries in that he has a religious outlook on life. He focuses on the dignity of each human being while simultaneously showing concern that each person should have opportunities to enhance his or her value to society. Brotherly love, understood as social equality, is an important desideratum for him. Opposed to the idea that art is an end in itself, Ahlin wants to draw the reader into his stories and have him or her identify with the characters, thus causing the reader's view of the world to be altered.

Ahlin had his debut with the novel *Tåbb med manifestet* (1943; Tåbb with the Manifesto), in which the character Tåbb recognizes that the ideas contained in Karl **Marx**'s *Communist Manifesto* (1848) are false and that he should support egalitarian social democracy rather than a system that promotes a hierarchy of value. *Inga ögon väntar mig* (1944; No Eyes Await Me) is a collection of short stories; other volumes in this genre include *Fångens glädje* (1947; The Joy of the Prisoner), *Huset har ingen filial* (1949; The House Has No Annex), and *Vaktpojkens eld* (1986; The Watch Boy's Fire).

Min död er min (1945; My Death Is My Own) deals with the destructive consequences of feelings of failure but also shows that such feelings can be overcome, albeit at times by extreme or even grotesque means. The novel *Om* (1946; If) exhibits strong anti-realism in that readers are constantly reminded by the narrator that they are reading a work of fiction. *Jungfrun i det gröna* (1947; The Virgin in the Grass) is thematically related to *Min död er min* in that it shows an average man may be able to accept himself as such through the love of a woman. *Egen spis* (1948; A Stove of One's Own) contrasts the pursuit of social and material ambition with true caring for others. *Fromma mord* (1952; Pious Murders) criticizes the kind of religiosity that leads some people to seek their own salvation without regard for the needs of other people.

The novel *Kanelbiten* (1953; tr. *Cinnamoncandy*, 1990) tells the story of a young girl with cinnamon-colored hair who grows up too fast, believing that a woman exists primarily through her relationship to the man in her life. The story was adapted for radio by Mia Törnkvist and broadcast in Sweden in 2004. *Stora glömskan: Zacharias' första bok* (1954; The Great Forgetfulness: Zacharias's First Book) has as its main character a 13-year-old boy named Zacharias, who is exceptionally attuned to other people. He also occurs in *Natt i marknadstältet* (1957; Night in the Fairground Tent), in which he observes the marital tragedy of the characters Leopold and Paulina Dahl. At the end of his career, Ahlin returned to Zacharias in *De sotarna! De sotarna! Zacharias' andra bok* (1990; The Chimney Sweeps! The Chimney Sweeps! Zacharias's Second Book).

After publishing *Bark och löv* (1961; Bark and Foliage), a novel about the relationship between author and audience, Ahlin published no books for approximately 20 years. Then, after co-authoring a novel with his wife, he returned to his previous themes with *Sjätte munnen* (1985; The Sixth Mouth), which describes the love that an 11-year-old boy has for his father in spite of the father's many shortcomings. The novel *Din livsfrukt* (1987; Fruit of Your Life) shows that achieving a sense of self-worth is hard for the rich as well as the poor. *Det florentinska vildsvinet* (1991; The Florentine Wild Boar) considers the role played by love in the development of a budding artist. Ahlin published collections of his earlier essays in 1994, 1995, and 1996. His two plays, *Lekpaus* (1948; Play Break) and *Eld av eld* (1949; Fire of Fire), have received little critical attention.

AHO, JUHANI (1861–1921). A Finnish novelist, and short story writer, Aho was the son of a Lutheran minister and worked as a newspaperman much of his life. He started out as an adherent of **realism**, but turned toward **impressionism** in the 1890s. One of Aho's major themes is the contrast between the traditional rural lifestyle and the urban life of artists and intellectuals. His first novel, *Rautatie* (1884; The Railroad), describes the fascination of an elderly rural couple for this newfangled mode of transportation. The railroad also figures prominently in his narrative *Helsinkiin* (1889; To Helsinki) and the novella *Yksin* (1890; Alone).

Like many other Scandinavian realists, Aho was concerned about the situation of **women** in the home and in society. Two novels, *Papin tytär* (1885; The Parson's Daughter) and *Papin rouva* (1893; The Parson's Wife) tell about a minister's daughter named Elli who is married off to a man she does not love and who is also a minister. Her father's wishes are the deciding factor. Her mother, who suffered the same fate in her youth, aids and abets her parson husband. Later this kind of behavior would be referred to as identification with the oppressor.

In Scandinavian literature as a whole, the early 1890s marked a turn away from social themes to an interest in the interior lives of human beings. Aho's oeuvre is also marked by this change, and in addition he is subject to a turn toward nationalism that in Finnish literature manifested itself as an interest in Karelia. His novel *Panu* (1897) is set there and takes place in the 17th century. Panu is a shaman who is in conflict with the local clergyman, who wins the battle because Panu is not completely true to the old ways. The novel *Kevät ja takatalvi* (1906; Spring and the Cold Spell) features the conflict between religiously awakened country dwellers and representatives of the intelligentsia in the 1840s. *Juha* (1911) is also a novel set in the Karelian forests; it is a penetrating psychological study of the love of an older and ugly man for his young and beautiful wife.

The novel *Rauhan erakko* (1916; Hermit of Peace), which is set in central Europe during World **War** I, has a pacifist message. Childhood memories are at the core of *Muistatko—?* (1920; Do You Remember—?), a novel about how to deal with loss and its resulting depression. Throughout his long career as a writer Aho also published eight volumes of shorter prose pieces that he called *Lastuja* (1891–1921; Wood Shavings).

ALMQVIST, CARL JONAS LOVE (1793–1866). A Swedish poet, playwright, novelist, short story writer, and essayist, Almqvist is a child of the **romantic** era who may also be thought of as an early **realist**. Accused of attempted murder, he left Sweden for America in 1851, at which time his literary career was effectively over and interest in his writings largely came to an end. Almqvist returned to Europe from the United States in 1866 but died in a hospital in Bremen, Germany. Rescued from oblivion by the writer Ellen Key in an essay written in 1894, Almqvist is now considered one of Sweden's most gifted and interesting men of letters.

Almqvist's romantic works include *Amorina* (written in 1822, but not published until 1839), which is characterized by such gothic motifs as incest, madness, and murder. The title character represents natural goodness in contrast with controlling religiosity of her stepfather. The story *Jaktslottet* (1832; The Hunting Lodge) was used as a frame story in the multivolume *Törnrosens bok* (1833–1840; The Book of the Briar Rose), which in successive editions included a large number of Almqvist's writings. The owner of the hunting lodge, Hugo Löwenstjerna, acts as the host of a gathering in which various stories are told. Poetry written by Almqvist is also acted out as *tableaux vivants*; these poems are referred to as "Songes" (Dreams).

One of the stories included in *Törnrosens bok* bears the title "Ormus och Ariman" (Ormazd and Ahriman) and is inspired by the Persian *Zend-Avesta*, a Zoroastrian sacred text. Ormus is an organizer and controller, while the seemingly evil Ariman is similar to the romantic artist. Also included in *Törnrosens bok* is a fascinating historical novel, *Drottningens juvelsmycke eller Azouras Lazuli Tintomara* (1834; tr. *The Queen's Diadem*, 1992), which mixes prose, drama, and poetry in its creation of the beautiful Tintomara, who appears as both male and female. With the murder of King **Gustav III** in 1792 at its center, *Drottningens juvelsmycke*, too, is a hybrid text of great complexity and endless fascination for its devotees.

Almqvist's ties to the thematic concerns of realism are best observed in his short novel *Det går an* (1839; tr. *Sara Videbeck*, 1919; *Why Not?*, 1994). Sara is a young woman who has inherited the right to work as a glazier from her father but, according to the law at the time, only as long as her mother is alive. During a boat trip she meets

Albert, with whom she falls in love and agrees to have an ongoing sexual relationship without the benefit of marriage. Sara insists that they must have separate living quarters, however, so that they will both preserve their independence. The Swedish authorities were shocked by this display of independence, and Almqvist lost his job as a school principal.

ANDERSEN, BENNY (1929–). A Danish poet, short story writer, novelist, and playwright, Andersen had his literary debut with the poetry collection *Den musikalske ål* (1960; The Musical Eel), which was followed by *Kamera med køkkenadgang* (1962; Camera with Kitchen Privileges) and *Den indre bowlerhat* (1964; The Inner Bowler Hat). With humor and self-irony, the poems in these collections discuss such fundamental issues of life as the relationship between nature and culture and between the individual and the community, and Andersen's work was perceived as meaningful by a large audience. Other collections with similar concerns are *Portrætgalleriet* (1966; The Portrait Gallery) and *Det sidste øh og andre digte* (1969; The Last Um and Other Poems).

Some of Andersen's later poetry shows a greater degree of social and political engagement. *Personlige papirer* (1974; Personal Papers) and *Himmelspræt eller kunsten at komme til verden* (1979; Blanket-Toss, or the Art of Being Born) express ethical views that show the influence of **Søren Kierkegaard**'s thought. The commitments that members of a family have to one another are seen as a workable model for both the national and the world community. Andersen's most recent volumes of poetry concern the aging process and human mortality. The poems in *Denne kommen og gåen* (1993; This Coming and Going) and *Sjælen marineret* (2001; The Marinated Soul) are life affirming and show that Andersen has maintained his mental and emotional flexibility.

The most important of Andersen's several collections of short stories is *Puderne* (1965; tr. *The Pillows*, 1983); the stories deal with various forms of maladjustment. *Over skulderen: Blå historier* (1983; Over the Shoulder: Blue Stories) offers portraits of a variety of characters in personal or social distress. Andersen has also written several plays. The most important is *Orfeus i undergrunden* (1979; Orpheus in the Underground), in which the author argues against

Danish membership in the European Common Market (later to become the European Union). His novel *På broen: Roman i ni episoder* (1981; On the Bridge: A Novel in Nine Episodes) describes life in Denmark during World **War** II.

ANDERSEN, HANS CHRISTIAN (1805–1875). A Danish **fairy tale** writer, novelist, dramatist, and poet, Andersen came from a working-class background and felt like an outsider all of his life. However, he is Scandinavia's best-known writer, and his stories are known and loved throughout the world. Andersen did not hit on the idea of writing tales until well into his career. His first significant published work was a collection of sketches entitled *Fodreise fra Holmens Canal til Østpynten af Amager i Aarene 1828 og 1829* (1829; A Walking Tour from Holmen's Canal to the Eastern Point of Amager in the Years 1828 and 1829), in which he described his observations while walking through Copenhagen. He also published an early poetry collection, *Digte* (1830; Poems), as well as *Phantasier og Skizzer* (1831; Fantasies and Sketches), which contains additional poems.

Andersen's main object in the early years of his career was to become a dramatist. An example of his efforts in this vein is his play *Mulatten* (1840; The Mulatto), an interracial love story set on the island of Martinique. His earliest success, however, came through his novels. Written after a journey to Italy, where it is set, the novel *Improvisatoren* (1835; tr. *The Improvisatore*, 1845) became a great success. Andersen also received much favorable attention for his other novels, *O. T.* (1836; tr. 1845), *Kun en Spillemand* (1837; tr. *Only a Fiddler*, 1845), *De to Baronesser* (1848; tr. *The Two Baronesses*, 1848), *At være eller ikke være* (1857; tr. *To Be, or Not To Be?* 1857), and *Lykke-Peer* (1870; tr. *Lucky Peer*, 1871). Most of these books contain autobiographical references.

Autobiographical elements are also present in Andersen's fairy tales, the genre which brought him his worldwide reputation. He produced a total of 156 tales that were published in 11 volumes with such titles as *Eventyr, fortalte for Børn* (1835; Tales Told for Children), *Historier* (1852; Stories), and *Eventyr og Historier* (1858; Tales and Stories). The tales vary greatly by content. Some are simply retellings of well-known folktales or **folklore**; others have a point that one would associate neither with a children's story nor with a folklore text. For example, "Skyggen" (1847; tr. "The Shadow," multiple publication dates) features a scholar who searches for the good, the true, and the beautiful, only to have his social position taken over by his shadow, who finally arranges to have the man killed. Other tales have slightly different messages for adults and children. For example, "Den grimme Ælling" (1844; tr. "The Ugly Duckling," multiple publication dates) makes a philosophical point that is probably lost on most children, namely, that memories of having been raised by ducks will color one's life even if most of it is lived among swans. Many of Andersen's tales owe their power to the presence of different layers of meaning as well as to the simple colloquial language Andersen employs.

Andersen traveled widely and used his experiences in a number of travel narratives, most of which were translated into English during his lifetime. He published several versions of his autobiography, the final version being *Mit Livs Eventyr* (1855; tr. and expanded as *The Story of My Life*, 1871). His diaries were published in 10 volumes 1971–1977. A selection in English bears the title *The Diaries of Hans Christian Andersen* (1990). *See also* CHILDREN'S BOOKS.

ATTERBOM, PER DANIEL AMADEUS (1790–1855). A Swedish poet and playwright, Atterbom was a major spokesperson for **romanticism** in Sweden. He was strongly influenced by the German romantics, and particularly Friedrich W. J. Schelling's *System of Transcendental Idealism* (1800) and Johann Gottlieb Fichte's *Science of Knowledge* (1794). As a student at Uppsala University, Atterbom was deeply involved in the debate between classicism and romanticism, even to the point of exhaustion. He was a central figure in the group Auraraförbundet (The **Aurora Society**), which sponsored the important journal *Phosphorus*.

Atterbom's first major publication was a cycle of poems, *Blommorna* (The Flowers), which was published in the annual *Poetisk kalender* (Poetic Calendar) in 1812. *Poetisk kalender* was very popular as a Christmas gift, and *Blommorna* reached a large audience. The poems in the cycle symbolized both the seasons of the year and different aspects of human life.

One of the major romantic genres was the **fairy-tale** play (*sagospel* or *eventyrspill*), and Atterbom tried his hand at it with his *Fågel* *blå*, a fragment of which was published in *Poetisk kalender* in 1818, but which remained incomplete. He did, however, complete his second effort in this genre, *Lycksalighetens ö* (1824–1827; The Isle of Bliss), in which the main character, King Astolf, spends 300 years in the company of the forever young Felicia. This poetic drama is Atterbom's major work as well as one of the great works of Swedish romanticism.

AURORA SOCIETY. Started by a group of Swedish students in 1808, Auroraförbundet (The **Aurora Society**) published the journal *Phosphorus*. The group promoted the ideas of **romanticism** in Sweden and emphasized the ability of the poet to be in touch with a transcendental reality beyond the visible world. Its greatest luminary was **Per Daniel Amadeus Atterbom**.

– B –

BAGGESEN, JENS (1764–1826). A Danish poet, Baggesen started writing poetry early and attracted the attention of, among others, the Danish preromantic poet **Johannes Ewald**. He had much success with a collection entitled *Comiske Fortællinger* (1785; Comic Tales), in which he put various anecdotes and tales into verse, much like the Dano-Norwegian poet **Johan Herman Wessel**. Baggesen also published collections of his occasional poetry. Baggesen is remembered chiefly as the author of Denmark's first truly artistic travel narrative, *Labyrinten* (1792–1793), an account of a three-year trip through Germany in which he was adaptable, got along well with a wide variety of people, and enjoyed himself very much; his readers also enjoyed his book. In the year 1800 Baggesen moved to Germany.

BANG, HERMAN (1857–1912). A Danish novelist, short story writer, poet, dramatist, and **critic**, Bang made a lackluster attempt at becoming an actor. He had considerable success as a cultural journalist in the Copenhagen press, however, and some of his journalism has been collected in the volumes *Realisme og Realister* (1979; Realism and Realists), *Kritiske Studier* (1880; Critical Studies), and *Herhjemme og Derude* (1881; At Home and Abroad).

Bang's first novel made use of his own experience as the child in a family where mental and physical illness were present. Entitled *Haabløse Slægter* (1880; Hopeless Generations), the book depicts both personal and family decline and is one of the first manifestations of the literature of decadence in Scandinavia. It was followed by the novel *Fædra* (1883) and the short story collections *Excentriske Noveller* (1885; Eccentric Stories) and *Stille Eksistenser* (1886; Quiet Existences), in which sexual desire is a significant theme. *Stille Eksistenser* includes the novella "Ved Vejen," (tr. *Kathinka*, 1990), an early example of **impressionism** in Scandinavian literature. Showing the influence of his Norwegian colleague **Jonas Lie**, Bang's novel *Stuk* (1887; Stucco) is an indictment of the foolish avarice of an entire city, Copenhagen in the 1880s. The novel *Tine* (1889; tr. *Tina*, 1984), on the other hand, portrays a doomed love affair during the 1864 **war** between Denmark and Prussia. Seduced by her master, the servant Tine commits suicide when she realizes that the man she loves has no lasting interest in her. The short stories in *Under Aaget* (1890; Under the Yoke) and the novel *Ludvigsbakke* (1896; tr. *Ida Brandt*, 1928) are equally pessimistic about the possibility for human happiness.

Several novels by Bang are partly autobiographical. *Det hvide Hus* (1898; The White House) and *Det graa Hus* (1901; The Grey House) offer realistic representations of Bang's childhood. *Mikaël* (1904) and *De uden Fædreland* (1906; tr. *Denied a Country*, 1927) depict socially marginalized artists hungry for love. *See also* WILLUMSEN, DORRIT.

BELLMAN, CARL MICHAEL (1740–1795). A Swedish lyric poet, Bellman was born into the family of a well-situated, mid-level civil servant and was provided with an education of very good quality. His study of literature included learning how to write poetry, and Bellman eventually wrote more than 1,500 poems. He was placed in several government jobs but did nothing to distinguish himself. In Bellman's day the drinking song was ever present in Swedish life. Many of these songs were written to popular melodies and often parodied other poems and songs. Bellman's achievement consists in taking this humble and unrecognized literary form and raising it to a genre that became impossible to ignore, while in the process creating songs and characters that have become an indispensable part of Sweden's literary and cultural heritage.

Bellman had the personality of an entertainer, loved to perform, and accompanied himself with a simple string instrument. He was a welcome guest everywhere and even attracted the attention of the Swedish king, **Gustav III**, who provided him with a financial subsidy. Bellman created a gallery of characters who appeared in his songs, and with his sound background in classical literature and mythology, he structured this group of figures as a parody on classical themes and constantly wove mythological references into the texts of his songs. The appeal of his poems thus consisted not only in the characters and situations that are described in them, but also in the surprising and humorous similarities and contrasts that arise between his Stockholm characters and situations and their classical literary and mythological frame of reference. Some of Bellman's characters are the prostitute Ulla Winblad, a tavern musician, a wig maker, a corporal, and so on. The patron saint of the whole enterprise was a watchmaker named Fredman who had lost his social respectability and finally drunk himself to death.

Two volumes of poems and songs were published during Bellman's lifetime. *Fredmans epistlar* (1790; Fredman's Epistles) was presented as epistles sent by Fredman to his fellow devotees of Bacchus, the ancient god of wine. *Fredmans sångar* (1791; Fredman's Songs) had little connection with Fredman himself; one should perhaps regard Fredman as a kind of trademark that Bellman had established for himself.

King Gustav III had literary and cultural interests and collaborated with many of the men of letters of the age. His attempt to enlist Bellman in his royal cultural enterprise was largely unsuccessful, for Bellman's talent seemed limited to the mode of expression that he had chosen for himself. However, Bellman is remembered as the most brilliant among the Gustavian poets.

BENEDICTSSON, VICTORIA (1850–1888). A Swedish novelist and short story writer, Benedictsson wrote under the male pseudonym Ernst Ahlgren. Raised as a tomboy by her father, her life was a bit like that of August Strindberg's Miss Julie, a character that was modeled after her. When her father refused to let her go to Stockholm to study art, Victoria married a widower 28 years her senior. The marriage allowed her time to write, and she had her debut with a collection of short stories, *Från Skåne* (1884; From Skåne). Her novel *Pengar* (1885; Money) told about the life of a protagonist named Selma who would like to pursue art but marries an older man, and who then achieves independence. Like many other Scandinavian novels of the 1870s and 1880s, it was very critical of social conditions. Benedictsson expresses her indignation as a means to reform, however, rather than just for its own sake.

A second volume of short stories bears the title *Folkliv och småberättelser* (1887; Folk Life and Minor Stories). The same year she published her second novel, *Fru Marianne* (1987; Mrs. Marianne), which she had written specifically to impress the Danish **critic Georg Brandes**, with whom she had fallen in love. The novel argues for monogamous relations between the sexes and tells about an upper-class woman who marries a farmer and adjusts just fine to her new life. Brandes was not impressed, and Benedictsson committed suicide by slitting her throat in a cheap hotel in Copenhagen. *See also* WOMEN.

BENEDIKTSSON, EINAR (1864–1940). An Icelandic poet and journalist, Benediktsson was the son of a notable politician and government administrator. Somewhat unruly as a young man, Benediktsson took a long time to finish a law degree in Copenhagen, where he spent a great deal of time developing his poetic gifts. He was much taken with the ideas of **Georg Brandes**, whose lectures he attended, but later adopted the individualist outlook of the **neoromantics**. Back in Iceland after his studies, he worked as a newspaperman and championed Iceland's independence. He was in favor of industrialization and other forms of economic development, including the development of radio as a means of communication between Iceland and the outside world. Some of his early poetry was published in the collection *Sögur og kvæði* (1897; Tales and Songs).

Benediktssson's poetry is highly intellectual and reflective. It unites a concern about form—Benediktsson is keenly aware of the poetic heritage from Old Norse literature—with a love for the natural world that is strongly present in such collections as *Hafblik* (1906;

Sea Calm), *Hrannir* (1913; Waves), and *Vogar* (1921; Billows). The ocean is one of his main sources of inspiration.

BERGMAN, HJALMAR (1883–1931). A Swedish novelist and playwright, Bergman was strongly influenced by **Freudianism** and wrote with great psychological insight but with a very pessimistic view of life. Most of his novels take place in the district of Bergslagen in the middle of Sweden. Born in the town of Örebro, Bergman knew the area well. Örebro is the model for his fictional town Wadköping, the setting for some of his most important works.

Bergman came from a well-to-do family and, until the death of his father in 1915, was able to devote himself entirely to writing with little thought to his financial life. After a series of novels that give little indication he was to become one of Sweden's most significant modernists, *Hans nåds testamente* (1910; tr. *The Baron's Will*, 1968) appeared. Set in Bergslagen, it is both a funny story of complex family relationships and a tale of rather irrational behavior, with an emphasis on the absurdity of existence. *Vi Bookar, Krokar och Rothar* (1912; We Books, Kroks, and Roths) is a story about the financial machinations of those well off and the sufferings of those who are not.

The modernist concern with the role of the artist comes to the fore in *Loewenhistorier* (1913; Loewen Stories). Bergman's pessimism is reflected by *En döds memoarer* (1918; The Memoirs of a Dead Man), in which the anti-realism of modernist prose is a major feature of the text. Artistically successful, it was less commercially so than the novel *Markurells i Wadköping* (1919; tr. *God's Orchid*, 1924), in which a story of both financial ruin and personal heartache is told with great hilarity. Its controlling protagonist, Markurell, is a reflection of Bergman's parents, and is similar to such figures as the title character in *Herr von Hancken* (1920; Mr. von Hancken) and the matriarch in *Farmor och Vår Herre* (1921; tr. *Thy Rod and Thy Staff*, 1937), who is brought to realize that what she thought of as her love was really attempts to control the behavior of her children. In *Chefen Fru Ingeborg* (1924; tr. *The Head of the Firm*, 1936) sexual jealousy is added to the protagonist's wish to dominate, as Ingeborg discovers that she has fallen in love with her future son-in-law. Bergman's last novel, *Clownen Jac* (1930; tr. *Jac the Clown*, 1995), is the author's pessimistic commentary on his own situation as a writer. The artist cannot be honest with the audience, which demands deception and lies in the name of entertainment.

Bergman wrote a number of dramas and screenplays, for many years as a collaborator with the great movie director Victor Sjöström. The three plays that make up *Komedier i Bergslagen* (1914–1916; Bergslagen Comedies) were well received. He also published a series of dramas that tend toward expressionism, of which *Herr Sleeman kommer* (1917; tr. *Mr. Sleeman Is Coming*, 1944) bears special mention. *See also* THEATER.

BJØRNEBOE, JENS (1920–1976). A Norwegian novelist, playwright, poet, and essayist, Bjørneboe was profoundly influenced by the culture of Continental Europe. His literary debut was a collection of poetry entitled simply *Dikt* (1951; Poems), which was followed by two more collections, *Ariadne* (1953) and *Den store by* (1958; The Great City). Restless by nature and deeply affected by the **war** experience, Bjørneboe wrote his first novel, *Før hanen galer* (1952; Before the Cock Crows), about medical experiments performed by Nazi doctors on concentration camp prisoners. It offers a portrait of a man whose mind is divided; he is a caring and sensitive person in his private life, but his scientific objectivity leads him to commit the most gruesome crimes. This book was controversial, but even more so was Bjørneboe's next novel, *Jonas* (1955; tr. *The Last of These*, 1959), which through a portrait of a dyslexic little boy attacked the Norwegian school system.

Under en hårdere himmel (1957; Under a Harder Sky) portrays Norway's treatment of Nazi wartime collaborators and is a severe indictment of the country's judicial authorities. *Blåmann* (1959) is a novel about artistic development, while *Den onde hyrde* (1960; The Evil Shepherd) argues that it is necessary to reform the way young criminals are treated; it is a good example of Bjørneboe's gadfly behavior vis-à-vis the Norwegian State Prosecutor's office. *Drømmen og hjulet* (1964; The Dream and the Wheel), a fictionalized account of the life of the Norwegian writer Ragnhild Jølsen (1875–1908), is another novel of artistic development. Jølsen was a promising novelist and short story writer when she ended her life with an overdose of sleeping powder.

The war experience caused Bjørneboe to become fascinated by the problem of evil. After discussing it in the context of the war in both *Før hanen galer* and *Under en hårdere himmel*, he offers a more general investigation in a trilogy commonly referred to as "The History of Bestiality." The first volume, *Frihetens øyeblikk* (1966; tr. *Moment of Freedom*, 1975), has as its narrator a certain servant of justice in a small European principality, a man who sets out to record the various evils and atrocities of Western civilization. The other two volumes, *Kruttårnet* (1969; tr. *Powderhouse*, 1999) and *Stillheten* (1973; tr. *The Silence*, 2000), continute the same line of inquiry. The theme of evil is also present in Bjørneboe's final novel, *Haiene* (1974; tr. *Sharks*, 1993). Its tone is more positive, however, for although it tells the story of the struggle between the crew members of a ship, there is hope for reconciliation in the end.

Bjørneboe's dramas were strongly influenced by the ideas of Bertolt Brecht and attempt to subvert the verisimilitude of such traditional **theater** as that associated with **Henrik Ibsen**. *Til lykke med dagen* (1965; Many Happy Returns) satirized the Norwegian penal system. Bjørneboe's best play, *Fugleelskerne* (1966; tr. *The Bird Lovers*, 1993), is set in an Italian village and thematizes the idea of ethical responsibility. A party of German bird lovers—former Nazi occupants of the area—wish to establish a bird sanctuary. They are recognized by some of the people whom they had tortured during the war, and the question is to what extent they are to be held individually responsible for their deeds 30 years earlier. Bjørneboe argues that ethical responsibility for such evils as the atrocities of war is collective, not individual. His next play, *Semmelweis* (1968; tr. 1996), tells the story of the Hungarian doctor who discovered the cause of childbirth fever, only to be silenced by the medical establishment of his time; it is once more a critique of authority. So is the parody *Amputasjon* (1971; tr. *Amputation*, 2003), in which society's members are literally trimmed to the desired length. *Dongry* (1975; Dungarees) is a satire on business life.

BJØRNSON, BJØRNSTJERNE (1832–1910). A Norwegian poet, novelist, and dramatist, Bjørnson was considered Norway's most important writer during his lifetime and heads a list of four 19th-century Norwegian writers commonly referred to as "de fire store" (the four great ones; the others are, in order, **Henrik Ibsen**, **Alexander Kielland**, and **Jonas Lie**). His significance to Norwegian literature, culture, and society cannot be overestimated; for half a century he used his preeminence as a writer to provide leadership both intellectually and artistically.

Bjørnson was the son of a Lutheran minister in Romsdal on the northwestern coast of Norway. He grew up among farmers and became thoroughly familiar with most aspects of rural life. After schooling in Molde and Christiania (now Oslo), he started writing cultural journalism for the Christiania paper *Morgenbladet* (The Morning Post) in 1854. He had a tremendous amount of energy and involved himself in a variety of causes, including Norway's first workers movement and the struggle to establish a Norwegian **theater**, as well as liberal politics in general.

He burst upon the literary scene in 1857, when he published both the historical drama *Mellem Slagene* (tr. *Between the Acts*, 1941) and a *bondefortelling* (peasant tale) entitled *Synnøve Solbakken* (tr. 1858), a prose narrative roughly the length of a short novel that was set in the type of environment that he knew so well from his youth. Both works were influenced by the ideas of **national romanticism** as well as those of the Dane **N. F. S. Grundtvig**, for Bjørnson wanted to show that contemporary Norwegian peasants were the natural heirs of the greatness of their ancient forbears. But his characters nevertheless come across as real human beings who must struggle to overcome personal problems before they can find happiness.

For the next several years, Bjørnson alternated between writing historical plays, which are generally referred to as "saga dramas," and peasant stories with a contemporary setting. Both forms, but particularly the latter, gave him a reputation as Scandinavia's foremost writer, and his peasant stories are still widely read in Norway. Two of his most important such tales, next to *Synnøve Solbakken*, are *Arne* (1859; tr. 1866) and *En glad Gut* (1860; tr. *A Happy Boy* 1870), both of which have male protagonists who have to overcome weaknesses of character. Among his most important saga dramas are *Halte-Hulda* (1858), *Kong Sverre* (1861; King Sverre), and *Sigurd Slembe* (1862; tr. 1888), which borrows heavily from **Snorri Sturluson**'s *Heimskringla*. A stay in Italy (1860–1862) removed Bjørnson from the political fray for a time and enabled him to focus more fully on his writing, and Rome also gave him a stronger sense of history and fostered his appreciation for such classical values as balance and equilibrium.

The breadth of Bjørnson's literary output during the 1860s was substantial. The play *Maria Stuart i Skotland* (1864; tr. *Mary, Queen of Scots*, 1897) was written partly in response to Friedrich von Schiller's treatment of the same material. A cycle of epic poetry, begun in 1860, was finished and published as *Arnljot Gelline* (1870; tr. 1917), and Bjørnson collected his poetry as *Digte og Sange* (1870; tr. *Poems and Songs*, 1915). He also wrote his first contemporary domestic play, *De Nygifte* (1865; tr. *A Lesson in Marriage*, 1911), which examines the situation of a **woman** who is forced to choose between her husband and her parents.

After again escaping the contemporary debate by going to Italy, this time in 1873, Bjørnson wrote two plays that introduced **realistic** drama to Scandinavia. *En fallit* (1875; tr. *The Bankrupt*, 1914) is thematically related to Henrik Ibsen's *Samfundets støtter* (1877; tr. *The Pillars of Society*, 1888) in that its subject is honesty and integrity in business and public life, while *Redaktøren* (1875; tr. *The Editor*, 1914) offers a portrait of a rather harsh man and pleads for tolerance in politics. Bjørnson's demand for truth is also the theme of *Kongen* (1877; tr. *The King*, 1914), which attacks the institution of the monarchy.

The most important development in Bjørnson's life in the late 1870s was that he abandoned his Grundtvigian-colored Christian beliefs, replacing them with a reliance on secular ethics and a trust in Charles Darwin's theory of evolution. *Det ny system* (1879; tr. *The New System*, 1913), a play about difficulties associated with telling the truth in a small country, records his spiritual struggle, and the drama *Leonarda* (1879; tr. 1911) shows that he was quick to adopt his new outlook. Taking a woman's right to divorce as its subject, *Leonarda* was, however, eclipsed by Ibsen's far superior play ***Et dukkehjem*** (1879; tr. *A Doll's House*, 1880).

Politics took much of Bjørnson's time in the 1880s, and his play *En handske* (1883; tr. *A Gauntlet*, 1886) is considered his intervention in the so-called morality debate that raged in the middle years of the decade. The social issue was whether women should be given the same freedom in sexual matters as had traditionally been claimed by men; Bjørnson's heroine argues that men should be held to the same standards as had traditionally been required of women. The author was consequently attacked from both the right and the left. These years also saw his first full-scale novel, *Det flager i byen og på havnen* (1884; tr. *The Heritage of the Kurts*, 1892), which argues for broader educational opportunities for women. There is a lighter touch in the comedy *Geografi og kærlighed* (1885; tr. *Love and Geography*, 1914), however, in which an egotistical scholar and husband is taught an important lesson in commitment.

Most of Bjørnson's works from the latter part of his career have not withstood the test of time. The most notable exception is his dramatic masterpiece *Over ævne I* (1883; tr. *Pastor Sang*, 1893), which probes the psychology of faith. Another fine play from his later years is *Paul Lange og Tora Parsberg* (1898; tr. *Paul Lange and Tora Parsberg*, 1899), which pleads for less cruelty in politics. Bjørnson's legacy is in large measure constituted by his best poems, many of which have become part of Norway's national patrimony and are known—and often sung—by large numbers of Norwegians.

BJØRNVIG, THORKILD (1918–2004). A Danish poet and essayist, Bjørnvig studied comparative literature and became a prize-winning literary scholar. Bjørnvig is thus aware that there is a close relationship between literary **criticism** and the literature on which it is based, and he sees a similar relationship between poetry and reality. The poet, for Bjørnvig, does not create reality linguistically, but the poem reflects and embodies reality. Bjørnvig's poetic epistemology is thus essentially of the premodern kind; knowledge is reality reflected in the glassy essence of the mind, and truth is so because it corresponds to reality.

Bjørnvig had his literary debut with the poetry collection *Stjærnen bag Gavlen* (1947; The Star behind the Gable), in which he expresses the view that poetry mediates our experience of the universe. Art's ability to help humans understand life is further stressed in the poetry collections *Anubis* (1955) and *Figur og Ild* (1959; Figure and Fire). **Nature** becomes comprehensible through poetry. The collection *Ravnen* (1968; The Raven) is the epitome of structure and order, thus indicating that humans and nature have a necessary rather than a contingent relation to one another. In his future volumes of poetry,

Bjørnvig takes the consequences of this realization: since the relation of human beings to nature is necessary, the condition of nature deeply affects what becomes of humanity. Environmentalism thus becomes a supreme ethical obligation, for the mental and spiritual purity of human beings is a consequence of the purity of nature.

These kinds of ideas were expressed in the poetry collections *Delfinen* (1975; The Dolphin), *Abeguden* (1981; The Monkey God), and *Epimeteus* (1990). Bjørnvig has also presented his views in volumes of essays, beginning with *Begyndelsen* (1960; The Beginning) and *Virkeligheden er til* (1973; Reality Exists), and continuing, with even greater explicitness, in *Også for naturens skyld* (1978; Also for the Sake of Nature) and *Barnet og dyret i industrisamfundet* (1979; The Child and the Animal in Industrial Society). Bjørnvig has used the term "ecological socialism" to designate his environmental program.

Like many other Danish writers, Bjørnvig has also written memoirs. His first book in this vein was *Pagten* (1974; tr. *The Pact*, 1983), in which he discusses his relationship with **Karen Blixen**. Later volumes include *Solens have og skolegården* (1983; The Garden of the Sun and the Schoolyard), *Hjørnestuen og månehavet* (1984; The Corner Room and the Moon Ocean), *Jordens hjerte* (1986; The Heart of the Earth), and *Ønsket* (1987; The Wish); together these four volumes cover the years 1918–1948.

BLICHER, STEEN STEENSEN (1782–1848). A Danish short story writer and poet, Blicher spent his life as a Jutland parson. Drawing on folk life and at times using the local dialect in his stories, he produced the earliest **realist** literature in Denmark and anticipated narrative techniques associated with **modernism**. Blicher's stories are of uneven quality. Many were written simply because he was in a financial bind, but the best of them have become classics in Danish literature. His first significant prose work bears the title *Brudstykker af en Landsbydegns Dagbog* (1824; tr. *The Diary of a Parish Clerk*, 1945), in which he utilizes the biography of the Danish noblewoman Marie Grubbe; this material was later to be used by **J. P. Jacobsen** as well. But it is the position of the narrator, the son of a parish clerk who later becomes a parish clerk himself, that is of the greatest interest in the story. An outside observer, the narrator views the events of the story with limited omniscience while Blicher manipulates his point of view so as to provide psychological insights into the characters.

Some of the other stories show surprisingly modern narrative techniques as well. In "Præsten i Vejlbye" (1829; tr. "The Parson at Vejlbye," 1945) Blicher uses both documents and diary narrative to uncover the wrongful execution of a local clergyman. "Sildig Opvaagnen" (1828; tr. "Tardy Awakening," 1945) uses retrospective narration to uncover a story of adultery and suicide. "Hosekræmmeren" (1829; tr. "The Hosier and His Daughter," 1945) employs two different narrators who together tell a story of misguided parental love and control. "E Bindstouw" (1842; "In the Knitting Room") dramatizes the narrative situation and adds a sense of realism through the use of Jutland dialect. Blicher's poetry collection *Trækfuglerne* (1838; The Migratory Birds) takes the transitoriness of life as its main theme.

BLIXEN, KAREN (1885–1962). A Danish short story writer and sometime novelist, Blixen is a major writer in both Danish and English; among speakers of English she is known as Isak Dinesen. Her first success came in the English-speaking world, but later she was recognized in Denmark as well and became a veritable cultural institution there. As a writer, Blixen reacted against the psychological and social realism of contemporary Danish literature and looked back to the romantic storytellers for inspiration. Her main theme is art and its role in human life, and her value system is that of a bygone era.

After living on a coffee farm in Kenya for a number of years, Blixen returned to Denmark after the farm failed. In her early youth she had published some tales under a pseudonym, and she had written more of them while in Africa; these tales found their way into her first book, which was published in English as *Seven Gothic Tales* (1934), and then in Danish as *Syv fantastiske Fortællinger* (1935). These stories are marked by a number of fantastic features, such as the shape shifting in the story "Aben" ("The Monkey"). The prioress of a home for older unmarried women owns a monkey that originally came from Zanzibar, and at times the "soul" of the monkey and that of the woman trade bodies; the prioress goes out in the form of a monkey, and vice versa. Art also plays an important role, as in "Syndfloden over Norderney" ("The Deluge of Norderney"), in which the actor Kasparsen has murdered Cardinal Hamilcar von Sehested in order that he may impersonate him, thus playing the role of his life.

Blixen's second book was a narrative based on her experiences on the coffee farm, *Den afrikanske Farm* (1937; tr. *Out of Africa*, 1937). It is both a book about a lost paradise and a memorial to Blixen's lover Denys Finch-Hatton, who had died when his private plane crashed shortly before Blixen's return to Denmark. Blixen's portrait of life in Africa is seductive, but she no doubt romanticized her experiences somewhat. *Skygger paa Græsset* (1960; tr. *Shadows on the Grass*, 1960) is a less engaging continuation of the story of her time in Africa.

Vinter-Eventyr (1942; tr. *Winter's Tales*, 1942) is the undisputed high point in Blixen's oeuvre. Several of its stories are central to understanding her work. "Den unge Mand med Nelliken" ("The Young Man with the Carnation"), which introduces the English-language edition, is a powerful expression of Blixen's theory of art. Its protagonist, Charlie Despard, discovers that he is not in control of his destiny as a writer, but that God has chosen him for this vocation and will give him just the right amount of pain to spur his creativity on. Blixen is thus in agreement with her countryman **Søren Kierkegaard** that art and pain are closely linked. "Skibsdrengens Fortælling" ("The Sailor-Boy's Tale") teaches not only that people living in northern Norway may have special powers, but that the eternal principle of justice cannot be violated. "Heloïse" ("The Heroine") shows that salvation may come through the actions of an exotic dancer just as well as from any other source.

The two volumes *Sidste Fortællinger* (1957; tr. *Last Tales*, 1957) and *Skæbne-Anekdoter* (1958; tr. *Anecdotes of Destiny*, 1958) contain such tales as "Det ubeskrevne Blad" ("The Blank Page"), which radically questions the origin and locus of meaning, and "Babettes Gæstebud" ("Babette's Feast"), which has been turned into an award-winning motion picture. "Babettes Gæstebud" is also a hymn to art, which is shown to have the atoning power generally associated with religion.

Blixen also wrote a novel occasioned by World **War** II, *Gengældelsens veje* (1944; tr. *The Angelic Avengers*, 1946), under the pseudonym Pierre Andrézel. Essays and letters from her time in Africa were published posthumously, as were *Efterladte Fortællinger* (1975; tr. *Carnival: Entertainments and Posthumous Tales*, 1977).

BOKMÅL. *See* RIKSMAAL.

BORGEN, JOHAN (1902–1979). A Norwegian short story writer, novelist, playwright, and cultural journalist, Borgen had a significant place in the intellectual and cultural life of his country for nearly 50 years. Born into an upper-middle-class family, he experienced the cultural upheaval associated with World **War** I, when the social and cultural hegemony, as well as the aristocratic values of his class, gave way to a relatively unbridled capitalism. Borgen reacted to these historical forces by becoming a social and economic radical; although he was unable to commit himself to the cause of communism, he had strong socialist sympathies throughout his life. But he was also occupied with the emotional consequences of rapid social change, and many of his best stories and novels focus on his characters' need to develop a durable sense of identity.

After writing short stories for various magazines, Borgen published his first book, a collection of stories entitled *Mot mørket* (1925; Toward Darkness), to a rather lackluster reception. After working briefly for the conservative *Morgenbladet* (The Morning Paper), he went to work for the liberal *Dagbladet* (The Daily Paper), with which he remained associated for most of his working life. During the 1930s he published his first novel, *Når alt kommer til alt* (1934; When Everything Is Said and Done), as well as several plays, the most remarkable of which is *Mens vi venter* (1938; While We Are Waiting), which departs from the realistic style, inherited from **Henrik Ibsen**, that was the standard in Norwegian **theater** at the time. The short stories in *Barnesinn* (1937; Children's Minds) feature children who have difficulties adjusting to a world in flux.

During World War II Borgen put his talents in the service of the resistance movement. Imprisoned by the Nazis for a while, he later fled to Sweden, where he tirelessly continued his resistance work, including journalism, plays, and a novel published in Swedish, *Ingen sommar* (1944; No Summer). He later published several plays as well as the novel *Kjærlighetsstien* (1946; Lovers' Lane), which satirizes the morals of the upper class and attacks residual Nazism. But his definitive breakthrough as a literary artist came with a series of three short story collections, *Hvetebrødsdager* (1948; Honeymoon), *Noveller om kjærlighet* (1952; Short Stories about Love), and *Natt og dag* (1954; Night and Day). Many of these stories focus on the search for personal identity. A story included in *Natt og dag*, "Elsk meg bort fra min bristende barndom" ("Love Me away from My Breaking Childhood") won him a shared first prize in the short story competition of the *New York Herald Tribune* in 1961 and shows how lovers may share each other's past through an almost uncanny intuition.

Borgen's most significant work is a trilogy about Wilfred Sagen, consisting of *Lillelord* (1955; tr. 1982), *De mørke kilder* (1956; The Dark Fountains), and *Vi har ham nå* (1957; We've Got Him Now). Strongly autobiographical, the trilogy follows Wilfred, nicknamed Lillelord, from his early childhood up to his suicide during World War II, as he struggles for a sense of who he really is, but spends most of his effort trying to perfect the roles that he believes he has been given by those around him. The Lillelord trilogy secured Borgen a major position in Norwegian literature, and he followed it up with several significant novels and short story collections. *Jeg* (1959; tr. *The Scapegoat*, 1993) is an experimental novel in which the protagonist is split into two personalities, one of which observes the actions of the other. *Blåtind* (1964; Blue Peak) is yet another novel in which questions of identity play a major role. Such novels as *Den røde tåken* (1967; tr. *The Red Mist*, 1973), *Min arm, min tarm* (1972; My Arm, My Intestine), and *Eksempler* (1974; Examples) all center on problems of personality and identity.

Nye noveller (1965; New Stories) won Borgen the **Nordic Literary Prize** in 1967. Three other collections of short stories bear the titles *Trær alene i skogen* (1969; Trees Alone in the Woods), *Lykke til* (1974; Good Luck), and *I dette rom* (1975; In This Room). *Barndommens rike* (1965; The Kingdom Childhood), originally written for a weekly radio program, tells about his own childhood. Borgen also published other novels and plays as well as many collections of journalism, essays, and miscellaneous prose.

BOYE, KARIN (1900–1941). A Swedish poet, novelist, short story writer, and essayist, Boye started out as a poet with the collection *Moln* (1922; Clouds), which was followed by *Gömda land* (1924;

Hidden Lands) and *Härdarna* (1927; The Hearths). Although most of her early poetry is rather traditional in form, many of her poems have a striking content, for example, "Sköldmön" (The Shield Maiden), in which a **woman** warrior fights and dies next to her male companion without him noticing it. This poem can be read as a feminist statement about the position of women in a man's world. In the poetry collection *För trädets skull* (1935; For the Tree's Sake) Boye abandoned traditional meter in favor of free verse.

After writing a number of literary and cultural essays and reviews, Boye published her first novel, *Astarte* (1931), a critique of contemporary advertising aimed at women as well as a more general investigation of modern myths and the meaning they conceal. Her next novel, *Merit vaknar* (1933; Merit Awakens), discusses marriage and sex roles from the perspective of a widow who is working through her past. *Kris* (1934; Crisis) is a novel about a crisis of faith brought about because the 20-year-old female protagonist has become sexually attracted to another woman. A volume of short stories, *Uppgörelser* (1934; Reckonings), is generally considered inferior to Boye's novels.

The novel *För lite* (1936; Too Little) deals with the conflict between art and family life. Boye's last novel, *Kallocain* (1940; tr. 1966), is set in a dystopia in the beginning of the third millennium, a society in which even a person's thoughts are known to the state. It expresses Boye's concern about both **Marxist** and Nazi totalitarianism.

BRANDES, GEORG (1842–1927). A Danish literary **critic**, Brandes is the greatest and most influential critic Scandinavia has produced. A very talented man, he played a crucial role in both Danish and Scandinavian literary life for three decades. Brandes had a long and productive life, during which he wrote a large number of books on European writers and artists. He was translated into all of the major European languages and was very influential not only in Scandinavia, but internationally as well.

Brandes came from a secular Jewish background and used his outsider status to launch an incisive and much needed critique of Danish literary and intellectual life. Having first been influenced by the Danish literary lion **Johan Ludvig Heiberg**, he traveled abroad and became taken with the ideas of the French critics Hippolyte Taine (1828–1893) and Charles-Augustin Sainte-Beuve (1804–1869). Taine practiced a positivistic historical-biographical form of criticism that also emphasized the psychology of the author; Sainte-Beuve preferred a systematic criticism based on historical determinism. An early collection of critical essays by Brandes entitled *Kritiker og Portræter* (1870; Critiques and Portraits) shows the influence of both French critics.

Brandes's prominence in Scandinavian literary life dates to 3 November 1871, when in the first lecture of a series held at the University of Copenhagen he called for a literary practice that would use literature to debate modern problems and issues. His strong personality either attracted or repelled people, and he soon gained a large following for his ideas, but also much opposition from the conservative Danish literary and political establishment. His lectures were eventually published as his most important work, the six-volume *Hovedstrømninger i det Nittende Aarhundredes Literatur* (1872–1890; tr. *Main Currents in Nineteenth-Century Literature*, 1901–1905).

Progressive Scandinavian writers generally found Brandes's ideas attractive, and the ensuing two decades, roughly 1870 to 1890, is a period referred to as the **Modern Breakthrough** in Scandinavia. Such **realists** and **naturalists** as the Danes **Henrik Pontoppidan** and **J. P. Jacobsen**, the Norwegians **Henrik Ibsen, Bjørnstjerne Bjørnson, Alexander Kielland, Arne Garborg**, and **Amalie Skram**, and the Swede **August Strindberg** were all deeply influenced by him, as were many others.

Together with his brother Edvard, Georg Brandes published the literary journal *Det Nittende Aarhundrede* (1874–1877; The Nineteenth Century), the chief forum for his radical critique of literature and culture. Brandes also summed up the early achievements of the Modern Breakthrough in his book *Det moderne Gennembruds Mænd* (1883; The Men of the Modern Breakthrough). In the 1880s he discovered the work of the German thinker Friedrich Nietzsche (1844–1900), whose writings he discussed in his essay "Aristokratisk Radikalisme" (1889; Aristocratic Radicalism) in the journal *Tilskueren* (The Spectator).

BRANNER, HANS CHRISTIAN (1903–1966). A Danish novelist, short story writer, and dramatist, Branner was in the forefront of

Danish literary life during the decades immediately after World **War** II. He had his debut with the novel *Legetøj* (1936; Toys), which is marked by the psychological **realism** of the interwar period. The new manager at a toy factory wants conformity and power, so he sows seeds of discord among the workers, who as a result lose their sense of solidarity with each other; this change in the microcosm of a small factory can be seen as a reference to social and political developments in Germany.

Barnet leger ved Stranden (1937; The Child Playing on the Beach) is influenced by psychoanalysis, as the narrator-protagonist searches his childhood for the causes of his present misery. **Freudianism** was also a significant influence on *Drømmen om en Kvinde* (1941; The Dream of a Woman), in which literary modernism is in evidence through interior monologue and stream-of-consciousness narration. The novel *Historien om Børge* (1942; tr. *The Story of Børge*, 1973) tells about an orphaned boy whose foster parents do not comprehend his sensitivity and imagination.

Branner's existential seriousness is also present in his short stories in the collections *Om lidt er vi borte* (1939; Soon We Are Gone) and *To Minutters Stilhed* (1944; tr. *Two Minutes of Silence*, 1966), as is his focus on the significance of childhood experiences. The motif of the authoritarian personality, first presented in *Legetøj*, returns in *Rytteren* (1949; tr. *The Riding Master*, 1951), in which Branner allows freedom and goodness to triumph over the urge to control others. The action in the novel *Ingen kender natten* (1955; tr. *No One Knows the Night*, 1958) takes place one night during Germany's occupation of Denmark in World War II and contains elements of Christian allegory. Myth and allegory are also significant features of the short stories in *Vandring langs floden* (1956; A Walk along the River).

Branner's stage dramas are rather traditional, but his radio plays are groundbreaking. His stage drama *Søskende* (1952; tr. *The Judge*, 1955) is inspired by psychoanalysis and concerns the relationship between three siblings and the consequences of having been raised by a controlling father. *Thermopylæ* (1958; tr. 1973) is an expression of humanist concerns.

BRANTENBERG, GERD (1941–). A Norwegian novelist, Brantenberg is considered Norway's foremost representative of **feminist** lesbian literature. She is also an outstanding lesbian and feminist activist who was instrumental in establishing the lesbian movement in Norway in 1975. Her first novel, *Opp alle jordens homofile* (1973; tr. *What Comes Naturally*, 1986), tells about being a lesbian in Norway in the early 1970s. Her next book, *Egalias døtre* (1977; tr. *Egalia's Daughters*, 1985), was widely translated and offers a satirical take on sex roles. It describes a society where **women** rule and where both social and linguistic structures serve their interests. *Ja, vi slutter* (1978; Yes, We Are Quitting) deals with the difficulty of giving up smoking.

The trilogy *Sangen of St. Croix* (1979; The Ballad of St. Croix), *Ved fergestedet* (1985; At the Ferry), and *For alle vinder* (1989; tr. *The Four Winds*, 1996) tells the story of a group of schoolgirls in Brantenberg's hometown, Fredrikstad, in the 1950s and 1960s. The main character eventually comes to terms with her lesbian identity. *Favntak* (1983; Embraces) is a novel in a similar vein; it portrays the situation of lesbian women who are trying to end their marriages.

Augusta og Bjørnstjerne (1997; Augusta and Bjørnstjerne) is a historical and largely documentary novel about the love relationship between the Norwegian writer **Bjørnstjerne Bjørnson** and Augusta Mjøen, Brantenberg's great-grandmother. A well-written and engaging story, it is also a tragic tale: the relationship did not lead to marriage because Mjøen's parents were against it and thwarted their daughter's efforts, even to the point of stealing the letters that went between the young lovers. Brantenberg wrote another big novel about another ancestor, her German grandmother Cläre Emilie, who married a Norwegian and spent her adult life in Norway. Entitled *Landssvikersken* (2003; The Female Collaborator), it describes what it was like for a German woman to live in Norway during two world wars and, as a supporter of Hitler, finally to be found guilty of treason after World **War** II. Brantenberg has also written essays and a children's book.

BREGENDAHL, MARIE (1867–1940). A Danish novelist, short story writer, and poet, Bregendahl was, like her husband **Jeppe Aakjær**, born in Jutland. Expected to become a farm wife, she spent some time at a folk high school, where she met Aakjær, and moved with him to Copenhagen. She had her literary debut with the novel

Henrik i Bakken (1904; Henrik down the Hill), which is written with a significant sense of psychological **realism**, of which she is one of the pioneers in Danish literature. The novel *En Dødsnat* (1912; tr. *A Night of Death*, 1931) exemplifies a groundbreaking narrative technique in that the death of the farm **woman** in the book—modeled on the death of Bregendahl's own mother—is focalized through her young children.

Bregendahl's major work is a suite of seven shorter narratives that were later published in two volumes with the collective title *Sødalsfolkene* (1935, originally published 1914–1923; The People of Sødal), in which preindustrial rural culture is portrayed. Social change and its effect on rural people is likewise the theme of a historical novel in two volumes, *Holger Hauge og hans Hustru* (1934–1935; Holger Hauge and His Wife). Bregendahl also wrote a number of short story collections. One of the major themes in the stories is the emotional price that has to be paid by the rural people who move to the cities because they have been displaced by structural economic changes in their home environments. She also published one volume of poetry, *Filtret Høst* (1937; Filtered Autumn).

BREMER, FREDRIKA (1801–1865). A Swedish novelist, Bremer has her roots in the **romantic** worldview. While the romantics often focus on the glorious past of the nation or on the rural people, however, Bremer depicted middle- and upper-class family life as she knew it. Her first book was a collection of stories, *Teckningar utur hvardagslifvet* (1828; Scenes from Everyday Life), which she wrote in order to finance charitable work. Her domestic novel *Famillen H**** (1830–1831; tr. *The H— Family*, 1853) makes it clear that she saw the home both as the center of human life and as the focus of her writing.

The novels *Presidentens döttrar* (1834; tr. *The President's Daughters*) and *Nina* (1835; tr. 1843) make use of her own negative experiences. In a manner similar to that of Norwegian novelist **Camilla Collett**, Bremer describes the pressure put on daughters to marry according to the wishes of their parents. The novels were not well received. The epistolary novel *Grannarna* (1837; tr. *The Neighbours*, 1972), on the other hand, which promotes tolerance and respect among people of different ages and social backgrounds, was less strident and more to the liking of her audience. It depicted idyllic family life at a Swedish manor and offered a stark contrast to the type of home that Bremer had grown up in. The ideas expressed in *Hemmet* (1839; tr. *The Home, or Life in Sweden*, 1853) are similar; Bremer continues to advocate for the right of **women** to govern themselves, which, to a minimal extent, Swedish women received in 1858 when a law was passed that granted unmarried women legal responsibility when they reached the age of 25. *Syskonliv* (1848; tr. *Brothers and Sisters*, 1848) is a further expression of Bremer's idealism as a social reformer.

Bremer traveled widely in the United States during the years 1850–1851, and her epistolary novel about her experiences, *Hemmen i nya världen* (1853; tr. *The Homes of the New World: Impressions of America*, 1854), offers an interesting, balanced portrait of American life. Her final novel, *Hertha, eller en själs historia* (1856; tr. *Hertha*, 1856), was found by many readers to be too **realistic** in its portrayal of social conditions and too radical in its demands for reform. It has since been recognized as one of Scandinavia's earliest and most interesting **feminist** novels.

BRØGGER, SUZANNE (1944–). A Danish novelist, essayist, epic poet, and playwright, Brøgger writes at the boundary between fact and fiction, on the line that separates her private life from the lives of her characters, including her first-person narrators. At times readers have not sufficiently distinguished between Brøgger's narrators and the person Brøgger, which she has exploited by creating a rapidly evolving mythic version of herself. Champions of residual Danish puritanism have been both attracted to and repulsed by the frank discussion of sexuality in her oeuvre.

In her first book, *Fri os fra kærligheden* (1973; tr. *Deliver us from Love*, 1976), Brøgger criticizes the middle class for having domesticated the erotic force and thus limited the potential for freedom inherent in human life. In *Kærlighedens veje og vildveje* (1975; Love's Paths and Pitfalls, 1975), she maintains that **women** have the capacity to free themselves from male domination solely by an act of will. Understandably, this argument struck many contemporary **feminists** as both naïve and excessively individualistic.

Crème Fraiche: En føljeton (1978; Crème Fraiche: A Feuilleton), the story of a woman who travels around the world in pursuit of self-understanding, includes an uninhibited celebration of the erotic. The similarities between Brøgger and the first-person narrator are striking, and many readers ignored the distance between narrator and author. In *Ja: Føljeton* (1984; Yes: Feuilleton) this narrator tries to extend her outward liberation to her inward self, and this quest is continued in *Transperence: Føljeton* (1993; Transparency: Feuilleton).

The novel *En gris som har været oppe at slås kan man ikke stege* (1979; tr. *A Fighting Pig's Too Tough to Eat*, 1997) constitutes an exploration of the impact on a small-town environment on a woman's search for autonomy. Set in Brøgger's own home community, it seems particularly informed by her personal experiences.

Much of Brøgger's essayistic and occasional writing is collected in *Brøg: 1965–1980* (1980; Brew: 1965–1980) and *Den pebrede susen: Flydende fragmenter og fixeringer* (1986; Peppered Hush: Flowing Fragments and Fixations), as well as in the essay collection *Kvælstof: 1980–1990* (1990; Nitrogen: 1980–1990). The volume *Tone* (1981) is an epic poem about a woman who lives her life according to the ideas presented in *Crème Fraiche*; the last third of the book, however, tells about her death from cancer. Brøgger has also written a successful drama, *Efter orgiet* (1992; After the Orgy), which mourns such aspects of the sexual revolution as the AIDS epidemic. The novel *Jadekatten: En Slægtssaga* (1997; The Jade Cat: A Family Saga) tells the story of a Danish Jewish family. *Et frit og muntert lig* (1998; A Free and Happy Corpse) extols everyday living, while *Linda Evangelista Olsen* (2001) offers portraits of Brøgger's two cats, juxtaposed with comments about her own life.

BURMAN, CARINA (1960–). A Swedish literary scholar and novelist, Burman is a skilful practitioner of the pastiche, and her work appeals strongly to an audience that shares some of her historical knowledge. Educated at Uppsala University, where she studied comparative literature, classics, and English, she wrote her doctoral dissertation on the oratorical practice of the Swedish writer **Johan Henric Kellgren**. Her biographical and historical studies for her dissertation laid the groundwork for her first novel. *Min salig bror Jean Hendrich* (1993; My Dear Departed Brother Jean Hendrich) is a clever mixture of fact and fiction. Supposedly containing two extended obituaries of Kellgren—one written by his brother and the other by his mistress—there is also an explanatory introduction, supposedly penned by the secretary of the Swedish Academy, as well as an epilogue in which Burman pretends to be the editor of these papers. This is an old trick of novelists, but it seems to work as well in **postmodernism** as it did for such writers as Nathaniel Hawthorne and **Søren Kierkegaard**.

Burman also did scholarly work on the Swedish writer **Fredrika Bremer** and followed it up with the novel *Den tionde sånggudinnan* (1996; The Tenth Muse). During a prologue in heaven—there are shades of Goethe's *Faust* here—its protagonist, the literary scholar Elisabet Gran, makes a bet with another literature professor named Georg Schlippenbach, a caricature of the high theory in the 1980s, that historical-biographical research can still be fruitful. In order to win the wager, Gran chooses to hunt for letters from Sophia Elisabeth Brenner (1659–1730), Sweden's first serious woman poet. The main text of the novel parodies both the epistolary novel and the diary novel, and it is also a pastiche on letters of a bygone era, as fictitious letters from Brenner are reproduced in the context of Gran's correspondence with two collaborators as well as in her own diary. Like the academic novels of the British writer David Lodge and, even more so, a philosophical epistolary "novel" such as Jacques Derrida's work *La carte postal* (1980), the book contains numerous allusions that are perhaps best appreciated by insiders.

A visit to Great Britain became the occasion for Burman's next novel, *Cromwells huvud: Antropologisk komedi* (1998; Cromwell's Head: An Anthropological Comedy). The story is centered on a fictitious college at Cambridge University, where a Swedish au pair named Malin gets involved with a couple of different men and where academic infighting, espionage, and even murder make an appearance. A postmodern mixture of high and low, new and old, it features an old-fashioned narrator who offers a commentary on the creative process itself. The letters of Burman's earlier works have been replaced by the e-mails that pass between one of the characters, the Swedish anthropologist G. G. Bondeson, and his estranged wife.

The novel *Islandet* (2001; The Ice Land), which includes the events narrated in an earlier short story, "Hammaren" (1999; The

Hammer), is set in Uppsala during the heyday of Swedish **romanticism**. Its cast includes mostly historical persons, but there is also the fictitious character Fransiska B***, who appears in the novel *Grannarne* (1837; tr. *The Neighbors*, 1842), by Fredrika Bremer.

The novel *Babylons gator* (2004; The Streets of Babylon) takes place in London in 1851 and features a Bremer-like character named Euthanasia Bondeson. A detective novel with strong echoes from Arthur Conan Doyle's stories about Sherlock Holmes, the plot of *Babylons gator* centers on Euthanasia's search for her young companion, Agnes, who has mysteriously disappeared. The book takes its title from Benjamin Disraeli's novel *Tancred* (1847), in which London is characterized as a modern Babylon, and Euthanasia becomes thoroughly acquainted with the city's seamy side. Burman may be indebted to Oscar Wilde's novel *The Picture of Dorian Gray* (1891) for the depiction of some of London's more sordid locales. But Euthanasia also moves in polite society and is introduced to some of the luminaries of British literature at the time, such as George Eliot and Charles Dickens.

– C –

CANTH, MINNA (1844–1897). A Finnish novelist, short story writer, and dramatist, Canth was Finland's most significant playwright after **Aleksis Kivi** and one of its most outspoken **realist** social critics, writing on themes similar to those of **Henrik Ibsen** and **Amalie Skram** in Norway. Canth began her literary career as a widow with seven children to support, and her own experience of life's harshness no doubt influenced her literary work.

Canth's first dramatic efforts were two comedies, *Murtovarkaus* (1882; The Burglary) and *Roinilan talossa* (1883; In the House of Roinila). Her social criticism comes to the fore, however, in *Työmiehen vaimo* (1885; A Worker's Wife), in which she speaks out against alcoholism and a husband's control of his wife's property. The wife in the play, Johanna, is married to a man who drinks up the money she brought into the marriage and steals the cloth she has contracted to produce for two women of the middle class, who, as a matter of course, abuse her when she is unable to deliver it because of her husband's irresponsibility.

The **feminist** message is also present in the novel *Hanna* (1886), in which the life of a young girl—and that of her mother—is contrasted to that of her brothers and father. Canth's criticism of the unequal distribution of wealth is continued in both the story *Köyhää kansaa* (1886; Poor Folks) and the play *Kovan onnen lapsia* (1888; Misfortune's Children), in which she, like Amalie Skram, also takes aim at the treatment of mentally ill people. Her novella *Kauppa-Lopo* (1889; The Peddler Lopo) contrasts the indifference of the well-to-do with the kindness of the scorned peddler. Intergenerational conflict is the theme of the play *Papin perhe* (1891; The Parson's Family), in which the minister father somewhat belatedly realizes that core Christian values apply to his conduct in his home.

Canth's play *Sylvi* (1893), written in Swedish, has a title character that in some ways looks like an extreme version of Nora in Ibsen's play ***Et dukkehjem*** (1879; tr. *A Doll's House*, 1880). Sylvi is treated like a doll and a child by her much older husband, falls in love with another man, poisons her husband in order to be free to remarry, and does it without understanding that what she has done is against the law. She is dumbfounded when her new lover rejects her as a criminal. In the play *Anna-Liisa* (1895; tr. 1997), on the other hand, Anna-Liisa's fiancé stands by her when she voluntarily confesses to a crime from her youth and is willing to take her punishment.

CARPELAN, BO (1926–). A Finland-Swedish poet and novelist, Carpelan had his literary debut with the poetry collection *Som en dunkel värme* (1946; Like a Dusky Warmth), which was quickly followed by *Du mörka överlevande* (1947; You Dark Survivor) and *Variationer* (1950; Variations). From the beginning of his career Carpelan had his own voice, even though he was influenced by both the Swedish and the Finnish **modernists**. While intrigued by the mystery of life, Carpelan also looks at life with a sense of humor, as evidenced by some of the prose poems in *Minus sju* (1952; Minus Seven). Additional prose poems are found in his collection *Jag minns att jag drömde* (1979; I Remember That I Dreamed). The three poetry volumes *Landskapets förvandlingar* (1957; The Landscape's Transformations), *Den svala dagen* (1960; tr. *The Cool Day*, as a part of *Homecoming*,

1995), and *73 dikter* (1966; 73 Poems) attest to increasing precision and conciseness in Carpelan's expression.

In the collection *Gården* (1969; tr. *The Courtyard*, 1982; also as a part of *Homecoming*, 1995), Carpelan offered poetic snapshots of life in an apartment building during his childhood in the 1930s. In *Källan* (1973; The Source), strength is found in love, while *I de mörka rummen, i de ljusa* (1976; In the Dark Rooms, and in Light), for which Carpelan received the **Nordic Literary Prize** in 1977, shows the interplay between life and death. *Dagen vänder* (1983; The Day Turns) and *Marginalia till grekisk och romersk diktning* (1984; Marginal Notes to Greek and Roman Poetry) express his sense of indebtedness to the tradition. *År som löv* (1989; tr. *Years like Leaves*, 1993; also as a part of *Homecoming*, 1995) pays tribute to acknowledged influences. After the collection *I det sedda* (1995; In What Is Seen), Carpelan returned to prose poems in the volume *Namnet på tavlan Klee målade* (1999; The Name on the Picture Klee Painted). *Ögonblickets tusen årstider* (2001; The Thousand Seasons of the Moment) contains 270 brief poems that in their minimalism are similar to those in *73 dikter*.

Carpelan's first novel, *Rösterna den sena timmen* (1971; tr. *Voices at the Late Hour*, 1988), tells about the start of a nuclear **war** and how different members of an extended family respond to what is most likely certain death. *Din gestalt bakom dörren* (1975; Your Figure behind the Door), a novel in the tradition of the doppelgänger, offers a frightening portrait of the human mind. *Vandrande skugga* (1977; Wandering Shadow) is a historical novel about murder and arson. *Axel* (1986; tr. 1998) tells the story of one of Carpelan's relatives, who was closely associated with the Finnish composer Jean Sibelius (1865–1957). *Urvind* (1993; tr. *Urwind*, 1997) is an epistolary novel; its protagonist, a secondhand bookseller, writes letters to his chemist wife, who is away doing research at Harvard. In *Benjamins bok* (1997; Benjamin's Book) a retired translator looks back on his life with an eye for both its tragic and its comic elements.

Carpelan has also written several books for both younger and older children, beginning with *Anders på ön* (1959; Anders on the Island) and *Anders i stan* (1962; Anders in the City); both were inspired by his son Anders. Another pair of books for young people are *Bågen* (1968; tr. *Bow Island: The Story of a Summer That Was Not*, 1971) and *Paradiset* (1973; tr. *Dolphins in the City*, 1976); the latter tells about a disabled boy. The protagonist in *Julius Blom: Ett huvud för sig* (1982; tr. *Julius Blom-Bvr 111*, 1992) is another sensitive child.

CENSORSHIP. Freedom of expression is guaranteed by the constitution of each Scandinavian country. Under the absolutist monarchs who ruled prior to the establishment of democracy, however, politically motivated censorship was common, even under such enlightened rulers as Sweden's **Gustav III**. Censorship returned to Denmark and Norway during World **War** II, when both countries were occupied by Nazi Germany. Since all of the Scandinavian countries have state churches, however, blasphemy was long considered illegal. For example, the Swedish dramatist **August Strindberg** had to stand trial on the charge of blasphemy in 1884 because of a remark about communion wine made in a volume of short stories entitled *Giftas* (1884; tr., with a second volume, as *Married*, 1913; also as *Getting Married*, 1972). He was acquitted, as was **Gustaf Fröding** when he was accused of pornography because of erotic language in his poem "En morgondröm" (1896; "A Morning Dream"). Public decency was an issue in Scandinavian literature throughout the periods of **realism** and **naturalism**, but with changing social mores sexual explicitness became increasingly tolerated. In the 1950s the Norwegian writer **Agnar Mykle** was accused of pornography after the publication of his novel *Sangen om den røde rubin* (1956; tr. *The Song of the Red Ruby*, 1961) but was acquitted by Norway's High Court. Ten years later his colleague **Jens Bjørneboe** published *Uten en tråd* (1966; tr. *Without a Stitch*, 1969), which was found by the courts to be pornographic and consequently confiscated. It is no longer considered likely, however, that a Scandinavian literary work will be censored for any reason.

CHILDREN'S BOOKS. Thanks to the popularity of such Scandinavian writers as **Hans Christian Andersen**, **Astrid Lindgren**, and **Tove Jansson**, Scandinavian children's literature has a worldwide reputation. Owing to the teachings of the Lutheran state churches in the Scandinavian countries, literacy among children developed relatively early and has remained very high. While the earliest Scandinavian books for children had didactic purposes, the tales and stories of

Hans Christian Andersen, published between 1835 and 1858, early laid stress on fantasy and everyday language. Later manifestations of the didactic spirit are found in the work of the Finn **Zacharias Topelius** and the Swede **Selma Lagerlöf**; the latter's *Nils Holgerssons underbara resa genom Sverige* (1906–1907; tr. *The Wonderful Adventures of Nils*, 1907, and *Further Adventures of Nils*, 1911) was written specifically in order to teach geography to Swedish schoolchildren. Other Scandinavian contributions to world literature for children include Astrid Lindgren's indefatigable Pippi Longstocking and Tove Jansson's family of Moomin trolls. *See also* BRANTENBERG, GERD; CARPELAN, BO; GAARDER, JOSTEIN; GRIPE, MARIA; KJÆRSTAD, JAN; LØVEID, CECILIE; OBRESTAD, TOR; SCHOULTZ, SOLVEIG VON; SEEBERG, PETER; SVENDSEN, HANNE MARIE; VIK, BJØRG.

CHORELL, WALENTIN (1912–1983). A Finland-Swedish novelist and dramatist, Chorell started his career as a writer with two undistinguished volumes of poetry, after which he produced two novels, the mystery story *Lektion för döden* (1947; Lesson for Death) and the more serious *Jörgen Hemmelinks stora augusti* (1947; Jörgen Hemmelink's Great August). The protagonist in the latter is the son of a Finland-Swedish mother and a Polish-Jewish father; he is the first of a large number of social misfits created by Chorell. The novels *Calibans dag* (1948; Caliban's Day), *Blindtrappan* (1949; The Dead End Staircase), and *Intim journal* (1951; Secret Diary) all offer portraits of characters with truly horrible lives. There is more hope in *Sträv gryning* (1952; Harsh Dawn), in which a killer serves his sentence and manages to adjust to life outside of prison. A trilogy comprising the novels *Mirjam* (1954), *Främlingen* (1956; The Stranger), and *Kvinnan* (1958; The Woman), tells about a girl who grows to womanhood and decides to raise her baby without marrying its father; she is a character with self-confidence and hope for the future.

Starting in the 1960s, Chorell created more miserable characters. The novels *Stölden* (1960; The Theft), *De barmhärtiga* (1962; Those with Mercy), *Saltkaret* (1963; The Salt Shaker), *Grodan* (1966; The Frog), *Agneta och lumpsamlaren* (1968; Agneta and the Rag Collector), and *Sista leken* (1970; The Last Game) all feature thieves, abusers, arsonists, and killers of various stripes who only have their lack of sanity in common.

Äggskalet (1972; The Egg Shell), *Knappen* (1974; The Button), and *Livstycket* (1976; The Bodice) is a trilogy about two young people from different social backgrounds who get married in the first volume. Predictably, the marriage deteriorates in the second volume and ends in divorce in the third. In the trilogy *Dockorna* (1978; The Dolls), *Rävsaxen* (1980; The Fox Trap), and *Lekhagen* (1981; The Playpen), an alcoholic writer and his wife, who is partly disabled from polio, are utterly miserable together. *Kvarteret barmhärtighet* (1982; The Block Named Mercy) is centered on an imagined mercy killing.

Chorell also wrote a very large number of plays for stage, television, and radio. Quite successful in their day, they are set in the same types of hopeless environments as his novels and have the same types of characters. Some of his better dramas are *Systrarna* (1955; tr. *The Sisters*, 1971), which tells about hateful siblings, and *Kattorna* (1963; tr. *The Cats*, 1978), in which a group of **women** employees unite in opposition to a woman supervisor. *See also* THEATER.

CHRISTENSEN, INGER (1935–). A Danish poet, novelist, and essayist, Christensen first published two volumes of poetry, *Lys* (1962; Light) and *Græs* (1963; Grass), that received relatively little attention. Her two early experimental novels, *Evighedsmaskinen* (1964; The Perpetual Motion Machine) and *Azorno* (1967), blur the distinction between the subject of the narrative and the process of narration itself and indicate that she developed an interest in the relationship between language and the world early in her career.

Christensen's breakthrough as a poet came with *Det* (1969; It), a long and highly structured poem divided into numerous subsections that establish complex patterns of organization. Itself an example of how language not only structures but actually creates human reality, it constitutes a creative act but also consciously presents language as the primary medium of creation. *Det* was very well received by the **critics** and the public at large and made Christensen one of Denmark's most popular writers.

In her next poetry collection, *Brev i april* (1979; Letter in April), Christensen retreats somewhat from the radical nominalism advocated in *Det*. Her attitude toward the reality that surrounds her is marked by a greater sense of humility as she asks if objects in the world could perhaps know that they are really named something else than what they are called by human beings. In the volume *alfabet* (1981; tr. *alphabet*, 2000), Christensen departs from her concern with language as constitutive of the world and recognizes that there is, out there in the world, an extralinguistic reality that language can be used to discover and name. She does not necessarily believe reality to be amorphous or chaotic, for her poem, which may be regarded as an attempt to reflect this extralinguistic reality, is a highly structured work.

Christensen's attraction to order is even more clearly visible in the following volume of poetry, *Sommerfugledalen: Et requiem* (1991; tr. *The Valley of the Butterflies*, 1999), a collection of 15 interconnected sonnets. The structure of this work is far more restrictive than what is dictated by the sonnet form, however, for each succeeding sonnet begins with the concluding line of the previous one, and sonnet number 15 consists of the beginning lines of sonnets one through 14. Such a highly structured and restrictive form suggests that the poet may have gone from satisfying her need for order by linguistic creation (in *Det*) to a standpoint where a sense of orderliness is achieved through a type of linguistic representation that is deeply committed to both the idea of representation and a belief in the indwelling orderliness of existence.

Although primarily known as a poet, Christensen has also written radio and television scripts as well as the play *Intriganterne: Et teaterstykke* (1972; The Schemers), which presents the world as marked by distortion and confusion. Her **postmodernist** novel *Det malede værelse: En fortælling fra Mantua* (1976; tr. *The Painted Room*, 2000) is set in the Italian Renaissance and gives an example of how the world and its representation may become one. Christensen's *Del af labyrinthen: Essays* (1982; A Part of the Labyrinth: Essays) offers commentary on her artistic assumptions and practice. A later volume, *Hemmelighedstilstanden* (1999; The State of Secretiveness), is a collection of previously written essays that offer reflections of Christensen's multifaceted world.

CHRISTENSEN, LARS SAABYE (1953–). A Norwegian novelist, poet, dramatist, and screenwriter, Christensen is one of Norway's most important contemporary writers. Some of his most important works have been translated into English, and he has received a number of literary prizes, including the prestigious **Nordic Literary Prize** (2002). Born and raised in Oslo, Christensen uses the city and its various problems as the setting and theme in his literary works.

After two privately printed collections of poetry as well as some poems published in anthologies, Christensen's debut came with *Historien om Gly* (1976; The Story about Gly), which tells about the sad life and suicide of a young outsider, whose poetry is also included in the volume. Then came the novel *Amatøren* (1977; The Amateur), which has as its protagonist another misfit, Christian Humle, whose life, in contrast to that of Gly, is portrayed with a good deal of humor. Christensen's next two books are characterized by despair; they are poetry collections entitled *Kamelen i mitt hjerte* (1978; The Camel in My Heart) and *Jaktmarker* (1979; Hunting Grounds). His best collection of poetry is *Paraply* (1982; Umbrella).

Christensen's fame rests on his novels. *Amatøren* was followed by *Billettene* (1980; The Tickets) and *Jokeren* (1981; tr. *The Joker*, 1991), both of which are crime stories. The former features a streetcar conductor who sells used tickets in order to save up enough money to escape from his miserable life; the latter tells about a bank robber who, after reading his own obituary in the paper, tries to find out who paid to have the obituary printed. But it was the novel *Beatles* (1984) that became both Christensen's definitive breakthrough and a runaway bestseller. Set in Oslo in the 1960s, it chronicles the lives of a group of teenage boys whose lives are centered on the music of the British band. It offers fascinating characters, particularly the narrator, Kim Karlsen, and is an interesting portrayal of the decade in which Christensen himself lived through his teen years.

The thriller *Sneglene* (1987; The Snails) garnered Christensen the Riverton Prize for the year's best mystery story. In *Herman* (1988; tr. 1992), another prize-winning novel, he returns to the 1960s and tells the story of a boy who loses his hair and has to cope with teasing and mood swings. It is a vivid portrait of life in a big city as seen through the eyes of a child. *Bly* (1990; Lead) continues the story of Kim Karlsen, the narrator in *Beatles*. A young boy is also the protagonist in *Gutten som ville være en av gutta* (1992; The Boy Who

Wanted to Be One of the Boys), a story about soccer, a ubiquitous pastime in Norway.

Christensen moved to Vesterålen in northern Norway in 1983. This is the part of the country where many of **Knut Hamsun**'s novels are set, and Christensen's novel *Jubel* (1995; Jubilation) offers portraits of characters that evoke some of Hamsun's figures. But *Halvbroren* (2001; tr. *The Half Brother*, 2003) is strikingly original; its theme is deception both as a means of getting along in the world and as a coping strategy. The novel *Maskeblomstfamilien* (2003; The Turtlehead Family) is another novel set in Oslo in the 1960s. Ever the prolific writer, Christensen has also published other volumes of prose, collections of poetry, books of photography for which he has provided poetic captions, dramas, and movie scripts.

CHRISTIANIA BOHEMIANS. The most radical of Scandinavia's writers in the 19th century, the Christiania bohemians advocated free love and an end to injustice. The group was centered in the city of Christiania (now Oslo), Norway. *See also* GARBORG, ARNE.

CLAUSSEN, SOPHUS (1865–1931). A Danish poet, Claussen was independently wealthy and was able to devote himself entirely to his artistic pursuits. He first studied law, then became a journalist for several provincial papers, and he spent time in France and Italy. His travel book *Antonius i Paris* (1896; Antonius in Paris) tells about his encounter with the French **symbolists**. Claussen affiliated with the circle around **Johannes Jørgensen**'s periodical *Taarnet* and became an apologist for a poetic practice that renounced **naturalist** dogma in favor of a more personal and less social conception of poetry. In Danish literary history Claussen stands as one of the most important forerunners of **modernism**.

Claussen's first poetry collection, *Naturbørn* (1887; Children of Nature), spoke in favor of sexual liberation. His second book, *Pilefløjter* (1899; Willow Whistles), on the other hand, was far removed from the social concerns of the 1880s; the poems in it were highly personal, ironic, and dealt with private erotic themes. The poems in *Djævlerier* (1904; Devilries) were written against the background of Claussen's travels, and some of them show influences from Charles Baudelaire (1821–1867). Two representative titles are "Trappen til

Helvede" (The Stairs to Hell) and "Sorte Blomst" (Black Flower); the latter portrays a prostitute. Later collections include *Danske Vers* (1912; Danish Verses) and *Heroica* (1925), which contains the prescient "Atomernes Oprør" (The Revolt of the Atoms), with images suggestive of nuclear **war**.

COLLETT, CAMILLA (1813–1895). A Norwegian novelist, Collett is the sister of the well-known Norwegian poet **Henrik Wergeland**. Collett received a traditional education for upper-class girls at the time, which left her unhappy about the place of **women** in her society. When she fell in love with **Johan Sebastian Welhaven**, the enemy of her brother and father, she was further angered by the injustice of her situation, and her diaries and letters from the 1830s testify to the despair with which she reacted when Welhaven told her that their mutual attraction could not lead to marriage. In 1841 she married Peter Jonas Collett, who encouraged her to write, and she did some writing while raising her four children.

Widowed in 1851, however, she focused increasingly on her literary work and soon published *Amtmandens Døttre* (1854–1855; tr. *The District Governor's Daughters*, 1992), which drew extensively on her own experiences and observations. Thematically Norway's first modern novel, its narrative technique is fairly traditional, as it includes letters and excerpts from diaries, numerous apostrophes to the reader, and a fairly convoluted syntax. None of the district governor's four daughters enjoys a happy marriage, as their parents give more weight to social considerations than to love when their daughters are married off. Collett's novel is an effective piece of social criticism.

Collett followed up the success of *Amtmandens Døttre* with a book of memoirs, *I de lange Nætter* (1862; During the Long Nights), which tells about her youth and offers vivid portraits of her father and brother. Most of her other writings from her later years were highly polemical; a representative title is *Fra de Stummes Leir* (1877; From the Encampment of the Mute), which criticizes what she sees as the almost universal denigration of women by male writers.

CRITICISM. Scandinavian literary critics have a long history of acting as intermediaries between producers and consumers of literary texts. New works are given a great deal of attention in the press, particularly in the national newspapers. **Scandinavian literary journals** regularly publish both longer essays and brief reviews. The beginnings of Scandinavian literary criticism may be found in antiquarian efforts during the Renaissance and the Reformation, when manuscripts of Old Norse texts were collected and **Snorri Sturluson**'s historical work *Heimskringla* was translated into Danish. Later, both **Ludvig Holberg** and **Olof von Dalin** discussed literature in their essays, which in Dalin's case were published in his journal *Then Swänska Argus* (1732–1734; The Swedish Argus). Various literary societies were also formed, the most important of which was the Swedish Academy, which today selects the recipients of the **Nobel Prize** in literature.

As neoclassicism gave way to preromanticism and then **romanticism**, the critic **Johan Henric Kellgren** published reviews in the newspaper *Stockholms Posten* (The Stockholm Post). The Norwegian-born philosopher Henrik Steffens (1773–1845) was very influential in Denmark during the romantic period, especially through a series of lectures on the German romantics held in Copenhagen and published as *Indledning til philosophiske Forelæsninger* (1803; Introduction to Philosophical Lectures). **Per Daniel Amadeus Atterbom** was romanticism's major spokesperson in Sweden, publishing in the important journal *Phosphorus*, while in Finland **Johan Ludvig Runeberg** was a major exponent of **national romanticism** through his work as a newspaper critic. The Dane **Johan Ludvig Heiberg** wrote a large number of literary essays, many of which were published in his journal *Københavns flyvende Post* (1827–1828, 1830, 1834–1837; The Copenhagen Flying Mail). Heiberg was influenced by Hegel, and even more so was the Norwegian philosopher and critic **Marcus Jacob Monrad** (1816–1897), who harmonized romantic idealism and early **realism**—the result was referred to as poetic realism—and was a prolific contributor to both newspapers and cultural journals. The Norwegian language reformer **Aasmund Olafsson Vinje** wrote on literary topics in his newspaper *Dølen* (1858–1870; The Dalesman).

Scandinavia's greatest literary critic is **Georg Brandes**, who in 1871 inaugurated the **Modern Breakthrough**. In addition to writing numerous books on literary topics, Brandes also published the literary journal *Det Nittende Aarhundrede* (1874–1877; The Nineteenth Century), the chief forum for his radical critique of literature and culture. His brother Edvard Brandes (1847–1931) was also a critic of note, who published in both newspapers and literary magazines. The 1890s saw Danish criticism written by **Johannes Jørgensen** and published in his magazine *Taarnet* (1893–1894; The Tower), while in Norway **Nils Kjær** (1870–1924) was active as a newspaper critic. In Sweden **Oscar Levertin** functioned in a similar role.

Many of the important 19th-century literary critics were also writers of poetry, fiction, and drama, and this pattern has continued in Scandinavia up to the present. After World **War** I, for example, both **Elmer Diktonius** and **Hagar Olsson** were important Finnish newspaper critics, while **Rabbe Enckell** was an equally valiant, although less prolific, defender of **modernism**. The Danes **Hans Kirk** and **Tom Kristensen** published criticism in both newspapers and magazines. The Norwegian **Sigurd Hoel** was Norway's most important critic from the 1920s until his death in 1960. The Dane **Klaus Rifbjerg** and the Swede **Agneta Pleijel** have continued the practice of combining newspaper and journal criticism with creative work. In Norway **Knut Faldbakken** is one of the country's most prolific fiction writers, a literary critic publishing in newspapers, and a contributor to such literary magazines as *Vinduet*, of which he is a past editor. *See also* BANG, HERMAN; FROBENIUS, NICOLAJ; HEIBERG, GUNNAR; KROG, HELGE; MYRDAL, JAN.

– D –

DAGERMAN, STIG (1923–1954). A Swedish novelist, short story writer, dramatist, and poet, Dagerman produced a large volume of work in the course of approximately five years. Mostly departing from **realist** conventions, his **modernist** fictional style tends toward **expressionism**. An example is his novel *Ormen* (1945; tr. *The Snake*, 1995), in which the snake symbolizes the guilt and fear of the book's characters, who tell stories in order to cope. The narrative in the novel *De dömdas ö* (1946; tr. *Island of the Doomed*, 1991) is largely expressionistic, as the lizards and blind birds that infest the island of a group of shipwrecked people signify the terror within them. The short story collection *Nattens lekar* (1947; tr. *Games of the Night*, 1959) contains a mixture of realistic and **symbolic** stories. The novel *Bränt barn* (1948; tr. *A Burnt Child*, 1950), however, is a psychologically sophisticated story that is realistically told. *Bröllopsbesvär* (1949; Wedding Trouble) is, by comparison to Dagerman's other novels, a lighthearted and comical tale. The "trouble" of the title refers to the appearance of the father of the child that the bride in the story is pregnant with as she is about to be married to another man.

Tysk höst (1947; tr. *German Autumn*, 1988) is a book about conditions in Germany following World **War** II. After his death many of his short stories and poems were collected in the volume *Vårt behov av tröst: Prosa och poesi* (1955; Our Need for Consolation: Prose and Poetry). Dagerman's six dramas were less technically advanced than his fiction. Some of the titles are *Den dödsdömde* (1947; tr. *The Condemned*, 1951), *Ingen går fri* (1949; Nobody Goes Free), and *Den yttersta dagen* (1952; The Day of Judgment). *See also* THEATER.

DALIN, OLOF VON (1708–1763). A Swedish essayist and poet, Dalin is his country's most important Enlightenment figure. The son of a minister and educated at Lund University, he did not get a degree but was asked to serve as a private tutor to a noble family. For two years he also wrote the content for and anonymously published a journal called *Then Swänska Argus* (1732–1734; The Swedish Argus), much in the style of Joseph Addison and Richard Steele's *The Tatler* (1709–1711) and *The Spectator* (1711–1714). Like an argus, a giant with many eyes in Greek mythology, Dalin's journal was to see things of importance and bring them to the attention of the readers in well-formed and clever essays. The style was satirical and at times a bit chatty; the attitude behind it was witty and urbane.

His work with the *Argus* gave Dalin an important position in Swedish society and letters. He first became the royal librarian and later the tutor of Crown Prince Gustav, the future king **Gustav III**. When a **theater** named the Swedish Comedy was formed in 1737, he contributed two plays to its repertoire, a comedy entitled *Den afvundsiuke* (1738; tr. *Envy*, 1876) and the tragedy *Brynhilda* (1738), a reworking of Old Norse material.

Dalin's most enduring prose work is the brief *Sagan om hästen*

(1740; The Tale of the Horse), an allegory of the relationship between Sweden and its kings. He wrote an elegy at the death of Queen Ulrika Eleonora, *Swenska friheten* (1742; Swedish Liberty), and he produced satires, pastorals, and a large amount of occasional poetry. Although not trained in history, Dalin spent the years 1747–1762 writing a Swedish history in four volumes.

DASS, PETTER (1647–1707). A Norwegian poet of the Baroque period, Dass is known chiefly for his long descriptive poem *Nordlands trompet* (1739; tr. *The Trumpet of Nordland*, 1954), which he worked on from 1678 to approximately the year 1700. Dass, a minister in the Helgeland district of northern Norway, also wrote religious poetry designed to edify his parishoners, most notably *Katechismus-sange* (1714; Catechism Songs), which were finished before 1698. With their down-to-earth presentation of religious doctrines and duties, Dass's songs reached a large audience, and the best of them are still included in the hymnal of the Norwegian Evangelical-Lutheran state church. Dass was thoroughly acquainted with life among the fishers and small farmers of Helgeland, for he had been born and spent his early childhood there, and although educated both at the Cathedral School in Bergen and at the University of Copenhagen, he never lost touch with his origins. Much loved and respected by the people to whom he ministered, he was regarded as a leader spiritually, economically, and socially. Both his insider perspective on Norwegian life and his sense of humor are evident in his secular verse, chief among which is "Den Nordske Dale-Viise" (1683; The Norwegian Valley Song), written in the 1670s and in which he, among other things, relates his experience with bad food and lice-infested bedding.

DELBLANC, SVEN (1931–1992). A Swedish novelist, essayist, playwright, and scriptwriter, Delblanc addressed the question of how to balance the individual's desire for freedom against the need for order in society. He had his literary debut with the novel *Eremitkäftan* (1962; The Hermit Crab), in which the protagonist leaves a highly structured society in search of freedom, only to return again in search of security. Delblanc's vision of the human quest for liberty is thus one of profound pessimism.

Prästkappan: En heroisk berättelse (1963; The Cassock: An Heroic Tale) is set in Frederick the Great's Prussia. One of the central characters, Hermann, is an idealist who goes from one defeat to another. His companion Lång-Hans, on the other hand, has a good sense of reality, and reality has a habit of vanquishing a person's ideals. The ideal of free will is also dealt a severe blow in *Homunculus: En magisk berättelse* (1965; tr. *Homunculus: A Magic Tale*, 1969), in which an inventor creates a humanlike being in his bathtub. The inventor, Sebastian, has to defend the being against U.S. and Soviet agents, and he becomes increasingly evil as he does so, finally choosing suicide as a means of protecting what remains of his humanity. *Nattresa* (1967; Night Journey) explores how an artist may combine his individualistic artistic vision with a commitment to socialism.

Delblanc spent a year as a visiting professor at the University of California in Berkeley during the 1968–1969 academic year. A result of this experience was the diary novel *Åsnebrygga* (1969; Bridge of Asses), which criticizes American society and politics and details the narrator's struggle against a sense of intellectual paralysis. *Zahak: Persiska brev* (1971; Letters from Persia) is a travelogue, while *Trampa vatten* (1972; Treading Water), a collection of brief essays, offers a variety of observations.

The core of Delblanc's oeuvre is two interlinked tetralogies. The first one consists of four historical novels about his hometown, which he has given the fictional name Hedeby. *Åminne* (1970; River Memory), *Stenfågel* (1973; Stone Bird), *Vinteride* (1974; Winter Lair), and *Stadsporten* (1976; The City Gate) cover the period from 1937 to shortly after World **War** II and record the transition from an older and more stratified society to an egalitarian one governed by social-democratic values.

The second series of novels is based on Delblanc's family history. The central characters in *Samuels bok* (1981; The Book of Samuel), *Samuels döttrar* (1982; The Daughters of Samuel), *Kanaans land* (1984; The Land of Canaan), and *Maria ensam* (1985; Maria Alone) are all modeled on his maternal grandfather and his descendants. There is a strong patriarchal tradition in this family line, and the **women** suffer as a result. There is also a tendency toward mental illness, but the main protagonist, the writer Axel, finds that his education is a source of mental health for him. Some of the characters in

Maria ensam are taken from the Hedeby novels, which it overlaps in time.

Three other novels focus on the relationship between artists and those who hold power in society. *Primavera: En konstnärlig berättelse* (1973; Primavera: An Artistic Tale) is an allegory of the relationship between artist and market, while *Kastrater: En romantisk berättelse* (1975; tr. *The Castrati: A Romantic Tale*, 1979) questions whether art is worth the sacrifices made for it. The novel *Grottemannen* (1977; The Cave Man) shows that art does not necessarily lead to freedom, at least not in a society that is in relentless pursuit of material things. Delblanc's cultural pessimism is further expressed in *Speranza: En samtida berättelse* (1980; tr. *Speranza: A Contemporary Tale*, 1983) and *Jerusalems natt* (1983; Jerusalem's Night); the latter is set during the siege of Jerusalem in the year 70.

The title of the novel *Moria land* (1987; The Land of Moriah) alludes to Abraham's binding of Isaac, but the father in Delblanc's book has turned his son over to the authorities in their dystopian future Swedish society. The title character in *Änkan* (1988; The Widow), by contrast, has acquired a means of regaining her youth and, with it, seemingly unlimited freedom. In the novel *Ifigenia: Berättelse i två upptåg* (1990; Iphigenia: A Tale in Two Acts), Delblanc radically reinterprets the reasons for Agamemnon's sacrifice of his daughter and many other facts of classical antiquity, thus suggesting that history is subject to the laws of social constructionism, as it is always written by the victors. Delblanc also wrote a number of scripts for radio and television and several plays, many of them adaptations of his novels.

DIKTONIUS, ELMER (1896–1961). A Finland-Swedish poet, novelist, and **critic**, Diktonius came from a working-class background, attended Finnish schools, which made him bilingual, and studied music in his youth. Although he had strong socialist sympathies, he did not actively involve himself in the Finnish civil **war** of 1918, and he served as a medic in the Finnish army after the victory of the Whites over the Reds. Next he went abroad to Paris and London, where his music studies suffered while he focused on politically radical poetry. His literary debut came with *Min dikt* (1921; My Poem), and additional works followed: the poetry volume *Hårda sånger*

(1922; Hard Songs), *Brödet och elden* (1923; The Bread and the Fire), a book of aphorisms, and the poetry collections *Taggiga lågor* (1924; Barbed Flames) and *Stenkål* (1927; Rock Coal). The conclusion of Diktonius's early poetic phase is *Stark men mörk* (1930; Strong but Dark), in which it becomes clear that his overemphasis on revolutionary poetry most likely stifled some of his more personal—and more valuable—poetic expression. This impression is strengthened by the early work found in the volume *Ringar i stubben* (1953; Rings in the Tree Stump), published by Jörn Donner after Diktonius became ill.

During these years Diktonius was also an extremely prolific newspaper critic. Other prose works were *Onnela: Finsk idyll* (1925; Onnela: Finnish Idyll), which celebrates rural Finland in a Swedish language that is replete with Finnicisms, and *Ingenting och andra novellistiska skisser* (1928; Nothing and Other Story-like Sketches). He also produced a collection of musical reviews. His most important work from this period, however, is the short novel *Janne Kubik: Ett träsnitt i ord* (1932; Janne Kubik: A Woodcut in Words), an episodic narrative about a coward and braggart. The short story volume *Medborgare i republiken Finland* (1935; Citizens of the Republic of Finland) contains satirical portraits of fictitious persons, among them both a necrophile and a pedophile; it was followed by *Medborgare: Andra samlingen* (1940; Citizens: Second Collection).

Also in the 1930s, Diktonius published the poetry collections *Gräs och granit* (1936; Grass and Granite) and *Jordisk ömhet* (1938; Earthly Tenderness). He began to show symptoms of illness and his poetry collection *Varsel* (1942; Portents) indicates that his powers were in decline. *Höstlig bastu* (1943; Autumnal Sauna) is a prose volume consisting mostly of previously published essays and other prose pieces. His last two volumes of poetry, *Annorlunda* (1948; Otherwise) and *Novembervår* (1952; November Spring), were published shortly before he was admitted to an institution.

DINESEN, ISAK. *See* BLIXEN, KAREN.

DITLEVSEN, TOVE (1917–1976). A Danish poet, novelist, and short story writer, Ditlevsen was born to a working-class family where she was actively discouraged from pursuing an education. Her relationship with both of her parents was strained, but that to her mother was particularly dysfunctional, which left Ditlevsen with a host of insecurities. Her later drug problems—she also attempted suicide, and was ultimately successful—may be traced to her childhood and youth. But these experiences also gave Ditlevsen a wealth of material for her writing, and her openness about her difficulties in life no doubt contributed to the fascination with her person that was exhibited by the media throughout her life.

Ditlevsen's literary debut was the poetry collection *Pigesind* (1939; A Girl's Mind), which contained poems about a young woman's insecurities and longing for love. Formally traditional, these poems were accessible and well received. The troubles and longings of young **women** return in Ditlevsen's first novel, *Man gjorde et Barn Fortræd* (1941; A Child Was Harmed), in which the protagonist is a young girl who feels that a shadow is resting on her. Only when she realizes that she has been sexually abused as a child and confronts the abuser does she develop the strength she needs to move ahead with her life. Ditlevsen here touches on a matter that has become an all too common reality in the decades since her novel was published.

The poems in *Lille Verden: Digte* (1942; Little World: Poems) are similar to those in *Pigesind*, but some of the **critics**—particularly male critics—looked down their noses at them because they did not adhere to the formal ideals of **modernism**, which started to manifest itself in Danish literature at this time. Ditlevsen is also a traditionalist in her novel *Barndommens Gade* (1943; The Street of Childhood), a realistic and psychological portrait of life among working-class people in Copenhagen in the 1920s and 1930s. The stories in Ditlevsen's first collection of short stories, *Den fulde Frihed* (1944; tr., with some additional texts, as *Complete Freedom and Other Stories*, 1982), are set in a similar environment. Her novel *For Barnets Skyld* (1946; For the Child's Sake) argues that divorce is harmful to children.

Ditlevsen had enormous popular success with her poetry collection *Blinkende Lygter* (1947; Blinking Lanterns), which was traditional in form and reflected her life experience as a woman. The short stories in *Dommeren* (1948; The Judge) and *Paraplyen* (1952; The Umbrella) reflect the harshness of Ditlevsen's own experiences. *Vi har kun hinanden* (1954; We Only Have One Another) was a novel commissioned by Denmark State Radio and was broadcast in installments. This was a popular feature of Danish radio programming, but the book was not an artistic success. Ditlevsen's artistic development is on display in the poetry collection *Kvindesind* (1955; A Woman's Mind), however, which is a more mature parallel to her earlier *Pigesind*.

The essays in *Flugten fra opvasken* (1959; The Escape from the Dishes) takes as its theme family life and its consequences for women; this was to become a much more significant theme in Scandinavian literature in the 1960s and 1970s. The novel *To some elsker hinanden* (1960; Two Who Love Each Other) tells about a husband's betrayal of his wife. This theme is continued in the poetry collection *Den hemmelige rude* (1961; The Secret Window) and the short stories in *Den onde lykke* (1963; Evil Joy).

Ditlevsen returned to her difficult childhood and youth in two volumes of memoirs, *Barndom* (1967; Childhood) and *Ungdom* (1967; Youth; tr. with *Barndom* as *Early Spring*, 1985). She treated her married life—she had been married four times—in *Gift* (1971; Married/Poison). *Tove Ditlevsen om sig selv* (1975; Tove Ditlevsen about Herself) is factual and informative. She continued her autobiographical work in the novel *Vilhelms værelse* (1975; Vilhelm's Room). Female creativity, especially as hindered by men, is the theme of the novel *Ansigterne* (1968; tr. *The Faces*, 1991), in which the protagonist descends into a psychotic state. In the poetry collection *De voksne* (1969; The Adults), Ditlevsen—finally, in the view of some critics—wrote poems in the style of modernist free verse, but she only partly made use of this style in her next volume of poetry, *Det runde værelse* (1973; The Round Room).

Ditlevsen also had a long career as a columnist for the daily and the weekly press. Much of this material has also been published in book form.

DOLL'S HOUSE, A. See *ET DUKKEHJEM*.

DUUN, OLAV (1876–1939). A Norwegian novelist and short story writer, Duun chose his home district of Namdalen in central Norway as the setting for his books. A teacher by profession and thus by necessity a part-time writer, Duun succeeded in creating some of the most complex characters in all of Scandinavian literature while at the same time writing extensive historical epics and providing some of the best descriptions of **nature** that Norwegian literature has to offer. After publishing a volume of short stories, *Løglege skruvar og anna folk* (1907; Oddballs and Other People), Duun had his literary breakthrough with *Paa tvert* (1909; Crosswise). His next several novels all concern the kind of conflicts between individuals that can be explicated according to the ideas of **Freudian** psychoanalysis: *Nøkksjølia* (1910; The Slope by Nixie Lake), *Hilderøya* (1912; Hilder Island), *Sigyn* (1913), *Tre venner* (1914; Three Friends), *Harald* (1915), *Det gode samvite* (1916; tr. *Good Conscience*), and *På Lyngsøya* (1917; At Heather Island).

Firmly rooted in traditional Norwegian folk culture with its focus on the extended family as life's organizing principle, Duun's masterwork is a series of six novels collectively entitled *Juvikfolke* (1918–1923; tr. *The People of Juvik*, 1930–1935), which covers six generations of the Juvik family. The first three novels—*Juvikingar* (1918; tr. *The Trough*, 1930), *I blinda* (1919; tr. *The Blind Man*, 1931), and *Storbrylloppe* (1920; tr. *The Big Wedding*, 1932)—all have as their protagonist a man named Per-Anders, whose values and general outlook on life can be traced back to the paganism of the Viking Age. The last three novels—*I eventyre* (1921; tr. *Odin in Fairyland*, 1932), *I ungdommen* (1922; tr. *Odin Grows Up*, 1934), and *I stormen* (1923; tr. *The Storm*, 1935)—tell about the life of Odin Setran, whose character is a combination of the old family traits and a sense of both Christian ethics and capitalist prudence. In the end he sacrifices his life in order to save that of an enemy. *Juvikfolke* can be read as a record of the transition from a mentality governed largely by a concern for self to one where there is a balance between the individual's attention to the needs of self and other, as well as the story of Norway's change from an economic system built on self-sufficiency supplemented with bartering to a monetary economy.

Duun was even more overtly preoccupied with the conflict between good and evil in his next major work, a trilogy consisting of the novels *Medmenneske* (1929; Fellow Man), *Ragnhild* (1931), and *Siste leveåre* (1933; The Final Year of Life), which covers the first 15 years or so of the 20th century in the life of the Dale family. The father, Didrik Dale, has turned over his farm to his son Håkon and his daughter-in-law Ragnhild, but he becomes increasingly mendacious and manipulative with the young couple. Ragnhild, fearing that he will corrupt Håkon, kills Didrik with an ax in a moment of frustration. Håkon becomes increasingly like his father, however, and after her release from prison, Ragnhild comes home to try to prevent him from being consumed with bitterness and evil. The final volume of the trilogy shows that she has a measure of success in helping her husband heal emotionally and spiritually.

The novels *Ettermæle* (1932; A Reputation Left Behind) and *Gud smiler* (1935; God Smiles) exhibit a strong reverence for common human beings and their internal strength. *Samtid* (1936; The Present Age) presents the frightening political situation of the 1930s in the guise of a conflict within a small community. The novel *Menneske og maktene* (1938; tr. *The Floodtide of Fate*, 1961) is an allegory of Nazism as it threatened to engulf Europe. A small group of people are caught on a low-lying island while the sea is rising, and Duun shows that human beings do have the internal resources that they need to maintain their dignity whatever their challenges.

In addition to his first collection of short stories, published in 1907, Duun made a valuable contribution to the genre with three additional volumes: *Gamal jord* (1911; Old Soil), *Blind-Anders* (1924; Blind Anders), and *Vegar og villstig* (1930; On the Road and Getting Lost). While thematically related to Duun's other works, many of these stories are technically and formally sophisticated.

– E –

EITHER/OR. See *ENTEN-ELLER*.

EKELÖF, GUNNAR (1907–1968). A Swedish poet and essayist, Ekelöf played a decisive role in introducing **modernism** to his homeland. Coming from a difficult family background, he felt like an outsider and thus had the temperament of someone who could bring about change. After a stay in Paris, he published his first volume of poetry, *Sent på jorden* (1932; tr. *Late Arrival on Earth*, 1967), which, among other inventions, contained no capital letters. His next three volumes of poetry, *Dedikation* (1934; Dedication), *Sorgen och stjärnan* (1936; The Sorrow and the Star), and *Köp den blindes sång* (1938; Buy the Blind Man's Song), show influence from **romanticism and symbolism**. *Färjesång* (1941; Ferry Song) attests to the impact of World War II on Ekelöf, as he tries to come to terms with a world where such forces as fascism and communism play dominant roles. The book was not well received, as it did little to bolster the morale of its Swedish readers. The title of the next collection, *Non serviam* (1945; I Will Not Be a Slave), emphasizes that Ekelöf had no wish to be identified with any kind of collective, and certainly not with the Swedish welfare state. *Om hösten* (1951; In the Autumn) contains "Röster under jorden" (Voices from Underground), which presents past and present as a single temporal continuum and which can also be read as a description of how the poet has passed into a dream world.

Ekelöf's *Strountes* (1955; Nonsense), *Opus incertum* (1959), and *En natt i Otocac* (1961; A Night in Otocac) were considered antipoetic by the poet, in that the meaning of language is presented as always deferred. *En Mölna-Elegi* (1960; tr. *A Mölna Elgy*, 1971) is highly allusive and shows influence from T. S. Eliot. One of the true masterpieces of Swedish poetry, it uses Latin graffiti on the left-hand page with Ekelöf's Swedish text on the right. The effect thus created is both a juxtaposition of past and present and a confrontation of two different cultural heritages.

While visiting Turkey in 1965, Ekelöf experienced an unusual moment of inspiration which resulted in a poetic trilogy consisting of *Dīvān över Fursten av Emigión* (1965; Dīvān about the Prince of Emigión), *Sagan om Fatumeh* (1966; The Tale of Fatumeh), and *Vägvisare till underjorden* (1967; tr. *Guide to the Underworld*, 1980). The Prince of Emigión undergoes much suffering, and *Sagan om Fatumeh* is a great love story. The final volume is an attempt to find harmony in a world of split and fragmented human experience. Ekelöf also published several volumes of essays that attest to his wide reading: *Promenader* (1941; Promenades), *Utflykter* (1947; Excursions), and *Blandade kort* (1957; Shuffled Cards).

EKELUND, VILHELM (1880–1949). A Swedish poet and essayist, Ekelund was born in the district of Skåne in southern Sweden. His first poetry collection, *Vårbris* (1900; Spring Breeze), celebrates that part of the country in the style of some of his contemporaries. His second volume, *Syner* (1901; Visions), was a significant breakthrough for him, however, for in it he turned to free verse, the first Swedish poet to do so consistently. Many of the poems in *Melodier is skymningen* (1902; Melodies in the Twilight) deal with the concept of poetry itself, while those in *Elegier* (1903; Elegies) touch on the theme of love. This theme becomes increasingly important in *Havets stjärna* (1906; The Ocean's Star) and *Dithyramber i aftonglans* (1906; Dithyrambs in Evening Splendor).

Influenced by the work of the German philosopher Friedrich Nietzsche (1844–1900), Ekelund produced such collections of essays and aphorisms as *Antikt ideal* (1909; The Ideal of Classical Antiquity) and *Nordiskt och klassiskt* (1914; Nordic and Classical). Throughout his long career, which included many additional volumes of poetry and prose, Ekelund was highly regarded by, and had great influence on, other poets in Sweden.

EKMAN, KERSTIN (1933–). A Swedish novelist who first became known as a writer of mystery stories, the best known of which is *De tre små mästarna* (1961; tr. *Under the Snow*, 1997), Ekman produced two additional notable works in a similar vein. In *Pukehornet* (1967; The Devil's Horn), she departed from the rigid conventions of the mystery novel by dispensing with the need for an identifiable crime. *Menedarna* (1970; The Perjurers), a mixture of mystery and historical novel, tells the story of the labor organizer Joe Hill, who was found guilty and executed on trumped-up charges in 1915.

Ekman's definitive breakthrough as a serious writer came with the novel *Mörker och blåbärsris* (1972; Darkness and Blueberry Brush). Set in a rural environment in northern Sweden, it tells a humorous but tragic story about a group of local people who eke out a living under depressing circumstances. Their most successful economic venture is the making and marketing of a type of moonshine that in quality far surpasses what is sold at the state-owned liquor stores. But Ekman also shows that sexual experimentation, as a departure from relatively strict norms of fidelity, has the potential for tearing up the fragile social and economic fabric of their community.

Ekman grew up in Katrineholm, a town south of Stockholm, and perhaps her most significant literary work is a tetralogy, *Kvinnorna och staden* (The Women and the Town), that recounts the town's growth and development after the coming of the railroad around 1870. Consisting of the volumes *Häxringarna* (1974; tr. *Witches' Rings*, 1997), *Springkällan* (1976; tr. *The Spring*, 2001), *Änglahuset* (1979; tr. *The Angel House*, 2002), and *En stad av ljus* (1983; A City of Light), the tetralogy makes use of a large number of **women** characters, most of whom are related by blood, adoption, or marriage, to tell the story of the town's social and economic progress, which mirrors that of Sweden in general. The **realism** is at times graphic, as the books are full of hard labor, emotional and sexual abuse, and mental and physical illness, but Ekman's women are tough survivors.

One of Ekman's cleverest stories is the novel *Rövarna i Skuleskogen* (1988; tr. *The Forest of Hours*, 1998), the protagonist of which is the troll Skord (the meaning of the name is *skog-ord* or forestword). As a troll, Skord has a life span that greatly surpasses that of humans, and thus Ekman is able to filter several hundred years worth of historical material through his consciousness. Skord is drawn to humans, learns to communicate with them, and becomes quite successful in a number of professions. He is ultimately able to integrate his troll nature with what he has learned from humans, and can thus be regarded as a symbolic bridge across the **nature**/culture divide.

In her novel *Händelser vid vatten* (1993; tr. *Blackwater*, 1997), Ekman successfully integrates some of the common features from her past as a mystery writer into her literary practice, thus, in the manner of **postmodernist** writing, mixing "high" and "low" stylistic elements. The novel takes place in the woods close to the Norwegian border and begins with a double murder that is investigated on two temporal levels separated by a period of 18 years. Intertextual references abound, such as the sex-crazed woman character Ylajali Happolati, a reference to Knut Hamsun's novel *Sult* (1890, tr. *Hunger*, 1899), who 18 years after having first been encountered has become a professor of **folklore** at the University of Helsinki. Ekman thus also indulges in humor and satire in the novel that garnered her the **Nordic Literary Prize** in 1994.

Gör mig levande igen (1996; Bring Me Back to Life) is set in Stockholm and features a women's discussion group, a device that allows Ekman to offer a cross-section of women's experience and attitudes toward Swedish society. An extension of and response to **Eyvind Johnson**'s Krilon trilogy (1941–1943), the book examines the power of communication to improve people's lives. It also has an element of the mystery story in it, as the body of a missing woman is found in a freezer; this detail should perhaps be read as an ironic postmodern response to Johnson's work of high **modernism**.

A recent large work is a trilogy with the common title *Vargskinnet* (The Wolf Hide), which consists of the volumes *Guds barnhärtighet* (1999; God's Mercy), *Sista rompan* (2002; The Last String), and *Skraplotter* (2003; Scratch Tickets). Its setting is the same locale as that found in *Händelser vid vatten*, a community named Svartvattnet (Blackwater) in the forest land where the district of Jämtland borders on Norway. Covering the years from 1916 to the present time, it introduces the reader to the beauties of the mountain landscape, the travails of the local Sámi culture, and the tension between traditional ways of life and the encroaching industrial and consumer society. Like **Sara Lidman**'s great *Jernbaneepos* (Railway Epic), it is a monument to the strength and endurance of women, as is Ekman's entire oeuvre.

EMIGRANTS, THE. See UTVANDRARNA.

ENCKELL, RABBE (1903–1974). A Finland-Swedish poet, novelist, dramatist, and **critic**, Enckell combined his career as a man of letters with that of an artist in oil painting and watercolor. His best work is his early poetry, published in such collections as *Dikter* (1923; Poems), *Flöjtblåsarlycka* (1925; Flute-Player's Happiness), *Vårens cistern* (1931; Spring's Cistern), and *Tonbrädet* (1935; The Sounding Board), in which he created miniature **modernist** poems of great power and beauty. The poems in *Valvet* (1937; The Vault) deal with a crisis in Enckell's life—his wife left him for another man, whom Enckell later knifed—and are powerful human documents. This crisis in his life figures prominently in the poetry collections *Lutad över brunnen* (1942; Bent over the Well) and *Andedräkt av koppar* (1946; Breath of Copper). His later collections of poetry, from *Sett och återbördat* (1950; Seen and Restored) to *Flyende spegel* (1974; Fleeing Mirror), which was published posthumously, express both a continued sense of melancholy and a bit of grumpiness about the direction his society and culture had taken.

Enckell's best critical essays from before World **War** II were collected in *Relation i det personliga* (1950; Relation in the Personal). Although not as prolific a critic as, for example, **Hagar Olsson** and **Elmer Diktonius**, Enckell had a sharp eye for changes and developments on the literary scene and valiantly defended literary modernism against its traditionalist detractors. He also wrote prose narratives. *Tillblivelse* (1929; Origination), *Ljusdunkel* (1930; Chiaroscuro), and *Ett porträtt* (1931; A Portrait) were accounts drawn directly from his own life and that of his wife, while *Landskapet med den dubbla skuggan* (1933; The Landscape with the Double Shadow) was a traditional novel with autobiographical elements. The short stories in *Herrar till natt och dag* (1937; Lords of Night and Day) reflect circumstances surrounding the end of his first marriage.

Enckell's dramas are of much less significance than his poetry. Drawn to the Greek classics, he both alluded to them in his other work and wrote a series of dramas that are largely retellings of Greek stories. *Orfeus och Eurydike* (1938; Orpheus and Eurydice), *Iokasta* (1939), *Agamemnon* (1947), *Hekuba* (1952), and *Mordet på Kiron* (1954; The Murder of Chiron) are all in this vein.

Enckell concluded his oeuvre with several volumes of mixed prose. *Traktat* (1955; Tractate) was followed by *Essay om livets framfart* (1961; An Essay on Life's Forward Motion). *Och sanning?* (1966; And Truth?) was a reply to those who had accused him of not showing sufficient political awareness in his work, while *Tapetdörren* (1968; The Secret Door in the Wallpaper) and *Resonören med fågelfoten* (1971; The Raisonneur with the Bird Foot) were both retrospective in nature. *See also* THEATER.

ENQUIST, PER OLOV (1934–). A Swedish novelist, playwright, and essayist, Enquist has been one of the foremost Scandinavian writers since the 1960s. He had his debut with the novel *Kristallöget* (1961; The Crystal Eye), a story of a young woman who comes to terms with her past by telling about it. His next novel, *Färdvägen* (1963; The Route), similarly features a narrator who learns to take responsibility for events in his past by repeatedly telling about them; each repetition adds details to the story. Enquist's literary breakthrough was the novel *Magnetisörens femte vinter* (1964; tr. *The Magnetist's Fifth Winter*, 1989), a fictionalization of the life of Franz Anton Mesmer (1734–1815), the German hypnotist who gave us Mesmerism. *Hess* (1966) appears to be a documentary novel about the Nazi Rudolf Hess, but the documents in question have been invented by the author. This technique, which may be called pseudo-documentarism, is an effective means for a writer who wants to investigate the nature of truth.

Legonärerna (1968; tr. *The Legionnaires*, 1973) secured Enquist's position as a major writer by giving him an international reputation. It tells about 167 soldiers from Estonia, Latvia, and Lithuania who were conscripted by the Germans during World War II but fled to Sweden and surrendered. Although they feared reprisals by the Soviets, these men were sent back home by force after the war, and this incident created an intense debate in Sweden at the time. Enquist's novel investigates this episode and presents it with some sympathy for the Soviet occupants of the Baltic States.

As a young man, Enquist had been active in sports as a high jumper. His novel *Sekonden* (1971; The Second) draws on his familiarity with the culture of track and field. The novel is built on the true story of a hammer thrower who sets new records by using an underweight hammer. Narrated by the man's son, the novel investigates why a successful athlete would have felt pressured to cheat. The essays in *Katedralen i München och andra berättelser* (1972; The Cathedral in Munich and Other Stories) critically examines both the Olympic movement and other aspects of sports as a cultural phenomenon.

Enquist's next novel, *Musikanternas uttåg* (1978; tr. *The March of the Musicians*, 1985), is set in northern Sweden, where he grew up. Informed by the history of the author's family, the story is centered on the general strike of 1909, a watershed event in Swedish labor history. Members of the same family are on different sides of the conflict, and some of Enquist's characters become so disenchanted that they emigrate to Brazil.

The 1970s saw a major shift in Enquist's work, as he turned to drama and became a very successful playwright. *Tribadernas natt: Ett skådespel från 1889* (1975; tr. *The Night of the Tribades: A Play from 1889*, 1977) presents the conflict between the Swedish dramatist

August Strindberg and Marie David, whom Strindberg suspected of being the lover of his estranged wife, Siri von Essen. Next he wrote *Till Fedra* (1980; To Phaedra), which reworks material from Greek mythology, and *Från regnormarnas liv: En familjetavla från 1856* (1981; From the Lives of Nightcrawlers: A Family Portrait from 1856), which tells about the relationship between the Danish writer **Hans Christian Andersen** and the famous Danish literary couple **Johan Ludvig Heiberg** and Johanne Louise Heiberg. *Strindberg: Ett liv* (1984; Strindberg: A Life) was the script of a six-part television series about the Swedish dramatist, while *I lodjurets timma* (1988; tr. *The Hour of the Lynx*, 1990) is a dramatic exploration of the relationship between religion, insanity, and crime. He later published *Tre pjäser: Magisk cirkel, Tupilak, Maria Stuart* (1994; Three Plays: Magic Circle, Tupilak, Maria Stuart), which deal with wartime collaboration, family dysfunction, and the history of Mary, Queen of Scots, respectively. *Hamsun: En filmberättelse* (1996; Hamsun: A Film Narrative) is the screenplay of Jan Troell's motion picture *Hamsun* (1996). *Bildmakarna* (1998; The Image Makers) tells about the life of the Swedish novelist **Selma Lagerlöf**, while the play *Systrarna* (2000; The Sisters) is based on Anton Chekhov's drama *The Three Sisters* (1901).

The short novel *Nedstörtad angel* (1985; tr. *Downfall: A Love Story*, 1986) discusses both the nature of love and the concept of identity. Characters from *I lodjurets timma* and *Musikanternas uttåg* reappear in the novel *Kapten Nemos bibliotek* (1991; tr. *Captain Nemo's Library*, 1992), in which Enquist returns to his childhood in northern Sweden. The action in the novel *Livläkarens besök* (1999; tr. *The Royal Physician's Visit*, 2001) is centered on the years 1770–1772 and depicts the conflict between Enlightenment ideas and conservatism during the reign of Christian VII of Denmark. *Lewis resa* (2001; Lewi's Journey) exhibits Enquist's trademark pseudo-documentarism as it tells the story of Lewi Pethrus, one of the founders of the Pentecostal movement in Sweden.

ENTEN-ELLER. A philosophical work in two volumes by the Dane **Søren Kierkegaard**, who published *Enten-Eller* (1843; tr. *Either/Or*, 1944) under the pseudonym Victor Eremita. *Enten-Eller* presents

Kierkegaard's theory of the aesthetic and the ethical spheres of existence and adumbrates what Kierkegaard calls the religious stage.

ET DUKKEHJEM. A drama by the Norwegian **Henrik Ibsen**, *Et dukkehjem* (1879; tr. *A Doll's House*, 1880) explores the role of **women** in the home and in society, concluding that a woman has not only the right but the duty to leave her husband and family if she is prevented by her marriage from realizing her full potential as a human being. The play has long been an inspiration to **feminism**.

EXPRESSIONISM. A movement in literature and art which has its origins in the German theater of the early 20th century, expressionism eschews **realist** representation in favor of a nonrealistic atmosphere. Expressionistic works tend to display a dreamlike quality of action, and to transmit impressions and moods through the use of objects or various literary devices. The foremost exponent of expressionism in Scandinavian literature is **Pär Lagerkvist**, who wrote the manifesto *Ordkonst och bildkonst* (1913; Verbal Art and Pictorial Art) upon his return to Sweden after a stay in Paris, as well as the essay *Modern teater* (1918; tr. *Modern Theatre*, 1961), in which he argued against the dramatic practice of the Norwegian playwright **Henrik Ibsen** and spoke in favor of the anti-realist dramaturgy of such plays as **August Strindberg**'s *Ett drömspel* (1902; tr. *A Dream Play*, 1929). From drama, expressionism spread to other literary forms, such as poetry and the novel. *See also* BERGMAN, HJALMAR; DAGERMAN, STIG; KRISTENSEN, TOM; MARTINSON, HARRY; OLSSON, HAGAR.

EWALD, JOHANNES (1743–1781). A Danish poet and dramatist, Ewald was plagued by ill health most of his life. A transitional figure between neoclassicism and **romanticism**, his work is marked both by adherence to the formal strictures of the neoclassicists and by romanticism's focus on the individual. Ewald's dramatic debut was a neoclassical play about the Fall entitled *Adam og Ewa eller Den ulykkelige Prøve* (1769; Adam and Eve, or, The Unlucky Test). It was followed by *Rolf Krage* (1770), an action drama with the subject taken from the Danish history written by Saxo Grammaticus, a 13th-century historian. Another drama on an Old Norse theme is *Balders*

Død (1774; tr. *The Death of Balder*, 1889), which inspired **Adam Oehlenschläger**. The play *Fiskerne* (1779; The Fishermen) tells about a daring rescue and contains one of Ewald's best-known poems, "Kong Christian stod ved højen Mast" (King Christian Stood by Lofty Mast).

Ewald's fragmentary autobiography bears the title *Levnet og Meeninger* (1773–1777; published 1804–1808; Life and Opinions), and it gives the reader a good sense of the challenges he had to face in his personal life. He is, however, remembered chiefly for his poetry. He was a master of the occasional poem, one of which is the ode "Rungsteds Lyksaligheder" (1775; The Joys of Rungsted), which not only celebrates a country place to which his mother had sent him in order to help him overcome his alcoholism, but which also expresses his religious faith. "Poenitenten" (1777; The Penitent One), "Følelser ved den hellige Nadvere" (1777; Feelings at Holy Communion), and "Til Sielen. En Ode" (1777; Ode to the Soul) all express his religious feelings. The ode "Til min Moltke" (1777; To My Moltke), on the other hand, expresses his gratitude toward an earthly benefactor. *See also* THEATER.

– F –

FAGERHOLM, MONIKA (1961–). A Finland-Swedish novelist and short story writer, Fagerholm writes about **women** and pays much less attention to men. Her women characters, as found in the prose text collections *Sham* (1987) and *Patricia* (1990), however, can be quite repulsive and do not seem calculated to conform to patriarchy's image of ideal femininity. Her great vacation novel *Underbara kvinnor vid vatten* (1994; tr. *Wonderful Women by the Sea*, 1998), on the other hand, tells about two culturally Americanized Finnish women, Rosa and Isabella, who try to imitate consumerist glamour as presented on the pages of *Life* magazine. When the world changes from a state of relative innocence to one of political engagement and activism during the summer of 1968, however, Rosa and Isabella are forced to reassess their approach to living.

The central figure and narrator in *Diva* (1998) is a girl, age 13, who has what can only be described as superhero powers, through which she constructs a highly personal and mythic perception of reality. *Den amerikanska flickan* (2004; The American Girl), which is conceived as the first volume of a series entitled *Slutet på glitterscenen* (The End of the Glitter Stage), has as its theme the loneliness and precarious friendship of youth.

FAIRY TALES. In Scandinavian literature, "fairy tale" refers to traditional folk narratives that nobody believes to be true to life, and to imaginative literature written in imitation of such stories. In the first sense of the term, fairy tales are an important **folklore** genre, while the second definition is best exemplified by the tales and stories of **Hans Christian Andersen**, published between 1835 and 1858. Fairy tale characters and motifs have also been used by other writers. **Per Daniel Amadeus Atterbom**'s fairy tale play *Lycksalighetens ö* (1824–1827; The Isle of Bliss), for example, is one of the major works of Swedish **romanticism**. Fairy tale motifs have also been used ironically, as in **Märta Tikkanen**'s novel *Rödluvan* (1986; Little Red Riding Hood). *See also* KROHN, LEENA; LUGN, KRISTINA; MARTINSON, MOA; PLEIJEL, AGNETA.

FALDBAKKEN, KNUT (1941–). A Norwegian novelist, short story writer, and dramatist, Faldbakken has had five of his novels translated into English. A practitioner of psychological **realism**, Faldbakken studied psychology for two years; his interest in deviant sexuality, a thematic staple in his works, may be a result of these studies.

Faldbakken's first novel, *Den grå regnbuen* (1967; The Gray Rainbow), is set in Paris and illustrates the old idea that a literary artist has to sacrifice human relationships in order to create. The narrator is a young man who abandons his girlfriend because he realizes that marriage is incompatible with his artistic aspirations. *Sin mors hus* (1969; His Mother's House) treats mother-son incest; not even a sexual relationship with an attractive and passionate woman his own age is able to pull the male protagonist away from his mother, who seduces him by appealing to his infantile curiosity about her body. *Maude danser* (1971; tr. *The Sleeping Prince*, 1988) offers a portrait of a woman who, at age 47, is still a virgin, and who appears to have been emotionally arrested by the experience of finding a dead man in the grass when she was a girl. At first she carries on an imaginary relationship with one of the residents of the boardinghouse in which she lives. After his death, she is pursued sexually by the boarder who replaces him, whom she murders, thus duplicating her girlhood experience of being close to a dead body.

Faldbakken's familiarity with the Norwegian literary tradition shows up in *Insektsommer* (1972; tr. *Insect Summer*, 1991), which evokes some motifs in **Knut Hamsun**'s *Pan*. It is a story about a young man's first encounter with the erotic, including the relationship between eroticism and power. Later Faldbakken offered a retelling of Hamsun's story in his book *Glahn* (1985), in which he changed the setting from rural northern Norway in the 1850s to Oslo in the 1980s.

Two ecological novels from the mid-1970s attracted much interest and favorable **critical** attention, culminating in a nomination for the **Nordic Literary Prize** in 1977. In *Uår: Aftenlandet* (1974; tr. *Twilight Country*, 1993) Faldbakken portrays a dystopian urban society where runaway capitalism and wanton exploitation of natural resources force his characters to move to the city dump in order to survive as scavengers. In *Uår: Sweetwater* (1976; tr. *Sweetwater*, 1994) there is a complete socioeconomic collapse, after which some of the residents of the former metropolis band together to establish an ecologically responsible society guided by socialist principles.

After the *Uår* novels Faldbakken returned to male-female relationship issues. *Adams dagbok* (1978; tr. *Adam's Diary*, 1988) is a narrative triptych of sorts, as the same story is narrated from the perspectives of three different characters called the Thief, the Dog, and the Prisoner. *Bryllupsreisen* (1982; tr. *The Honeymoon*, 1987) mixes violence with marriage difficulties, and the author was criticized for appearing to condone physical abuse. But *Bryllupsreisen* also explores the intricacies of literary creativity, for the protagonist believes that striking his wife in her face has freed him to write. Creativity is a core issue in *Bad Boy* (1988), where the middle section of the book is part of a first-person novel that the protagonist in the rest of the book is trying to write, and in which he offers a highly fictionalized version of the reality that is presented in the first and last section. A willingness to experiment with behavior that is not normally part of one's repertoire, for example, cross-dressing, is presented as a means to unleashing one's creativity. *Ormens år* (1993; The Year of the Serpent) represents a return to Faldbakken's earlier focus on pathological sexuality; the protagonist is an outpatient at a mental hospital who creates elaborate mythic structures in order to cope with the fact that he killed his father for sexually abusing his sister.

Three novels from the second half of the 1990s form a kind of trilogy. *Når jeg ser deg* (1996; When I See You), *Eksil* (1997; Exile), and *Alt hva hjertet begjærer* (1999; All That the Heart Desires) are freestanding narratives that are related thematically and share many of the characters. At their center is the question of how it is possible to form and maintain love relationships; all too often personal choice seems to give way to coincidence in the way relationships are formed and how they end.

Faldbakken's most insightful, and also most frightening, novel about sexual abuse is *Frøken Snehvit* (2000; Miss Snow White), in which some young teenagers are preyed on by a woman who claims to be a teacher. The narrator, one of the teens who tells the story as an adult many years later, shows how lives are lost and futures are destroyed by pedophiles. The luridness of the theme is balanced by the author's moral earnestness.

Faldbakken has also written short stories and plays, as well as a book-length essay on literary creativity, *Tør du være kreativ? Et personlig essay om kreativitet* (1994; Dare You Be Creative? A Personal Essay on Creativity), and some additional novels of minor significance, including two mystery stories.

FALKBERGET, JOHAN (1879–1967). A Norwegian novelist, Falkberget was a Christian socialist who grew up near the mining town of Røros in southern Trøndelag, Norway, and spent much of his childhood and youth working in the mines. His numerous novels and stories are centered on the history of mining in the area, as well as the conflicts between the various segments of its population. A careful researcher, Falkberget created a body of literature that has both historical and artistic value. But there was also a clear connection between his portraits of the past and his commitment to promoting social justice in the present; his reconstructions of past events showed that many injustices had not been done away with in Norweigan society.

After writing several locally printed stories, Falkberget's true literary debut was the short novel *Svarte Fjelde* (1907; Black Mountains), which combines detailed descriptions of mining life with expressions of his love of the mountain landscape. Many other novels about hardworking people and their economic struggles—as well as their trials in various love relationships—followed, one of the more notable being *Lisbet paa Jarnfjeld* (1915; tr. *Lisbeth of Jarnfjeld*, 1930), a tragic story of passion and death in the Røros area. *Brændoffer* (1917; Burnt Offering), on the other hand, shows the inhumanity of capitalism as a family moves to Christiania, now Oslo, and suffers the bleak fate of many proletarians. But Falkberget could be funny as well, as is demonstrated by *Bør Børson jr.* (1920), a satire at the expense of those who wanted to get rich quickly in the stock market during the years following the end of World **War** I.

Falkberget's first truly great novel was *Den fjerde nattevakt* (1923; tr. *The Fourth Night Watch*, 1968), a novel about sin, guilt, and redemption. Its protagonist is the proud and ambitious minister Benjamin Sigismund, who serves as the Røros community's pastor early in the 19th century. After falling in love with—and committing adultery with—a peasant woman named Gunhild Bonde, Sigismund experiences a crisis of faith from which he emerges only after a great deal of personal suffering.

Two multivolume series of novels, both of them dealing with mining life, are considered Falkberget's greatest achievement. *Christianus Sextus* (1927–1935), in six volumes, gets its title from a copper mine that is the unifying element in an otherwise episodic narrative. *Nattens brød* (1940–1959), in four volumes, is centered on An-Magritt, a strong-willed woman of the people who leads a life of suffering and toil but also achievement both spiritually and materially.

FEMINISM. The beginnings of feminism in Scandinavian literature can be found in the works of such writers as **Mathilde Fibiger**, **Camilla Collett**, and **Fredrika Bremer**, who promoted **women**'s right to select marriage partners and to have economic independence, including the legal right to control property and the right to paid employment. These issues became paramount in the literature of the **Modern Breakthrough** in the 1870s and the 1880s, when **Henrik Ibsen**'s play *Et dukkehjem* (1879; tr. *A Doll's House*, 1880) was received as a clarion call to women's liberation. Many writers of the period, for example, **Amalie Skram** and **Victoria Benedictsson**, portrayed the situation of women as both oppressive and injurious. More attention was paid to the situation of women in the family and the world of work than in political life, for example, in the novels of **Elin Wägner** and the plays of **Minna Canth**. The franchise was extended to women in Finland in 1906, in Norway in 1913, in Denmark and Iceland in 1918, and in Sweden in 1921, but the struggle for women's right to vote is not a major theme in Scandinavian literature.

The second wave of feminism started around 1960 and deeply affected many Scandinavian writers. The rights of a female minority such as lesbians is a major theme in the work of **Gerd Brantenberg**. Radical feminism, and especially its emphasis on the role of patriarchy in the oppression of women, has influenced such writers as **Svava Jakobsdóttir**, **Cecilie Løveid**, **Kristina Lugn**, and **Bjørg Vik**. Third-wave feminism can be observed in the work of such younger writers as **Hanne Ørstavik**, who in her novel *Presten* (2004; The Minister) links the social situation of Sámi women to the colonial oppression of their forebears by the Norwegian government. *See also* BOYE, KARIN; BRØGGER, SUZANNE; HEIBERG, GUNNAR; JENSEN, THIT.

FIBIGER, MATHILDE (1830–1872). A Danish novelist, Fibiger was the first writer in her country to introduce issues of justice for **women** into literature. In her first novel, *Clara Raphael: Tolv Breve* (1850; Clara Raphael: Twelve Letters), which was published under the pseudonym Clara Raphael, Fibiger describes the effort of a young governess to create independence for herself. She laments the fact that Danish society offers no significant opportunities for intellectual growth to highly talented women and that women's only viable option in society is marriage. The novel set off a heated debate in Copenhagen, in which Fibiger intervened with a second epistolary novel, *Et Besøg* (1851; A Visit), which expands on her views concerning the oppression of women. Her novel *Minona* (1854) goes further still by criticizing the institution of marriage and the double standard in sexual matters.

FIVE YOUNG MEN, THE GROUP OF. The group got its name from an anthology of **modernist** poetry, *5 unga* (1929; Five Young

Men), that was perceived as a challenge to traditional Swedish verse. The two most illustrious contributors were **Artur Lundkvist** and **Harry Martinson**.

FLØGSTAD, KJARTAN (1944–). A Norwegian novelist, short story writer, and poet, Fløgstad is the most significant **postmodernist** in Norwegian literature. His first two published books were poetry collections, *Valfart* (1968; Pilgrimage) and *Seremoniar* (1969; Ceremonies). He soon found his narrative voice, however, with the books *Den hemmelege jubel* (1970; The Secret Jubilation) and *Fangliner* (1972; Painters), both volumes of short prose. Then followed the novel *Rasmus* (1974). These books all drew on Fløgstad's experiences as a sailor and as a factory worker and provided true-to-life descriptions of life in the merchant marine and on the factory floor. Unlike the works of many of Fløgstad's socialist **realist** contemporaries, they were written to be read by common people.

Fløgstad's first postmodern work, the novel *Dalen Portland* (1977; tr. *Dollar Road*, 1989), became his definitive literary breakthrough and also garnered him the **Nordic Literary Prize** in 1978. The book mixes features of popular literature with the conventions of belles lettres, intermingles old-fashioned literary conventions with **modernist** ones, alternates segments of realistic narration with outlandish fantasy, and tells its story of industrialization in western Norway through a veritable chorus of sometimes competing voices. The author even appears as one of the story's characters, and the activity of writing is figured as this character's knocking with a wrench on the side of a boiler in a factory, listening for hollowness in the language.

Other novels are even more characteristic of postmodernism. Partly set in the fictional industrial community Lovra, *Fyr og flamme* (1980; Fire and Flame) is subtitled "Av handling" (Dis Sertation/ From Action); it tells a story of industrial development and subverts the story that is told. *U3* (1983), which takes its title from the U2 incident of the Cold War in which the Soviet Union shot down a U.S. spy plane, mixes a reasonably realistic tale, rich in detail, with such improbable devices as a "retrospectoscope" that allows the narrator to look back into the past and thus know the details of his story. This novel also has a strong political message, as it warns about the consequences of Norwegian membership in the North Atlantic Treaty Organization (NATO) and the resulting potential for United States dominance of Norwegian foreign policy.

Fløgstad's most problematic book, at least from the perspective of his typical reader, is *Det 7. klima* (1986; The Seventh Climate), which twists Norwegian and European intellectual history and wryly comments on the problems and practices of the Norwegian mass media in the guise of a fictional autobiography of a certain Salim Mahmood, a Pakistani immigrant to Norway. *Det 7. klima* is such a radically open work, in Umberto Eco's sense, that there is no critical agreement as to its meaning.

Kniven på strupen (1991; The Knife to the Throat), on the other hand, gives the reader a clearer sense of the author's intentions. As in *Dalen Portland* and *Fyr og flamme*, the history of Norwegian industrial development figures prominently. Set in the 1980s, however, *Kniven på strupen* presents life under late capitalism, when factory workers have mostly been replaced by machines and the traditional work ethic of the people has given way to greed and crime. With many elements of the traditional mystery story present, the novel presents a tale of murder, theft, and robbery with captains of industry in the leading roles. In spite of Fløgstad's irony, humor, and legendary punning, it is a bitter book that mourns the direction that Norwegian society has taken. The same anger at social conditions is present in *Fimbul* (1994), which also is a novel about crime, this time with an admixture of terrorism. Set in 1978, when the Nobel Peace Prize is to be awarded to Anwar Sadat and Menachem Begin in Oslo, the story centers on the theft of a mortar that is to be used in a fictional assasination attempt. The attempt is foiled, but not before Fløgstad has managed to assault the Norwegian language with his numerous bad puns.

Fløgstad's social criticism is continued in his magic realist novel *Kron og mynt* (1998; Heads and Tails), but this novel is not nearly as acerbic as its two predecessors. Fløgstad is much more playful as he constructs a linguistic universe that clearly takes precedence over the segments of reality that are depicted. Anything can happen in Fløgstad's imagination, and his command of the language is superb. This is also the case in *Paradis på jord* (2002; Paradise on Earth), which tells the story of a Chilean boy named José Andersen (a pun on the name of the Danish writer **Hans Christian Andersen**), the illegitimate son of a Norwegian engineer and a South American native, who travels to Norway in search of his patrimony. The result is a truly adventurous narrative in which Fløgstad once again offers a funhouse image of his homeland.

Fløgstad has also written travelogues and several volumes of essays, mostly of cultural and social criticism. He writes in **nynorsk**.

FOGELSTRÖM, PER ANDERS (1917–). A Swedish novelist, Fogelström was born and raised in Stockholm, a city that he has memorialized in a large number of novels. His first important novel, however, was *Sommaren med Monika* (1951; The Summer with Monica), which became well known because it had the same title as the film by Ingmar Bergman, for which Fogelström wrote the screenplay. Fogelström's first Stockholm novels were in a series consisting of five volumes that depict the city's transition from a preindustrial town to a modern metropolis: *Mina drömmars stad* (1960; City of My Dreams), *Barn av sin stad* (1962; Children of Their City), *Minns du den stad* (1964; Do You Remember the City), *I en förvandlad stad* (1966; In a Transformed City), and *Stad i världen* (1968; City in the World).

Fogelström portrays his own generation in a series of novels with the collective title *Kamrater* (Comrades), consisting of the volumes *Upptäckarna* (1972; The Explorers), *Revoltörerna* (1973; The Rebels), *Erövrarna* (1975; The Conquerors), and *Besittarna* (1977; The Possessors). Stockholm during the reign of King **Gustav III** and the decades thereafter is depicted in a trilogy consisting of *Vävarnas barn* (1981; Children of the Weavers), *Krigens barn* (1985; Children of the Wars), and *Vita bergens barn* (1987; Children of the White Mountains District). Fogelström used his own family history as material in *Komikern: Roman om en teaterfamilj* (1989; The Comedian: A Novel about a Theatrical Family), while Stockholm again serves as the background for his fictional narrative *Mödrar och söner* (1991; Mothers and Sons).

FOLKLORE. Folklore is a term used to designate the mostly oral traditions of a group of people; it includes such oral forms as legends, **fairy tales**, and ballads. Legends are typically short narratives that are anchored in a particular time and place recognizable and meaningful to the audience. A large number of the legends that were collected in traditional Scandinavian society tell about contact with beings of the normally invisible world. These creatures were spirits of mountains, forests, lakes, and rivers, as well as household spirits. Trolls and the hidden folk, two common terms for such beings, lived inside mountains and hills as well as underground, and they were believed to have an economic or sexual interest in humans; the latter was thought to be so because these beings could not obtain Christian salvation except through marriage to a Christian. Some of the spirits were clearly malevolent; for example, water sprites such as the nixie lured people to their deaths. Others behaved in ways that exemplified both fairness and good will.

Fairy tales are longer narratives than the legends and are less tied to a particular time and place. While most traditional audiences believed that legends were true, nobody but a small child would think so about a fairy tale. One of the most common motifs of the Scandinavian fairy tales is that of the young boy, the Ashlad, who through his cunning, wit, and courage wins a princess and half of her father's kingdom.

Medieval ballads have been collected all over Scandinavia and are similar to both legends and fairy tales in content. Many of them have their origin in printed texts owned and sung by the nobility; later these texts entered popular culture. Ballad singing appears to have accompanied ring dancing, and this practice has survived up to modern times in the Faroes.

Folkloristic texts had a very strong influence on Scandinavian literature, particularly during the **romantic** period. In Norway **Johan Sebastian Welhaven** wrote a series of narrative poems that are essentially retellings of legends. The Dane Hans Christian Andersen modeled his widely read fairy tales on actual stories told by the folk. In one of his best-known dramas, *Peer Gynt* (1867; tr. 1892), **Henrik Ibsen** uses legendary material to great dramatic and comical effect. *See also* GOLDSCHMIDT, MEÏR ARON; HEIBERG, JOHAN LUDVIG; LÖNNROT, ELIAS; RYDBERG, VICTOR; STRINDBERG, AUGUST.

FORSSELL, LARS (1928–). A Swedish poet, playwright, and novelist, Forssell has produced an eclectic oeuvre, with both serious and more popular texts. One theme is role-playing, as in his second collection of poetry, *Narren* (1952; The Jester). The poetry collections *Telegram* (1957), *Röster* (1964; Voices), and *Jack uppskäraren* (1966; Jack the Ripper) combine seriousness and whimsy, fear and a sense of security. Forssell has reached a large audience with his less serious poetry, found in the volume *Snurra min jord och andra visor* (1958; Spin, My Earth, and Other Songs). There is a significant political dimension to *Visor svarta och röda* (1972; Songs Black and Red). The **war** in Vietnam had a strong impact on Forssell, who objected to the U.S. bombing of Hanoi in *Försök* (1972; Attempt), which followed *Oktoberdikter* (1971; October Poems), a volume of less specific political poetry. But Forssell also has a strong sense of the poetic tradition, as evidenced by a volume of sonnets, *Sånger* (1986; Songs).

Forssell's numerous plays move from an early concern with people's use of masks to a preoccupation with politics. Examples of the former are *Narren som tillhörde sina bjällor* (1953; The Jester Who Belonged to His Bells) and *Galenpannan* (1964; The Madcap), which deals with the life of the dethroned Swedish king Gustaf IV Adolf. Two of his political dramas are *Sverige, Sverige eller Borgerlighetens fars* (1967; Sweden, Sweden, or, The Farce of the Middle Class) and *Borgaren och Marx* (1970; The Bourgeois and Marx). Many of Forssell's plays have historical settings; for example, *Bergsprängaren och hans dotter Eivor* (1989; The Dynamite Blaster and His Daughter Eivor) takes place in the 1930s.

Forssell's novel *De rika* (1976; The Rich) constitutes an unmasking of middle-class norms. Its ideas are similar to those of his political poetry and drama.

FOSSE, JON (1959–). A Norwegian novelist, poet, essayist, and playwright, Fosse is Norway's foremost dramatist after **Henrik Ibsen**. His work has been translated into 30 languages and is frequently performed abroad, especially in Germany. He has received numerous literary prizes and is Norway's best-known writer internationally. Fosse writes in a minimalist yet lyrical **nynorsk** and takes as his theme simple and everyday occurrences.

Fosse started out as a novelist and had his literary debut with *Raud, svart* (1983; Red, Black), a story about teenage depression and suicide. *Stengd gitar* (1985; Closed Guitar) has as its protagonist a single mother who wanders the streets while her baby has been left at her apartment, from which she has been locked out. Neither novel has a clear resolution of the story. The novel *Blod: Steinen er* (1987; Blood: The Stone Is) likewise has no clear ending, and the central element of the plot, whether or not a man is the murderer of his dead wife, is also left unresolved. All three books have in common that the protagonists are confused and that their confusion is reflected in the disjointed language that is used consciously by Fosse to give a sense of its representationalist limits.

Around the time when he was separating from his first wife, Fosse published the novel *Naustet* (1989; The Boathouse), a story about youthful love triangles and their repetition later in the lives of the narrator and the book's other characters. *Flaskesamlaren* (1991; The Bottle Collector), presents a protagonist whose identity is as uncertain and fragmented as those of the individuals he encounters and fictionally represents in the text. In the novel *Bly og vatn* (1992; Lead and Water) a married journalist happens upon an intoxicated young woman, takes her with him to his hotel room, experiences the complete collapse of his ability to function professionally and socially, and then discovers that he has fallen in love with the woman. He, too, is one of Fosse's many decentered characters.

Fosse has commented on his artistic practice in such collections of essays as *Frå telling via showing til writing* (1989; From Telling via Showing to Writing) and *Gnostiske essay* (1999; Gnostic Essays), in which he acknowledges his debt to such philosophers as Theodor Adorno, Herbert Marcuse, Martin Heidegger, and Jacques Derrida.

Fosse became a dramatist after his second marriage in 1993 and has published a large number of plays, starting with *Og aldri skal vi skiljast* (1994; And Never Shall We Be Separated). Both this play and those that followed are characterized by a lack of emphasis on plot and a corresponding focus on the limitations of language; the characters, often unnamed, rarely manage to express what they want. The theme of *Og aldri skal vi skiljast* is how difficult it is for couples to remain married, and this problem is also explored in *Namnet* (1995; tr. *The Name*, 2002), in which a couple is expecting a child, which highlights their difficulties in communication. Communication is also the issue in *Nokon kjem til å komme* (1996; tr. *Someone Is Going to Come*, 2002), in which a marriage breaks down subsequent to the arrival of a third person. Three plays published together in 1997, *Barnet* (tr. *The Child*, 2002), *Mor og barn* (Mother and Child), and *Sonen* (The Son), all highlight the problem that children, present or absent, can be to a marriage. In *Barnet* the problem is the lack of a child, as the woman miscarries, while the other two plays deal with conflicts about and with children.

Both the love triangle and conflicts involving children are thematized in *Natta syng sine songar* (1998; tr. *Nightsongs*, 2002), in which the father of a baby is also trying to become a writer. This drama, too, has a pessimistic outcome, as there is a failure to communicate and the mother of the baby leaves for another man. In *Ein sommars dag* (1998; A Day in Summer) the failure of the man and the woman to communicate effectively plays itself out on two temporal levels, as it is filtered through the memories of the woman after she has grown old. Both the elderly woman and her younger self are characters in this play, and a brief meeting between them reinforces the theatricality of the piece. *Draum om hausten* (1999; Autumn Dream) also juxtaposes the past and the present, neither of which is stable in the memory and experience of the characters. The three plays *Besøk* (2000; Visit), *Vinter* (2000; Winter), and *Ettermiddag* (2000; Afternoon) continue the themes of jealousy, isolation, and failure of communication. In the play *Vakkert* (2001; Beautiful) another love triangle from the past reemerges.

Dødsvariasjonar (2002; Variations on Death) is yet another play about loneliness and features a family of three: father, mother, and daughter. The daughter regards death as a good friend, but she is ambivalent when she finally chooses suicide. *Jenta is sofaen* (2003; The Girl in the Sofa) juxtaposes a grown woman with her pubescent self as she fails to bring healing to wounds sustained in her early teens. *Lilla* (2004) deals with teen sexuality and power struggles, while *Suzannah* (2004) is a dramatic presentation of the life of Suzannah Thoresen, the wife of Henrik Ibsen.

His success as a dramatist has not kept Fosse from writing novels. *Melancholia I* (1995) and *Melancholia II* (1996) present the life and family of the Norwegian painter Lars Hertervig. *Morgon og kveld* (2000; Morning and Evening) takes place partly after the death of the protagonist, as he continues to exist in a spiritual realm. *Det er Ales*

(2004; It Is Ales) tells about love, death, and the ocean in the lives of several generations of one family. *See also* THEATER.

FREUDIANISM. The theories of Sigmund Freud (1856–1939) became very influential in Scandinavian literature after World **War** I. **Hans Kirk**, a Danish **Marxist**, depended heavily on Freud in his social analysis and, in particular, in his depiction of religion. The early work of **Hans Christian Branner** is strongly marked by the Freudian inspired psychological **realism** of the interwar period. In Norway, both **Olav Duun** and **Sigurd Hoel** were influenced by Freudian psychoanalysis, and Hoel particularly so in his portrayal of childhood in his novel *Veien til verdens ende* (1933; The Road to the End of the World). *See also* BERGMAN, HJALMER; KYRKLUND, WILLY.

FRIDEGÅRD, JAN (1897–1968). A Swedish novelist and short story writer, Fridegård was the son of *statare*, people who lived serflike lives on large estates, where they provided the farm labor. With very little education, he took whatever work he could find as a young man. His major literary work is a trilogy about his former self, written from the perspective of a more mature man, consisting of *Jag, Lars Hård* (1935; tr. *I, Lars Hård*, 1985), *Tack för himlastegen* (1936; tr. *Jacob's Ladder*, 1987), and *Barmhärtighet* (1936; tr. *Mercy*, 1987), in which the protagonist is a cynical and lazy young man who has little sense of solidarity with his class. Fridegård continued the story about Lars Hård in the novels *Här är min hand* (1942; Here Is My Hand) and *Lars Hård går vidare* (1951; Lars Hård Keeps Going).

Another trilogy is set during the Viking Age. Consisting of the volumes *Trägudars land* (1940; tr. *Land of Wooden Gods*, 1989), *Gryningsfolket* (1944; tr. *People of the Dawn*, 1990), and *Offerrök* (1949; tr. *Sacrificial Smoke*, 1990), it portrays the coming of Christianity to Sweden and offers a detailed psychological portrait of a Viking Age slave named Holme, whose life is not unlike that of the *statare* almost a thousand years later. The novels *Lyktgubbarna* (1955; The Will-o'-the-wisps), *Flyttfåglarna* (1956; The Migratory Birds), and *Arvtagarna* (1957; The Heirs) arc set in the district of Uppland during Fridegård's childhood. He also wrote a five-volume series of novels—commonly referred to as *Soldatsviten* (The Soldier

Suite)—that take place before and after the year 1800, when Sweden was at **war** more often than not.

Many of Fridegård's short stories were collected in the volumes *Statister* (1939; Extras), *Kvarnbudet* (1944; The Message from the Mill), and *Kvinnoträdet* (1950; The Woman Tree). He also wrote four volumes of memoirs, *På oxens horn* (1964; On the Horns of the Ox), *Lättingen* (1965; Lazybones), *Det kortaste strået* (1966; The Short End of the Stick), and *Tre stigar* (1967; Three Paths).

FROBENIUS, NIKOLAJ (1965–). A Norwegian novelist and social critic, Frobenius had his debut with *Latours katalog* (1996; tr. *De Sade's Valet*, 2000), a novel about a man who is unable to feel pain and who therefore inflicts pain on others in an attempt to learn what pain is like. As an assistant to the notorious Marquis de Sade, he also tries to comprehend his employer. It was a huge success both in Norway and abroad, and was followed by *Den sjenerte pornografen* (1999; The Shy Pornographer), in which a young boy enters a society of the future where life is completely centered on the production and consumption of pornographic images. Frobenius successfully expresses his critique of the sexualization of contemporary life. *Andre steder* (2001; Other Places) probes the boundary between reality and fiction, truth and lies. The protagonist, a young man named Christopher, responds to his father's disappearance by leaving his ill mother and his girlfriend for a year and a half. Upon his return he can remember only a few things from the time he was gone and has no clear sense of his own identity.

Det aller minste (2003; The Very Least) contains, in the form of an interior monologue, the response of a 17-year-old to his mother's suicide. It is a highly fragmented text that effectively conveys the condition of a mind that is in the process of deteriorating. It is built on Frobenius's play *Mikromani* (Micromania), which was performed, without much success, at the National Theater in Oslo in January 2003. *Teori og praksis* (2004; Theory and Practice) is a well-written but highly personal book that barely fictionalizes the autobiogrpahical material on which it is based.

FRÖDING, GUSTAF (1860–1911). A Swedish poet, Fröding suffered from mental illness for much of his life and in 1898 suffered a breakdown that effectively put a stop to his work. A perpetual outsider, he should be regarded as an early **modernist**, who had his debut with the collection *Gitarr och dragharmonika* (1891; tr. *Guitar and Concertina*, 1926). As indicated by the title, this volume contains two types of poems, the more somber and serious ones, suitable for guitar accompaniment, and the lighter and funny ones, the sort that one could imagine accompanied by a concertina. The latter type made Fröding one of the most beloved poets in Swedish literature.

Some of the poems in *Nya dikter* (1894; New Poems) express Fröding's views on social issues, while *Stänk och flikar* (1896; Sprinklings and Tatters) alludes to how difficult it is to arrive at a coherent worldview; the old view of reality is in tatters, and nothing has yet replaced it. In this collection Fröding introduces the image of the Holy Grail, which represents the lost ability to hold all of reality in a single vision. One of the poems, "En morgondröm" (A Morning Dream), landed Fröding in court, accused of pornography; he was, however, acquitted.

The collection *Nytt och gammalt* (1897; New and Old) was followed by *Gralstänk* (1898; Sprinklings from the Grail), which further deal with the fragmentation of modern reality. Two prose works, *Om livsmonader* (1898; About Life's Monads) and *Grillfängerier* (1898; Flights of Fancy), are in a similar vein. The collections *Efterskörd* (1910; Late Harvest), *Reconvalescentia* (1913), and *Återkomsten* (1964; The Return) were published posthumously.

FRÖKEN JULIE. A modern drama by the Swede **August Strindberg**, *Fröken Julie* (1887; tr. *Miss Julie*, 1912) is an excellent example of **naturalism** in Scandinavian drama.

FROSTENSON, KATARINA (1953–). A Swedish poet and dramatist, Frostenson writes poetry that avoids both any kind of story line and the use of metaphor. Instead, she juxtaposes the beautiful and the grotesque and emphasizes sound and rhythm. The **critical** consensus is that her poetry is very difficult. Frostenson knows Western literature well and has a degree in comparative literature, film, and drama. Frostenson had her debut with the poetry collection *I mellan* (1978; In Between), which refers to the significance of the gap between the two terms in a binary opposition. It was followed by *Rena land*

(1980; Pure Lands), *Den andra* (1982; The Other), and *I det gula* (1985; In the Yellow). The male/female opposition is significant in the poetry collections *Samtalet* (1987; The Conversation) and *Strändarna* (1989; The Shores). Later poetry collections include *Joner: Tre sviter* (1991; Ions: Three Suites), *Tankarna* (1994; The Thoughts), and *Korallen* (1999; The Coral).

In collaboration with her husband, Jean-Claude Arnault, a French photographer, Frostenson has published three books, *Överblivet* (1989; Left Over), *Vägen till öarna* (1996; The Way to the Islands), and *Endura* (2002). They have also collaborated on other projects. Arnaud opened a gallery and multimedia stage in Stockholm in 1989, and Frostenson wrote her first play, the one-act *Sebastopol* (1989), for this stage. She more or less invented a type of compact monologue that she termed "monodrama" and later published a volume containing four of them, *4 monodramer* (1990; Four Monodramas), with which she had a great deal of success. Later dramas include *Traum* (1996; Dream) and *Sal P* (1996; Ward P); the latter explores the methods used by Jean-Martin Charcot (1825–1893) in the treatment of **women** suffering from hysteria at his hospital in Paris. She also wrote the libretto for the opera *Staden* (The City), which opened in Stockholm in 1998. Two further plays are *Kristallvägen* (2000; The Crystal Road) and *Safirgränd* (2000; Sapphire Lane). *See also* THEATER.

– G –

GAARDER, JOSTEIN (1952–). A Norwegian novelist and short story writer, Gaarder is known primarily for his novel *Sofies verden* (1991; tr. *Sophie's World: A Novel about the History of Philosophy*, 1994), which was the world's best-selling work of fiction in 1995, but he has produced many other books that straddle the boundary between literature for young adults and adults. Educated in philosophy, the history of ideas, and Scandinavian literature, he had, with several collaborators, published several titles in the areas of religion and ethics by the time he produced his first work of fiction, *Diagnosen, og andre noveller* (1986; The Diagnosis and Other Stories), which continues his work on ethics and religion. Two children's books followed, *Barna fra Sukhavati* (1987; The Children of Sukhavati) and *Froskeslottet* (1988; tr. *The Frog Castle*, 1999).

Gaarder's first adult novel, *Kabalmysteriet* (1990; tr. *The Solitaire Mystery: A Novel about Family and Destiny*, 1996), features an inquisitive child named Hans Thomas who travels through Europe with his father in search of his mother. The journey is one of education both outwardly and inwardly, for Hans Thomas learns to know both himself and the world of history and intellect. The relationship between him and his father is a Socratic one, but the boy increasingly takes responsibility for his own education.

Sofies verden is structurally similar to *Kabalmysteriet* but has two pairs of learners and mentors. The reader is first introduced to Sofie Amundsen, a teenager who is receiving notes about the history of philosophy from a mysterious figure who calls himself Alberto Knox. After they meet, their relationship continues as a Socratic dialogue. But each of the two has a double, a Norwegian United Nations observer named Albert Knag and his daughter Hilde. The book soon takes a **postmodern** turn, however, as the reader learns that Sofie and Alberto Knox are nothing but characters in a novel about the history of philosophy that Hilde is reading. Hilde thus becomes the reader's double as well, and the reader turns out to be the real recipient of the information that is transmitted in the book.

One of the main themes in *Sofies verden* is the healthy curiosity of children, which returns in Gaarder's next book, *Julemysteriet* (1992; tr. *The Christmas Mystery*, 1996). It has a frame story in which a boy named Joakim opens the windows of his Advent calendar and is drawn into an adventure that takes place in Palestine in 1948. There are also strong spiritual overtones in *I et speil, i en gåte* (1993; tr. *Through a Glass, Darkly*, 1998), and didactic history lessons resurface in *Bibbi Bokkens magiske bibliotek* (1993; Bibbi Bokken's Magical Library). The necessity of questioning life returns as the theme of *Hallo? Er det noen her?* (1996; tr. *Hello? Is Anybody There?*, 1997), while *Vita Brevis: Floria Aemilias brev til Aurel Augustin* (1996; tr. *Vita Brevis: A Letter to Saint Augustine*, 1997) is a meditation on the church's attitude toward **women** in late antiquity.

The novel *Maya* (1999; tr. 2000) combines Gaarder's concern with ethics with an inquiry into the nature of science. *Sirkusdirektørens datter* (2001; tr. *The Ringmaster's Daughter*, 2002) tells the story of the separation of a father and his daughter; only as she dies does he discover her identity. *Appelsinpiken* (2003; tr. *The Orange Girl*, 2004) is another juvenile novel about the separation of parent and child. See also CHILDREN'S BOOKS.

GARBORG, ARNE (1851–1924). A Norwegian novelist, short story writer, poet, playwright, and essayist, Garborg was the oldest son, and thus the allodial heir, in a farm family in the Jæren district of southwestern Norway. He grew up with an extreme form of rural religious pietism that long soured him on both religion and rural life. After leaving home in order to become a teacher, he learned, at the age of 18, that his father had committed suicide. This gave him deep and lasting feelings of guilt, for he feared that his own rejection of his ancestral farm had contributed to the depression that led to his father's death. After a period of teaching, Garborg went to Oslo in order to qualify for admission to the university; he reached this goal in 1875 with superior marks. Around the same time he abandoned all traces of the conservative religiosity with which he had been raised, becoming increasingly radical in his thinking and writing. One aspect of that radicalism was his choice of literary medium; for most of his writing he choose the dialect-based **Landsmaal** (later known as **nynorsk**) rather than the Danish-colored standard **Riksmaal** (later known as bokmål).

Garborg's first significant literary effort was the short novel *Ein Fritenkjar* (1878; A Freethinker), which details the prejudice that meets a sincere individual who wants to build his personal worldview on reason rather than dogma. But Garborg's definitive literary breakthrough came with *Bondestudentar* (1883; Peasant Students), a detailed depiction of life in Norway during the author's youth. The protagonist of *Bondestudentar* is a gifted young man from Garborg's home district of Jæren named Daniel Braut, and the book chronicles his path from childhood until, as a student of theology, he for pecuniary reasons commits to marry an upper-class woman he does not love. The cultural-historical value of the book is considerable, as it offers vivid portraits of some of the most significant inhabitants of Norway's public sphere in the 1860s and 1870s, among them the writer **Aasmund Olafsson Vinje**, the Hegclian professor of philosophy **Marcus Jacob Monrad**, and the radical student leader Olaus

Fjørtoft, and it offers thumbnail sketches of some of the central issues of the day.

In the middle of the 1880s Garborg associated with some of the most radical writers of the time, the **Christiania bohemians**, who wanted to do away with traditional morality by allowing free love to take the place of bourgeois marriage, and even to replace society's whole conception of justice. Garborg's naturalistic novel *Mannfolk* (1886; Menfolk), in which he continues his exploration of some of the characters in *Bondestudentar*, constitutes an investigation of the various male-female relations that are possible in Norway in the 1880s. Covering a time period of roughly one year, it offers a number of case studies in love and eroticism that, on the whole, supports the pessimistic cultural diagnosis of the bohemians.

Mannfolk was not banned by the authorities, as several books by Garborg's bohemian friends had been, but Garborg was punished by being fired from his government job. Married to Hulda Bergersen in 1887, he needed money badly and quickly, and assisted by Hulda wrote *Hjaa ho Mor* (1890; Living with Mama), which is partly based on Hulda's life. It tells the story of the development of its protagonist, Fanny Holmsen, from when she is a young girl until she consents to marry a man more than twice her age, whom she does not love. She does love another character in *Hjaa ho Mor*, a man named Gabriel Gram, who was one of the men in *Mannfolk*; however, he is too emotionally divided to accept Fanny's love by proposing marriage to her.

The Garborg family (a son was born to them at this time) spent this difficult time in a small and drafty mountain cabin at Kolbotn in Norway's southeast interior. There Garborg wrote the play *Uforsonlige* (1888; The Uncompromising), an attack on the liberal government's lack of support for the arts. *Kolbotnbrev* (1890; Letters from Kolbotn) is another small volume, originally published piecemeal in the newspaper *Fedraheimen* (The Home of the Fathers), in which Garborg offers both beautiful **nature** descriptions and ironic comments on his domestic life.

Garborg's greatest success was *Trætte Mænd* (1891; tr. *Weary Men*, 1999), a diary novel in the style of the decadent writing of the 1890s. Its narrator-protagonist is the same Gabriel Gram who appears in both *Mannfolk* and *Hjaa ho Mor*. *Trætte Mænd* presents his relationship with Fanny Holmsen from his point of view, and Garborg is at pains to show why Gram has developed his defects of personality. But Garborg also offers an interesting representation of the role that religion had come to play in the 1890s and ironically shows that Gram seeks the comfort of the church as consolation after he has lost Fanny.

Religion is also a major theme in Garborg's next several books. *Fred* (1892; tr. *Peace*, 1929), a novel set in his home district of Jæren, tells the story of the mental illness, religious delusions, and death of Enok Haave, who is Garborg's own father in fictional form. The play *Læraren* (1896; The Teacher) as well as the two slender novels *Den burtkomne Faderen* (1899; tr. *The Lost Father*, 1920) and *Heimkomin Son* (1908; The Returned Son) all have members of the Haave family as protagonists and debate what constitutes true and ethical Christianity. These themes were also discussed in expository form in *Jesus Messias* (1906) and *Den burtkomne Messias* (1907; The Lost Messiah), in which Garborg presents alternatives to fundamentalist Christianity.

Garborg was also a gifted poet. The life-affirming poetic cyle *Haugtussa* (1895; The Mountain Maid) has as its setting Jæren before the advent of pietism. It is centered around Veslemøy, a young woman gifted with second sight who overcomes evil and adversity because of her goodness and her capacity for love. She is Garborg's chief exponent of his own values.

GARDELL, JONAS (1963–). One of the best-known public personalities in 21st-century Sweden, Gardell is a stand-up comic, poet, novelist, essayist, and filmmaker. His early years were very difficult, as his father abandoned the family, leaving Gardell with bitter feelings that caused him to look for solace in drugs. He had his literary debut while still a teenager with the poetry collection *Den tigande talar/ 4937* (1981; The Silent One Speaks/4937). His first novel was *Passionsspelet* (1985; The Passion Play). The novel *Odjurets tid* (1986; The Time of the Beast) depicts characters who create the illusions they need to cope with life. *Präriehundarna* (1987; The Prairie Dogs) satirizes contemporary Swedish society, while *Vill gå hem* (1988; Want to Go Home) offers satirical portraits of two sisters. *Fru Björks öden och äventyr* (1990; The Wonderful Adventures of Mrs.

Björk) tells the story of a woman who takes revenge on her former husband.

En komikers uppväst (1992; A Comedian Grows Up) is an autobiographical novel that offers many details about Gardell's own life. The story about his two main characters, Juha and Jenny, continues in *Ett ufo gör entré* (2001; A UFO Shows Up). *Frestelsernas berg* (1995; The Mount of Temptations) deals with the history of a dysfunctional family. Taking its title from a well-known Swedish evening hymn, *Så går en dag ifrån vårt liv och kommer aldrig åter* (1998; Thus a Day Passes from Our Lives and Never Comes Back) tells about the lives of a group of everyday people.

Gardell has published a volume of drama, *Isbjörnarna; Cheek to cheek; Människor i solen: tre pjäser* (1997; The Polar Bears; Cheek to Cheek; People in the Sun: Three Plays). He has also written the screenplay for such films as *Pensionat Oskar* (1995; also distributed as *Like It Never Was Before*) and *Livet är en schlager* (2000; also distributed as *Once in a Lifetime*). He continues to produce live shows.

Mormor gråter och andra texter (1993; Grandma Cries and Other Texts) contains both poetry and prose. The title piece, "Mormor gråter" (Grandma Cries), is a Christmas story that is well on its way to achieving the status of a Christmas classic in Sweden. The essay collection *Oskuld och andra texter* (2000; Innocence and Other Texts) is of interest chiefly because of Gardell's reflections on matters of religion. These concerns also animate his book *Om Gud* (2003; About God), in which he offers a historical introduction to the Christian concept of the divine.

GEIJER, ERIK GUSTAV (1783–1847). A Swedish poet, Geijer was, with **P. D. A. Atterbom**, Sweden's greatest proponent of **romanticism**, which for him had a decidedly nationalistic slant. He studied at Uppsala University and eventually got a professorship in history there. He was also active in one of Uppsala's several associations, Götiska förbundet (The Old Norse League), and published some poems in its journal, *Iduna*. Two of these poems bear mention, as they gesture at the two main strands within **national romanticism**. "Vikingen" (The Viking) is an example of the interest that the national romantics took in the ancient history of Scandinavia, especially the Viking Age. Geijer was, however, more interested in the Viking as a personality type than in the factual history of the Vikings. The other poem, "Odalbonden" (The Yeoman Farmer), ties in with national romanticism's admiration for the common folk of the rural districts, who lived close to **nature** and were direct descendents of the ancient Scandinavians.

Geijer started out as a cultural and political conservative. With the passage of time, however, his ideas became more liberal, and this development can be studied in *Den blå boken* (1837; The Blue Book), which contains articles and aphorisms. Geijer also wrote several historical works.

GIANTS IN THE EARTH. The first volume of a trilogy by the Norwegian immigrant writer **Ole E. Rølvaag**, *Giants in the Earth: A Saga of the Prairie* (1927) was a translation by Lincoln Colcord of two novels, written in Norwegian and published in Norway, entitled *I de dage* (1924; In Those Days) and *Riket grundlægges* (1925; The Kingdom Is Founded), which tell the story of a handful of emigrants from Rølvaag's home district of Helgeland in northern Norway who settle on the prairie of America's Dakota Territory.

GOLDSCHMIDT, MEÏR ARON (1819–1887). A Danish novelist, short story writer, and journalist, Goldschmidt first became notorious in Danish cultural life as the editor of and main contributor to the satirical weekly journal *Corsaren* (1840–1846; The Corsair). After traveling abroad Goldschmidt started another journal, *Nord og Syd* (1847–1859; North and South), which offered facts and opinion about European society and politics.

Goldschmidt's first novel, *En Jøde* (1845; tr. *A Jew*, 1852, 1990), tells about a Jewish man who gets engaged to a Christian woman, but who is not strong enough to handle the cultural differences. The short stories in *Fortællinger* (1846; Stories) also treat the situation of Jews living in Denmark. The three-volume novel *Hjemløs* (1853–1857; tr. *Homeless*, 1861) represents a further development of the theme of the outsider. The protagonist of *Hjemløs* has failed the woman he was supposed to marry and as a result has become a wanderer. He spends the rest of his life suffering and trying to find peace, for there is retribution in the world, and he must pay the price for what he has done.

After Goldschmidt moved to London and Paris, he published three volumes of *Fortællinger og Skildringer* (1863–1865; Stories and Sketches). The first two volumes consist of stories, but the third one contains the novel *Arvingen* (The Heir), which is reminiscent of *Hjemløs*. Goldschmidt's best novel is *Ravnen* (1867; The Raven), a combination of **realistic** narrative and some **folklore** motifs. It represents a further development of his theory of retribution. Goldschmidt also published two volumes of short stories entitled *Smaa Fortællinger* (1868–1869; Small Stories), the short story volume *Kjærlighedshistorier fra mange Lande* 1867; Love Stories from Many Countries), and several other volumes of prose.

GÖSTA BERLINGS SAGA. A novel by the Swedish **Selma Lagerlöf**, *Gösta Berlings saga* (1891; tr. *The Story of Gösta Berling*, 1898) is set in the author's home district of Värmland at the end of the 1820s and tells a semi-mythical story of good and evil.

GRESS, ELSA (1919–1988). A Danish essayist, novelist, and dramatist, Elsa Gress was also an inveterate traveler, translator, and sharp-tongued participant in public debate. Her greatest artistic achievement is likely her memoirs, published as *Mine mange hjem* (1965; My Many Homes), *Fuglefri og fremmed* (1971; Free as a Bird and a Stranger), and *Compania 1–2* (1976), in which she writes with exemplary openness about her life. Gress wrote three novels in the early part of her career, including her debut *Mellemspil* (1947; Interlude), which draws on her experiences as a resistance fighter in Denmark during World **War** II. Toward the end of her working life she published two more novels, *Salamander* (1977) and *Simurghen* (1986), in which art is portrayed as a painful vocation.

The essay was arguably Gress's best genre, and she published 15 volumes designated as such throughout her career, starting with *Strejftog* (1945; Raids) and *Nye strejftog* (1957; New Raids), in which she expresses her thorough knowledge and love of American culture. Other titles are *Fugle og frøer* (1969; Birds and Seeds), *Fanden til forskel* (1978; One Hell of a Difference), and *Blykuglen* (1984; The Lead Bullet). Some of these titles may give an idea of how strident Gress could be in her public discourse. Closely related to her essays is her book *Det uopdagede køn* (1964; The Undiscovered Sex), in which she argues in favor of androgyny.

Gress had a great love of drama, but she was not a successful playwright. *Den sårede Filoktet* (1970), which she had self-published in an English-language version the previous year as *Philoctetes Wounded* (1969), may be considered her breakthrough as a dramatist.

GRIEG, NORDAHL (1902–1943). A Norwegian poet, novelist, playwright, and journalist, Grieg first published a volume of poetry, *Rundt Kap det gode Haab* (1922; Around the Cape of Good Hope), which was followed by a novel, *Skibet gaar videre* (1924; tr. *The Ship Sails On*, 1927). Both were inspired by a period of work as a sailor in the merchant marine. Grieg's first drama, *Barrabas* (1927), dealt with the question of whether pacifism or armed resistance when attacked is more conducive to world peace. An extended stay in the Soviet Union put its mark on the play *Vår ære og vår makt* (1935; tr. *Our Honor and Our Glory*, 1971), which discusses **war** profiteering in the shipping industry. This drama is particularly interesting because of Grieg's use of techniques borrowed from film. The play *Nederlaget* (1937; The Defeat) has the Paris Commune of 1871 as its setting but strongly alludes to the Spanish Civil War.

GRIPE, MARIA (1923–). A Swedish writer of **children's books**, Gripe is not quite as well known as her colleague **Astrid Lindgren**, but she is widely read in Sweden and her work has been translated into many languages, including English. Her books emphasize children's fantasy life and characters that experience significant psychological development in the course of the story. This is the case in her series about Hugo and Josephine, *Josefin* (1961; tr. *Josephine*, 1969), *Hugo och Josefin* (1962; tr. *Hugo and Josephine*, 1971), and *Hugo* (1966; tr. 1971), as well as in *Elvis Karlsson* (1972; tr. *Elvis and His Secret*, 1976) and its sequels, one of which is *Elvis! Elvis!* (1973; tr. *Elvis and His Friends*, 1976). Gripe's novel *Glasblåsarens barn* (1964; tr. *The Glassblower's Children*, 1973) tells about children who are taken into a fantasy world; it also discusses the nature of parental love.

GRUNDTVIG, NIKOLAJ FREDERIK SEVERIN (1783–1872). A Danish poet and theologian, Grundtvig took a degree in theology but did so without an active Christian faith. The experience of falling in love, as well as his reading of some of the major writers of **romanticism**, cased him to catch a glimpse of the possibility of uniting matter and spirit. Influenced by both the ideas of universal romanticism and the tenets of its nationalist variety, Grundtvig came to see a parallel between the neoplatonist contrast between spirit and matter, and the Old Norse division between gods and giants. He first expressed these ideas in *Lidet om Sangene i Edda* (1806; Something about the Songs in the Edda). He went further along the same lines in *Nordens Mythologi* (1808; Norse Mythology), in which the end of the world that was foretold among the ancient Scandinavians was interpreted as a result of sin against a deity who was essentially a stand-in for the Christian god.

Having thus developed a coherent **national romantic** vision, all Grundtvig needed was a Christian awakening before he could see Nordic paganism as a fallen religion, but nevertheless one structurally similar to Christianity. His dramatic poem *Optrin af Kiempelivets Undergang i Nord* (1809; Scenes from the End of Heroic Life in the North) is marked by his preconversion vision, while *Optrin af Norners og Asers Kamp* (1811; Scenes from the Battle of the Norns and the Gods) shows that he had experienced a religious crisis that caused him to develop a strong personal Christian faith. He applied that faith to a reading of Danish history and concluded that Denmark was a strong nation in times of strong Christian faith, and weak in times of doubt and spiritual lukewarmness. This vision of history was expressed in *Roskilde-Riim* (1814; The Roskilde Rhymes), a versified history book.

In addition to having a strong personality, Grundvig also seems to have suffered from bipolar disorder. Guided by his personal faith, which allowed him to hold Danish history and Christian doctrine in a single vision, he vehemently attacked those theologians who did not share his views. As a result he was marginalized professionally, and his response is expressed in the mystery play *Paaske-Lilien* (1816–1817; The Easter Lily), in which he sees Christ's resurrection replicated both in his own spiritual awakening and in the religious movement that he was trying to get under way in Denmark.

The capstone of Grundtvig's religious system was his discovery that Martin Luther had not been completely right when insisting that the relationship between human beings and the deity is mediated primarily by the word of God as found in sacred scripture. In place of an emphasis on a written text, which is subject to all manner of interpretations, including those based on extreme rationalism, Grundtvig stressed what he called the living word, which comes to a person through such sacraments as baptism and communion and addresses itself to people's emotions. This idea was an effective tool in his fight against those tendencies among the Danish clergy that were not to Grundtvig's liking.

Two aspects of Grundtvig's activity as a spiritual leader bear mention. As a poet he was an immensely productive writer of hymns, many of which have become part of Danish church life. Grundtvig's hymns address themselves to the Christian fellowship more than to individual Christians. Also, his pedagogical ideas were groundbreaking. Instead of an educational system that emphasized rote learning and theory, Grundtvig wanted balanced human development. The Danish folk high school came to be the vehicle for this kind of education, and it remains a strong tradition in the Scandinavian countries up to the present time.

GUNNARSSON, GUNNAR (1889–1975). An Icelandic novelist, short story writer, playwright, and poet, Gunnarsson was born in Iceland but moved to Denmark at the age of 18. Before moving to Denmark, Gunnarsson published two slender volumes of poetry in Icelandic and one in Danish; the loss of his mother at the age of seven is an important theme in his poems. While living in Denmark, Gunnarsson, who married a Danish woman, was a very prolific and successful novelist who was especially well regarded in Germany. He returned to Iceland shortly before the German attack on Denmark on 9 April 1940, during World **War** II.

Gunnarsson's first significant literary success was a tetralogy entitled *Borgslægtens Historie* (1912–1914; tr. *Guest the One-Eyed*, 1920), which dealt with a long period of Icelandic history. The three novels *Livets strand* (1915; The Shore of Life), *Varg i Veum* (1917; A Wolf in the Temple), and *Salige er de enfoldige* (1920; tr. *Seven Days Darkness*, 1930) all demonstrate how fine a line there is between sanity and madness. *Edbrødre* (1918; tr. *The Sworn Brothers*, 1920) tells about the earliest settlement of Iceland.

Gunnarsson's greatest literary achievement is an autobiographical series of novels in five volumes, collectively known as *Kirken paa Bjerget* (1923–1928; tr. as *Ships in the Sky* and *The Night and the Dream*, 1938). His protagonist, Uggi, grows up in Gunnarsson's home district, then loses his mother, publishes two pamphlets of poetry, travels to Denmark, and finds success as a writer. After his success with this series, Gunnarsson wrote a number of historical novels set in Iceland. The most important one is *Svartfugl* (1929; tr. *The Black Cliffs*, 1967), which tells the story of a double murder and the court case that followed. Of Gunnarsson's many other novels, volumes of short stories, and plays, the most significant is the novel *Advent* (1937; tr. *The Good Shepherd*, 1940), in which the protagonist, a farmer named Benedikt, struggles to save his sheep that have gotten lost in the mountains during a snowstorm.

GUSTAFSSON, LARS (1936–). A Swedish poet, novelist, short story writer, and essayist, Gustafsson has a doctorate in philosophy from Uppsala University, and his works give evidence of a strong interest in existential and epistemological questions. He has also been well received in the English-speaking world and has been a faculty member at the University of Texas, Austin, since 1983. In his native Sweden, however, he has often been criticized for being too self-absorbed, arrogant, and excessively theoretical.

Although Gustafsson also wrote prose, in the early part of his literary career he was more important as a poet and published several volumes of poetry. Selections from some of these early collections appeared in English as *The Stillness of the World before Bach: New Selected Poems* (1988); this book also contains a portion of Gustafsson's long poem *Kärleksförklaring till en sefardisk dam* (1970; Declaration of Love to a Sephardic Lady), a watershed event in his oeuvre, in which he introduces the Jungian concept of the anima as his image of womanhood. Another successful volume of poetry was *Varma rum och kalla* (1972; tr. *Warm Rooms and Cold*, 1975).

Gustafsson's earliest prose works are rather unremarkable. In the 1960s he published three novels. One of these, *Bröderna: En allegorisk berättelse* (1960; The Brothers: An Allegorical Story), introduces the difficulties of childhood into his work. The short story collection *Förberedelser till flykt och andra berättelser* (1967; Preparations for

Flight and Other Stories) introduced motifs that were to become central to Gustafsson's next several novels.

Five prose works written during the 1970s—*Herr Gustafsson själv* (1971; Mr. Gustafsson Himself), *Yllet* (1973; Wool), *Familjefesten* (1975; The Family Celebration), *Sigismund: Ur en polsk barockfurstes minnen* (1976; tr. *Sigismund: From the Memories of a Baroque Polish Prince*, 1985), and *En biodlares död* (1978; tr. *The Death of a Beekeeper*, 1981)—all share a protagonist named after the author, Lars. A mixture of social criticism and philosophical themes, they were later published together as *Sprickorna i muren* (1984; The Cracks in the Wall). The joy of intellectual activity is strongly present in *Tennisspelarna* (1977; tr. *The Tennis Players*, 1983). Set in Austin, Texas, it reflects Gustafsson's stint there as a visiting professor. At this time he also published two collections of poetry, *Sonnetter* (1977; Sonnets) and *Artesiska brunnar cartsianska drömmar: Tjugotvå lärodikter* (1980; Artesian Wells, Cartesian Dreams: Twenty-two Didactic Poems).

Gustafsson's novels from the 1980s show the influence of **postmodernist** ideas about writing. The action in *Sorgemusik för frimurare* (1983; tr. *Funeral Music for Freemasons*, 1987) takes place on several continents, and it is unclear who is the novel's protagonist. *Bernard Foys tredje rockad* (1986; tr. *Bernard Foy's Third Castling*, 1988) offers three interrelated stories. The novel *En kakelsättares eftermiddag* (1991; tr. *A Tiler's Afternoon*, 1993) was intended as a thematic sequel to *En biodlares död* and focuses on an aging man's relationship to the past. *Historien med hunden: Ur en texansk konkursdomares dagböcker och brev* (1993; tr. *The Tale of a Dog: From the Diaries and Letters of a Texan Bankruptcy Judge*, 1998) is set in Austin, Texas, and features the killing of a dog as well as the murder of a Belgian-born professor who, as it turns out, had published some anti-Semitic articles in his native land during World War II. In a literary context it is difficult not to think about the Belgian-born deconstructionist Paul de Man, whose character was in the process of being assassinated by some at the time Gustafsson's novel was written.

More recently, Gustafsson has published the novels *Tjänarinnan: En kärleksroman* (1996; The Maid: A Love Story), *Windy berätter* (1999; Windy Narrates), *Blom och den andra magentan* (2001; Blom and the Second Magenta), a thriller that features the search for a rare postage stamp, and *Dekanen* (2003; The Dean), a combination of mystery story and philosophical novel. A recent collection of poetry is *En tid i Xanadu* (2002; A Time in Xanadu). Gustafsson has also written philosophical, cultural, and literary essays.

GUSTAV III (1746–1792). The king of Sweden from 1771 until his assasination during a masked ball in 1792, Gustav III had deep literary and cultural interests and forged strong cultural ties with France. Having had **Olof von Dalin** as his tutor, the king later collaborated with **Johan Henric Kellgren** on several librettos. King Gustav III was a patron of the great poet **Carl Michael Bellman** and is often credited with having created Swedish **theater**. *See also* ALMQVIST, CARL JONAS LOVE.

GYLLEMBOURG, THOMASINE (1773–1856). A Danish short story writer, Gyllembourg was the mother of **Johan Ludvig Heiberg**, who published the stories she started writing at the age of 54. She kept writing anonymously, most likely because she saw a conflict between her role as a woman and her activity as a writer. Her portrayal of **women** is done with great psychological insight, and the middle-class environment of her stories is realistically portrayed.

Gyllembourg's literary debut was *Familien Polonius* (1827; The Polonius Family), which was followed by *En Hverdags-Historie* (1828; An Everyday Story), in which the first-person narrator tells about his complicated love relationships. In *Slægtskab og Djævelskab* (1830; Kinship and Devilry) the female protagonist rebels against the wishes of her family and marries the man she wants. *Drøm og Virkelighed* (1833; Dream and Reality) has a significant component of social criticism as it describes how a man of the upper classes seduces a servant. Thematically, Gyllembourg's stories anticipate the debate about women's position in the family and in society that became common in Scandinavian literature in the 1870s. She is also very much alive to the question of how a woman should adjudicate between her role as a wife and mother and erotic desires that seek satisfaction outside the bonds of marriage. Gyllembourg's significance to Danish literature consists in her willingness to discuss such issues, however pseudonymously.

GYLLENSTEN, LARS (1921–). A Swedish novelist and essayist, Gyllensten has pursued two apparently different careers, one as a medical doctor and specialist in histology, and one as a writer. However, both endeavors are centered on a search for truth, which Gyllensten early realized is problematic scientifically and philosophically, as the observer cannot remove himself or herself from the observation situation. Hence, all formulations of truth are marked by the subjectivity of the observer, which entails that finding truth is a process with no end in sight. Gyllensten examines the full consequences of this realization in his literary oeuvre, as each of his works represents a stage on the process toward truth, while his oeuvre as a whole embodies the entire process as constituted by his activity as a writer. In the manner of the Danish philosopher and writer **Søren Kierkegaard**, Gyllensten experiments with various standpoints that one may take with regard to truth, and from Hegel he has learned that the structure of the process is likely to be dialectical. Gyllensten is thus one of the most philosophical or theoretical writers in Scandinavian literature.

The basic standpoint of the inquirer, for Gyllensten, is one of skepticism. A skeptical attitude toward already formulated truth is necessary if the process of truth-seeking is to continue. If this process is allowed to stop, the result may be such reified versions of "the truth" as that found in **Marxist**-Leninism or Nazism, or in various religions. Gyllensten is fundamentally skeptical about the ability of human beings to come to a knowledge of the world, but he is also committed to the proposition that we must never give up trying.

Gyllensten's first book of any significance was *Moderna myter* (1949; Modern Myths), an unmasking of various systems of belief. His next book, the novel *Det blå skeppet* (1950; The Blue Ship), has a protagonist who does the exact opposite by choosing to stake his all on the idea of the miraculous. These two standpoints represent a Hegelian thesis and its antithesis. *Barnabok* (1952; Child's Book) offers a portrait of the infantile and constitutes no synthesis of the standpoints in the two previous books, for the process of looking for something to rely on cannot ever be allowed to stop. Gyllensten's next book, *Carnivora* (1953), anatomizes Nazism's attitude toward life and thus offers an illustration of what may happen when people think they have found absolute truth. *Senilia* (1956) is offered as an antithesis to *Barnabok* and describes negative attitudes associated with old age.

Senatorn (1958; The Senator) is a graphic illustration of what working within a specific ideological system can do to a person, here illustrated by communism. In *Sokrates' död* (1960; The Death of Socrates), Socrates is willing to drink the fatal hemlock in order that he and his ideas may be remembered; the parallel with Christ's death on the cross is obvious. The antithesis to that kind of reliance on an ideology is represented by Socrates's wife, Xanthippe, who offers the commitment **women** make to bearing children, and the risks associated with that, as superior to any ideology. In *Desperados* (1962) Gyllensten applies that term to those who suffer from an excessive firmness of convictions; however, he playfully realizes that his own statement may be read as an instance of what he opposes, and thus be deemed incoherent.

Gyllensten elaborates on these ideas in a long series of novels. One of the most significant is *Kains memoarer* (1963; tr. *The Testament of Cain*, 1967), which contains the supposed record of a sect that worships the iconoclasts Cain and Satan. The antithesis to iconoclasm as an ideal is found in *Diarium spirituale* (1968), in which Gyllensten seeks to construct meaning rather than just tear it down. His main point is that human beings have the power to create their own reality. This general idea undergirds the narratives in *Palatset i parken* (1970; The Palace in the Park), *Grottan i öknen* (1973; The Cave in the Desert), *I skuggan av Don Juan* (1975; In Don Juan's Shadow), *Baklängsminnen* (1978; Backward Memories), and several other books.

In *Det himmelska gästabudet* (1991; The Heavenly Symposium) the search for meaning takes place in heaven, as each person present tells a story in order to find meaning in their earthly lives. *Anteckningar från en vindskupa* (1993; Notes from a Garret) features a protagonist named Johannes whose personal structures of meaning are profoundly negative. *Ljuset ur skuggornas värld* (1995; The Light from the World of Shadows) features another narrator named Johannes—the negativity of Kierkegaard's Johannes the Seducer comes to mind—and is another story of decay and destruction. *Kistbrev* (1998; Letters from a Chest) is a frame story that further explains the fictional origins of the two previous novels.

The idea that human beings are meaning-making animals certainly did not originate with Gyllensten. But there are surely few writers who have been as relentless in ferreting out the consequences of that idea, and of illustrating it in both works of fiction and in the volumes of essays that Gyllensten has also published.

– H –

HAAVARDSHOLM, ESPEN (1945–). A Norwegian novelist and short story writer, Espen Haavardsholm, like his better-known colleague **Dag Solstad**, started out with a focus on such **modernist** themes as alienation and absurdity. Many of the stories in his first book, *Tidevann* (1966; Tidewater), discuss anxiety as a force in human life. The novel *Munnene* (1968; The Mouths) portrays four young people whose social interaction limits their self-expression. *Den avskyelige snømannen* (1970; The Abominable Snowman) contains eight short stories about emotional alienation. A semi-documentary collection of seven texts, *Zink* (1971; Zinc) argues in favor of a **Marxist**-Leninist revolution in Norway. *Grip dagen* (1973; Seize the Day) centers on Norway's referendum concerning membership in the European Economic Community, held on 25 September 1972; it argues that Norwegian society is sacrificing its traditional values of liberty and equality in favor of economic growth at any price. *Historiens kraftlinjer* (1975; The Power Lines of History) offers Albania as an example of an ideal society. Like many other radical writers in Norway at the time, Haavardsholm began to depart from orthodox Marxism-Leninism in the 1980s. *Drift* (1980; Floating) tells the story of a teacher who becomes disenchanted with communism following a visit to East Berlin.

Svarte fugler over kornåkeren (1981; Black Birds over the Grain Field) contains four stories about love and its problems. The autobiographical novel *Store fri* (1983; Big Break) presents the existential problems of Haavardsholm's peers, the children of Norwegian radicals of the 1930s. *Roger, gult* (1986; Roger, Yellow) is yet another novel about teenage angst in Oslo in the 1960s. In the first-person novel *Huleskyggen* (1990; The Cave Shadow), a middle-aged painter tries to comprehend the consequences of his own childhood and youth for his daughter. The multilayered mystery novel *Ikke søkt av sol* (1994; Unseen by the Sun) is also centered on the main character's self-analysis.

The protagonist of the novel *Det innerste rommet* (1996; The Innermost Room) is a psychiatrist named Endre Sand, who, like many other Haavardsholm characters, looks for self-understanding in his childhood and youth, and especially in his relationship with his friends Uno and Katja, who later married each other. *Italienerinnen* (1998; The Italian Woman), one of Haavardsholm's most successful novels, combines the story of a contemporary love triangle with the narrative of a shipwreck in the Lofoten archipelago in 1431. The novel *Lilit* (2001; Lilith) is a continuation of *Det innerste rommet*; Katja brutally murders her husband Uno, and Endre tries to figure out why.

Haavardsholm returned to autobiographical narration in *Gutten på passbildet* (2004; The Boy in the Passport Photo), which combines a story set in 1959 with notes to an autobiography and family pictures. He has also written books for young adults as well as biographies of **Aksel Sandemose** and **Johan Borgen**.

HAGALÍN, GUÐMUNDUR GÍSLASON (1898–1985). An Icelandic novelist, short story writer, and biographer, Hagalín hailed from the isolated West Fjords, but he received an education and traveled abroad, including an extended stay in Norway. An extremely productive writer, his earlier books are of greater literary significance than his later works. His literary debut was a collection of prose and poetry entitled *Blindsker* (1921; Submerged Rock), the stories of which have the Icelandic coast as their setting. A second collection bears the title *Strandbúar* (1923; Coastal Dwellers), and one of the strengths of its stories is the naturalness of the language spoken by the characters. His first novel, set in the same locale, is *Vestan úr fjördum: Melakongurinn* (1924; From the West Fjords: The King of Melar), in which very strong-willed characters are pitted against one another, with particular attention to the conflict between young and old. It was followed by the novel *Brennumenn* (1927; Firebrands), in which the conflict is between socialists and a local capitalist in a fishing village.

The characters of *Kristrún í Hamravík* (1933; Kristrún of Hamravík) are also endowed with great strength; the title character, an old woman, is willing to fight against all kinds of obstacles in order to see her farm occupied by her family for generations yet to come. The novel *Sturla í Vogum* (1938; Sturla from Vogar) also sings the praises of simple rural living. *Blítt lætur veröldin* (1943; The Lure of the World) tells about a young boy who, under the influence of an older girl, learns to perceive the beauty and goodness of life. *Módir Ísland* (1945; Mother Iceland) deals with the corruption that was brought about by British and American influences during World **War** II.

After World War II, Hagalín's conservatism caused him to be out of touch with the emerging literary audience in Iceland. Between 1951 and 1979 he continued to publish novels, short stories, and essays, but his emphasis was on a multivolume autobiography and on writing biographies of living persons.

HALLGRÍMSSON, JÓNAS (1807–1845). An Icelandic poet and short story writer, Hallgrímsson studied law and natural science at the University of Copenhagen. While there he became familiar with the ideas of **national romanticism**, including the notion that one should look back to the glorious past of the nation as a source of inspiration for the present. In Hallgrímsson's day, Iceland had been under Danish colonial rule for many centuries and was marked by poverty and lack of development. In 1835 Hallgrímsson and three of his friends founded the annual *Fjölnir*, which published his poems and short stories, as well as articles about Iceland's geology and related fields. Hallgrímsson used both traditional Old Icelandic meter and modern poetic form in his poetry; he was the first person to write a sonnet in Icelandic. He also affected the development of the modern Icelandic written language. A linguistic purist, he advocated finding native terms that could be used instead of loan words, and he worked to rid Icelandic of Danicisms.

HAMSUN, KNUT (1859–1952). A Norwegian novelist, short story writer, poet, and playwright, Hamsun was born Knut Pedersen on a small farm in Norway's central valley, Gudbrandsdalen, but is one of the few Norwegian writers who belong to world literature. When he was a young boy his family moved to Hamarøy in northern Norway, where they lived on a farm called Hamsund that was owned by his maternal uncle. Knut had to work for this man, who mistreated him. After his confirmation he spent the next five years in a variety of jobs, among them that of an itinerant peddler. Among other goods, Knut sold cheaply made books, and at the age of 18 he made his first contribution to literature, a novella entitled *Den gaadefulde* (1877; An Enigmatic Man).

Den gaadefulde is not only a testament to Knut's literary ambitions but also points to many of the themes of his more mature works. A young man named Knud Sonnenfield suddenly appears in a rural community. Supposedly the son of a cotter, he falls in love with the daughter of the richest farmer around. According to the norms of the time, their relationship is a mismatch, but everything ends well because it turns out that Sonnenfield is not a cotter's son after all, but rather the son of a city merchant. The motif of the outsider who suddenly shows up and tries to win the most desirable local woman recurs in several of Hamsun's novels from the 1890s.

During the 1880s Hamsun, who got the name by which he is known from the farm where he had lived, minus its final "d" when it was accidentally dropped by a printer, struggled very hard to become a writer. These years included two stays in America, where he had hoped to become recognized as a man of letters. When he returned from his second stay in 1888, he published, in the Danish periodical *Ny Jord* (New Ground), a chapter of what was to become his breakthrough novel, a first-person and partly autobiographical narrative entitled **Sult** (1890; tr. *Hunger*, 1899). Set in Christiania, it tells about its narrator's mental self-experiments; he periodically starves himself so as to observe the effects of starvation on his mind. An aspiring writer, the narrator eventually gives up the experiment and goes to sea.

As an example of a truly psychological literature, *Sult* was hailed as a completely new kind of novel. Emboldened by his success, Hamsun next published *Mysterier* (1892; tr. *Mysteries*, 1927), in which the motif of the outsider who pursues a desirable local woman figures prominently. The protagonist of *Mysterier*, Johan Nilsen Nagel, is traveling aimlessly along the coast of southern Norway when he happens on a small town that he likes and decides to stay there for a while. His eccentric dress and behavior attract the attention of the townspeople, but he fails to successfully woo the daughter of the local minister, Dagny Kielland, and commits suicide in the end.

After two relatively unimportant books, *Redaktør Lynge* (1893; Editor Lynge) and *Ny jord* (1893; tr. *Shallow Soil*, 1914), Hamsun published one of his finest works, the novel *Pan* (1894; tr. 1920). Set in northern Norway, it is a lyrical tale about the power of love, but also about relationships of power. In 1855 Lieutenant Thomas Glahn has taken leave from his commission and has come to a place named Sirilund to commune with **nature**, and very possibly to try to become a writer. While at Sirilund he is sexually involved with two of the local women and has a more conventional, or chaste, love relationship with Edvarda Mack, the daughter of the local storekeeper. When Edvarda discovers that Glahn has become the lover of her father's mistress, her attaction to him is replaced by jealousy and hatred, and she and Glahn torment each other until Glahn finally leaves. An epilogue to the novel reveals that Glahn is unable to forget Edvarda and that he later goads a hunting companion into killing him in order to escape his memories.

Victoria (1898; tr. 1923) is Hamsun's final novel from the 1890s, and the last one that is specifically a love story. At this time he also published several unsuccessful dramas, two collections of short stories, a travelogue, and an unremarkable collection of poetry. After the turn of the century he wrote a short novel entitled *Sværmere* (1904; tr. *Dreamers*, 1921), which is entertaining but of limited literary value. In 1908 he published two novels set in the same locale and with overlapping characters, *Benoni* (tr. 1925) and *Rosa* (tr. 1926), which tell about a man of limited means who works his way up the social ladder and ends up with the woman he desires; Rosa is even a minister's daughter.

Hamsun also wrote a trilogy in which the protagonist is a writer named Knut Pedersen, who, like Glahn in *Pan*, has escaped from the city in order to find inspiration. *Under høststjærnen* (1906; Under the Autumn Star) and *En vandrer spiller med sordin* (1909; A Wanderer Plays on Muted Strings) have been published together in English as *Wanderers* (1922); the third volume is *Den siste glæde* (1912; tr. *Look Back on Happiness*, 1940). These novels are notable for the portrait they offer of an artist who is getting a bit on in years.

Around the time of World **War** I, Hamsun turned increasingly toward depicting what he considered the problems of modern society. *Børn av tiden* (1913; tr. *Children of the Age*, 1924) and *Segelfoss by* (1915; tr. *Segelfoss Town*, 1925) are set in a fictional town in northern Norway (perhaps modeled on Selfors near Mo i Rana) and portray the evils of industrialization and the deterioration of the old mercantile aristocracy. *Markens grøde* (1917; tr. *Growth of the Soil*, 1920) tells about a homesteader in the far north of the country. Isak Sellanrå carves a prosperous farm out of raw nature, but the ways of the city, together with a copper mine located on his property, threaten to undermine his work. The romantic portrait of hard physical labor given in this book may seem attractive to some readers, especially to those who do not know such labor by their own experience. Hamsun received the **Nobel Prize** for this novel in 1920.

Hamsun's critique of civilization was continued in *Konerne ved vandposten* (1920; tr. *The Women at the Pump*), in which he offers a portrait of small-town life at its worst. Hamsun also takes on the culture of the English, modern education, and labor organizing. His next novel, *Siste kapitel* (1923; tr. *Chapter the Last*, 1929), is very pessimistic; it takes place at a mountain sanatorium and has death as its main theme.

Feeling that his creativity had gone stale, Hamsun turned to pychoanalysis, and the result was one of his very finest novels. *Landstrykere* (1927; tr. *Vagabonds*, 1930) tells about Edevart Andersen and his friend August, a man of many ideas and projects. August's restlessness causes numerous problems for the two friends, but it also makes for an entertaining narrative that, while critical of modern society, is not nearly as pessimistic and bitingly satirical as Hamsun's previous books. The lyrical story of the love between Edevart and the beautiful Lovise Magrete Doppen is reminiscent of Hamsun's love stories from the 1890s. *Landstrykere* is the first volume of a trilogy and takes place partly in the fictitious community Polden, where the next volume, *August* (1930; tr. 1931), is also set and continues the story of August's many undertakings. In volume three, *Men livet lever* (1933; tr. *The Road Leads On*, 1934), however, the action moves to Segelfoss, the setting of *Børn av tiden* and *Segelfoss by*, and Hamsun brings back the central characters of those two novels in addition to continuing the story about August, who dies at the end of the book. *Men livet lever* can thus be regarded as a common concluding volume in two different trilogies.

Hamsun wrote only one more novel before the onset of World War II. *Ringen sluttet* (1936; tr. *The Ring Is Closed*, 1937), although unfinished, recapitulates many of his major themes and is thus a fitting summary to his work as a writer. But Hamsun lived on to make the biggest mistake of his life, as he supported the German occupants during the war, although he also used his influence to secure the release of some Norwegians who had been arrested by the Nazis. After the war the collaboration of the country's foremost living writer was a great embarrassment to the Norwegian authorities, and the question of how to deal with him was a matter of some delicacy. Hamsun was examined by two psychiatrists who declared that he suffered from permanently impared mental faculties, and this diagnosis was used as a pretext to exempt him from criminal prosecution. Instead he was given a fine equal to 85 percent of his net worth, but the fine was later reduced. The author's own account of this difficult episode is found in *Paa gjengrodde stier* (1949; tr. *On Overgrown Paths*, 1967), the artistic qualities of which show that the aged Hamsun was anything but mentally impaired. See also HANSEN, THORKILD.

HANSEN, ERIK FOSNES (1965–). A Norwegian novelist, Fosnes Hansen had his literary debut with *Falketårnet* (1985; The Falcon Tower), a historical novel set at the time of the crusades. The protagonist is the young son of a knight. Wolfgang, who understands the language of birds and is happy only when in the company of his four hunting falcons, is portrayed through his relationship to Suzanne, the daughter of an executioner, and to his power-hungry and evil uncle. The book is well written and has an exciting story line, and the **critics** marveled that it was produced by someone who was only 19 years old. Fosnes Hansen's next novel, *Salme ved reisens slutt* (1990; tr. *Psalm at Journey's End*, 1996), tells the life stories of seven musicians who are on board the *Titanic* at the time of its sinking. All of them have had difficulties coping with life, and their individual fates are portrayed with great sensitivity and an impressive breadth of perspective on Western culture at the time of its transition into modernity.

In *Beretninger om beskyttelse* (1998; tr. *Tales of Protection*, 2002),

Fosnes Hansen also uses the technique of linking several stories together and presenting them within a frame. Each of the book's four major sections contains several shorter narratives. Set at the end of the 20th century, the frame story presents the disembodied thoughts of the recently deceased industrialist and engineer Wilhelm Boldt, whose body is about to be cremated. Bolt is also the protagonist of the first story, which tells about his retirement years as a bitter old man. He likewise figures prominently in the fourth story, which is set in Asia during World War II, but which also contains a long segment of retrospective narration that gives the background for his bitterness by describing his boyhood and early manhood. Set in 1897, the second section takes place at a lighthouse on an island in the Baltic Sea. The third and longest section takes place in Renaissance Italy during the years shortly before 1500. Through these various stories, the book discusses the idea of serialization, the notion that apparently random events are connected in some manner. One of the finest Norwegian stylists of his generation, Fosnes Hansen has also written *Underveis: Et Portrett av Prinsesse Märtha Louise* (2003; En Route: A Portrait of Princess Märtha Louise).

HANSEN, MARTIN A. (1909–1955). A Danish novelist, short story writer, and essayist, Hansen had rural roots and later became a teacher. He was keenly aware of the crisis in the Danish farming communities in the 1930s and published two novels which proffered **Marxism** as a solution to contemporary economic problems. Hansen's first significant novel, *Jonatans Rejse* (1941; Jonathan's Journey), uses the legendary motif of the blacksmith who has confined the devil to a bottle as part of a commentary on the existential and moral situation of modern human beings. Hansen believes that the old farm society has lessons of responsibility and ethics to teach to modern men and women.

The novel *Lykkelige Kristoffer* (1945; tr. *Lucky Kristoffer*, 1974) tells about two men, Kristoffer and Martin, who travel to Copenhagen at the time of the Reformation, which is also a time of bloody conflict. Owing to his cleverness, Martin survives and profits from their circumstances, while Kristoffer dies. But Kristoffer has acted ethically and is truly the luckier of the two, while Martin is devoid of both integrity and true humanity. There is a parallel between Kristoffer and the Danish resistance fighters who died during World War II, whom Hansen admired for their courage and sacrifice.

Ethical and existential themes also dominate the short stories in the volumes *Agerhønen* (1947; The Partridge) and *Tornebusken* (1946; The Briar Bush). Such concerns take center stage in the novel *Løgneren* (1950; tr. *The Liar*, 1954), which was serialized on Danish State Radio. Its narrator-protagonist, Johannes Vig, is extremely conscious of his ethical weaknesses, but he is still dishonest in his narrative, which is addressed to an imaginary reader named Nathaniel. The biblical character Nathaniel, for whom Hansen's addressee is named, was a man utterly without deceit, while Johannes Vig has deceit built into his name, as *svig* means "deceit" in Danish. *Løgneren* is thus ultimately a story about fidelity and honesty as contrasted with dishonesty and betrayal. It highlights the existential choice of the literary artist, who must choose between fidelity to lived truth and dishonestly using life as material for art.

Hansen turned away from fiction in *Orm og Tyr* (1952; Serpent and Bull), which discusses the coming of Christianity to Scandinavia. Hansen believes that Christian ideas enriched Scandinavian life, but he also holds that many of the ethical norms ascribed to Christianity were already present in the indigenous culture. For most of the rest of his active life as a writer, Hansen wrote mainly travel books.

HANSEN, MAURITS CHRISTOPHER (1794–1842). A Norwegian novelist and short story writer, Maurits Hansen is one of Norway's earliest prose writers in modern times, and an extremely prolific one. Often forced to write under pressure in order to supplement his income as a teacher, however, he produced few works of lasting value, even though he was much admired in his day. Influenced by German *Rauberromantik*, some of his stories are reminiscent of the gothic novel, with highly complicated plots and incredible story lines. His first novel, *Othar af Bretagne* (1819; Othar of Brittany), is about a knight's battles against evil powers. His best longer work is the novel *Keadan eller Klosterruinen* (1825; Keadan, or, the Monestary Ruin), which, while reasonably well constructed, relies on letters and various documents and has a narrator who frequently addresses explanatory comments to the reader.

Hansen's short stories are of greater interest. "Luren" (1819; The

Shepherd's Horn) inaugurated the peasant tale, later popularized by **Bjørnstjerne Bjørnson**, into Norwegian literature. "Luren" tells the story of a young couple, Ragnhild and Guttorm, who are prevented from marrying by Ragnhild's proud father, the farmer Tord. They have a baby out of wedlock, and are finally reconciled with Tord through the good offices of the story's narrator, Carl Møhlmann, whose powers of persuasion are no match for the farmer. But persuasion also operates on many other levels of the text, including the relationship between Guttorm and Ragnhild, which subverts the story's happy ending. "Novellen" (1827; The Short Story) is of interest because of what it reveals about Hansen's theory of literary meaning; interesting narratives are the result of the imaginative reworking of striking memories.

HANSEN, THORKILD (1927–1989). A Danish novelist, travel writer, essayist, and journalist, Hansen produced early work that was a harbinger of the documentary movement in Scandinavian literature in the 1960s and later. After publishing a book of literary scholarship at the age of 20, Hansen spent five years in Paris, where he studied French literature and philosophy while serving as a correspondent for a Danish newspaper. Returning to Denmark in 1952, he earned a living as a journalist. He also traveled widely in Europe, Africa, and the Middle East.

Hansen published several volumes about his travels, later including edited versions of his diaries from his youth and years as a newspaper journalist. His literary breakthrough came with the historical and documentary novel *Det lykkelige Arabien: En dansk ekspedtion 1761-67* (1962; tr. *Arabia Felix: The Danish Expedition of 1761–1767*, 1964). This novel is both a faithful historical account of an expedition to Yemen that was doomed from the start—five of its six members perished, with only the German Carsten Niebuhr making it back to Denmark—and a statement on the human condition that emphasizes randomness and meaninglessness. While thus influenced by French existentialist thought, Hansen goes a step further and claims that failure and anonymity are necessary preconditions to true understanding and remembrance. Niebuhr is a paradigm case, as he returns from Yemen stripped of whatever arrogance and social ambition might otherwise have clouded his vision throughout his life.

With a knack for identifying forgotten episodes in the history of Danish national ambition, Hansen next studied the case of the Arctic explorer Jens Munk. The result was the novel *Jens Munk* (1965; tr. and abridged as *North West to Hudson Bay: The Life and Times of Jens Munk*, 1970). Hansen's character Jens Munk is another case of a man humbled by circumstances. Although he returned from the expedition as only one of three survivors, there were no rewards for him and he died in obscurity.

Hansen's greatest literary achievement is a trilogy that deals with the Danish slave trade. Set in the 1700s, it describes a common triangular trade route at the time. Ships sailed from Europe to West Africa loaded with weaponry and other goods, then continued to the Americas with a cargo of slaves, and then returned to Europe with a load of sugar. Denmark had a colony in the Caribbean, three islands that comprised the Danish West Indies (since 1917 the U.S. Virgin Islands), where African slaves worked the sugar plantations. The trilogy's first volume, *Slavernes kyst* (1967; The Coast of the Slaves), describes the capture and treatment of the slaves in Africa. *Slavernes skibe* (1968; The Ships of the Slaves) describes, with illustrations, the horrendous conditions the slaves had to endure while being transported across the Atlantic. *Slavernes øer* (1970; The Islands of the Slaves) details their lives on the islands of St. Thomas, St. John, and St. Croix. Hansen's work shined a bit of daylight on some embarrassing facts from the past, including Denmark's reluctance to outlaw slavery, and the Enlightenment writer **Ludvig Holberg**'s financial involvement with a company that participated in the slave trade. Hansen was rewarded for his literary achievement with the **Nordic Literary Prize** in 1971.

After almost a decade as a public figure and highly respected writer, Hansen published his final novel, *Processen mod Hamsun* (1978; The Case against Hamsun), in which he described the postwar trial of the great Norwegian novelist **Knut Hamsun**, who had expressed strong Nazi sympathies during World **War** II. Hansen questioned whether Hamsun had been treated according to principles of justice, and a heated debate ensued, especially in Norway. Some of Hansen's critics believed that he had gone too easy on Norway's Nazi sympathizers, and Hansen's reputation suffered when historical inaccuracies were found in his book. Hansen also published an autobiographical volume entitled *Søforhør: Nærbillede af Thorkild Hansen* (1982; Maritime Inquest: Close-up of Thorkild Hansen), which, in the form of an extended interview and illustrated with photographs from the author's life, looked like an autobiographical apology.

HAUGE, ALFRED (1915–1986). A Norwegian novelist and poet, Hauge is one of very few significant Norwegian writers who have been able to combine a personal commitment to Christianity with significant literary achievement. With his origins in a pietistic community in southwestern Norway, he studied theology for a while, but later became a teacher and finally a cultural journalist in the daily *Stavanger Aftenblad* (Stavanger Evening Paper).

Hauge wrote his first novel, *Septemberfrost* (1941; September Frost), about Norway's difficult years of national isolation prior to 1814. Published during the German occupation of Norway during World War II, its patriotic theme was intended to strengthen Norwegian national resistance. *Ropet* (1946; The Call) describes his own situation as a writer who is torn between his artistic commitment and the frequent condemnation of fiction that is found in his fundamentalist environment. After experiencing a significant religious development that led him to abandon some of the more conservative notions of his childhood faith, Hauge published two related novels that together gave him his artistic breakthrough. *Året har ingen vår* (1948; The Year Has No Spring) and *Fossen og bålet* (1949; The Waterfall and the Bonfire) are set in Hauge's home district and detail a family's search for salvation. Two other novels have regret as their theme. The protagonist in *Ingen kjenner dagen* (1955; Nobody Knows the Day), a minister, has sacrificed his talent as an artist for his religion, while the middle-aged man in *Kvinner på Galgebakken* (1958; Women on Gallows Hill) belatedly realizes that he has sacrificed the legitimate needs of others for his own vain ambition.

The story of the Norwegian emigration to America had long fascinated Hauge, especially because an early organizer of this movement named Cleng Peerson hailed from Hauge's home district. Hauge combined the story of Cleng's life and the history of the emigration into a trilogy, named for its protagonist, that is narrated by Cleng as an old man living in Bosque County, Texas. The first volume, *Hundevakt* (1961; Midwatch), tells about the social and economic background of the movement. The second volume, *Landkjenning* (1964; Landfall), tells the story of the journey of the vanguard, on board the sloop *Restaurationen* (The Restoration), from Stavanger to New York in 1825. The final volume, *Ankerfeste* (1965; Anchorage), tells about the westward movement of the Norwgian settlers, from upstate New York to the Fox River valley in Illinois, and for some of them, to Texas. Hauge emphasizes the spiritual conditions among the emigrants, showing that life in America was both economically and religiously unsettling. The trilogy is a representative example of the historical novel and the novel of emigration, which in Scandinavian literature has been practiced by such masters as **Vilhelm Moberg** and to a lesser extent by Johan Bojer. An English translation was published in two volumes as *Cleng Peerson*, on the occasion of the 150th anniversary celebration of Norwegian emigration to America in 1975.

Hauge's most complex work is his Utstein Monastery Cycle, which consists of five novels and two volumes of poetry. The poetry volumes are *Det evige sekund* (1970; The Eternal Second) and *I Rindbrads land* (1983; In Rindbrad's Country). The first novel in the cycle is a highly experimental work entitled *Mysterium* (1967; Mystery), in which Hauge attempts to analyze the qualities of tenderness and empathy. A Jungian *Bildungsroman* that illustrates the ideals of Christian ethics, it is a book about suffering and about our obligation as human beings to assist others when they have to cope with the adversities of life. It was followed by *Legenden om Svein og Maria* (1968; The Legend of Svein and Maria), a reworking of Hauge's earlier book *Vegen til det døde paradiset* (1951; The Way to the Dead Paradise), which, like its model John Bunyan's *Pilgrim's Progress*, is an allegorical representation of the struggle of good against evil. The second half of the cycle has the common title *Århundre* (Century), and consists of the novels *Perlemorstrand* (1974; Mother-of-Pearl Shore), *Leviathan* (1979), and *Serafen* (1984; The Seraph). Set in Hauge's home district of southwestern Norway, the trilogy examines the spiritual and environmental crises of the 20th century. Hauge finds that the ultimate cause of the misery of the century is those all too human emotions, greed and fear, which Christianity has largely unsuccessfully attempted to bridle. Hauge has also written three volumes of autobiographical narrative.

HEIBERG, GUNNAR (1857–1929). A Norwegian dramatist, **critic**, and essayist, Heiberg was overshadowed by the achievement of **Henrik Ibsen**. His first play, *Tante Ulrikke* (1884; Aunt Ulrikke), offers a dramatic representation of the struggle of one of Norway's leading early **feminists**, Aasta Hansteen (1824–1908). *Kong Midas* (1890; King Midas) accused **Bjørnstjerne Bjørnson** of being self-righteous, while *Kunstnere* (1893; Artists) and *Gerts have* (1894; Gert's Garden) have a lighter mood. *Balkonen* (1894; tr. *The Balcony*, 1922) and *Kjærlighedens tragedie* (1904; tr. *The Tragedy of Love*, 1921) explore the tension between erotic love and everyday reality. *Jeg vil værge mit land* (1912; I Shall Defend My Country) is set in 1905 and deals with the dissolution of the union between Norway and Sweden. Heiberg's essays abundantly attest to familiarity with contemporary culture and his keen sense of stagecraft. Two important volumes are *Ibsen og Bjørnson på scenen* (1918; Ibsen and Bjørnson on the Stage) and *Norsk teater* (1920; Norwegian Theater). *See also* THEATER.

HEIBERG, JOHAN LUDVIG (1791–1860). A Danish poet and dramatist, Heiberg was an influential arbiter of taste and the most important Danish man of letters of his generation. As a young man he lived in Paris for several years, where he became acquainted with the plays of Eugène Scribe (1791–1861) and was intrigued by his vaudevilles. He also met Georg Wilhelm Friedrich Hegel (1770–1831) and was much taken with his dialectical thinking. Back in Denmark, Heiberg introduced Hegelianism to his countrymen and based his own theory of literature on it. He saw drama as a synthesis of lyric poetry and the epic, and he regarded the vaudeville as a synthesis of poetry and music. He explained his ideas in *Om Vaudevillen* (1826; On Vaudeville) and in numerous essays.

Heiberg wrote several vaudevilles, the first being *Kong Salomon og Jørgen Hattemager* (1825; King Salomon and George Hatter), which combines a story of mistaken identity with a convoluted love story. *Recensenten og Dyret* (1826; The Critic and the Animal) satirizes **critics** who write just for money without any real knowledge of their subject. He also wrote more traditional dramas, for example, the romantic folklore plays *Elverhøi* (1828; The Elves' Hill) and *Alferne* (1835; The Elves). The elves are portrayed as superior to the skeptics and materialists of Heiberg's own time. The lovers in *Syvsoverdag* (1840; Late Sleepers Day) find their happiness in poetry, the antithesis of middle-class strivings.

One of the leading intellectual lights in Heiberg's Copenhagen was the theologian Hans L. Martensen (1808–1884), under whose influence Heiberg gradually turned toward Christianity. Martensen's influence is visible in Heiberg's *Nye Digte* (1841; New Poems), which consists of several parts and includes the comedy *En Sjæl efter Døden* (tr. *A Soul after Death*, 1991). Its protagonist is a lower-middle-class man who, after his death, is able to get into neither heaven nor the classical Elysium; he feels perfectly comfortable in hell, however. Another section of *Nye Digte*, "Gudstjeneste" (Sunday Service) extols Christian love over romantic nature worship.

After a long career as a freelance intellectual, toward the end of his life Heiberg spent several years as the director of Copenhagen's Royal Theater, where his wife Johanne Luise was the leading actress. *See also* THEATER.

HEIDENSTAM, VERNER VON (1859–1940). A Swedish poet and novelist, Heidenstam was one of the most important figures in the literary life of his country during the fin-de-siècle and a leader in the **neoromantic** reaction against the aesthetics of **naturalism**. An aristocrat by birth, Heidenstam traveled widely during his youth and visited most of the countries of the eastern Mediterranean. After pursuing art in Rome he went to Paris, where he became acquainted with the beginnings of the decadent movement. His first collection of poetry, *Vallfart och vandringsår* (1888; Pilgrimage and Years of Wandering), is characterized by a focus on the individual, aestheticism, a love of the exotic, and Heidenstam's admiration for the cultures of the classical past. His next volume of poetry, *Dikter* (1895; Poems), contains poems in a similar vein.

Heidenstam laid out his literary program in the essay *Renässans* (1889; Renaissance), in which he argued that the scientific worldview of the naturalists was outdated, and he added a strong current of nationalism. The novel *Endymion* (1889) pits Western barbarism, a stand-in for naturalism, against Eastern culture and beauty, which may be read as signifying the new kind of writing that Heidenstam had in mind.

In both poetry and prose, the novel *Hans Alienus* (1892) tells about a young Swede who revels in the life and culture of the Catholic Church, visits the past through a sojourn in Hades, and finally returns to Sweden. Heidenstam's next novel marks a nationalistic turn in his oeuvre. The novel *Karolinerna* (1897–1898; tr. *The Charles Men*, 1920) is the story of the ill-fated attempt of King Karl XII to bring the Baltics back under Swedish rule. The king is cast as a classical hero, with the Russians playing the role of the barbarians. *Heliga Birgittas pilgrimsfärd* (1901; St. Birgitta's Pilgrimage) unites Heidenstam's nationalism with his aesthetic admiration of Catholicism. *Folkungaträdet* (1905–1907; tr. *The Tree of the Folkungs*, 1925) gives an idealized account of the rise of Sweden.

Heidenstam's nationalism gradually turned to conservatism, as demonstrated by two volumes of poetry, *Ett folk* (1902; One People) and *Nya dikter* (1915; New Poems). He received the **Nobel Prize** in 1916.

HEIMSTADDIKTNING. A Scandinavian form of the German *Heimatdichtung*, *heimstaddiktning* refers both to literature that has a writer's rural home district as its setting and that celebrates or memorializes this setting. The heyday of this type of writing in Scandinavia was the period 1900–1940, and the Jutland novels of **Jeppe Aakjær** are its outstanding example.

HEINESEN, WILLIAM (1900–1991). A Faroese and Danish novelist, short story writer, and poet who wrote in Danish, Heinesen is known mostly for his novels. Educated in Copenhagen, Heinesen started out writing novels that emphasized groups of people rather than single individuals and were thus similar to the Danish collective novel at the time. Heinesen's examples of the genre are *Blæsende Gry* (1934; Windswept Dawn) and *Noatun* (1938; tr. *Niels Peter*, 1939), which offer a humorous and satirical treatment of popular religious movements and other changes in Faroese society, thereby transcending the common social **realism** of the period. The action in *Den sorte Gryde* (1949; tr. *The Black Cauldron*, 1992) takes place during the British occupation of the Faroes in World **War** II and takes war profiteering as its theme. *De fortabte spillemænd* (1950; tr. *The Lost Musicians*, 1972) deals with the move to abolish the use of alcoholic beverages in the Faroes, but Heinesen's main purpose is to offer an almost mythical representation of the conflict between good and evil, death and life.

In *Moder Syvstjerne* (1952; tr. *The Kingdom of the Earth*, 1973) Heinesen presents a paean to womanhood, which he identifies with the forces of life. Myth-making is similarly present in *Tårnet ved verdens ende* (1976; tr. *The Tower at the Edge of the World*, 1981). The conflict between life and death is also found in the epistolary novel *Det gode Håb* (1964; The Good Hope), which is a fictionalization of the life of a Danish minister who worked in the Faroe Islands during the 1600s. This novel won him the **Nordic Literary Prize** in 1965.

Heinesen has also written several collections of short stories with themes similar to those of his novels, starting with *Det fortryllede lys* (1957; Enchanted Light). The title story in *Don Juan fra Tranhuset* (1970; Don Juan from the Whale Oil Factory) is set in Tórshavn, the capital of the Faroes, in the 1890s and tells about the arrival of a Maltese man who arouses much interest among the locals. Myth-making is central to *Laterna Magica* (1985; tr. 1987). The title of *Her skal danses* (1980; The Dance Shall Go On) alludes to the Faroese ring dance, a central form of cultural expression. Other short story collections are *Gamaliels besættelse* (1960; Gamaliel's Possession), *Kur mod onde ånder* (1967; A Cure for Evil Spirits), *Fortællinger fra Thorshavn* (1973; Stories from Tórshavn), and *Grylen og andre noveller* (1975; Grylen and Other Stories).

As a poet Heinesen was at first derivative of the style of the Danish poetry of the 1890s, as exemplified by the poems in *Arktiske Elegier* (1921; Arctic Elegies). *Høbjergning ved Havet* (1924; Hay-Cutting by the Sea) emphasizes the cycle of life and the place of human life in the natural world. Other volumes of poetry are *Sange mod Vaardybet* (1927; Songs toward the Depth of Spring), *Stjernerne vaagner* (1930; The Stars Awaken), *Den dunkle Sol* (1936; The Dark Sun), *Panorama med regnbue* (1972; Panorama with Rainbow), and *Digte* (1990; Poems).

HENNINGSEN, AGNES (1868–1962). A Danish novelist and dramatist, Henningsen advocated both equality between men and **women** and the right for women to fully express themselves erotically. Her literary debut was the novel *Glansbilleder* (1899; Glossy Pictures), which together with her next novel, *Strømmen* (1899; The Current), argues that women need paid work. *Polens Døtre* (1901; The Daughters of Poland), which Henningsen wrote after a visit to Poland, was well received. It portrays two women who both love the same man, but their adherence to convention drives them to unhappiness and frigidity. Several other novels argued that male-dominated society naturally leads to frigidity and fear of sexuality in women. Frigidity was pretty much a taboo at the time, so Denmark's middle class did not appreciate Henningsen's works. This was especially true when she published the novels *Den elskede Eva* (1911; Beloved Eva) and *Den store Kærlighed* (1917; The Great Love), which cost Henningsen a governmental stipend.

A trilogy consisting of *Kærlighedens Aarstider* (1927; Love's Seasons), *Det rige Efteraar* (1928; The Rich Autumn), and *Den sidste Aften* (1930; The Last Evening) offers a more optimistic view of the possibilities of women's happiness in love. Henningsen is still aware of the problems that society throws in the way of women who seek self-realization, however.

Two of Henningsen's plays were published, *Den Uovervindelige* (1904; The Indomitable One) and *Elskerinden* (1906; The Mistress). The latter offers a frank portrait of the life of a mistress, for whom the man in her life means everything but who is regarded mostly as a plaything by him. Henningsen's most enduring literary work is her eight volumes of memoirs (1941–1955), which, in addition to offering her recollections of her life, also provide a survey of Danish social history, including that of women, during the author's lifetime.

HJARTARSON, SNORRI (1906–1986). An Icelandic poet and novelist, Hjartarson showed an early interest in writing poetry but did not pursue this interest and went to Norway to study art instead. His literary debut was as a novelist in Norway with *Høit flyver ravnen* (1934; The Raven Flies High), in which an Icelandic artist living in Norway is torn between a Norwegian and an Icelandic woman.

Hjartarson's debut as a poet came with the volume *Kvæði* (1944; Poems), which was followed by *Á Gnitaheiði* (1952; On Gnita Heath). Both volumes lay stress on coloration, which one might expect from a painter turned poet, and there is a strong emphasis on the portrayal of **nature**, a concern also visible in *Høit flyver ravnen*. His poetry endows nature with transcendence, as nature, beauty, and goodness work together to protect human beings from the forces of exploitation and greed. The poems in *Lauf og stjörnur* (1966; Leaves and Stars) and *Hauströkkrið yfir mér* (1979; The Autumn Mist above Me) have a simplicity of language that borders on minimalism, but there is also more optimism than in Hjartarson's earlier works. He received the **Nordic Literary Prize** in 1981.

HØEG, PETER (1957–). A novelist and short story writer, Høeg is Denmark's internationally best-known contemporary writer. His books have been translated into numerous languages, and all of them have appeared in English. Høeg wrote his first novel, *Forestilling om det tyvende århundrede* (1988; tr. *The History of Danish Dreams*, 1995), during a six-year, self-directed apprenticeship as a writer. With features of narrative technique that transcend traditional **realism**, it shows influence from both magic realism and other elements of **postmodernism**. Present are also such serious motifs as a general critique of Danish society and criticism of the brutality with which children have often been raised. Høeg also meditates on what time is, how it can be understood, and how some people use the concept of time, not just time itself, for self-serving ends. *Fortællinger om natten* (1990; tr. *Tales of the Night*, 1997), Høeg's second book, is a volume of short stories about the conditions of love at a specific point, during the night of 19 March 1929. Høeg writes not only about romantic love, but also about the love of children, knowledge, and art.

Høeg's greatest international success came with the novel *Frøken Smillas fornemmelse for sne* (1992; tr. *Smilla's Sense of Snow*, 1993), which contains elements of the thriller or crime story. The first-person narrator, Smilla, a Danish woman of Inuit descent, doubts the conclusion of the police that the death of a young boy named Isaiah was an accident. Smilla is an erudite amateur detective who pursues the case until she discovers that a corporate conspiracy with far-reaching tentacles is connected with Isaiah's death, and that there is a plan to profit from the discovery of a potentially very dangerous meteorite found on Greenland. Some of the people involved in the conspiracy are well-known scientists who want to use the discovery to further their careers. This scheme is then presented by the author as a metaphor for both how Danish colonialism has exploited the Greenlanders and for the way children have been mistreated. The narrator-protagonist in *De måske egnede* (1993; tr. *Borderliners*, 1994) is a man named Peter who, as a child, had been passed from boarding school to boarding school. His experience is presented as paradigmatic of the lives of some of the weakest members of society, orphans, who are being subjected to attempts at forced socialization and threatened with a future as social outcasts if they do not conform.

The novel *Kvinden og aben* (1996; tr. *The Woman and the Ape*, 1996) extends a critique of the scientific mind-set that is also found in *Frøken Smillas fornemmelse for sne*. The protagonist in *Kvinden og aben* is a Danish-born woman, Madelene, who is married to Adam, a deranged biologist whose ambition is to become the director of the London Zoo. Madelene discovers that Adam is hoping to reach that goal by experimenting on a unique and very intelligent ape named Erasmus, whom he is holding captive in a building behind their home. Madelene frees Erasmus, after which the woman and the ape become lovers and Madelene becomes Erasmus's tutor, helping him learn English and Danish. *Kvinden og aben* argues in favor of respect for others, including animals, shows the need to have reverence for **nature**, and severely criticizes human selfishness and greed.

HOEL, SIGURD (1890–1960). A Norwegian novelist, Hoel is also considered one of Norway's major novelists of the 20th century. The heir of both **neoromanticism** and **realism** in Norwegian literature, Hoel decisively altered his country's literary landscape by making **Freudianism** a staple in Norwegian fiction, particularly in his portrayal of relationships between men and **women**. Hoel was also a cultural journalist, **critic**, and editor at Norway's foremost publishing house, Gyldendal. His impact on Norway's cultural life was second to none.

Hoel's literary debut took place in 1922, when he published a collection of short stories, *Veien vi går* (The Road We Walk), which shows that he had already been influenced by Freud. *Syvstjernen* (1924; The Seven-Pointed Star) is a rather tedious allegory. Hoel's definitive breakthrough came with the novel *Syndere i sommersol* (1927; tr. *Sinners in Summertime*, 1930), which satirizes the way a group of middle-class graduate students conduct themselves while insisting that they, in contrast to their elders, are able to avoid self-deception. Male rivalry is a major theme, but so is men's fear of commitment. Many years later Hoel wrote a sequel in which the characters are 30 years older, *Jeg er blitt glad i en annen* (1951; I Am in Love with Someone Else), but it is not as charmingly entertaining as *Syndere i sommersol*.

Although born in the countryside, Oslo, Norway's capital, had long been Hoel's home. *Ingenting* (1929; Nothing) is the first of many Hoel novels that are set in Oslo. Like the first-person narrator in **Knut Hamsun**'s *Sult*, Hoel's protagonist wanders the streets but remains dissatisfied with his life. *En dag i oktober* (1931; tr. *A Day in October*, 1932) also deals with unsatisfied longing and men's inability to extend themselves emotionally. Considered an example of the collective novel, it is set in an apartment building and tells a detailed story of one particular dysfunctional couple, which is presented in the context of several unhappy marriages.

Freud's theories of childhood are on display in the autobiographical novel *Veien til verdens ende* (1933; The Road to the End of the World), in which Hoel draws on his childhood memories. These memories also inform the stories in *Prinsessen på glassberget* (1939; The Princess on the Glass Mountain). He also felt a need to understand himself better through psychoanalysis and became a patient of the psychiatrist Wilhelm Reich (1897–1957), who lived in Norway after fleeing his native Austria. Strongly influenced by this experience, Hoel published *Fjorten dager før frostnettene* (1935; A Fortnight before the Frost Nights), which presents the midlife crisis of a physician, the emotionally barren Knut Holmen. Echoing the process of analysis, Holmen goes on a search for a woman whose love he had betrayed while in his early 20s.

Hoel's gift for satire is on display in *Sesam, sesam* (1938; Open Sesame), in which he caricatures many of Norway's leading cultural figures. *Ved foten av Babels tårn* (1956; At the Foot of the Tower of Babel) is an example of satire turning into bitterness.

During World **War** II Hoel was occupied with resistance work and had to flee to Sweden. After the war he probed the causes of Nazism in his novel *Møte ved milepelen* (1947; tr. *Meeting at the Milestone*, 1951), one of Norway's finest novels about the trauma of occupation and the tragedy of collaboration with the enemy. The first-person narrator, a former resistance fighter, discovers that his own betrayal of a woman he loved has contributed to some of the wartime problems, and that his conscience is not as clear as he used to think. The less successful novel *Stevnemøte med glemte år* (1954; Rendevous with Forgotten Years) deals with similar issues.

Before fleeing to Sweden during the war, Hoel had published the novel *Arvestålet* (1941; The Family Dagger), in which issues of love and marriage figure prominently. Set in the region of Telemark in the 1800s, its male protagonist, Håvard, indirectly causes the suicide of the woman who loves him, Tone, by becoming interested in the attractive widow Rønnaug. In the sequel *Trollringen* (1958; tr. *The Troll Circle*, 1991), Håvard has married Rønnaug and has moved to her farm in a different community, where his stepdaughter Kjersti falls in love with him. When Rønnaug dies in an accident, Håvard is accused of murdering her, is found guilty and executed, and Kjersti is hounded to suicide by the women in the community. Again, it is a man's inability to commit himself emotionally that causes the disaster.

HOEM, EDVARD (1949–). A Norwegian novelist, poet, and dramatist, Hoem is considered one of the foremost stylists in contemporary Norwegian literature. He started out as a poet but has since devoted most of his energy to the **theater** and the novel. A **Marxist**-Leninist in the 1970s, he had his literary debut with a collection of 31 poems and three short prose texts, *Som grøne musikantar* (1969; Like Green Musicians). It was followed by a book of 60 poems that together form a lyrical novel, *Landet av honning og aske* (1970; The Land of Honey and Ashes), and then by the book that gave him his literary breakthrough, the novel *Anna Lena* (1971). Inspired by socialist **realist** doctrines, it depicted the exploitation of low-paid workers in the Norwegian countryside; it is also notable for the author's violations of narrative conventions, which Hoem, following the German dramatist Bertold Brecht (1898–1956), hoped would cause readers to have an analytical attitude toward his story rather than reading it chiefly for entertainment.

Capitalism's push for centralization of the rural population is the related theme of *Kjærleikens ferjereiser* (1974; tr. *The Ferry Cross-*

ing, 1989) which, while critical of the policies of the Norwegian government, also exhibits **postmodern** traits. As in **Dag Solstad**'s *Arild Asnes, 1970*, published three years earlier, the book ends as the Marxist-Leninist paper *Klassekampen* (The Class Struggle) is being sold door to door.

The influence of Brecht is strongly visible in Hoem's dramatic works from the 1970s. *Kvinnene langs fjorden* (1973; The Women by the Fjord) depicts the plight of low-paid seamstresses. *Musikken gjennom Gleng* (1977; The Music through Gleng) and *Tusen fjordar, tusen fjell* (1977; A Thousand Fjords, a Thousand Mountains) argue in favor of keeping small rural communities alive. The historical play *Der storbåra bryt* (1979; Where the Big Wave Breaks), set at the end of the Napoleonic wars, uses satire while depicting people's reactions to the new ideas of liberty.

In 1978 Hoem began an intended trilogy with the title *Gi meg de brennende hjerter* (Give Me the Burning Hearts). The first volume, *Melding frå Petrograd* (1978; Report from Petrograd), adheres closely to ideas of socialist realism as expressed by the Hungarian literary critic György Lukács (1885–1971). The next volume, *Fjerne Berlin* (1980; Distant Berlin), sets the class struggle aside in favor of portraying private relationships. The third volume has not appeared, possibly because Hoem became disenchanted with Marxist-Leninism.

Hoem collected some of his poetry in the volume *Du er blitt glad i dette landet* (1982; You Have Become Fond of This Country), and the same year published his play *God natt, Europa* (1982; tr. *Good Night, Europe*, 1989), in which an old politician and **war** hero tries to come to terms with his past. He also wrote several significant novels. *Prøvetid* (1984; Rehearsal) depicts the midlife crisis of its protagonist, Johannes Bergmann. *Heimlandet barndom* (1985; The Homeland Childhood) is a sensitive fictionalized account of the author's youth. *Ave Eva: Herregårdsroman* (1987; tr. *Ave Eva: A Norwegian Tragedy*, 2000), while using John Milton's *Paradise Lost* (1667) as intertext, offers a satirical take on contemporary Norway as the protagonist struggles to save his family farm only to lose it to the oil industry.

The play *Sankt Olavs skrin* (1989; Saint Olav's Reliquary) explores another period of cultural transition, namely that from Catholicism to Lutheranism in Norway. A sequel to *Prøvetid*, the novel *I Tom Bergmanns tid* (1991; In Tom Bergmann's Time), has Johannes Bergmann's cousin Tom as its protagonist and critiques financial practices of the 1980s. A third Bergmann novel, *Tid for klage, tid for dans* (1996; A Time to Mourn, a Time to Dance), is set among artists and intellectuals in Oslo in the 1990s.

The novel *Engelen din, Robinson* (1993; Your Angel, Robinson) discusses what has become of the generation that came of age in the 1960s. Hoem also published an essay entitled *Mitt tapre språk* (1996; My Brave Language), in which he argued that **nynorsk**—Hoem's medium of expression—is not just a language for rural people. The novel *Frøken Dreyers musikkskole* (2000; Miss Dreyer's Music School) features the trials of a German violinist, while the drama *Audun Hestakorn* (2002) commemorates the 700th anniversary of the hanging of an advisor to King Magnus the Lawgiver. Hoem has also written other play scripts, essays, and religious texts.

HØJHOLT, PER (1928–2004). A Danish poet, novelist, and essayist, Højholt has had a great deal of influence on the poetry of his country but is largely unknown outside Denmark. After a couple of minor poetry collections, he had his breakthrough as a writer with *Poetens hoved* (1963; The Poet's Head). The volume *Min hånd 66* (1966; My Hand 66) contains poems that are very self-reflective and refer only indirectly to an extralinguistic reality. His theory of poetry is presented in the essays *Cézannes metode* (1967; Cézanne's Method) and *Intethedens grimasser* (1972; The Grimaces of Nothingness), and is further illustrated in *Turbo* (1968; Turbo), a volume of unusual poetic energy.

In addition to a series of more traditional volumes of poetry, Højholt published 12 volumes with the common title *Praksis* (1977–1996; Praxis), which contain both poems and prose texts, as well as what Højholt, employing a nonsensical neologism, has termed "kvababbelser." These are satirical poems dealing with current issues, and they have been very popular in radio broadcasts, as has a series of monologues in the Jutland dialect spoken by a woman character, Gitte. Højholt also wrote *Auricula* (2001), a fantastic novel about Europe during the 20th century, in which a large number of human ears are conceived and born and spread out over the continent.

HOLBERG, LUDVIG (1684–1754). A poet, playwright, novelist, and essayist, Holberg is considered Scandinavia's foremost Enlightenment figure. He was born into a family mostly of farmers and merchants, but his father had worked his way up from a private to a liuetenant colonel in the Dano-Norwegian army. Well educated at the Bergen Cathedral School and the University of Copenhagen, Holberg never lost touch with practical life during a lifetime as an academic and a writer. He consistently valued useful activity above learning for the sake of learning and the vernacular above Latin; his attitudes are largely those of a middle class that was about to eclipse the old aristocracy.

After years of study and travel and having laid the groundwork for a brilliant academic career, including books on European history as well as natural and international law, Holberg started writing satirical poetry shortly before 1720. A mock-heroic epic in four books, *Peder Paars*, was published in 1719–1720 and gave him quite a reputation as a creative writer. It describes the journey of one Peder Paars from the city of Kallundborg to Aars for the purpose of visiting his fianceé, but owing to the enmity of some pseudo-classical gods, he is driven off course and shipwrecked on an island named Anholt. The island of Anholt is a microcosm of Denmark, and Holberg portrays life there so as to exhibit a long catalogue of human foibles.

Holberg was soon given additional opportunities to hold human failings up to ridicule. In the fall of 1722 a Danish-language **theater** was established in Copenhagen, and the second play performed there was Holberg's comedy *Den Politiske Kandestøber* (tr. *The Political Tinker*, 1915), which satirized common people who want to get involved in political life. Other comedies have touches of the tragic. *Jeppe paa Bierget* (1722; tr. *Jeppe of the Hill*, 1915), for example, presents the miserable life of a drunken peasant. *Erasmus Montanus* (1731, tr. 1915), a satire on learning for its own sake, also shows how easily truth may be compromised.

Comedies by Plautus and Molière were among Holberg's readings and served as examples for him, but he is far more than simply an imitator. His characters, although mostly types, are anchored in a realistically portrayed social and economic environment, and Holberg has a gift for depicting the absurd. His output was truly phenomenal, for by the time the theater closed in 1727 because Denmark's new king, the pietistic Christian IV, was opposed to it, Holberg had written 26 comedies. Six more were written after the theater was reopened in 1748. Many of his comedies are still performed regularly in Scandinavia. By the time the theater closed, however, Holberg had largely exhausted his poetic inspiration and returned to scholarship. Many volumes of historical, topographical, and biographical studies ensued, but Holberg also wrote a long utopian novel in Latin, *Nicolai Klimii Iter Subterraneum* (1741; tr. *Journey to the World Underground*, 1742), as well as seven volumes of essays and three Latin autobiographies.

HULDÉN, LARS (1926–). A Finland-Swedish poet and short story writer, Huldén occupies a unique position in Finland-Swedish letters. As a philologist and professor at Helsinki University for 25 years, he made both academic and literary contributions, among them the many poems that he provided on festive academic occasions. Witty and cheerful, yet with an undercurrent of melancholia and pessimism, Huldén's work is both deceptively accessible and an embodiment of artistic seriousness.

Huldén had his literary debut with the poetry collection *Dräpa näcken* (1958; Killing the Nixie), which was followed by *Speletuss* (1961; Blithe Spirits) and *Spöfugl* (1964; Whipperwit); these volumes attest to the fun-loving play with language found in Huldén's rural background. *Enrönnen* (1966; The Lone Mountain Ash) and *Herr Varg!* (1969; Mr. Wolf!) are darker—the wolf in the latter collection eats the speaker of the poem about it—and more serious, too. Other collections bear the titles *Dikter i fosterländska ämnen* (1967; Poems on National Themes), *Herdedikter* (1973; Pastoral Poems), *Läsning för vandrare* (1974; Reading for Wanderers), and *Island i december* (1976; Iceland in December).

Hailing from Ostrobothnia, Huldén has felt a great kinship with **Johan Ludvig Runeberg**, and that relationship is expressed in *J. L. Runeberg och hans vänner* (1978; J. L. Runeberg and His Friends), the poems in which both comment on Runeberg's texts and imitate his style. This is also the case with some of the poems in *Dikter vid säskilda tillfällen* (1979; Poems on Special Occasions). The three collections *Jag blir gammal, kära du* (1981; Darling, I Am Growing

Old), *Mellan jul och ragnarök* (1984; Between Christmas and the End of the World), and *Judas iskariotsamfundets årsbok 1987* (1987; The Judas Iscariot Society Yearbook 1987) are statements from a man who knows he is approaching the end of his productive life. *Psalmer för trolösa kristna* (1991; Hymns for Christians without Faith) has appeal for believers and nonbelievers alike, while *När flaggorna flög* (1992; When Flags Were Flown) is a collection of occasional poems. Recent volumes are *Sånger, allvarsamma* (2000; Serious Songs) and *Sångbok från scen och kabaré* (2000; Songbook for Stage and Cabaret). The poetry collections *Vegas färd* (1997; Vega's Journey) and its continuation *Återkommen från Atlanta* (2005; Back from Atlanta) deal with what it is like to be growing old.

Huldén has also written a number of scripts for radio and stage, including a play about **Edith Södergran**, *Resen till Raivola* (1992; The Journey to Raivola). *Hus* (1979; Houses) is a collection of short stories. *Berättelser ur mitt förflutna liv* (1990; Stories from My Past Life) and *Berättelser om mig själv och andra* (1992; Stories about Myself and Others) contain made-up as well as possibly factual narratives.

HUNGER. See SULT.

– I –

IBSEN, HENRIK JOHAN (1828–1906). A Norwegian playwright and poet, Ibsen is recognized as one of the world's greatest dramatists but was also, especially during his lifetime and in his native Norway, considered a notable poet. Born into a middle-class family in the town of Skien in the county of Telemark, he lost the social and economic advantages of that birth through his father's bankruptcy while Henrik was yet a small boy. Education beyond elementary school was out of the question, and at the age of 16 he had to leave home to earn a living as a druggist's apprentice in the nearby town of Grimstad.

While in Grimstad, Ibsen fathered an illegitimate child by one of his employer's maids, a woman 10 years his senior, which brought him both social and pecuniary embarrassment. Perhaps through his work for the druggist, he also hit on the idea of pursuing a career in medicine. This necessitated passing his university matriculation examinations, for which he prepared by self-study. He also wrote poetry. While studying his Latin curriculum, he came across the account of the Roman rebel Catiline; he became so taken with this story that he shaped it into a play, *Catilina* (1850; tr. *Catiline*, 1900). After moving to Christiania (now Oslo) in order to further his education, he completed his second drama, *Kjæmpehøjen* (performed 1850, published 1902; *The Warrior's Barrow*, 1922), a Viking history play after the manner of **national romanticism**.

In 1851 Ibsen was given an appointment at the recently founded Norwegian theater in Bergen. One of his duties was to provide an original play each year, and Ibsen's time in Bergen became an opportunity for him to thoroughly learn his craft. He was assisted by a travel grant that allowed him to study **theater** in Germany and Denmark. Most of the plays written in Bergen are of minor significance, however. An exception is the historical tragedy *Fru Inger til Østeraad* (1855; tr. *Lady Inger of Østråt*, 1890), written in prose and with lifelike characters.

After returning to Christiania in 1857, where he was associated with the Norwegian Theater, he completed a second significant historical play, *Hærmændene paa Helgeland* (1858; tr. *The Vikings at Helgeland*, 1890), which was inspired by several Icelandic family sagas. But financially this was a difficult period for Ibsen, who had recently married and as of 1859, with the birth of his son Sigurd, had a family to support. *Kjærlighedens komedie* (1862; tr. *Love's Comedy*, 1890) was a witty commentary on love and marriage, full of funny situations. But Ibsen was also plagued with depression and doubt about his artistic gifts, which he expressed in another historical tragedy, *Kongs-emnerne* (1863; tr. *The Pretenders*, 1890).

After receiving two small grants to enable him to collect **folklore**, Ibsen was given funds designed to support a year's residence abroad and left Norway for Italy in 1864. His outlook on life changed dramatically, and he soon published two of his major works, the verse dramas *Brand* (1866; tr. 1891) and *Peer Gynt* (1867; tr. 1892). The character Brand is an extreme idealist in the spirit of the Danish philosopher **Søren Kierkegaard**, while Peer Gynt is his unprincipled and hedonistic counterpart.

Ibsen remained abroad, chiefly in Italy and Germany, until 1891, when he again settled in Christiania. These were highly productive years for him, even though it took 10 additional years before he began writing the 12 modern plays for which he is best known in the English-speaking world. After publishing *De unges forbund* (1869; tr. *The League of Youth*, 1890), he finished his longest play—consisting of 10 acts divided into two evenings of performance—which has the title *Kejser og Galilæer* (1873; tr. *Emperor and Galilean*, 1876). The protagonist is the emperor Julian the Apostate, who tried to reestablish paganism as the state religion of the Roman Empire in the fourth century. Ibsen considered it his best play, but today that opinion is rarely shared.

Ibsen's 12 modern prose dramas can be divided into three groups of four plays each. The first group consists of dramas that are critical of social conditions. *Samfundets støtter* (1877; tr. *The Pillars of Society*, 1888) excoriates deception and hypocrisy in business and concludes that the spirit of truth and freedom are the real pillars of society. ***Et dukkehjem*** (1879; tr. *A Doll's House*, 1880) explores the role of **women** in the home and in society, concluding that a woman has not only the right but the duty to leave her husband and family if she is prevented by her marriage from realizing her full potential as a human being. *Gengangere* (1881; *Ghosts*, 1885) also offers a portrait of a marriage; its main focus, however, is on such ghosts from the past as the received ideas that people may have jettisoned intellectually but that still exert an emotional influence over them. Additionally, Ibsen discussed in the play such a delicate matter as syphilis that is passed on from a father to his unborn child (this used to be considered medically possible) and euthanasia, and for this he was censured. *En folkefiende* (1882; tr. *An Enemy of the People*, 1888) dramatizes the conflict between an exceptional intellect and the community in which he lives. Dr. Stockmann has discovered that the water at the local baths is polluted, but he is silenced when he tries to make people aware of his discovery. He is then branded an enemy of the people for suggesting that the actual pollution is but a symbol for the spiritual and political pollution in his town. Ibsen does not view Stockmann without irony, however, for at the end of the play he appears to have developed a strong Messiah complex.

The second group of plays have in common that Ibsen relies heavily on **symbolism** as he probes middle-class family life. In *Vildanden* (1884; tr. *The Wild Duck*, 1890), a teenage girl commits suicide because she does not believe her father loves her anymore, while her father uses his illusions as a crutch to cope with life's difficulties. Both of these characters, and several others, are illuminated by the symbol of the wild duck, which, wounded by a hunter, lives as a pet in an attic in the company of chickens and rabbits. Although the duck is never actually seen on stage, it figures prominantly in the dramatic economy, as it becomes a figure for characters that have been wounded by life in various ways. The conflict in *Rosmersholm* (1886; tr. 1891) concerns a widower, Rosmer, and Rebekka West, the woman who drove his former wife to jump into a millrace, killing herself. In the end, the white horses of Rosmersholm, which signify that someone is going to die, come back one more time, after which the millrace claims Rebekka and Rosmer as well. *Fruen fra havet* (1888; tr. *The Lady from the Sea*, 1890) probes the relationship between a widower, Dr. Wangel, and his second wife, Ellida, who, as a mermaid of sorts, has myserious ties to the sea, as well as to a seaman she had at one time promised to marry. The eponymous Hedda in the play *Hedda Gabler* (1890; tr. 1891) leads an utterly boring life as a new bride, amused only by a pair of pistols—a symbol of her dissatisfaction with her gender roles—that she has inherited from her father. In the end each pistol claims a life, as Hedda gives one of them to a former love interest so that he can use it to commit suicide, and then, when his death is not as beautiful as she wishes it were, she uses the other pistol to take her own life.

The final group consists of plays that in one way or another comment on the situation of the artist at the end of his career. *Bygmester Solness* (1892; *The Master Builder*, 1893) shows us the artist in the guise of an aging architect who has taken advantage of those around him and who now fears life's retribution. *Lille Eyolf* (1894; tr. *Little Eyolf*, 1895) presents a man who has used his work as an excuse for neglecting his wife. *John Gabriel Borkman* (1896; tr. 1897) adds crime to simply taking advantage; the protagonist has compromised his fiduciary duties in order to raise the funds needed for him to follow his calling as an industrialist. *Når vi døde vågner* (1899; tr. *When We Dead Awaken*, 1900) has as its protagonist a sculptor who has betrayed the love of his life for the sake of art.

It is a testimony to the power and enduring value of Ibsen's dramas that they continue to be performed all over the world.

IMPRESSIONISM. Borrowed from painting, the term impressionism captures one aspect of the general revolt against **realism** and **naturalism** that took place in the early 1890s. Rather than striving to faithfully represent reality, such impressionist writers as the Finn **Juhani Aho** and the Dane **Herman Bang**, in some of their works, attempted instead to render the writer's own impressions of observed objects, with a corresponding emphasis on moods and individual attitudes. *See also* MODERNISM; SYMBOLISM.

INDEPENDENT PEOPLE. See SJÁLFSTÆTT FÓLK.

ISAKSSON, ULLA (1916–2000). A Swedish novelist and screenwriter, Isaksson wrote mostly about **women** who, in one way or another, find themselves in extreme situations. Isaksson grew up in a strongly pietistic middle-class family, and her first novels were overtly religious. *Trädet* (1940; The Tree) and *I denna natt* (1942; In This Night) both won prizes in competitions sponsored by the Swedish Evangelical National Foundation, but it was not until Isaksson became divorced that her career as a secular writer took off. *Ytterst i havet* (1950; By the Outermost Edge of the Sea) recounts her spiritual crisis following the end of her marriage; it questions the power of a loving God in a world of evil and misery. *Kvinnohuset* (1952; The House of Women) depicts the lives of a series of different women, all of whom have moments of doubt and whose illusions are damaged by the truth. Isaksson's survey of types of women was continued in the short story collection *"Dödens faster"* (1954; "The Aunt of Death"), in which the title character is a truly horrifying person who preys on those around her in their moments of greatest weakness.

Isaksson's interest in the time of the witch trials is evident in *Dit du icke vill* (1956; Whither Thou Wouldst Not Go), which offers heartrending portrayals of the treatment of women accused of witchcraft. *Klänningen* (1959; The Dress) analyzes relationships between mothers and daughters as they are gradually transformed through the passage of time. Isaksson speaks in favor of illusion as a power for good in human life; human beings are simply not sufficiently strong to be able to bear the unvarnished truth. *De två saliga* (1962; tr. *The Blessed Ones*, 1970) further anatomizes love as both a supportive and destructive force.

The novel *Amanda eller den blå spårvagnen: En roman om dröm och verklighet* (1969; Amanda, or, the Blue Streetcar: A Novel about Dream and Reality) questions the perception, common at the time, that Sweden had created an ideal society. *Paradistorg* (1973; Paradise Market) offended some radical **feminists** by seeming to suggest that women have a particular responsibility for serving as nurturers, while the novel *Födelsedagen* (1988; The Birthday) returns to the theme of how mothers and daughters relate to one another. *Boken om E* (1994; The Book about E) recounts the descent of Isaksson's husband, Erik Hjalmar Linder, into Alzheimer's disease.

Isaksson also wrote several motion picture screenplays, most notably those of Ingmar Bergman's movies *Nära livet* (1958; released in the United States as *Brink of Life*) and *Jungfrukällan* (1960; released in the United States as *The Virgin Spring*).

– J –

JACOBSEN, JENS PETER (1847–1885). A Danish novelist, short story writer, and poet, Jacobsen is one of the most important writers of the **Modern Breakthrough** in Scandinavia. Most of his works are centered on the theme of dream versus reality and offer various examples of how this conflict can be adjudicated in the lives of individual human beings. Jacobsen's first published prose work was the novella *Mogens* (1872; tr. *Mogens, and Other Stories*, 1926, 1972, 1977, 1994), which is also the first **naturalist** work in Danish literature. At first the young Mogens acts like an animal; only later does he overcome his instinctual hedonism and find happiness in a lasting love relationship. He is able to make this transition once he has overcome his tendency to dream and has replaced fantasy with action.

The novel *Fru Marie Grubbe* (1876; tr. *Marie Grubbe*, 1917) is likewise a story about love and the dream of its satisfaction. Marie, of noble birth, is unable to find erotic happiness with her two husbands and a lover with backgrounds similar to her own, but then she runs off with a servant with whom she finds the happiness she craves. She is clearly driven by her sexual instincts, for she violates the norms of her class and relinquishes the advantages of her birth. This is an example of naturalism with a vengeance, as the power of biological inheritance triumphs not only over free will, but also over the power of the social environment. But Marie is also motivated by her dream of something better than what she has, and she is lucky enough to find it.

Jacobsen's most enigmatic novel is *Niels Lyhne* (1880; tr. 1919, 1990), which is set in the middle of the 1800s and discusses whether it is possible for people to completely overcome their inherited religious faith. Niels is an avowed atheist, and he repeatedly makes personal sacrifices for his nonfaith. He is repeatedly disappointed in love, however, and on her deathbed his own wife turns to God even though she knows that it hurts him deeply. Niels is perpetually unhappy, and at a moment when his atheism falters, leading him to pray, he gets no answer. He finally meets his death in the **war** between Denmark and Prussia in 1864.

Jacobsen's short stories express the same kind of bleakness as that found in his novels. In "To Verdener" (1879; tr. "Two Worlds," 1994) a sick woman uses magic to transfer her illness to an innocent stranger. "Pesten i Bergamo" (1882; tr. "The Plague in Bergamo," 1994) shows how the social order, as well as accepted spiritual truths, come to nothing in a moment of extreme stress. "Et Skud i Taagen" (1875; "A Shot in the Fog," 1994) is a study in jealousy and murder. Jacobsen is also known in Danish literary history for several poems, but his poetic production was not published in book form until after his death.

JACOBSEN, JØRGEN-FRANTZ (1900–1938). A Faroese and Danish novelist and essayist writing in Danish, Jacobsen was a cousin of the well-known Faroese writer **William Heinesen**, who edited some of Jacobsen's letters after his death. Jacobsen became an internationally known writer on account of a single novel, *Barbara* (1939; tr. 1939), which retells a Faroese legend of an evil woman named Beinta, who caused the death of her three husbands, all of them pastors. In Jacobsen's version of the story, the woman becomes an embodiment of immediacy as well as of the erotic. Barbara's husband in

Jacobsen's novel is the priest Poul, who, when leaving Copenhagen, renounced the world and its attractions. Alas, his meeting with Barbara changes all that, but her utter amorality and lack of principles bring him to the end of his wits.

Denmark's rule over the Faroe Islands was a grief to Jacobsen, and he tirelessly worked for greater freedom for the islanders. His journalism in Denmark served this purpose, as did his topographical and cultural work *Færøerne: Natur og Folk* (1936; The Faroes: Nature and People).

JÆGER, FRANK (1926–1977). A Danish poet, novelist, short story writer, and essayist, Jæger kept himself aloof from the social engagement of most of his contemporary writers and devoted himself to personal themes. Jæger's early poetry is marked by the lyricism of his volumes *Dydige Digte* (1948; Virtuous Poems), *Morgenens Trompet* (1949; The Morning's Trumpet), and *De 5 aarstider* (1950; The Five Seasons). The poems in *Tyren* (1953; The Bull) focus on the erotic and the absurdities of life. His later poetry, such as that found in *Idylia* (1967), presents the erotic as a significant danger.

The fun-loving Jæger is present in the supposedly autobiographical narrative *Den unge Jægers lidelser* (1953; The Sufferings of Young Jæger), the title of which is a pun on Johann Wolfgang von Goethe's *Die Leiden des Jungen Werther* (1774; tr. *The Sorrows of Young Werther*, 1775). Jæger's playfulness also marks his brief novel *Iners* (1950) and the short stories in *Hverdagshistorier* (1951; Everyday Stories). He fully embraces **realism**, however, in a story of the life of Joan of Arc, *Jomfruen fra Orleans* (1955; The Maid of Orleans), as well as in the stories in *Kapellanen og andre fortællinger* (1957; The Curate and Other Stories). In the three narratives in *Danskere* (1966; Danes), as well as in the book *Døden i skoven* (1970; Death in the Forest), realism is combined with humor, satire, and a sense of the fantastic.

Jæger also wrote numerous essays, which were published in such collections as *Velkommen, Vinter og andre essays* (1958; Welcome, Winter, and Other Essays), *Drømmen om en sommerdag* (1965; The Dream of a Summer Day), and *Naïve rejser* (1968; Naïve Journeys). Volumes of essays mixed with short stories are *Alvilda: Sengelæsning for Unge og Gamle* (1969; Alvilda: Bedtime Reading for Young and Old) and *Udsigt til Kronborg: Sængelesning* (1976; A View of Kronborg: Bedtime Reading). Taken together, these books constitute a celebration of the uncomplicated aspects of life and show that Jæger was largely at peace with himself and with existence. Jæger also wrote radio plays.

JAKOBSDÓTTIR, SVAVA (1930–2004). An Icelandic novelist, short story writer, and playwright, Jakobsdóttir started out in the tradition of social and psychological **realism** but quickly moved in the direction of the fantastic, which became a dominant trait in her work. Writing mostly about the lives of ordinary **women**, she also displays a strong **feminist** tenor in her oeuvre. Jakobsdóttir had her literary debut with *12 konur* (1965; Twelve Women), a collection of short stories mostly in the realist mode. Her next collection, *Veizla undir grjótvegg* (1967; Party under a Stone Wall), contained a mixture of realist and fantastic stories, but the feminist component was sufficiently strong that the Icelandic women's movement found Jakobsdóttir's work useful to their cause, and Jakobsdóttir was elected a member of the Icelandic parliament in 1971. Some of the stories are grotesque. In one story, the children in a family split their mother's head open and remove her brain in order to see what it looks like. The mother's functioning in family and society is not at all impeded, however. A third collection of short stories bears the title *Gevfið hvort öðru . . .* (1982; Give to One Another . . .).

Jakobsdóttir's first novel, *Leigjandinn* (1969; tr. *The Lodger and Other Stories*, 2000), tells about a married couple who build a house and then accept a boarder. After a while the border and the husband merge into a single two-headed figure, which has been read as Jakóbsdottir's commentary on Iceland's membership in the NATO alliance and the American military base located close to Reykjavík, with its attendant cultural influence. The novel *Gunnladar saga* (1987; The Saga of Gunnlöd) also employs fantastic narration, but it is less grotesque and tends more toward the use of myth. Narrated by the mother of a young girl named Dís, who has been accused of stealing a prehistoric urn from Denmark's National Museum of Art, the story merges two temporal levels, for Dís travels back in time so that her identity is fused with that of the mythical figure Gunnlöd, whom, according to Old Norse mythology, the god Odin seduced in order to get hold of the magic mead of poetry. The vessel that Dís has stolen from the museum is the urn that contained the poetry, and Gunnlöd has essentially come back to modern times in the form of Dís in order to retrieve her property. The Danish police have a hard time accepting this explanation, however, which shows that Jakobsdóttir was not entirely lost in the fantastic.

The short story collection *Undir eldfjalli* (1989; Under the Volcano) is similar in tone to *Gunnladar saga*. Jakobsdóttir has also written several dramas, including the stage plays *Hvað er í blýhólknum* (1970; What Is in the Lead Pipe), *Friðsæl veröld* (1974; A Peaceful World), *Æskuvinir* (1976; Childhood Friends), and *Lokaæfing* (1983; Final Rehersal), as well as the radio play *Í takt við tímana* (1980; In Step with the Times). In general, the plays deal with social and political topics, including the fear of nuclear **war**. *See also* JAKOBSSON, JÖKULL; THEATER.

JAKOBSSON, JÖKULL (1933–1978). An Icelandic playwright, novelist, and short story writer, Jakobsson is the brother of the more successful and better known **Svava Jakobsdóttir**. Jakobsson had his literary debut with the novel *Tæmdur bikar* (1951; Emptied Cup), which was generally thought to be an immature piece of work; it was published when the author was only 17 years old. But his next three novels, published in 1956, 1958, and 1960, did not fare much better, and Jakobsson turned his attention to drama. His first play, *Pótók* (Potok), was produced in 1961 and was well received by the public, albeit not by the **critics**. The play, which is very critical of modern society, was one of very few Icelandic plays written at the time. Jakobsson had a difficult time financially, however, so he tried to earn money writing short stories, a volume of which were published under the title *Næturheimsókn* (1962; Night Visit).

Throughout the years Jacobsson worked in a variety of jobs while writing plays on the side. His most popular play was *Hart í bak* (1965; Hard to Port), which premiered in 1962 and ran 205 times. *Sjóleidin til Bagdad* (performed 1965; tr. *The Sea Route to Baghdad*, 1973), in which the female protagonist has to choose between her drunken husband and her teenage love, was considerably less well received than *Hart í bak*.

Jakobsson continued to write plays for the stage as well as for radio and television, which at that time was a new medium in Iceland. He wrote several travel books to support himself but was largely unsuccessful. He had some success with the novel *Feilnóta í fimmtu sinfóníunni* (1975; Wrong Note in the Fifth Symphony), the story of a middle-aged woman who discovers that being a wife and mother is not sufficiently fulfilling for her. A character from this novel reappears in the posthumously published *Skilabod til Söndru* (1981; A Message to Sandra). *See also* THEATER.

JANSSON, TOVE (1914–2001). A Finland-Swedish novelist, short story writer, and author of **children's books**, Tove Jansson is the world's best-known Finland-Swedish writer. Most readers know her as the author of a series of novels about the Moomin Trolls, but she has also written books for adults. The Moomins are shaped like miniature hippopotami that walk upright on their hind legs. They live at a place called Moominvalley, which is surrounded by mountains. They hibernate during the winter, but during the rest of the year they are active, and at times they travel considerably. Moominvalley is their permanent home, however, and that is where their security is to be found.

The first book about the Moomins was published in 1945, but the most significant titles are *Trollkarlens hatt* (1949; tr. *Finn Family Moomintroll*, 1950), *Muminpappans bravader* (1950; tr. *The Exploits of Moominpappa*, 1952), *Farlig midsommar* (1954; tr. *Moominsummer Madness*, 1955), *Trollvinter* (1957; *Moominland Midwinter*, 1958), *Pappan och havet* (1965; tr. *Moominpappa at Sea*, 1966), and *Sent i november* (1970, tr. *Moominvalley in November*, 1971). The stories feature some kind of natural catastrophe that requires the Moomins to cooperate extensively in their efforts to save their home. The novels teach such values as kindness, social cooperation, respect for others, and the ability to laugh at one's own foibles. In *Farlig midsommar*, for example, there is a great flood, and the Moomins find a floating theater that challenges their ability to tell the difference between reality and theatrical illusions, especially when Moominpappa gets involved in having his own verse drama performed there.

Among Jansson's books for adults is an autobiographical novel of sorts, *Bildhuggarens dotter* (1968; tr. *The Sculptor's Daughter*,

1969), which may shed some light on the origins of the Moomins in Jansson's own childhood. Two volumes of tales are *Lyssnerskan* (1971; The Listening Woman) and *Dockskåpet* (1978; The Doll Cupboard). Her most popular novels for adults are *Sommarboken* (1972; tr. *The Summer Book*, 1977) and *Solstaden* (1974; tr. *Sun City*, 1976). Two later novels are *Den ärliga bedragaren* (1982; The Honest Swindler) and *Stenåkern* (1984; The Stony Field). Three books about various topics may be considered fictionalized memoirs: *Resa med lätt bagage* (1987; Journey with Light Baggage), *Rent spel* (1989; Honest Play), and *Brev från Klara* (1991; Honest Play).

JENSEN, JOHANNES V. (1873–1950). One of Denmark's greatest and most prolific poets and novelists, Jensen deeply affected Danish literary and cultural life, ultimately winning the **Nobel Prize** in literature in 1944. He was raised in the district of Himmerland in northern Jutland, and his works are strongly influenced by life there; Jensen believed the area to be the homeland of the Goths, whom he saw as the driving force in the development of Western civilization. His home district is celebrated in his three volumes of *Himmerlandshistorier* (1898–1910; Stories from Himmerland).

Jensen's works are permeated by a strong historical consciousness. Many of the poems in his collection *Digte* (1906; Poems; enlarged editions in 1917, 1921, 1943, and 1948) celebrate the technological and industrial innovations of modernity; a paradigm example is "Paa Memphis Station" (At the Memphis Train Station). Jensen celebrates the man of action at the expense of the contemplative spirit, and he therefore was deeply impressed with American culture, especially its pragmatism, which he regarded as a healthy counterweight to European metaphysical speculation.

After writing two novels that are critical of the self-reflexivity and inwardness of the literature of the 1890s, Jensen published *Kongens Fald* (1900–1901; tr. *The Fall of the King*, 1933 and 1992), which demonstrates how dangerous it can be when excessive thinking is allowed to take the place of action. A central figure of the novel is Danish king Christian II (1489–1559), who is portrayed as losing his power due to his inability to act decisively. The contrast between contemplation and action is further illustrated by Christian's companion, the thinker Mikkel, and Mikkel's opposite, the man of action

Axel. But Axel dies, and Jensen clearly holds that human life is ultimately futile.

Jensen traveled widely, including visits to the United States. The novels *Madame D'Ora* (1904) and *Hjulet* (1905; The Wheel) depict American life, and stories written at this time are set in America, China, and Java. But his 11 volumes of *Myter* (1907–1944; Myths) have been more durable expressions of his ideas, especially as work preparatory to his great six-volume cycle of novels, *Den lange Rejse* (1908–1922; tr. *The Long Journey*, 1923). Thoroughly Darwinian, this cycle of novels tells the story of human society and culture from before the Ice Age to the height of the industrial period. Jensen's mythic imagination localizes humanity's evolutionary beginnings to the primordial rain forests of his native Jutland, and the Nordic people, or Goths, come into being as a single couple refuses to be forced south by the advancing glacier. The Goths are characterized by a longing for the sun and its warmth, and this longing ultimately motivates such decisive historical events as the Viking expeditions and the journeys of Columbus. Longing for the sun also results in religious feeling and a longing for paradise, the ultimate cultural expression of which is the Gothic cathedral. After receiving the **Nobel Prize** in literature in 1944, Jensen largely turned away from fiction and advocated his Darwinian worldview mostly in articles and essays. *See also* JENSEN, THIT.

JENSEN, THIT (1876–1957). A Danish novelist, short story writer, and playwright, Jensen was committed to the idea of fairly traditional marriage and motherhood for **women** but also believed that one should distinguish between procreation and sexuality, which led her to campaign strongly for informing women about birth control. She also wanted women to have access to education and their own sources of income. A spiritualist, she believed strongly in reincarnation and was interested in parapsychology. Her strongly held convictions, coupled with a remarkable ability as a public speaker, made her a well-known person in her day. The famous Danish writer **Johannes V. Jensen** was her brother.

Thit Jensen had her literary debut with the novel *To Søstre* (1903; Two Sisters) and wrote a number of other novels and collections of short stories on contemporary topics. *Ørkenvandring* (1907; Desert

Walk), *Elskovsforbandelse* (1911; Cursed Love), and *Jorden* (1915; The Earth) are novels. *Sagn og Syner* (1909; Legends and Visions), *Det banker* (1911; There Is Knocking), and *Jydske Historier* (1916; Jutland Stories) are short story collections that express Jensen's love for her native Himmerland (a district in Jutland) and her interest in the paranormal. Her **realist** style was well suited to her **feminist** message in such novels as *Gerd* (1918) and its sequel, *Aphrodite fra Fuur* (1925; Aphrodite from Fuur), in which she traced the development of modern women.

In the late 1920s Jensen started writing historical novels, such as *Jørgen Lykke* (1931) and *Rigets Arving* (1946; The Heir to the Kingdom), which were widely read. She also wrote a play that is set in medieval Iceland and a volume of memoirs that emphasized her spiritualist beliefs, *Hvorfra? Hvorhen?* (1950; Wherefrom? Whereto?).

JERSILD, PER CHRISTIAN (1935–). A Swedish novelist and essayist, Jersild has produced work with **critical** and popular appeal. Trained in medicine, which he practiced full-time for much of his career as a writer, he has observed hospitals, medical research organizations, and other hierarchies with a keen eye and sharp wit. After publishing a collection of short stories and two novels, one of which, *Till varmare länder* (1961; To Warmer Lands), takes place partly in hell, Jersild had his literary breakthrough with *Calvinols resa genom världen* (1965; Calvinol's Voyage throughout the World), a doctor's fantastic journey through time and space. His first big success, however, was the novel *Grisjakten* (1968; The Pig Hunt), which tells about the eradication of swine on the Swedish island of Gotland. Jersild shows that the bureaucratic efficiency with which the book's narrator-protagonist goes about his task is related to such historical phenomena as the Holocaust and other instances of genocide. The technocratic mind-set is further explored in *Vi ses i Song My* (1970; See You in Song My), in which Swedish soldiers are being trained to act in ways contrary to reason.

The novel *Djurdoktorn* (1973; tr. *The Animal Doctor*, 1975) tells about a woman veterinarian who, in a dystopian future, looks after the health of research animals that are being unnecessarily experimented on. In *Barnens ö* (1976; tr. *Children's Island*, 1986) a 10-year-old boy deceives his mother by pretending to be away at summer camp, while instead staying home, reflecting on the big questions of life. *Babels hus* (1978; tr. *House of Babel*, 1987) has a large hospital as its setting, and Jersild portrays both its stratified society and the lack of communication that mark the relationships between such groups as doctors, nurses, and patients.

The main character in *En levande själ* (1980; tr. *A Living Soul*, 1988) is, quite literally, a brain in a vat, kept alive by laboratory scientists and experimented on by them for financial gain. Jersild has taken a philosophical concept—the brain in a vat is a popular contemporary version of René Descartes's famous "evil deceiver" argument—and uses it to probe the limits of what it means to be human.

Jersild's dystopian vision is also present in the novel *Efter floden* (1982; tr. *After the Flood*, 1986), in which a small group of survivors of a nuclear **war** find their humanity gradually slipping away. As they struggle for survival, often by brutal means, they are destroyed by a virus. Dan Brown's blockbuster novel *The Da Vinci Code* (2003) is anticipated by Jersild's fantasy novel *Den femtionde frälsaren* (1984; The Fiftieth Savior), in which a direct descendant of Jesus and Mary Magdalene shows up in Venice in the 1790s. Captured and tortured by officials of the Roman Catholic Church, he escapes briefly and impregnates a marchioness, whose child then becomes the 51st generation descendant of Christ.

Drawing on one of the great classics of Swedish literature, **Selma Lagerlöf**'s *Nils Holgerssons underbara resa genom Sverige* (1906; tr. *The Wonderful Adventures of Nils*, 1907), Jersild created a sequel to the story of the boy Nils in his novel *Holgerssons* (1991). *En lysande marknad* (1992; A Splendid Market), on the other hand, is a detective story that is strongly critical of Swedish society. A major theme of *En gammal kärlek* (1995; An Old Love) is the question of when euthanasia is morally defensible. *Ljusets drottning* (2000; The Queen of Light), tells about a young man who discovers that his adopted mother is really his biological mother, and that his biological father is a famous, but anonymous, sperm donor. The story is a major satire on life in Sweden during the final decades of the 20th century. Set in medieval Stockholm, *De ondas kloster* (2003; The Monastery of the Evil Ones) investigates the potential for evil found within religion.

Two collections of Jersild's essays are *Humpty Dumptys fall: Liv-*

såskådningsbok (1990; The Fall of Humpty Dumpty: An Outlook on Life) and *Darwins ofullbordade: Om människans biologiska natur* (1997; Darwin Unfinished: On Humanity's Biological Nature); the latter presents Jersild's philosophy of mind. He has also written a memoir of his youth, *Fem hjärten i en tändsticksask* (1989; Five Hearts in a Matchbox).

JOENPELTO, EEVA (1921–2004). A Finnish novelist, Joenpelto grew up in a middle-class family in Lohja, a small town in southwestern Finland. Her first novel, *Kaakerholman kaupunki* (1950; The Town of Kaakerholm) has that type of a community as its setting, and later Joenpelto named a series of four novels for her hometown. Her next book, *Veljen varjo* (1951; A Brother's Shadow), investigates how a person who was lost during the **war** is remembered by the survivors. In the novel *Johannes vain* (1952; Just Johannes) the protagonist leaves the materialism of the city behind in order to be at one with **nature**. The theme of *Neito kulkee vetten päällä* (1955; tr. *The Maiden Walks upon the Water*, 1991) is how a strong woman can get along with a weak man.

Joenpelto also published a large number of other novels that were well received. In the 1970s she wrote a series of novels that have her hometown as their setting, consisting of the books *Vetää kaikista ovista* (1974; A Draft from Every Door), *Kuin kekäle kädessä* (1976; Like Holding a Red Hot Coal in Your Hand), *Sataa suloaista vettä* (1978; Salty Rain), and *Eteisiin ja kynnyksille* (1980; Into the Hallways and onto the Thresholds). The action takes place after 1918 and tells about social and political change in Lohja, which symbolizes all of Finland.

Other novels of significance are *Elämän rouva, rouva Glad* (1982; tr. *The Bride of Life*, 1995), which tells about a woman with a knack for making money, and *Avoin, hellä ja katumaton* (1991; Open, Tender, Unrepentant), in which the characters, who come from very different social backgrounds, have something of both the decent person and the crook in them. Joenpelto's final novel was *Tuomari Müller, hieno mies* (1994; Judge Müller, a Fine Man).

JOHNSON, EYVIND (1900–1976). A Swedish novelist, Johnson was the son of a disabled railroad worker and had to fend for himself starting at the age of 14. With little formal schooling, he read widely, eventually rising to be one of Sweden's foremost writers, and he was honored with the **Nobel Prize** in 1974. Johnson's first books were written while he lived in Berlin and Paris, where he became acquainted with the work of Europe's foremost **modernists**. Such volumes as *De fyra främlingarna* (1924; The Four Strangers), *Timan och rättfärdigheten* (1925; Timan and Justice), *Stad i mörker* (1927; City in Darkness), and *Stad i ljus* (1928; City in Light) were the works that taught him his craft. *Stad i ljus*, which tells about a writer who is starving in Paris, shows influence from **Knut Hamsun**'s novel *Sult*. *Minnas* (1928; Remembering) portrays memory as linked to repression. *Kommentar till ett stjärnfall* (1929; Commentary to a Falling Star) is set in Stockholm during the 1920s and is Sweden's first novel that uses the stream-of-consciousness technique.

Many of Johnson's novels from the 1930s feature the character Mårten Torpare, who often appears as the author's mouthpiece. In the novel *Avsked till Hamlet* (1930; Farewell to Hamlet), Mårten eschews vacillation and comes to terms with his own past. *Bobinack* (1932) satirizes capitalist society and briefly suggests that a cure may be found in a return to **nature**. *Regn i gryningen* (1933; Rain at Dawn) is likewise an experiment with primitivist ideas.

Johnson became well known for a series of four autobiographical novels about a character named Olof. *Nu var det 1914* (1934; tr. *1914*, 1970), *Här har du ditt liv* (1935; Here's Your Life), *Se dig inte om!* (1936; Don't Look Back), and *Slutspel i ungdomen* (1937; Finale in Youth) tell about Olof's life during the first five years after he has left home at the age of 14.

Right before World **War** II Johnson wrote two novels warning people about the evils of Nazism, *Nattövning* (1938; Night Maneuvers) and *Soldatens återkomst* (1940; The Soldier's Return), in which he argues for the use of force to prevent violence and the loss of freedom. The wartime Krilon trilogy, an allegory of the war, consists of the volumes *Grupp Krilon* (1941; Group Krilon), *Krilons resa* (1942; Krilon's Journey), and *Krilon själv* (1943; Krilon Himself).

After World War II Johnson wrote several historical novels. *Strändernas svall* (1946; tr. *Return to Ithaca*, 1952) is a retelling of the story of Odysseus's journey home. As he kills Penelope's suitors, he tries to obtain peace by force, but it is not clear that he succeeds. *Dröm-*

mar om rosor och eld (1949; tr. *Dreams of Roses and Fire*, 1984) is set in 17th-century France under Cardinal Richelieu. While following the procedures of the *Malleus Maleficarum*, a manual that describes how to detect witches, the cardinal's minions work to get rid of his enemies. There are clear parallels with the Moscow trials of the 1930s. *Hans nådes tid* (1960; tr. *The Days of His Grade*, 1968) chronicles Charlemagne's rise to power; the narrative includes the story of a failed rebellion in Lombardy that is reminiscent of the events in Hungary in 1956.

Johnson capped his career with *Livsdagen lång* (1964; Life's Long Day), a love story; *Favel ensam* (1968; Favel Alone), a book about concentration camp survivors; and *Några steg mot tystnaden* (1973; A Few Steps toward Silence), which tells about characters who in various ways are held captive by the past.

JØRGENSEN, JOHANNES (1866–1956). A Danish poet and novelist, Jørgensen came to the forefront of Danish cultural life through his editorship of the literary magazine *Taarnet* (1893–1894; The Tower), through which he championed the literary ideas of the 1890s in opposition to the **naturalists**. His poetry collection *Bekendelse* (1894; Confession) and his brief novel *Sommer* (1892; Summer) both fail to live up to the ideals of **symbolism** but express a strong romantic longing for the past. After his conversion to Roman Catholicism in 1896, Jørgensen was very much at peace with himself, as shown, for example, by the poetry collection *Af det Dybe* (1920; From the Depths). A vigorous apologist for Roman Catholicism, Jørgensen wrote several books about saints. His autobiography bears the title *Mit Livs Legende* (1916–1928; tr. *Jørgensen, An Autobiography*, 1928–1929).

– K –

KALEVALA. *See* LÖNNROT, ELIAS.

KALLAS, AINO JULIA MARIA (1878–1956). A Finnish novelist, short story writer, and playwright, Kallas was born in Finland but married the Estonian **folklorist** Oskar Kallas; his service as an Estonian diplomat brought her to several European capitals, including a 20-year residency in London. One of the few Finnish writers from the early 20th century whose works were widely translated, she wrote for a large audience but was not much associated with other Finnish writers and did not greatly influence the development of Finnish literature.

Kallas's move to Estonia took her from a country that had enjoyed a high degree of liberty to one that was still suffering from the influence that Germany and Russia had exerted on it. The lives of the common people had been marked by serfdom, which Kallas described in two volumes of short stories, *Meren takaa* (1904–1905; From Beyond the Sea). In the story "Häät" (The Wedding), a young bride wants to kill the local lord, who has demanded his "first night right" from her, thus taking her away from her husband on her wedding night. Another story tells about the wife of a merchant who leaves home while in the middle of baking bread. She follows a group of people to Tallinn, believing that a white ship will come and take her to freedom. Later the smell of bread restores her to her senses and she returns home. The short story collection *Lähtevien laivojen kaupunki* (1913; The Town of the Departing Ships) shows the influence of **symbolism**. Efforts to remedy Estonia's lack of a national culture are vividly portrayed in the short novel *Ants Raudjalg* (1907), which tells the story of a man whose efforts end in defeat as he leaves the country in order to find work in Russia.

Kallas's most important works are three novels that portray the effects of a great passion and take place in Estonia in the 16th and 17th centuries. She uses archaic language and sentence structure—which she had experimented with in the short story collection *Vieras veri* (1921; Strange Blood)—in order to achieve the appropriate mood. *Barbara von Tisenhusen* (1923; tr. 1925, 1927, 1975) tells the story of a young Russian noblewoman who falls in love with a man of inferior rank. They elope and experience great happiness, but she is caught and killed by her family. In *Reigin pappi* (1926; tr. *The Clergyman of Reigi*, 1927, 1975) the wife of a pastor, the narrator of the book, falls in love with his assistant. She, too, is caught and killed. In both of these cases, love has transgressed social boundaries and must be punished. Forbidden love is also punished in *Sudenmorsian* (1928; tr. *The Wolf's Bride*, 1930, 1975), in which a woman becomes a werewolf and finds happiness with the local pack and by consorting with the forest demon. She has transgressed the boundary between the natural and the supernatural and is killed by a silver bullet, fired from her husband's gun.

Kallas's best-known play, *Bathseba Saarenmaalla* (1932; tr. *Bath-Sheba of Saarenmaa*, 1934), was successfully adapted as an opera. Her journals have been published (1952–1956), as has some of her correspondence, with the title *Kolme naista, kolme kohtaloa* (1988–1989; Three Women, Three Fates).

KALLIFATIDES, THEODOR (1938–). A Swedish novelist, poet, and essayist, Kallifatides was born in Greece but emigrated to Sweden in 1964. Intent on making Swedish his working language, he published his first book in Swedish, *Minnet i exil* (1969; The Memory in Exile), only five years later. It was followed by the novel *Utlänningar* (1970; Foreigners), which tells about the situation of immigrants in Sweden. This theme is continued in *Et nytt land utanför mitt fönster* (2001; A New Land outside My Window).

Many of Kallifatides's novels are set in Greece, such as the trilogy consisting of *Bönder och herrar* (1973; tr. *Peasants and Masters*, 1977), *Plogen och svärdet* (1975; The Plow and the Sword), and *Den grymma freden* (1977; The Cruel Peace), which describes the impact of World **War** II on life in a Greek village. *En fallen ängel* (1981; A Fallen Angel) discusses life under the Greek junta, while *Brännvin och rosor* (1983; Liquor and Roses) describes the struggle of the Greeks against the Nazis. *En lång dag i Aten* (1989; A Long Day in Athens) tells about Kallifatides's father.

Kallifatides writes about love in the novels *Kärleken* (1978; Love) and *De sju timmarna i paradiset* (1998; Seven Hours in Paradise), a novel about intense and all-consuming passion. *En kvinna att älska* (2003; A Woman to Love) tells about friendship. The novel *Det sista ljuset* (1995) is set in an immigrant neighborhood and accuses some immigrants to Sweden of having become welfare cheats. *Ett liv bland människor* (1994; A Life among Humans) is an autobiographical narrative, while *Afrodites tårar* (1996; The Tears of Aphrodite) is a volume of essays.

Kallifatides has also published two volumes of poetry, *Tiden är inte oskyldig* (1971; Time Is Not Innocent) and *För en kvinnas röst*

(1999; For the Voice of a Woman). In recent years he has turned to writing mystery stories and has published *Ett enkelt brott* (2001; A Simple Crime), *Den sjätte passageraren* (2002; The Sixth Passenger), and *I hennes blick* (2005; In Her Eyes).

KAMPMANN, CHRISTIAN (1939–1987). A Danish novelist and short story writer, Kampmann took middle-class life as his subject and explored it in a large number of short stories and novels. He had his literary debut with the short story collection *Blandt venner* (1962; Among Friends), which was followed by another collection, *Ly* (1965; Shelter). An important issue in these stories is that bourgeois values simply do not promote people's real involvement with each other. The need for security is the theme of Kampmann's earliest novels. *Sammen* (1967; Together), *Nærved og næsten* (1969; Near and Nearly), and the short story collection *"Vi elsker mere"* (1970; "We Love More") are all marked by the irony of their titles. *Nok til hele ugen* (1971; Enough for the Whole Week) documents the marital crisis of a middle-aged woman who gets her sense of meaning from reading weekly magazines.

Kampmann's greatest artistic achievement is a series of novels that depict the life of the upper middle class in Denmark during the period 1954–1974. Consisting of the volumes *Visse hensyn* (1973; Certain Considerations), *Faste forhold* (1974; Regular Relationships), *Rene linjer* (1975; Clear Lines), and *Andre måder* (1975; Other Ways), this tetralogy about the life of the fictional Gregersen family has been very popular among the Danish reading public and has also been filmed. The series is a saga about the changes that Danish society underwent during these two decades, from the rather quiet lives of people in the 1950s to a time when traditional marriage was being questioned while people's material prosperity was growing rapidly, but with the presence of the energy crisis of the 1970s hanging as a shadow over their paradise of consumption.

Before Kampmann was murdered in 1987, he wrote an autobiographical trilogy consisting of *Fornemmelser* (1977; Sensations), *Videre trods alt* (1979; Onward in Spite of Everything), and *I glimt* (1980; Seen as Glimpses), as well as other books. The novel *Gyldne løfter* (1986; Golden Promises) tells about an attempt to solve one's problems in life through meditation.

KÁRASON, EINAR (1955–). An Icelandic novelist, short story writer, and screenwriter, Kárason first studied literature at the University of Iceland. He had his literary debut with an unremarkable collection of poetry in 1979, and two years later he published his first novel, *Þetta eru asnar Gudjón* (1981; They Are All Fools), which describes a group of young men who try to make it in the commercial fishing industry after spending most of their previous lives in school. Kárason next embarked on a trilogy consisting of the volumes *Þar sem djöflaeyjan rís* (1983; tr. *Devil's Island*, 2000), *Gulleyjan* (1985; Treasure Island), and *Fyrirheitna landið* 1989; The Promised Land), in which he tells about life in Reykjavík during the years following World War II. British and American forces left a large number of barracks behind, and people from the countryside migrating to Reykjavík found shelter in this temporary housing. Through a story that involves three generations of one family, Kárason vividly depicts the social changes in Iceland during the 1950s.

During this period Kárason also published a volume of short stories, *Söngur villiandarinnar og fleiri sögur* (1987; The Song of the Wild Duck and Other Stories), in which he depicts strange characters and awkward situations. A second collection of stories about unusual characters is *Þættir af einkennilegum mönnum: smásögur* (1996; Tales of Peculiar People: Short Stories).

Another family saga consists of the volumes *Heimskra manna ráð* (1992; Worst Laid Plans) and *Kvikasilfur* (1994; Quicksilver) and depicts the problems that some formerly poor people have when they get rich. Kárason's male characters are flawed by their inability to appreciate the beauty of the everyday, and instead go off in pursuit of wealth that they are not prepared to handle. In the novel *Norðurljós* (1998; Northern Lights), which is set in the 18th century, the protagonist seeks material advancement through lawsuits, as his chief talent is his ability to say bad things about others. Another historical novel is *Óvinafagnaður* (2001; Meeting of Foes), which takes place in the late Middle Ages; like the age in which it is set, the novel is extremely violent. Kárason has also written plays and screenplays that are based on some of his novels.

KARLFELDT, ERIK AXEL (1864–1931). A Swedish poet, Karlfeldt hailed from the province of Dalarna, which he celebrated in verse throughout his career as a **neoromantic** and regionalist poet. After studying literature and English, he had his debut with the collection *Vildmarks- och kärleksvisor* (1895; Songs of Wilderness and Love), in which he dwells on the harmony between humans and **nature** and where subconscious forces are given such symbolic expression as the Greek god Pan and the more homey witches. In his next two volumes of poetry, *Fridolins visor och andra dikter* (1898; Fridolin's Songs and Other Poems) and *Fridolins lustgård och Dalmålningar på rim* (1901; Fridolin's Pleasure Garden and Dalarna Paintings in Rhyme), Karlfeldt introduces the character Fridolin, apparently modeled on **Carl Michael Bellman**'s Fredman, but whose retinue of compatriots are of much less interest than those of the older poet. *Flora och Pomona* (1906; Flora and Pomona) takes its title from the names of the goddesses of flowers and fruit and is replete with references to the classical world. This is also the case with Karlfeldt's next volume of poetry, *Flora och Bellona* (1918; Flora and Bellona), in which World **War** I—Bellona is the goddess of war—and the Russian Revolution are juxtaposed with the poet's longing for his beloved Dalarna of the past. Karlfeldt's final volume of poetry, *Hösthorn* (1927; Autumnal Horn), represents a nostalgic return to a relatively uncomplicated past that is contrasted with a rapidly changing present. The poet was awarded the **Nobel Prize** posthumously in 1931.

KELLGREN, JOHAN HENRIC (1751–1795). A Swedish poet and **critic**, Kellgren had his roots in neoclassical tastes and Enlightenment thought, but also showed appreciation for the preromanticism of the late 1700s. Born into a clerical family and afflicted with tuberculosis most of his adult life, Kellgren was educated at Åbo University in Finland, where he studied classical literature. His numerous allusions to Greek and Roman writers make his poetry less accessible to contemporary readers.

Kellgren was attracted to Stockholm by the literary and cultural flowering associated with the court of King **Gustav III**. He became associated with the newspaper *Stockholms Posten* (The Stockholm Post) and was also a leading member of the literary society Utile Dulci (Usefulness and Pleasure)—named after a core dictum in Horace's *Ars Poetica*—in which he had some editorial responsibilities. His position as cultural leader was consolidated when he was asked to collaborate with the king on the opera *Gustaf Wasa*, which premiered 19 January 1786. King Gustav produced a prose draft in French, which Kellgren then turned into Swedish verse. The two of them similarly produced the libretto for *Gustaf Adolf och Ebba Brahe* (1786–1787; Gustaf Adolf and Ebba Brahe), after which Kellgren got tired of the collaboration. While Kellgren was at first critical of the work of **Carl Michael Bellman**, he later wrote an appreciative introduction to Bellman's *Fredmans epistlar* (1790; Fredman's Epistles), in which he acknowledged the poet's genius.

KIANTO, ILMARI (1874–1970). A Finnish novelist, Kianto (originally Calamnius) was an immensely productive writer who kept publishing into the 1950s. Drawing extensively on his own experience, he wrote most interestingly about poor backwoods people in the district of Suomussalmi, close to the Russian border in north central Finland. He had strong patriotic leanings that caused him to also wish for that border to be moved farther east, so as to include Russian Karelia as part of Finland. These sentiments were expressed in *Suomi suureksi, Viena vapaaksi* (1918; For a Greater Finland, and a Free Russian Karelia).

In his youth Kianto studied in Moscow and later became a teacher of Russian. He rebelled against his childhood Lutheran faith—his father was a pastor—in the book *Vapaauskoisen psaltari* (1912; The Freethinker's Psalter). But his first novel was *Väärällä uralla* (1896; In the Wrong Career), which tells about a young man with military aspirations who realizes that it is the wrong thing to do. After a few collections of rather undistinguished poetry, Kianto wrote several novels that have love as their theme, *Pyhä viha* (1908; Sacred Wrath), which is critical of the church, *Kärsimys* (1909; Suffering), and *Pyhä rakkaus* (1910; Sacred Love), in which the erotic becomes an increasingly strong force.

One of Kianto's most important novels is *Punainen viiva* (1909; The Red Line), which tells about the promise of free elections as it relates to the life situation of poor backwoods people. The red line of the book's title is first and foremost the line used to mark the ballots in the elections of 1906; however, a much more meaningful red line in the lives of Kianto's characters is the streak of blood running from the neck of the book's protagonist, who gets killed while fighting a bear. Another novel set in the same poor, rural environment is *Ryysyrannan Jooseppi* (1924; Joseph of Ryysyranta), a humorous tale of a rather indolent but all too enterprising peasant who tries to make money on moonshine. In his inquiry into the fundamental reasons for poverty in Finland, Kianto writes with great sympathy for the downtrodden and the oppressed, and his protagonists in both of these novels are shown to be people whose human worth is indisputable. But with large families to support and little opportunity to develop lasting economic security, somebody's need for booze offers more promise for the future than political self-determination.

KIELLAND, ALEXANDER LANGE (1849–1906). A Norwegian novelist and short story writer, Kielland is considered one of the finest stylists in Norwegian literature. He was born into a wealthy merchant family in the city of Stavanger, Norway. After graduating from the town's Latin School, he took a law degree at the university in Christiania (now Oslo), married, and purchased a brickworks near his hometown. Dissatisfied with his life, however, he read, among others, the Danish philosopher **Søren Kierkegaard**, and in 1878 he left Stavanger for Paris, hoping to become a writer. His first book appeared, through the assistance of **Bjørnstjerne Bjørnson**, as *Novelletter* (1879; tr. *Tales of Two Countries*, 1891). Encouraged by the Danish **critic Georg Brandes**, Kielland next wrote a novel, *Garman og Worse* (1880; tr. *Garman and Worse*, 1885), in which he drew heavily on his own family history; the book combines biting satire with a realistic portrait of Stavanger life in a bygone age.

Kielland's purpose was not to write cultural history, but rather to castigate numerous social ills: class distinctions, hypocrisy and the abuse of power by state church ministers and other religious leaders, the stupidity of the school system, and lack of integrity in business and industry. His next novel, *Arbeidsfolk* (1881; Workers), is extremely polemical, but without the wit, style, and grace of his best works. Similarly to *Arbeidsfolk*, his several next novels privileged heavy-handed satire over style and characterization. *Else* (1881; tr. *Elsie: A Christmas Story*, 1894) castigated the rich for their lack of concern for the poor, and *Skipper Worse* (1882; tr. 1885), a prequel to *Garman og Worse*, offers a satirical account of how religion can be used to obtain power. But a slender volume of short stories, *To*

Novelletter fra Danmark (1882; tr. in *Norse Tales and Sketches*, 1896), shows that Kielland had not lost his skills as a writer. The short story "Karen," contained in that volume, is a masterpiece of irony and wit, but without the satire that, as practiced in most of Kielland's novels, could only detract from his artistry.

Three of Kielland's next novels are set in Stavanger, but in the author's own time. *Gift* (1883; Poison) and *Fortuna* (1884; Fortune; both are translated as *Professor Lovdahl*, 1904) attack, respectively, the Latin School and the questionable ethics of the business world. *Sankt Hans Fest* (1887; Saint John's Festival) excoriates religious bigotry, and *Sne* (1886; tr. *Snow*, 1887), also set in southwestern Norway, shows what happens when fundamentalist religion mixes with conservative politics.

Kielland was not much of a dramatist, but he wrote several light and entertaining plays, including *Tre Par* (1886; tr. *Three Couples*, 1917), *Bettys Formynder* (1887; Betty's Guardian), and *Professoren* (1888; The Professor), which became notorious for its unflattering portrait of the philosophy professor **Marcus Jacob Monrad**. The novel *Jacob* (1891) concludes Kielland's fictional oeuvre. It has been suggested that he may have exhausted his poetic gifts, but also that changes in the literary climate, which no longer favored social criticism as much as before, may account for his sudden abandonment of creative writing. In the final 15 years of his life he turned his talents to writing letters and is known as Norway's most artful correspondent.

KIERKEGAARD, SØREN (1813–1855). A Danish philosopher and man of letters, Kierkegaard is considered the father of existentialism, an important movement in 20th-century European philosophy and culture. Raised by a well-to-do merchant father from whom he inherited a predisposition toward depression, Kierkegaard grew up in Copenhagen and attended the university there, taking degrees in theology and philosophy. His father's wealth freed him from the necessity of earning a living, so he was able to focus entirely on his writing projects. There are few external events of much significance in Kierkegaard's life. The influence of a short-lived engagement to a young woman named Regine Olsen can be discerned in some of his writings about young men and love, as can a mysterious experience that he refers to as "the great earthquake," possibly a moment of insight into his father's religious life, which led Kierkegaard to leave home for a period of time.

Kierkegaard's literary debut was an essay in literary **criticism** entitled *Af en endnu Levendes Papirer* (1838; tr. *Early Polemic Writings: One Still Living*, 1990). He also published his M.A. thesis in philosophy, *Om Begrebet Ironie med stadigt Hensyn til Socrates* (1841; tr. *The Concept of Irony with Constant Reference to Socrates*, 1989), a critique of romantic irony, which Kierkegaard considered it irresponsible to indulge in.

Having broken the engagement to Regine Olsen, Kierkegaard spent a period of time in Berlin that marks the beginning of a 13-year period of immense productivity. Under the pseudonym Victor Eremita he soon published ***Enten-Eller*** (1843; tr. *Either/Or*, 1944), in which he presented his theory of the aesthetic and the ethical spheres of existence. The Kierkegaardian esthete is focused on either sensual or intellectual pleasure and is typified by the immediate or the reflective seducer, while the ethical person is centered on living responsibly as a member of society. But *Enten-Eller* also adumbrates what Kierkegaard calls the religious stage, which, along with the aesthetic and the ethical, is further discussed in *Stadier paa Livets Vei* (1845; tr. *Stages on Life's Way*, 1940). The religious stage is further analyzed in *Gjentagelsen* (1843; tr. *Repetition*, 1941), narrated by the pseudonymous Constantin Constantius. At the same time Kierkegaard also published *Frygt og Bæven* (1843; tr. *Fear and Trembling*, 1939), in which Abraham's intended sacrifice of his son Isaac is presented as a means of obtaining a kind of faith that is beyond reason and thus paradoxical.

The paradox of faith is also discussed in *Philosophiske Smuler* (1844; tr. *Philosophical Fragments*, 1936), while original sin, the sin inherited from the transgression of Adam and Eve, is the topic of *Begrebet Angest* (1844; tr. *The Concept of Dread*, 1944). *Afsluttende uvidenskabelig Efterskrift* (1846; tr. *Concluding Unscientific Postscript*, 1941), a sequel to *Philosophiske Smuler*, argues that truth is found in subjectivity because only individuals, not groups of people, are able to gain true religious faith through a consciousness of sin.

Having been subjected to ridicule by the editor of a Copenhagen satirical magazine, Kierkegaard largely withdrew from human company and intensified his writing. *Kjerlighedens Gjerninger* (1847; tr. *Works of Love*, 1946) emphasizes the idea that the paramount duty of human beings is to follow the will of God, while *Sygdommen til Døden* (1849; tr. *The Sickness unto Death*, 1941) catalogues various forms of despair, which are regarded as a consequence of ignoring God's will. *Indøvelse i Christendom* (1850; tr. *Training in Christianity*, 1941) suggests that martyrdom is a necessary component of true faith; this idea led Kierkegaard to become increasingly critical of the Danish church. A series of pamphlets with the common title *Øieblikket* (1855; tr. *Kierkegaard's Attack upon "Christendom,"* 1844) vigorously argued that the church had become lukewarm and given to compromise.

Synspunktet for min Forfatter-Virksomhed (written in 1848, but published posthumously in 1859; tr. *The Point of View for My Work as an Author*, 1939) explains that the true purpose of all of Kierkegaard's writings, including the aesthetic ones, was fundamentally religious. Such works as *Atten opbyggelige Taler* (1843; tr. *Eighteen Edifying Discourses*, 1943–1946), which like *Kjerlighedens Gjerninger* was published under the author's own name, further support that assertion.

KIHLMAN, CHRISTER (1930–). A Finland-Swedish novelist, Kihlman has his social background in upper levels of the Swedish-speaking minority, against whose value system he rebelled strongly in his writing. After publishing two volumes of poetry in the early 1950s, Kihlman achieved notoriety with an essay entitled "Svenskhetens slagskugga" (1959; tr. "The Shadow Cast by Swedishness," 1986), in which he accused his social and linguistic group of cultural narrowness and moral hypocrisy. The novel that he published the following year, *Se upp Salige!* (1960; Look Out, You Blessed!), was a harsh and satirical attack on a number of big names in the history of Finland-Swedish culture.

In *Den blå modern* (1963; tr. *The Blue Mother*, 1990) and *Madeleine* (1965), Kihlman offers further descriptions of decadence and lack of ethics in the lives of prominent figures—however fictional—in Finland-Swedish society. In *Människan som skalv: En bok om det oväsentliga* (1971; The Human Who Trembled: A Book about the Inessential), he lays blame on both capitalist society and remnants of Christianity. *Dyre prins* (1975; tr. *Sweet Prince*, 1983) features the corruption of international business. In *Alla mina söner* (1980; tr. *All My Sons*, 1984) Kihlman attracted much attention to his frank portrayal of his relationship with an Argentine male prostitute named Juan; this theme is continued in *Livsdrömmen rena: Bok om maktlöshet* (1982; The Pure Dream of Life: A Book about Powerlessness). *På drift i förlustens landskap* (1986; Adrift in a Landscape of Loss) describes the raging jealousy of a bisexual man, while *Gerdt Bladhs undergång* (1987; tr. *The Downfall of Gerdt Bladh*, 1989) returns to Kihlman's favorite subject matter, the description of weakness, lack of integrity, and general degeneration among Finland-Swedes. *Om hopplöshetens möjligheter* (2000; On the Possibilities of Despair) contains an exchange of letters with the Finland-Swedish poet, short story writer, and journalist Mårten Westö (1967–), one of Finland's most promising young men of letters writing in Swedish.

KINGO, THOMAS (1634–1703). A Danish poet, Kingo was the embodiment of the baroque. With great intensity of feeling he wrote florid and hyperbolic poetry in praise of both God and man. Many of his occasional poems have been preserved, but his most significant achievement is his large number of religious poems and hymns, which have had a prominent place in the hymnals of both the Danish and the Norwegian state churches. Having taken a degree in theology, Kingo served in various ecclesiastical positions throughout his life, ultimately rising to the level of bishop.

Many of Kingo's occasional poems were for the entertainment of friends at the Danish manor houses, but *Hosianna* (1671; Hosannah) was written for the crowning of King Christian V. Two long topographical poems are *Kroneborgs korte Beskrivelse* (1672; Short Description of Kronborg) and *Samsøes korte Beskrivelse* (1675; Short Description of Samsø). During the **war** against Sweden in 1675–1679, Kingo wrote verse descriptions of the events of the war, *Ledings-Tog* (1676–1677; War Expedition).

Kingo's religious poetry was published in the two-part *Aandelige Sjunge-Kor* (1674–1681; Spiritual Singing Chorus), which contained morning songs, evening songs, versified versions of some of the psalms of David, and songs for various occasions; these songs were intended chiefly for use in the home. Two of the best-known songs are "Far, Verden, far vel" (Farewell, World) and "Sorrig og Glæde de vandre til Hobe" (Sorrow and Joy Walk Together). They express Kingo's view of the human condition in general.

Having received a commission to produce a new Danish hymnal, Kingo wrote a number of hymns that were published as *Vinter-Parten* (1689; The Winter Part) and intended for use at church services. Many of these hymns emphasize humankind's obligation to submit to the will of God. In a social system where there was little distinction between divine and royal authority, Kingo served his king well.

KIRK, HANS (1898–1962). A Danish journalist, **critic**, and novelist, Kirk took a law degree in 1922 and started his literary career as a journalist and critic in radical journals as well as the communist newspaper *Arbejderbladet* (The Workers' Paper). After publishing a number of short stories, he had his literary breakthrough with the book *Fiskerne* (1928; tr. *The Fishermen*, 1999), a collective novel set in Jutland. Influenced by both **Marxism** and **Freudianism**, Kirk tells the story of a group of fishermen and their families who relocate from a harsh coastal area to Limfjorden, a relatively sheltered district. Devout Christians of the Danish Inner Mission type, the parental generation watches as their children adopt less restrictive moral views that seem more appropriate to them in their less challenging surroundings. Kirk's talent for storytelling is also on display in two novels that discuss the process of industrialization in rural Denmark, *Daglejerne* (1936; tr. *The Day Laborers*, 2001) and *De ny Tider* (1939; tr. *The New Times*, 2001), in which small farmers become factory workers who experience life under capitalism but are largely unable to share Kirk's own Marxist convictions.

In the aftermath of World **War** II Kirk was disappointed that the defeat of Nazism did not result in much radical social change in Denmark. The novels *Vredens søn* (1950; The Son of Wrath) and *Slaven* (1948; tr. *The Slave*, 2000) are allegorical historical accounts in which social criticism trumps traditional artistic considerations. A book of memoirs, *Skyggespil* (1953; Play of Shadows), engagingly tells about Kirk's years growing up as the son of a country doctor who hated injustice and instilled in his son a commitment to social responsibility and human decency.

KIVI, ALEKSIS (1834–1872). A Finnish novelist, poet, and dramatist, Kivi is the father of the Finnish novel. Although he wrote only one, *Seitsemän veljestä* (1870; tr. *Seven Brothers*, 1929, 1973, 1991), it is the best-known novel in Finnish, and its contents are familiar to virtually all Finns. It has been translated into a number of languages. Kivi is also the originator of drama in the Finnish language, and his plays still have a significant presence on the Finnish stage.

Kivi was the son of a village tailor and had great difficulties being admitted as a student at Helsinki University. Not a particularly good student, he nevertheless read widely and tried his hand at writing. His comedy *Nummisuutarit* (1864; tr. *The Heath Cobblers*, 1993) won a prize and established Kivi as an important man of letters. During the next few years, while living in the home of a woman several years his senior, he displayed a truly amazing level of productivity, writing 12 plays and a considerable amount of highly original poetry. Partly on account of some negative **critical** response to his novel, Kivi was forced to enter a mental hospital, from which he was discharged a broken man; he died at the home of his brother a few months later.

Kivi's first play was the tragedy *Kullervo* (1864; tr. 1993), which takes its subject from the *Kalevala*. Kivi stays close to the epic but emphasizes Kullervo's inability to control his own nature. When Kullervo, in the manner of classical tragedy, takes his life in the end, it is because he is a truly flawed character who is unable to adjust to living with other human beings. Some of Kivi's other dramas are the tragedy *Karkurit* (1866; Escapees) and the one-act comedy *Yö ja päivä* (1867; Night and Day).

Seitsemän veljestä is not only Kivi's best-known work but an exceptional work even in the context of world literature as a whole. The story is about seven orphaned brothers who resist a variety of social constraints, including the demand that they learn to read. Seeking refuge deep in the woods, they survive by fishing and hunting but eventually start farming. Each brother is a distinct individual whose character and personality are revealed by his actions, as Kivi is a quite unobtrusive narrator. The brothers learn many lessons from their struggle for survival and eventually become prepared to go back to civilization. The novel ends with a summary of what becomes of them; all but one end up with families of their own. An immensely rich literary work, *Seitsemän veljestä* can be read on many different levels and from many different perspectives, and this is partly the reason for its enduring power. Kivi's poetry was so radically different from what was written by other Finns during his lifetime that it took almost a hundred years before it became fully appreciated. He published only a single volume, *Kanervala* (1866; Where the Heath Grows), but left many more poems in manuscript.

KJÆR, NILS (1870–1924). A Norwegian essayist, **critic**, and dramatist, Kjær published several collections of literary and other essays, among them *Essays—Fremmede Forfattere* (1895; Essays on Foreign Writers), *Bøger og Billeder* (1898; Books and Images), *Smaa Epistler* (1908; Small Epistles), *Nye Epistler* (1912; New Epistles), and *Svundne Somre* (1920; Summers of the Past). His first play, *Regnskabets Dag* (1902; The Day of Reckoning), takes aim at moral and ethical relativism, while *Det lykkelige Valg* (1913; The Happy Election) is a witty and satirical comedy in which a longtime member of parliament loses an election to his wife.

KJÆRSTAD, JAN (1953–). A Norwegian novelist and short story writer, Kjærstad has been active both as a writer and as a participant in literary debate. He has been an important presence on the Norwegian parnassus since his debut with the short story collection *Kloden dreier stille rundt* (1980; The Planet Quietly Rotates). With an advanced degree in theology from the University of Oslo, and having written on the theologians Rudolf Bultmann, Reinholt Niebuhr, and Leszek Kolakowski, Kjærstad writes about such ethical issues as pollution, drugs, and racism. His first novel, *Speil: Leseserie fra det 20. århundre* (1982; Mirrors: A Series of Readings from the 20th Century), also takes issue with the contemporary use of technology. His definitive breakthrough, however, came with *Homo falsus, eller Det perfekte mord* (1984; Homo Falsus; or, The Perfect Murder), which was well received by both the **critics** and the public. A highly metafictive text, it foregrounds its own creation to an extraordinary degree. A young woman named Greta (after the movie actress Greta Garbo) lures three men to their deaths by first sending them letters and then taking them to borrowed apartments, where they disappear physically through sexual acts that have a mystical, and thus unexplained, component that may be labeled tantric. The narrator, who is Greta's fourth victim, barely escapes with his life, but he is later placed in a psychiatric hospital after Greta has taken over as narrator of the book. The question of who is really telling the story, Greta or the narrator, is never resolved.

Kjærstad's next novel, *Det store eventyret* (1987; The Great Fairy Tale), turns Oslo into the capital of a country in the developing world, an island located somewhere in the Indian Ocean. Its numerous intertextual references, unorthodox typography, and mixture of genres made it tough for some critics to accept. Other critics have appreciated it as an interesting example of literary **postmodernism**. The postmodern features in *Rand* (1990; Edge) are even more pronounced. A murder mystery with a serious message and carefully constructed characters, it mixes genres and conventions, thus appearing "impure" and confusing to some. But *Rand* also celebrates Kjærstad's hometown, Oslo, in a manner reminiscent of **Knut Hamsun**'s novel *Sult*.

Kjærstad's most significant work is a three-volume fictional biography of one Jonas Wergeland, but each volume presents a different version of the man. *Forføreren* (1993; tr. *The Seducer*, 2003), the first volume, is narrated by an Indian ethnographer, who presents Wergeland as a promising young man whom women find very attractive. The second volume, *Erobreren* (1996; The Conqueror), is narrated by Wergeland's sister, Rakel, who casts him as a famous television personality riddled with personal problems. The third volume, *Oppdageren* (1999; The Discoverer), is narrated partly by Wergeland himself and partly by his daughter Kristin. By offering multiple perspectives on the subject of the supposed biography, Kjærstad moves readers to reconsider their perception of truth and to abandon the idea that truth is something unchanging or objective. *Oppdageren* garnered the author the **Nordic Literary Prize** in 2001.

Tegn til kjærlighet (2002; Signs of Love) features a graphic designer who, on a quest for the perfect type font, falls in love with a storyteller; she causes him to die because she uses one of his stories for a wildly successful novel she writes. She brings him back to life by wrapping his body in a text, but she still loses him as her lover.

Kjærstad's fragmented narration and allegorical plot leave the story open to many different interpretations.

Kjærstad has also published **children's books** and collections of essays on literature and culture. His essays show that he is very well informed about both contemporary world literature and literary theory.

KRISTENSEN, TOM (1893–1974). A Danish poet, novelist, and **critic**, Kristensen came from a lower-middle-class background, the values of which he wanted to transcend. His literary debut was a collection of poetry, *Fribytterdrømme* (1920; Dreams of a Freebooter), which was marked by **modernism**'s rebellion against traditional poetic forms. His next volume of poetry, *Paafuglefjeren* (1922; The Peacock Feather), was inspired by a trip to China and Japan. The poems in *Mirakler* (1922; Miracles), however, show that Kristensen was attracted to Christianity, and particularly Roman Catholicism. The travel book *En Kavaler i Spanien* (1926; A Cavalier in Spain) also contains many important poems, and *Verdslige Sange* (1927; Worldly Songs) discusses the contrast between woman as a sexual being and woman as Madonna. Death, seen from a Christian perspective, is the subject of the poetry collection *Mod den yderste Rand* (1936; Toward the Outermost Edge), while *Digte i Døgnet* (1940; Poems at All Hours) contains memorial poems. Kristensen's undogmatic Christian outlook is also found in his final volume of poetry, *Den sidste Lygte* (1954; The Last Lamp).

To Danish literature, Kristensen is more significant as a novelist than as a poet. His first novel, *Livets Arabesk* (1921; The Arabesque of Life), is written in the style of **expressionism** and contains ideas similar to those in *Fribytterdrømme*. The novel *En Anden* (1923; Someone Else) is, like the poetry collection *Paafuglefjeren*, influenced by his travels in Asia and tells about a man's desperate search for a sense of identity through reflections on his childhood. Identity is also a major theme in Kristensen's most significant novel, *Hærværk* (1930; tr. *Havoc*, 1968), which is set in Copenhagen in the 1920s and details the self-destructive behavior of the literary critic Ole Jastrau, Kristensen's alter ego. Together with the character Steffensen, a poet and communist, Jastrau seeks for life's meaning in both alcohol and a flirtation with Catholicism, which Steffensen finally embraces, thus being saved from complete disintegration. Jastrau is not quite that lucky, however, as his existential quest is not exactly crowned with success, but there is a glimmer of hope in the end. After *Hærværk*, which was a tremendous success, Kristensen wrote no more novels. He maintained his interest in Catholic religion, however, as demonstrated by a travel narrative, *Rejse i Italien* (1951; Travel in Italy). He was very productive as a literary critic and brought many important writers to the attention of the Danes. His criticism can be found in a number of collections.

KRISTIN LAVRANSDATTER. A trilogy by the Norwegian **Sigrid Undset**, *Kristin Lavransdatter* consists of the volumes *Kransen* (1920; tr. *The Bridal Wreath*, 1923), *Husfrue* (1922; tr. *The Mistress of Husaby*, 1925), and *Korset* (1922; tr. *The Cross*, 1927). Set in medieval times, it tells the story of Kristin's life from her childhood to her death from the bubonic plague.

KROG, HELGE (1889–1962). A Norwegian dramatist, **critic**, and essayist, Krog started out with two plays about social injustice. *Det store vi* (1917; The Big We) dealt with abuse of the power of the press, and *Jarlshus* (1923; Earl's House) presented a labor conflict. Krog's most successful dramas, however, depict unconventional **women** in a lighthearted manner. The female protagonist in *Konkylien* (1929; The Conch Shell) goes from one man to the next in her search for ideal love, while the heroine in *Underveis* (1931; tr. *On the Way*, 1939) refuses to marry in spite of the fact that she is pregnant. In *Opbrudd* (1936; tr. *Break-Up*, 1939), the protagonist, Vibeke, rejects both her husband and her lover for their selfish individualism.

KROHN, LEENA (1947–). A Finnish novelist, short story writer, poet, and essayist, Krohn began her literary career by publishing a collection of **fairy tales**, *Vihreä vallankumous* (1970; The Green Revolution), which was followed by one more such volume and then by some stories, *Viimeinen kesävieras* (1974; The Last Summer Guest). Next Krohn published a fairy-tale-like novel, *Ihmisen vaatteissa* (1976; In Human Garb), that featured such conflicts as those between **nature** and civilization. Her career took off when she published *Donna Quijote ja muita kaupunkilaisia* (1983; tr. *Doña Quixote and Other Citizens; Gold of Ophir*, 1995); this book is a collection of short stories which share the same protagonist, an eccentric woman living in a city. In Krohn's next book, *Tainaron* (1985; tr. 2004), an epistolary novel of sorts, the characters are insects. Another book about the eccentric lady followed, entitled *Oofirin kultaa* (1987; tr. *Doña Quixote and Other Citizens; Gold of Ophir*, 1995). In the novel *Umbra* (1990) the title character is a collector of paradoxes.

A later volume of short stories entitled somewhat paradoxically *Älä lue tätä kirjaa* (1994; Do Not Read This Book) was followed by another short story collection, *Ettei etälsyys ikäväisi* (1995; That Distance Shall Not Yearn). Then came *Pereat mundus, romaani, eräänlainen* (1998; Pereat Mundus: A Novel of Sorts), several other novels, and *Unelmakuolema* (2004; A Dream Death), which tells about Lucia, an anesthetist who suffers from insomnia and works two jobs, one at a clinic that helps people to die easily and one where they freeze you in order to thaw you again once a cure for your illness has been found.

Krohn's essays have been published as *Rapina ja muita papereita* (1989; Rustling and Other Papers), *Tribar* (1993), *Kynä ja kone* (1996; The Pen and the Machine), and *3 sokeaa miestä ja 1 näkevä* (2003; Three Blind Men and One You Can See). Krohn's poetry emphasizes metrical patterns.

KRUSENSTJERNA, AGNES VON (1894–1940). A Swedish novelist, Krusenstjerna was descended from **Erik Gustaf Geijer** and was born into a noble family. In poor mental health much of her life, she produced a semi-autobiographical series about a woman named Tony, consisting of *Tony växer upp* (1922; Tony Grows Up), *Tonys läroår* (1924; Tony's Apprenticeship), and *Tonys sista läroår* (1924; The Last Year of Tony's Apprenticeship), in which Tony is portrayed as suffering a mental breakdown. Her seven novels with the common title *Fröknerna von Pahlen* (1930–1935; The Misses von Pahlen) gave rise to a heated debate about her portrayal of female sexuality. Krusenstjerna's final work was a tetralogy, *Fattigadel* (1935–1938;

Impoverished Nobility), in which she exposed the private lives of members of her family.

KYRKLUND, WILLY (1921–). Recognized as a masterful practitioner of Swedish prose, Kyrklund is best known for his short stories and novels, although he has also written plays. He had his literary debut with a collection of stories, *Ångvälten och andra noveller* (1948; The Steamroller and Other Stories), which gave nine examples of his trademark style: a mixture of **realism**, myth, and exotic ideas with an emphasis on irony and parody. Other books in a similar vein are *Hermelinens död* (1954; The Death of the Ermine) and *Den överdrivne älskaren* (1957; The Exaggerated Lover), the last of which focuses on folly associated with love, which for Kyrklund is a very fertile field of study. Emotions in a more general sense constitute the theme of *Den rätta känslan* (1974; The Right Feeling), in which the stories ironically explore emotions gone awry. The narratives in *8 variationer* (1982; Eight Variations) illustrate a statement by the Greek philosopher Heraclitus to the effect that the future belongs to the rising generation; they are further unified by their reliance on musical terms. Notable among them is "Återtaget drag" (Retracted Move), in which the legend of William Tell is told with a significant twist: Tell ends up as a poor shoemaker rather than a hero.

Kyrklund's novels are brief, too, and are perhaps even less conventional than his short stories. *Tvåsam* (1949; Twosome) features two characters, Övervaktmästaren (the Janitorial Supervisor) and Vaktmästaren (the Janitor), who are at odds with each other in the manner of a **Freudian** ego and super-ego, and who may be regarded as different aspects of the same individual. By problematizing the identity of his protagonist, Kyrklund questions traditional narrative conventions in a manner that prefigures the **postmodern** novel. Tension between characters is also a feature of *Mästaren Ma* (1952; Master Ma), which draws on Kyrklund's studies in Chinese culture. The master's teachings are contradicted both by his wife Yao and his disciple Li, leaving readers free to articulate their own personal wisdom.

One of the chief characteristics of Kyrklund's works is that they are maddeningly difficult to classify. Best thought of as a collage, *Polyfem förvandlad* (1964; Polyphemus Transformed) uses Ovid's *Metamorphoses* as an intertext, but with such twists as when the story of Odysseus's escape from the eponymous Cyclops is narrated from Polyphemus's point of view.

Classical literature is also present in Kyrklund's drama *Medea från Mbongo* (Medea from Mbongo; collected in *Från Bröllopet till Medea*, 1967; From the Wedding to Medea), in which the story of Jason and Medea has been both radically simplified and given a semimodern setting. Also inspired by Greek mythology, *Gudar och människar* (1978; Gods and Humans) has a strong political message, as it offers a critique of technology and international business that is very much in the spirit of the 1970s.

– L –

LAGERKVIST, PÄR (1891–1974). A Swedish poet, dramatist, short story writer, and novelist, Lagerkvist is a major figure in Scandinavian literature and was awarded the **Nobel Prize** in 1951. Born in Växjö in Småland, he briefly attended Uppsala University, after which he traveled to Paris. Introduced there to the most recent currents in modern art, and particularly to cubism, he wrote the manifesto *Ordkonst och bildkonst* (1913; Verbal Art and Pictorial Art) upon his return to Sweden. Speaking against **realism** and in favor of **expressionism**, Lagerkvist became one of the foremost exponents of **modernism** in Scandinavia.

After some lackluster literary experiments, Lagerkvist published *Järn och människor* (1915; tr. *Iron and Men*, 1988), a volume of short stories dealing with World War I. His literary breakthrough came with the poetry collection *Ångest* (1916; Anguish), a monument to the modernistic sensibilities of the time, as it emphasized fragmentation, loneliness, and absence of meaning. *Ångest* was succeeded by *Kaos* (1919; Chaos).

Lagerkvist maintained that the chaos and violence of the modern age called for a new kind of drama. His essay *Modern teater* (1918; tr. *Modern Theatre*, 1961) argued against the dramatic practice of the Norwegian playwright **Henrik Ibsen** and spoke in favor of the antirealist dramaturgy of such plays as **August Strindberg**'s *Ett drömspel*. He then wrote a series of plays in which he attempted to put these ideas into practice. *Sista människan* (1917; tr. *The Last Man*, 1988) is set at a time when most of the population of the earth has been wiped out by some type of catastrophe, and the three one-act plays of *Den svåra stunden* (1918; tr. *The Difficult Hour*, 1961) all deal with death. *Himlens hemlighet* (1919; tr. *The Secret of Heaven*, 1966) presents the human quest for meaning as utterly futile. *Det eviga leendet* (1920; tr. *The Eternal Smile*, 1934) and other prose works from this period are constructed around similar ideas. Children are presented as a source of joy in *Det eviga leendet*, however, but the prose piece "Far och jag" ("Father and I") in *Onda sagor* (1924; Evil Tales) belies the idea that childhood is necessarily a happy time. The autobiographical novel *Gäst hos verkligheten* (1925; tr. *Guest of Reality*, 1936) also indicates that Lagerkvist's childhood and youth were not particularly happy, but rather a process of gradual disenchantment with the religious beliefs of his family, accompanied by fear and guilt.

Lagerkvist was exceptionally far-sighted in his perception of the changes in European politics in the 1930s. Travels in Germany and Italy opened his eyes to the threat to humanism posed by the respective regimes of the two countries, and he lifted his voice in a warning against the Fascist ideology earlier than most other writers. *Bödeln* (1933, tr. *The Hangman*, 1936) shows that the cruelty of the Middle Ages was far surpassed by the barbarism of Nazi Germany. A number of prose works written in the 1930s, among them *Den knutna näven* (1934; tr. *The Clenched Fist*, 1988), had as their purpose to alert a broader audience to the threat and to remind them of the values of humanism. The drama *Mannen utan själ* (1936; tr. *The Man without a Soul*, 1944) had a similar purpose, as did several other plays written in the 1940s, namely, *Midsommardröm i fattighuset* (1941; tr. *Midsummer Dream in the Workhouse*, 1953), *Den vises sten* (1947; tr. *The Philosopher's Stone*, 1966), and *Låt människan leva* (1949; tr. *Let Man Live*, 1951).

After World **War** II, Lagerkvist wrote mostly novels. An exception is his final poetry collection, *Aftonland* (1953; tr. *Evening Land*, 1975), which expressed ideas similar to those found in his prose writings. The novel *Dvärgen* (1944; tr. *The Dwarf*, 1945) is a study in evil set in Renaissance Italy. Narrated by the title character, it expresses his complete lack of comprehension of human love and shows that he has no understanding of the value of art and science, except as tools of warfare. *Barabbas* (1950; tr. 1951) tells the story of the criminal who was set free instead of Jesus at the time of the crucifixion. Like Lagerkvist himself, Barabbas is drawn to Christianity, but his doubts are too great for him to overcome them. The novel *Sibyllan* (1956; tr. *The Sybil*, 1958) has as its protagonist Ahasuerus, of the legend of the Wandering Jew, who tries to understand why God has cursed him with the inability to die.

Lagerkvist's last several books all deal with the situation of human beings in relation to the divine. *Ahasverus död* (1960; tr. *The Death of Ahasuerus*, 1962), *Pilgrim på havet* (1962; tr. *Pilgrim at Sea*, 1964), and *Det heliga landet* (1964; tr. *The Holy Land*, 1966) show that even though people are a mixture of good and evil, most people may still eventually be able to come to terms with the divine. These ideas are further explored in the more pessimistic novel *Mariamne* (1967; tr. *Herod and Mariamne*, 1968), in which Herod's love for Mariamne is insufficient to redeem him from the evil he carries within him. *See also* THEATER.

LAGERLÖF, SELMA (1858–1940). A Swedish novelist, Lagerlöf became world renowned and received the **Nobel Prize** in 1909. She had her literary debut at the time of the transition from the **naturalism** of the 1880s to the **neoromanticism** of the 1890s, Scandinavia's version of **symbolism** in literature. Her first book, the novel *Gösta Berlings saga* (1891; tr. *The Story of Gösta Berling*, 1898), exemplifies this transition. Set in Lagerlöf's home district of Värmland at the end of the 1820s, it tells the story of Ekeby Manor, its mistress Margareta Celsing, and the 12 cavaliers whom she supports in a life of refined idleness. The cavaliers have entered into a pact with the devil, represented by the cantankerous squire Sintram, that they will bring all economic activity at Ekeby to a halt for one year. They succeed, but at great cost to the local community. The story of the defrocked priest Gösta Berling is at the center of the novel, as he is both one of the leading cavaliers and one of the book's several characters in need of reformation of character. Ultimately, Lagerlöf's theme in *Gösta Berlings saga* is the age-old conflict between good and evil, and she offers psychological as well as mythical depictions of how good will triumph in the end. Her ethical concerns are also at the core of a collection of stories entitled *Osynliga länkar* (1894; tr. *Invisible Links*, 1899).

Lagerlöf makes extensive use of Christian imagery, which can be found, for example, in some of the stories in the volume *Drottningar i Kungahälla jämte andra berättelser* (1897; tr. *The Queens of Kungahälla and Other Tales*, 1917). In her second novel, *Antikrists mirakler* (1897; tr. *The Miracles of Antichrist*, 1899), she compares Christianity and socialism, while *Kristuslegender* (1904; tr. *Christ Legends*, 1908) recounts many tales of saints.

Extreme or abnormal states of mind are depicted in many of Lagerlöf's books. The novel *En herrgårdssägen* (1899; tr. *From a Swedish Homestead*, 1901), for example, presents a mentally ill man who is rescued and brought back to health through the efforts of the woman who loves him. The great epic novel *Jerusalem I-II* (1901–1902; tr. *Jerusalem 1 and 2*, 1915–1918) tells about a group of Swedish farmers who believe that God has called them to leave their ancestral homes and emigrate to Palestine. The protagonist in *Herr Arnes penningar* (1903; tr. *Herr Arne's Hoard*, 1923) is Elsalill, who has fallen in love with the leader of a band of men who murdered the priest Arne and his entire household, including Elsalill's foster sister. The ghost of the foster sister makes certain that Elsalill finally recognizes the murderer as such, after which Elsalill takes her life in order to prevent the murderers from escaping their fate.

Nils Holgerssons underbara resa genom Sverige (1906–1907; tr. *The Wonderful Adventures of Nils*, 1907, and *Further Adventures of Nils*, 1911) has taught geography to generations of Swedish schoolchildren. The young Nils is unkind to animals, and as punishment he is shrunk by a gnome, after which he travels around Sweden on the back of a goose. Like the characters in *Gösta Berlings saga*, he eventually reforms and is allowed to return to his normal size. The novel teaches moral lessons as well as lessons in geography.

In the shadow of the impending World **War** I, Lagerlöf's next books were darker in tone. The novel *Körkarlen* (1912; tr. *Thy Soul Shall Bear Witness*, 1921) offers an all too realistic portrait of a tyrannical husband and father, while *Kejsarn av Portugallien* (1914; tr. *The Emperor of Portugallia*, 1917) features a father who has lost his sanity. In her novel *Bannlyst* (1918; tr. *The Outcast*, 1920), Lagerlöf speaks in favor of pacifism. In her last major work, a trilogy consisting of the novels *Löwensköldska ringen* (1925; tr. *The General's Ring*, 1928), *Charlotte Löwensköld* (1925, tr. 1928), and *Anna Svärd* (1928; tr. 1931), Lagerlöf tells the story of a man who may or may not be capable of redemption. It is thus a more ambivalent tale than the relatively edifying narratives that preceeded it and is perhaps a result of the traumas of World War I.

LANDSMAAL. A written form of Norwegian created in the 19th century by **Ivar Aasen**, Landsmaal (country language) is based on Norway's many different popular dialects and was offered as an alternative to the Danish-influenced Riksmaal (later known as bokmål, or book language). A simpler version of Landsmaal was created by **Aasmund Olafsson Vinje**. The standard is now the less old-fashioned **nynorsk**.

LAXNESS, HALLDÓR KILJAN (1902–1998). An Icelandic novelist, short story writer, poet, essayist, and dramatist, Laxness was an extremely prolific writer from his debut in 1927 until becoming disabled with progressive dementia in the 1990s. A **Nobel Prize** winner in 1955, he is Iceland's best-known modern literary artist. His debut was the autobiographical novel *Vefarinn mikli frá Kasmír* (1927; The Great Weaver from Kashmir), which he wrote after several years of travel in Europe and which offers a young man's rash opinions about the cultural and moral ideas of the age. A stay in the United States during the difficult late 1920s made him a socialist, which is reflected in his two novels about a young woman named Salka Valka, who becomes involved in social justice work in an Icelandic fishing village; the novels bear the titles *Þú vívíður hreini* (1931) and *Fuglinn í fjörunni* (1932; tr. together as *Salka Valka*, 1936). Another novel about poor but resilient Icelanders is *Sjálfstætt fólk* (1934–1935; tr. *Independent People*, 1945–1946), which tells about the life of a sheep farmer. The trilogy *Heimsljós* (1937–1940; tr. *World Light*, 1969) has a poor local poet as its protagonist.

In 1944 Iceland became politically independent for the first time in almost seven centuries, and the publication of Laxness's trilogy *Íslandsklukkan* (1943–1946; Iceland's Bell) coincided with this event. The trilogy gives a faithful historical representation of life in Iceland at the turn of the 18th century. There is also a political dimension to the diary novel *Atómstöðin* (1948; tr. *The Atom Station*, 1961), in which a young housemaid from the countryside tells about her experiences during a year's stay in Reykjavík, at a time when Icelandic politicians were dealing with a demand from the United States for the right to establish a permanent military base there. *Grepla* (1952; tr. *The Happy Warriors*, 1958), on the other hand, draws on the Old Icelandic sagas, but it too has a strongly pacifist message.

The novel *Brekkukotsannáll* (1957; tr. *The Fish Can Sing*, 1966) has as its setting Reykjavík around the year 1900, the time when the narrator grew up there, but the events are viewed from a point in time when the narrator has long been an adult. A novel about the conditions and demands of art, it has many parallels with Laxness's own life. So does, to a certain extent, the novel *Paradísarheimt* (1960; tr. *Paradise Reclaimed*, 1962), which takes as its theme the search for a spiritual paradise on earth. As a young man, Laxness had converted to Roman Catholicism, and he maintained an interest in spiritual matters throughout his life. The protagonist in *Paradísarheimt* finds his personal paradise among the Mormons in Utah, but when he goes back to Iceland as a missionary and chances upon his old farmstead, he comes to realize that paradise had been right under his nose all along.

In *Kristnihald undir Jökli* (1968; tr. *Christianity at Glacier*, 1972), in which a young theologian is charged with investigating the activities of a distant pastor, Laxness probes the limits of objectivity and the conditions under which truth may be established. These concerns also dominate his final two novels, *Innansveitarkronika* (1970; A Local Chronicle) and *Gudsgjafapula* (1972; A List of God's Gifts), which tells about how a young writer gets a start in life.

Laxness also wrote four volumes of memoirs from his early youth. A volume of poetry, *Kvædakver* (1930; Small Book of Poems), was republished in an augmented edition in 1949. Of his several plays, one bears mention: *Dúfnaveislan: skemtunaleikur í fimm þáttum* (1966; tr. *The Pigeon Banquet*, 1973). He also published several volumes of short stories and numerous essays.

LEHTONEN, JOEL (1881–1934). A Finnish novelist, short story writer, and poet, Lehtonen never knew his father and became a ward of the community owing to his mother's poverty and doubtful reputation. Raised by the kind widow of a local minister, he received an education and worked as a journalist for some time. The young Lehtonen adopted a **neoromantic** and Nietzschean view of life and quickly produced several works: the long poem *Perm* (1904; Perm), the novel *Paholaisen viulu* (1904; The Devil's Fiddle), the short story collection *Villi* (1905; Savage), and *Mataleena* (1905; Magdalen), a novel that commented on his own origins. These books featured artistically inclined rebels and were well received.

Some travel in Europe broadened Lehtonen's outlook and helped him develop a more tolerant attitude. He bought property in his home district of Savonlinna, published a couple of collections of folktales, and returned to his travels, during which time he was very active as a translator of classical European literature. A travel book from this time is *Myrtti ja alppiruusu* (1911; Myrtle and Rhododendron).

During these years Lehtonen also published four collections of poetry: *Nuoruus* (1911; Youth), *Rakkaita muistoja* (1911; Beloved Memories), *Markkinoilta* (1912; From the Fair), and *Munkki-kammio* (1914; The Monk's Cell). But his greatest achievement is the Putkinotko books, three novels and a collection of short stories that feature a common cast of characters. The novel *Kerran kesällä* (1917; Once in Summer) represents a turning away from neoromanticism toward **realism** and criticizes those of his educated contemporaries who were stuck in the past. *Kuolleet omenapuut* (1918; Dead Apple Trees) contains short stories. *Putkinotko* (1919–1920) is a very long novel that attempts to capture the events of a single summer day and suggests that the beauty of summer, like the pleasant aspects of life, may be compensation for a person's unpleasantries and toil. The series concludes with the novel *Korpi ja puutarha* (1923; Wilderness and Garden). Lehtonen also wrote two books about his early childhood and his summers: *Onnen poika* (1925; Son of Fortune) and *Lintukoto* (1929, Birdhouse).

Lehtonen's personal life during these years was plagued by illness and pain, and his outlook on life gradually became increasingly pessimistic. Such novels as *Rakastunut rampa* (1922; A Cripple in Love), the two-part *Sorron lapset—Punainen mies* (1923–1925; The Oppressed—The Red Man), and *Henkien taistelu* (1933; Struggle of the Spirits) all offer extremely negative representations of Lehtonen's society. He voluntarily ended his life in 1934.

LEINO, EINO (1878–1926). A Finnish poet, novelist, and dramatist, Leino did for Finnish poetry what **Aleksis Kivi** had done for the Finnish novel. Highly gifted and very productive, Leino showed that the Finnish language had the resources that were needed to create great poetry in it. Leino stands as the originator of Finnish poetry, and his influence has been acknowledged by all of his successors. Leino was also a skilled translator and wrote enduring essays about Finnish literature.

Leino grew up in a middle-class family in northeastern Finland, close to Karelia. He received a good education and published his first poetry collection, *Maaliskuun lauluja* (1896; March Songs), at the age of 18. Of his nearly 30 collections of poetry, *Helkavirsiä I* (1903; tr. *Whitsongs*, 1978) is generally thought to be his finest; the long epic ballads are connected to the *Kalevala* tradition both thematically and formally. A companion volume, *Helkavirsiä II* (1916; Whitsongs), is reflective of the pessimistic mood during World **War** I.

Leino wrote poems about all manner of subjects, from such universal topics as **nature** and love to the current events of his day. He also wrote several novels, but they are considered much inferior to his poetry. *Päivä Helsingissä* (1905; A Day in Helsinki) is a satirical treatment of contemporary issues. The presentation of contemporary life is also the strength of a series of novels: *Tuomas Vitikka* (1906), *Jaana Rönty* (1907), and *Olli Suurpää* (1908). A series of plays in six parts bears the title *Naamioita* (1905–1911; Masks).

LENNGREN, ANNA MARIA (1754–1817). A Swedish poet of the Enlightenment, Lenngren is still very popular in her native country. This is no doubt in part due to the colloquial style in which she wrote, as well as to the humor and gentle Horatian satire of her view of life. Born into a well-educated family—her father taught Latin at Uppsala University—she distanced herself from the pietistic religious views of her home and appears to have been happy with her middle-class life. She married Carl Petter Lenngren, who was associated with the newspaper *Stockholms Posten* (The Stockholm Post), and for many years she wrote anonymously for the paper. Two of her satirical poems are "Min salig man" (My Blessed Departed Husband), a poem about a drunkard, and "Några ord till min kära Dotter, i fall jag hade någon" (A Few Words to My Dear Daughter, in Case I Had One), which offers satirical "advice" to a young woman. Lenngren would not allow her poetry to be published in book form while she was alive, but *Skaldeförsök* (1819; Poetic Attempts) came out after her death.

LEONORA CHRISTINA (1621–1698). A Danish writer, Leonora Christina was the daughter of King Christian IV and his second wife. She was married to a young noble named Corfitz Ulfeldt, who later acted treasonously toward the crown. For this reason, Leonora Christina was jailed from 1663 to 1685. She is remembered chiefly for a memoir she wrote mostly in the 1690s, *Jammers Minde* (published 1869; Memory of Woe; tr. *Memoirs by Leonora Christina, Daughter of Christian IV of Denmark*, 1929). She also wrote an autobiography in French (completed 1673).

LEVERTIN, OSCAR IVAR (1862–1906). A Swedish poet, novelist, short story writer, and **critic**, Levertin had little sympathy with the interest in folk culture that came to the fore in the 1890s; he preferred the city and the Greco-Roman past. His role as a newspaper critic was of great significance to Swedish literature, and his wide reading and highly cultivated taste made him a central figure in Swedish literary life. He started out as a **realist** with two collections of stories, *Småmynt* (1883; Small Change) and *Konflikter* (1985; Conflicts), but a meeting with **Verner von Heidenstam** had a strong impact on him. Together Heidenstam and Levertin wrote the satirical essay "Pepitas bröllop" (1890; Pepita's Wedding), which was published as a pamphlet and argued against the aesthetics of **naturalism** and in favor of a greater concern with the interior lives of literary characters.

Levertin's first poetry collection, *Lengender och visor* (1891; Legends and Songs), is characterized by his concern with the themes of love and death and exemplifies the subjectivism of the 1890s. Other volumes of poetry are *Nya dikter* (1894; New Poems), *Dikter* 1901; Poems), *Kung Salomo och Morolf* (1905; King Solomon and Morolf), and the posthumously published *Sista dikter* (1907; Last Poems).

Livets fiender (1891; The Enemies of Life) is a decadent novel that shows influence from the French writer Joris-Karl Huysmans (1848– 1907), as well as from the Dane **Herman Bang**'s novel *Haabløse Slægter* (1880; Generations without Hope), in that the protagonist is a hypersensitive and nervous scion of a noble family in decline. Another brief novel is *Magistrarne i Österås* (1900; The Scholars of Österås). A collection of short stories from the same time period bears the title *Rococo-noveller* (1899; Rococo Stories).

LIDMAN, SARA (1923–). Recognized as one of Sweden's foremost writers of her generation, Lidman is a best-selling novelist and playwright who is also widely known for her political activism. Born in a small village in northern Sweden, she contracted tuberculosis during her youth and spent considerable time at sanatoriums. Her opportunities for education were limited, but she managed to prepare for her university matriculation examinations by correspondence study, after which she studied French, English, and pedagogy at Uppsala University. After a stint as a teacher she published her first novel, *Tjärdalen* (1953; The Tar Pit), which has as its setting a fictional village, Ecksträsk, that is modeled on her home community. Stylistically, Lidman's debut novel is a mixture of **modernism** and the speech patterns of the people among whom she had grown up, while thematically it sets the tone for her lifelong concern for how the weak are exploited by the strong. Its language often has a biblical ring, reflecting the religious traditions of the author's home district.

Lidman's next novel, *Hjortronlandet* (1955; Cloudberry Country), takes its title from the prolific and highly prized cloudberries of northern Scandinavia, and the action takes place in an area of homesteaders similar to the setting in **Knut Hamsun**'s novel *Markens Grøde* (1917; tr. *Growth of the Soil*, 1920). A collective novel, it celebrates the culture and linguistic resourcefulness of the people that Lidman knows and loves.

The two novels *Regnspiran* (1958; tr. *The Rain Bird*, 1962) and *Bära mistel* (1960; Bearing Mistletoe), by contrast, have a traditional protagonist, the young woman Linda Ståhl, who also hails from Lidman's fictional Ecksträsk but whose complex personality makes it difficult for her to find happiness. In both novels, family dynamics play a major part. Concerns with family return in *Jag och min son*

(1961; My Son and I), in which the first-person narrator is a Swedish expatriate in South Africa who is working to be able to go back home to northern Sweden and take care of his son. By this time Lidman had traveled extensively in Africa, particularly in South Africa and Kenya, where she lived for a while. Her second Africa novel, *Med fem diamanter* (1964; With Five Diamonds), attests to her intimate understanding of Kenya and its culture. Its protagonist is a young man named Wachira who goes to Nairobi in order to earn money to pay the bride price that is customary in his tribal culture. However, his life is destroyed by the colonialist social and economic system he encounters in the city.

For the next decade Lidman abandoned traditional fiction writing. A vocal opponent of the **war** in Vietnam, she wrote books and articles and gave numerous speeches against the actions of the United States and its supporters. Turning her attention to what she perceived as gross injustices in her native Sweden, she became a pioneer of literary documentarism in Scandinavia. Her best-known book in this vein is *Gruva* (1968; The Mine), which contains interviews with the workers at several government-owned iron ore mines in northern Sweden.

She returned to fiction in the mid-1970s with *Jernbaneepos* (Railway Epic), a series of novels about the bringing of the railroad to northern Sweden. Consisting of *Din tjänare hör* (1977; Thy Servant Obeys), *Vredens barn* (1979; The Children of Wrath), *Nabots sten* (1981; tr. *Naboth's Stone*, 1989), *Den underbare mannen* (1983; The Marvelous Man), and *Järnkronan* (1985; The Iron Crown), this work draws on her own family history as it shows how local subsistence farmers were transformed into loyal and effective cogs in the capitalist machinery that was used to extract huge profits from Sweden's northern forests. Greed, materialism, and consumerism combine to destroy the traditional way of life, and the ethical and moral damage done by the railway project is epitomized by the bankruptcy and conviction for embezzlement of the railroad's main local advocate, the charismatic but impractical leader Didrik. Two additional novels, *Lifsens rot* (1996; The Root of Life) and *Oskuldens minut* (1999; A Minute of Innocence), depict the life of Didrik's family in the wake of their economic catastrophe.

Two plays by Lidman bear mention. Her first drama, *Job Klockma-*

kares dotter (The Daughter of Job Watchmaker) was commissioned by the director of the Gothenburg City Theater. First performed on 26 December 1954, it was a huge success in Gothenburg, Stockholm, and Oslo, as well as on tour. *Aina*, with a sanatorium as its setting, was first performed on 25 August 1956 and was also very successful. Lidman is the recipient of several prizes, the most prestigious being the **Nordic Literary Prize**, which she received in 1980. *See also* THEATER.

LIE, JONAS (1833–1908). A Norwegian novelist and short story writer, Lie was raised mostly in the northern Norwegian town of Tromsø, where his father was a government official. He later attended school in Bergen and took a law degree at the University of Oslo, after which he was a businessperson for several years. Speculation in lumber led to a bankruptcy in 1868, however, and Lie, who had already published a poetry collection in 1866, decided to become a writer in order to make enough money to pay off his debts. Drawing on his experiences in Nordland, his first serious work was the novel *Den Fremsynte eller Billeder fra Nordland* (1870; tr. *The Visionary, or Pictures from Nordland*, 1894), which, while structurally convoluted, offered a striking psychological portrait as well as the love story of its protagonist, a man gifted with clairvoyance. But equally impressive are the **nature** descriptions, which, on account of Lie's eye for detail, in power and freshness rival those of **Petter Dass**, and the book was considered a major achievement. Lie followed it up with *Tremasteren "Fremtiden"* (1872; tr. *The Barque "Future,"* 1879), which is also set in the north and is considered Norway's first novel about business affairs.

Lie's next novel, *Lodsen og hans Hustru* (1874; tr. *The Pilot and His Wife*, 1876), is also set in a coastal community, but this time in the south of Norway. It combines a description of life at sea with a penetrating analysis of jealousy in marriage. The following two novels, *Thomas Ross* (1878) and *Adam Schrader* (1879), are psychologically interesting but less successful. *Rutland* (1880), on the other hand, combines two of his favorite themes, the sea and marriage, into a first-rate story. *Gaa paa!* (1882; Forge Ahead) follows up its success by portraying a small community that is a microcosm of Norway, where the youth and their new ideas are in conflict with the old and the conservative.

Lie was primarily a **realist** and motivated by a desire to improve society through his art. In *Livsslaven* (1883; tr. *One of Life's Slaves*, 1895), however, he tends toward **naturalism** as he presents the fate of a young man of illegitimate birth. There is also social criticism in *Familjen paa Gilje* (1883; tr. *The Family at Gilje*, 1920), which has the 1840s as its setting and debates the right of **women** to follow their hearts in matters of love and marriage. In *En Malstrøm* (1884; A Maelstrom) he returns to the subject of business ethics and the evils of speculation, while *Kommandørens Døtre* (1886; tr. *The Commodore's Daughters*, 1892), the title of which self-consciously evokes **Camilla Collett**'s *Amtmandens Døttre*, is another discussion of forced marriage. *Et Samliv* (1887; A Life Together), another novel of married life, shows that internal forces constitute the greater threat against love. *Maisa Jons* (1889) constitutes a return to the theme of social conditions and offers a portrait of the seamstress as a social type suspended between her lower-class origins and the attractive life of her middle-class employers.

While Lie, who spent most of his writing career abroad, largely kept himself aloof from the literary fashions of the time, there is a correlation between the concern with individual psychology that is a hallmark of Norwegian literature in the 1890s and his next works. The novel *Onde Magter* (1890; Evil Powers), which outwardly is a novel of business affairs, is also a study of those forces of the mind that lead to the destruction of human relationships. His next two books, two collections of stories about the dark powers of the mind entitled *Trold* (1891–1892; tr. *Weird Tales from Northern Seas*, 1893), contain masterful **symbolic** explorations of these forces within.

Lie's later novels are also strongly psychological. *Niobe* (1893; tr. 1897) deals primarily with the relationship between parents and children, while *Naar Sol gaar ned* (1895; When the Sun Sets), like some of Lie's earlier works, explores jealousy in marriage. *Dyre Rein* (1896) is a study of the irrational forces that lead a young man to commit suicide the day before he is to be married. *Faste Forland* (1899), like the earlier novel *En Malstrøm*, probes the mind-set that leads to wanton speculation in business, while *Naar Jerntæppet fal-*

der (1901; When the Iron Curtain Drops) explores people's reactions under stress. The passengers on an ocean liner learn that a bomb has been planted on board and is set to go off in precisely an hour. The bomb threat is subsequently revealed to be a hoax, but not before the experience has shaken many of the characters out of their long-standing habits of thought. *Ulfvungerne* (1903; The Ulfvung Family) takes greed and the lust for power as its theme, while *Østenfor Sol, vestenfor Maane og bagom Babylons Taarn* (1905; East of the Sun, West of the Moon, and Behind the Tower of Babylon) explores the theme of professional jealousy.

LINDEGREN, ERIK (1910–1968). A Swedish **modernist** poet, Lindegren studied philosophy at the University of Stockholm and had his debut with a volume of rather ordinary poems, *Posthum ungdom* (1935; Posthumous Youth). His most important collection is *Mannen utan väg* (1942; tr. *The Man without a Way*, 1969), in which he avoided the use of capital letters and punctuation. It contains 40 poems that consist of 14 lines each, and these fragmented sonnets give the impression of a disintegrated world. The meaning of the texts is also difficult to grasp, which is consistent with Lindegren's ides that truth and meaning are unattainable. The next collection, *Sviter* (1947; Suites), was more accessible. It was followed by *Vinteroffer* (1954; Winter Sacrifice).

LINDGREN, ASTRID (1907–2002). A Swedish author of **children's books**, Lindgren is arguably as well known in the English-speaking world as any other Swedish writer, and perhaps even better. Her best-known character is surely her indefatigable Pippi, a girl with superhuman strength, who appears in *Pippi Långstrump* (1945; tr. *Pippi Longstocking*, 1950) and its sequels *Pippi Långstrump går ombord* (1946; tr. *Pippi Goes on Board*, 1957), *Känner du Pippi Långstrump?* (1947; tr. *Do You Know Pippi Longstocking?*, 1999), *Pippi Långstrump i Söderhavet* (1948; tr. *Pippi in the South Seas*, 1959), and *Pippi Långstrump i Humlegården* (1949; tr. *Pippi Longstocking in the Park*, 2001). Lindgren also uses a girl as her protagonist in *Barnen på Bråkmakargatan* (1958; tr. *The Children on Troublemaker Street*, 1964) and *Madicken* (1960; tr. *Mischievous Meg*, 1962).

Lindgren's fantasy novel *Mio, min Mio* (1954; tr. *Mio, My Son*, 1956) violates the conventions of its genre by not letting Mio return to the "real" world. In *Bröderna Lejonhjärta* (1973; tr. *The Brothers Loonheart*, 1975) Lindgren introduces death into the story. In *Emil i Lönneberga* (1963; tr. *Emil and His Piggy Beast*, 1973) she lets her boy protagonist undergo significant personal development. The protagonist of *Ronja rövardotter* (1981; tr. *Ronia, the Robber's Daughter*, 1983) is somewhat similar to Pippi but does not have her superhuman abilities. An innocent and lyrical love story, the novel takes place against the backdrop of two rival robber bands in a distant forest in a distant time.

LINDGREN, TORGNY (1938–). A Swedish novelist, short story writer, and poet, Lindgren is an intensely private person who has provided little information about himself. Born in northern Sweden, he has worked as a teacher; he has a degree in religious studies and converted to Roman Catholicism. Lindgren began his literary career with three volumes of poetry: *Plåtsax, hjärtats instrument* (1965; Tin Snips, the Instrument of the Heart), *Dikter från Vimmerby* (1970; Poems from Vimmerby), and *Hur skulle det vore om man vore Olof Palme? Fragment ur en anarkists dagbok* (1971; What Would It Be Like to Be Olof Palme? Fragments from the Diary of an Anarchist). He has since considered these works mere preparatory exercises, but his focus on power, a persistent theme throughout his work, is present in this early poetry.

Power is also at the core of his first novel, *Skolbagateller medan jag försökte skriva til mina överordnade* (1972; School Trivia, While Trying to Write to My Superiors). Here he attacks the Swedish educational system, as his Norwegian colleague **Jens Bjørneboe** had done in the novel *Jonas* (1955; tr. *The Last of These*, 1959) a number of years earlier. *Övriga frågor* (1973; Additional Questions) extends Lindgren's critique to political life in general. *Brännvinsfursten* (1979; The Liquor Prince) gives a historical slant to his criticism, while *Skrämmer dig minuten* (1981; Are You Frightened by This Moment) is a satirical novel about marriage.

The novel *Ormens väg på hälleberget* (1982; tr. *The Way of the Serpent*, 1990) gave Lindgren a reputation as a major writer, and its almost minimalist style was highly acclaimed by the **critics**. A tale of both economic and sexual exploitation, it takes place in northern Sweden in the 1800s. The volume of short stories *Merabs skönhet: Berättelser* (1983; tr. *Merab's Beauty and Other Stories*) is stylistically similar. Lindgren's next novel, *Bat Seba* (1984; tr. *Bathsheba*, 1989), makes use of the biblical story of King David as it probes the connections between power and religion. David arranges for Bathsheba's husband, Uriah, to be killed in battle so that he can marry her, but Bathsheba is adept at political maneuvering and becomes increasingly powerful, ultimately succeeding in making her son David's successor. Lindgren's use of biblical themes continues in the short story collection *Legender* (1986; Legends).

In *Ljuset* (1987; tr. *The Light*, 1992), which was very well received, Lindgren returns to northern Sweden at the time of the plague. It was followed by *Till sanningens lov: Rammakaren Theodor Marklunds egen redogörelse* (1991; tr. *In Praise of Truth: The Personal Account of Theodor Marklund, Picture-framer*, 1994), a meditation on the relationship between truth and lies. In the short story collection *I Brokiga Blads vatten* (1999; In Brokiga Blad's Water), Lindgren's satire is mixed with humor and directed against such varied subjects as politics, mass-produced art, and uxoriousness.

Another achievement is the literary triptych consisting of the novels *Hummelhonung* (1995; tr. *Sweetness*, 2000), *Pölsan* (2002; tr. *Hash*, 2004), and *Dorés bibel* (2005; Doré's Bible), which all have the district of Västerbotten as their setting. *Hummelhonung* tells about two brothers who are locked in mutual hatred, from which they may finally be released only at the end of their lives. *Pölsan*, nominally a story about pulmonary tuberculosis and a quest for the perfect sausage, is in reality a novel about art and its conditions. *Dorés bibel* is narrated by a dyslexic man whose imagination has been nourished by Gustave Doré's bible illustrations, and whose story attests to the power of both pictorial and literary art.

LINNA, VÄINÖ (1920–1992). A Finnish novelist, Linna was born into a working-class family and worked in a variety of jobs, finally settling in as a factory worker in the city of Tampere while educating himself at the local library. After serving in Finland's Continuation

War of 1941–1944, he returned to his former employment and started writing on the side. His first novel, a poorly disguised autobiography with the title *Päämäärä* (1947; The Goal), tells about a young man's struggles to became a writer. His second novel, *Musta rakkaus* (1948; Black Love), is set in the city of Tampere and shows that tragedy, including murder, often results from jealousy and other negative emotions. One of the book's merits is its vivid descriptions of Finnish life.

Linna's finest novel is *Tuntematon Sotilas* (1954; tr. *The Unknown Soldier*, 1957), which was informed by his own wartime experiences. Telling the story of a platoon of machine-gunners during the Continuation War, Linna offers both a message of pacifism—war is ultimately futile and a wanton destruction of life and property—and a tribute to the courage and strength of the Finns who make up the platoon. They hail from all over the country, and by characterizing them through the use of their local dialects, Linna creates both a microcosm of Finland and many humorous situations. There is also a powerful and culturally influential anti-authoritarian tenor in the book—even to the point that an excessively rule-oriented person may be referred to as a "Lammio" in contemporary Finnish—and an equally strong emphasis on the kind of solidarity that manifests itself as true and intelligent friendship on the battlefield, as opposed to the blind obedience of well-trained automata so highly prized by military strategists.

Linna's other great literary work is the trilogy *Täällä pohjantähden alla* (1959–1962; tr. *Under the North Star*, 2001–2003), which tells about a Finnish farm family from the 1880s to the 1940s. Finland's major historical events during this period, such as the plight of tenant farmers around the turn of the century, the issue of socialism, and the civil war, are seen through the lens of a small group of people, the Koskela family. The trilogy became very popular, and Linna won the **Nordic Literary Prize** for its concluding volume in 1963. Linna published collections of essays and talks in 1967 and 1990.

LITERARY JOURNALS. *See* SCANDINAVIAN LITERARY JOURNALS.

LOE, ERLEND (1969–). A Norwegian novelist, Loe is considered one of the most promising young writers in Norway. He had his debut with the novel *Tatt av kvinnen* (1993; Taken by Woman), the title of which is a pun on the Norwegian translation of Margaret Mitchell's classic novel *Gone with the Wind* (1936), or *Tatt av vinden* (1937). In a satirical representation of love and marriage in Norway in the 1990s, a strong young woman moves in with a weak young man, who soon finds his life taken over by her and her unborn child by another man. Loe's verbal situation comedy is balanced by hints that the essence of the story is perhaps not too uncommon. Humor is also an important characteristic of Loe's next novel, *Naiv. Super.* (1996; tr. *Naïve. Super.*, 2001), in which the protagonist, whose weakness of personality is similar to that of the narrator in *Tatt av kvinnen*, is obsessed with finding the meaning of life, including the origin of the universe. His hyperreflectivity makes for a great deal of comedy, including his experiences during an extended visit to New York.

Loe's gifts as a satirist are also displayed in *L* (1999), a first-person narrative about an expedition to an island in the Pacific Ocean where, supposedly, a group of seven "explorers" will be looking for skates used by Native Americans at a time when the Pacific was covered with ice. *L* is an effective satire on the literature of exploration as represented by such Norwegian luminaries as Roald Amundsen (1872–1928) and Thor Heyerdahl (1914–2002).

The protagonists of Loe's first three novels all share a concern about finding their place in society. They fear change, and that fear is given a more serious treatment in Loe's fourth novel, *Fakta om Finland* (2001; Facts of Finland), in which hydrophobia serves as its metaphor. In the novel *Doppler* (2004), the protagonist rebels against pressures to perform and conform by leaving city life in favor of a tent in the woods. Loe can still be funny, but his humor is tempered by a serious critique of civilization.

LO-JOHANSSON, IVAR (1901–1990). A Swedish novelist, short story writer, and essayist, Lo-Johansson came from a background of oppressed agricultural laborers called *statare*, a class of people who lived serflike lives on large estates, where they provided the farm labor that was needed there. Lacking in formal schooling, he educated himself by reading and traveling widely. After publishing several travel narratives and the novel *Måna är död* (1932; Måna Is Dead), Lo-Johansson wrote *Godnatt, jord* (1933; tr. *Breaking Free*, 1990), a collective novel that detailed the predicament of the *statare*. He continued to write about them in three volumes of short stories, *Statarna* (1936–1937; The Estate Workers) and *Jordproletärerna* (1941; Proletarians of the Land), in which he traced the history of this mistreated social group. The novel *Kungsgatan* (1935; King's Street) told about youth who left the rural areas for the city, while *Traktorn* (1943; The Tractor) discussed issues associated with the modernization of agriculture.

One of Lo-Johansson's finest novels is *Bara en mor* (1939; tr. *Only a Mother*, 1991), which tells the story of a *statare* woman whose life is ruined by the ignorance and narrowmindedness of her fellow estate workers. In 1951 Lo-Johansson started a series of autobiographical novels; the first volume, *Analfabeten* (1951; The Illiterate), deals with the life of his father, while other volumes in the series, for example, *Gårdfarihandlaren* (1953; tr. *Peddling My Wares*, 1995) and *Journalisten* (1956; The Journalist), draw on the author's own experiences.

Between 1975 and 1985 Lo-Johansson also published four volumes of memoirs. He returned to the genre of the short story in 1968, and by 1972 he had published seven collections dealing with the seven deadly sins.

LÖNNROT, ELIAS (1802–1884). A Finnish folklore collector and philologist, Lönnrot created the *Kalevala*, a history of the ancient Finns based on epic poems of Finnish **folklore**. Lönnrot's work may be understood both as an outgrowth of the nation-building movement in 19th-century Finland and as a manifestation of **national romanticism**. Lönnrot's family made many sacrifices to allow him to get an education, and he eventually received a medical degree; his thesis was written about Finnish folk medicine. While serving as a medical officer in Karelia, Lönnrot made a number of trips in order to collect the traditional songs of people there as well as in neighboring areas. He also studied the relationships between various Finnic languages, including Finnish, Ingrian, Karelian, and Estonian.

Lönnrot did not discover the existence of Finnish oral folk poetry, but he studied materials that had already been collected and collected additional songs himself. Of the main divisions of such poetry—the lyric, magic, and epic songs—he focused on the epic poems as he set out to create a coherent poetic history of the ancient Finns. His purpose was to prove that the Finns had a national poetic heritage every bit as good as that of their neighbors, and even one that in beauty and heroism could rival that of the ancient Greeks.

The *Kalevala* was published in two versions, the old *Kalevala* (1835) and the new *Kalevala* (1849), which is almost twice as long as the first version. Lönnrot used mostly traditional songs, but he arranged them in a sequence of his own making and occasionally composed segments himself. The epic begins with the creation of the world and the peopling of the land of Kaleva and then tells about the exploits of such heroes as Väinämöinen, Ilmarinen, and Lemminkäinen, as well as the tragic figures Kullervo and Aino. The story is organized in quests of various kinds, but particularly for brides, and features such magical objects as the *sampo*, made by the people of the land of Kaleva as a bride prize. The story ends with the departure of the ancient heroes and the coming of Christianity. Lönnrot also published a companion compilation of lyric poetry, the *Kanteletar* (1840–1841).

LØVEID, CECILIE (1951–). A Norwegian poet, novelist, and playwright, Løveid is one of the most innovative writers of her generation. She started out writing poetry that tended toward narrative, and narrative that tended toward poetry. Anchored in the Norwegian **feminist** movement of the 1970s, she chose themes that were compatible with her social and political views. The fragmentary novel *Most* (1972), her literary debut, features three **women** who have been seduced by the same man, while Julia, the protagonist in *Tenk om isen skulle komme* (1974; What If the Ice Were to Come), has been exploited as an actress in pornographic movies. *Alltid skyer over Askøy* (1976; Always Clouds over Askøy), while depicting the life of a single mother, also gives flashbacks into the life of women in past generations. *Fanget villrose* (1977; Captured Wild Rose) links the oppression of women to capitalism and **war**. The novel *Sug* (1979; tr. *Sea Swell*, 1986), in which the protagonist of *Alltid skyer over Askøy* returns, tells the poignant story of an unwed mother's search for love and a sense of self after she has been abandoned by her married lover. It is the most significant of Løveid's early works.

Løveid's greatest contribution to Norwegian literature has, however, been to drama. A prolific playwright, she started out writing radio plays in the late 1960s and the 1970s. Her dramatic breakthrough came with the play *Måkespisere* (1983; tr. *Seagull Eaters*, 1989), set in Løveid's hometown of Bergen before and during World War II. With strong intertextual references to **Henrik Ibsen**'s *Gengangere* (1881; tr. *Ghosts*, 1890) and echoes of the work of the German playwright Bertolt Brecht, it tells the story of a young working-class woman who dreams of becoming an actress but who is exploited sexually and left in misery. *Vinteren revner* (1983; The Winter Cracks) portrays the relationship between a mother and her daughter, while *Balansedame* (1984; Tightrope Walker) depicts a woman who must balance her roles as a wife and mother against her desire for self-fulfillment. *Fornuftige dyr* (1986; Rational Animals) shows that human beings are in reality irrational, especially in matters of love. *Dobbel nytelse* (1988; tr. *Double Delight*, 1994) features an archeological dig that turns into a digging into the past of the female protagonist; it emphasizes the instability and malleability of human beings captured by the forces of desire.

A series of three plays about historical figures constitutes Løveid's most significant dramatic achievement. *Barock friise, eller kjærligheten er en større labyrint* (1993; Baroque Frieze; or, Love Is a Larger Labyrinth) explores the life and times of Zille Gad, a woman with strong intellectual interests born in Bergen in the late 1600s. *Maria Q* (1994) is an attempt to understand the Ukrainian-born wife of the Nazi collaborator Vidkun Quisling (1887–1945), who was executed in 1945. *Rhindøtrene* (1996; Daughters of the Rhine) features the life of the medieval mystic Hildegard von Bingen (1098–1179).

Henrik Ibsen's enduring importance for Norwegian dramatists is demonstrated not only by the significance of *Gengangere* to *Måkespisere*, but even more so in *Østerrike* (1998; Austria), in which Løveid radically reinterprets the character Agnes in Ibsen's *Brand* (1866; tr. 1894), pairing her up with the Austrian philosopher Ludwig Wittgenstein (1889–1951), who in his fanatical commitment to his discipline parallels Ibsen's character Brand's commitment to religion. Much in Wittgenstein's spirit, *Østerrike* is an interesting meditation on the power and limits of language.

Løveid returned to poetry with the collection *Spilt* (2001; Played). She has also written drama and fiction for children. *See also* THEATER.

LUGN, KRISTINA (1948–). A Swedish poet and dramatist, Lugn is also one of Sweden's foremost **postmodern** writers as well as a **feminist** critic of social conditions and observer of the roles of **women**. A master of irony, parody, and pastiche, she had her debut with the poetry collection *Om jag inte* (1972; If I Didn't), which features as its speaker a middle-aged Swedish woman who dies of loneliness. Lugn's next volume of poetry, *Till min man, om han kunde läsa* (1976; To My Husband, If He Were Able to Read), introduces one of Lugn's favorite literary motifs, violent death. The woman speaker talks about shooting her husband, but it is unclear whether she has actually done it or if it is just a fantasy on her part, as the husband of the title could simply be illiterate. Two more poetry collections, *Döda honom!* (1978; Kill Him!) and *Om ni hör et skott . . .* (1979; If You Happen to Hear a Shot . . .), take the idea of murder to the next level, as it is shown to be generally present as a possibility in Swedish middle-class, consumerist, and claustrophobic life.

The alienation of contemporary life in Sweden is also presented in *Percy Wennerfors* (1982), a book of poems that parodies well-known fairy tales as it presents a little girl who resists her female role by communicating through animal noises. *Bekantskap önskas med äldre bildad herre* (1983; Seeking an Older, Cultivated Man) presents an unnamed woman who is desperately looking for a man who can rescue her from her quotidian existence, and the theme of alienation is further emphasized in the prize-winning *Hundstunden: Kvinnlig bekännelseslyrik* (1989; The Dog Hour: Female Confessional Poetry).

The year 1979 marked Lugn's debut as a dramatist, and she has been a strong and very visible presence in Swedish **theater** ever since. Her plays tend to be brief, with few characters and a minimalist dialogue that is nevertheless pregnant with meaning. In addition to having had several unpublished pieces performed, Lung is particularly well known for *Idlaflickorna* (1993; tr. *The Old Girls*, 1995), and *Tant Blomma* (1993; tr. *Aunt Blossom*, 1995). The former illustrates the instability of female identity in modern Swedish society, while the latter is a study in the absurdity of modern life. *Nattorienterarna* (1998; Night Orienteers) is a study of loss in general and bereavement in particular.

LUNDKVIST, ARTUR (1906–1991). A Swedish poet, essayist, and novelist, Lundkvist was the most prolific Swedish man of letters of his generation, with well over 80 books to his credit. He also wrote scores of essays and articles. The sheer volume of his literary production may thus seem forbidding, but his work is structured by a major principle: his desire to investigate and describe the interplay between such opposed forces as **nature** and culture, reason and the subconscious, and reality and the imagination.

Although born into a rural family with little literary culture, Lundkvist was determined to become a writer and started producing journalism at the age of 16. Later he associated with a group of young men of similar background, the so-called Fem unga (**Five Young Men**), who were inspired by works of high **modernism** and rebelled against the traditionalism of contemporary Swedish poetry. Lundkvist's first poetry collections, *Glöd* (1928; Ember), *Naket liv* (1929; Naked Life), and *Svart stad* (1930; Black City), contain poems written in free verse and the same positive view of technology that is to be found also in the works of the Danish modernist **Johannes V. Jensen**, such as Jensen's poem "Paa Memphis Station" (At the Memphis Train Station).

Lundkvist's admiration of modern technology did not last long, however. The poetry collections *Vit man* (1932; White Man), *Nattens broar* (1936; Bridges of the Night), *Sirensång* (1937; Siren Song), and *Eldtema* (1939; Fire Theme) chronicle his interest in surrealism. Surrealism is also an important theme in a collection of essays entitled *Ikarus' flykt* 1939; The Flight of Icarus). During these same years Lundkvist traveled in Africa, which resulted in the travelogue *Negerkust* (1933; Negro Coast). He later traveled extensively in Asia and the Soviet Union, and these travels resulted in the books *Indiabrand* (1950; India Fire) and *Vallmor från Taschkent: En resa i Sovjet-Unionen* (1952; Poppies from Tashkent: A Journey in the Soviet Union).

The experience of World **War** II made Lundkvist increasingly conscious of the significance of politics. Trying to steer a middle course between the ideologies of the two superpowers, he understood that both Western-style capitalism and **Marxist**-Leninism had their limitations. Such poetry collections as *Spegel för dag och natt* (1953; A Mirror for Day and Night) and *Vindrosor* (1955; Wind Roses) express his sympathies with those who want to throw off oppression and exploitation. His novel *Darunga* (1954) describes a revolution in a Latin American country and points toward Castro's takeover in Cuba.

In keeping with his interest in mediating between opposites, Lundkvist experimented extensively with bringing prose and poetry together into the prose poem or poetic prose. Most of his work in the late 1950s and the 1960s was in this vein. Representative titles are *Berget och svalorna* (1957; The Mountain and the Swallows), *Det talande trädet* (1960; tr. *The Talking Tree*, 1982), and *Sida vid sida* (1962; Side by Side). The long poem *Agadir* (1961; tr. 1980) tells about his impressions of a destructive earthquake in Morocco.

Lundkvist also wrote several historical novels that depict moments in history when cultures meet and are transformed. Their disparate settings include Skåne in Sweden and ancient Babylonia. In the 1970s he further experimented with the mixing of such genres as essays, poems, and biography. Some titles from this period are *Lustgårdens demoni* (1973; The Demonism of Paradise), *Fantasins slott och vardagens stenar* (1974; The Castles of the Imagination and the Stones of Every Day), and *Flykten och överlevandet* (1977; Flight and Survival). *Färdas i drömmen och föreställningen* (1984; tr. *Journeys in Dream and Imagination*, 1991) contains prose poems that tell about his dreams while in a coma subsequent to a stroke.

– M –

MADSEN, SVEND ÅGE (1939–). A Danish novelist and dramatist, Madsen started out as an experimental writer but gradually turned to a more accessible narrative technique, which includes using psychological **realism** when appropriate. He has, for some time, been one of Denmark's most productive writers, and his popularity has soared in tandem with his increased use of more traditional techniques.

Madsen had his literary debut with the novel *Besøget* (1963; The Visit), which was followed by *Lystbilleder* (1964; Images of Desire), *Otte gange orphan* (1965; Eight Times an Orphan), and *Tilføjelser* (1967; Additions). These novels all deal with the familiar **modernist** themes of meaninglessness in an existential void, and they offer portraits of characters, many of them first-person narrators, who are devoid of substance until they are, so to speak, narrated into being.

The Danish reading public had understandable difficulties with these narratives, which presented them with characters unbounded in terms of time and space, without history and geographical attachment. Starting in the late 1960s, Madsen changed his focus from the characters' lack of anchorage in space-time to a certain relativism of meaning. The short story collection *Maskeballet* (1970; The Masquerade) and three novels were published during the next few years: *Liget og lysten* (1968; The Corpse and the Desire), *Tredje gang så tar vi ham* (1969; We'll Get Him the Third Time), and *Sæt verden er til* (1971; Let's Assume the World Exists). By exploding traditional structures of meaning and unmasking habitual ways of looking at the world, Madsen manages to create a sense of freedom for his characters and thereby give them hope.

The novel *Dage med Diam eller livet om natten* (1972; tr. *Days with Diam, or, Life at Night*, 1994) is structured according to the principle of choice. At regular junctures in the text the protagonist has to choose one thing or another. Subsequent to the presentation of the choice, the narrative splits as each of the choices is followed up and the respective consequences presented. A series of different narrative pathways is thus created in the text, and individual readers can choose those paths of reading that appeal to them and lead to happy or sad endings, and so on. The idea of choice is thus enthroned as the ruling principle both in the activity of writing and in that of reading.

Madsen turned to social criticism in his novel *Tugt og utugt i mellemtiden* (1976; tr. *Virtue and Vice in the Middle Time*, 1992). The book has a clearly recognizable setting in space and time (the Danish town Århus in the 1970s), but the narrator is a historian of the future who from a temporal distance of approximately 200 years tries to re-create its society and culture, including the cultural phenomenon known as "the novel," for intellectual reasons. Much of Madsen's humerous and satirical accomplishment in this book consists in the tension between what the reader knows to be the actual features of the culture that is being reconstructed and the sometimes wildly inaccurate reconstructions by the narrator/historian.

Madsen published a large number of novels in the years since *Tugt og utugt i mellemtiden*. By allowing characters from earlier books to come back in later ones, he has managed to weave a narrative fabric that is not delimited by the boundaries of his individual texts. This fabric is in principle without bounds and is limited only by Madsen's ability to add new books to it.

One of Madsen's most interesting recent novels is *Kvinden uden krop* (1996; The Woman without a Body), in which a dying woman is able to come up with an invention that transfers her spiritual and mental essence into the body of her husband, with the result that the two of them share one mortal human body. A number of ludicrous situations ensue, until the two of them are killed by the police. Rather than regarding the ending as a symbol for the limitations of the kind of fiction that Madsen writes, it is possible to think of their death as an attempt to purify literature of its fantastic elements.

Some of Madsen's humor is connected with his overt metafictionality. In the novel *Levemåder* (2004; Ways of Living), a budding writer is portrayed as working on a book that seems identical to *Levemåder*. This is not an original metafictional motif on Madsen's part, but his use of it underscores his belief in the interconnectedness of all objects and experiences. Madsen has also written scripts for stage, television, and radio.

MANNER, EEVA-LIISA (1921–1995). A Finnish poet, novelist, and playwright, Manner published her first collection of poetry in 1944 but has since distanced herself from her earliest work. The poetry collection *Tämä matka* (1956; This Journey) is her real debut; it shows that she perfectly mastered the **modernist** forms of expression that came to the forefront in Finnish poetry in the 1950s.

Manner's poetry is critical of the Western rationalism developed by such philosophers as René Descartes, Baruch Spinoza, and Ludwig Wittgenstein—against whom she places Eastern ways of looking at the world, particularly Taoism. She also finds inspiration in the child's view of reality, which emphasizes magic and perception through images rather than language. Manner has published with unusual regularity, and some of her most central volumes of poetry are *Farenheit 121* (1968), *Paetkaa, purret, kevein purjein* (1971; Flee Ships, with Light Sails), *Kuolleet vedet* (1977; Dead Waters), *Kamala kissa* (1976; A Horrible Cat), and *Kauhukakara ja Superkissa* (1982; Little Terror and Supercat). The last two show that Manner can be very funny.

World events have also influenced Manner's poetry. After the Soviet repression of democratic stirrings in Czechoslovakia, she published *Jos suru savuaisi* (1968; If Smoke Would Rise from Sorrow). Politics also motivated her novel *Varokaa, voittajat* (1972; Victors, Beware), which discusses oppression in Spain. Having traveled widely in that country, she knows Spanish history and culture well, and her novel is a plea for tolerance and justice. Manner's plays are appreciated but not performed very often. An example is *Eros ja Psykhe* (1959; Eros and Psyche), which, like her poetry, has an important mythic side to it.

MARTINSON, HARRY (1904–1978). Generally recognized as one of the leading figures in 20th-century Swedish literature, Martinson wrote poetry, novels, dramas, and essays, for which he was awarded the **Nobel Prize** in 1974. He was one of several self-educated writers of working-class origins who started writing in the late 1920s. Together with **Artur Lundkvist** and others he formed the group "Fem unga" (**Five Young Men**) and worked to promote **modernism** in Sweden.

Martinson had a very difficult childhood and youth. After the death of his father and his mother's departure for California, he was a ward of the community and was passed along from one foster family to another. He ran away and went to sea as a coal stoker in 1920, had many varied experiences, and returned home to Sweden for good in 1927. His literary debut came with the poetry collection *Spökskepp* (1929; Ghost Ship), which was informed by his experiences as a seaman, as was the volume *Nomad* (1931), which celebrates the outsider's ability to give truthful representations of phenomena only dimly visible to insiders. Some critical and financial success came to Martinson through two prose narratives that drew on his experiences as a sailor and wanderer. *Resor utan mål* (1932; Journeys without

Destination) and *Fap Farväl!* (1933; tr. *Cape Farewell*, 1934) are narrated with a strong admixture of lyricism.

By the mid-1930s Martinson's poetry changed in the direction of **expressionism** and surrealism. The collection *Natur* (1934; Nature), which testifies to the poet's appreciation for the realm of **nature**, also attests to the influence of his fellow poet Artur Lundkvist. It was received less enthusiastically than his earlier volumes of poetry, and Martinson returned to prose, this time to the experiences of his childhood and youth for inspiration. *Nässloran blomma* (1935; tr. *Flowering Nettle*, 1936) and *Vägen ut* (1936; The Way Out), while not conventional autobiography, cover Martinson's life up to the time presented in *Resor utan mål*. These books were written during his marriage to **Moa Martinson**, a writer 14 years his senior, whom he later divorced. Martinson also tried his hand at radio plays. Three of them were produced, the most successful being *Lotsen från Moluckas* (1937; The Pilot from the Moluccas Islands), which tells about Magellan's circumnavigation of the earth.

Events leading up to World **War** II, as well as the experiences of the war itself, caused Martinson to express his disenchantment with Western-style technological civilization and the popular culture associated with it in such books as *Det enkla och det svåra* (1939; The Simple and the Difficult), a collection of essays about humans' relationship to nature, and *Den förlorade jaguaren* (1941; The Lost Jaguar), his third book about life at sea. The poetry collection *Passad* (1945; Trade Wind) similarly questions the human value of technological advances.

The vagabond novel *Vägen til Klockrike* (1948; tr. *The Road*, 1955) is a story about several tramps whose philosophy of life is far more humane than that of many so-called successful people. It was followed by Martinson's most significant literary work, the space epic *Aniara* (1956; tr. 1958, 1963, and 1991), which is set in a future when earth has been contaminated by nuclear radiation and groups of people have to flee to other planets. The space ship *Aniara*, however, is thrown off course by a near collision with an asteroid, after which it heads into deep space, leaving its passengers with the prospect of living out their lives on board without ever finding a new home. This is depressing not only to the passengers, but also to the ship's supercomputer. Called the Mima, the computer is not just a machine but possesses a soul and self-destructs when it is confronted with incoming images of earth's final and utter destruction. Martinson's cosmic representation of the human condition is one of the truly great contributions to 20th-century literature.

Literary culture was extremely politicized in Sweden during the late 1960s and the 1970s, and Martinson's concern with nature, expressed in such volumes as his final poetry collection, *Tuvor* (1973; Tussocks), was not always appreciated. Some critics also questioned the choice of Martinson as a recipient of the **Nobel Prize** for literature in 1974. Martinson responded by publishing little of what he wrote. Some of this material has been published posthumously.

MARTINSON, MOA (1890–1964). A Swedish novelist and poet, Martinson came from a background of abject poverty in the slums of the town of Norrköping. She gave birth to five children, two of whom drowned in a creek, and she experienced the gruesome suicide of her first husband, who blew himself up with dynamite. In spite of all her adversity, Martinson worked hard to educate herself and wrote articles for the socialist and anarchist press. She married writer **Harry Martinson** in 1929; they were later divorced.

Moa Martinson's first novel, *Kvinnor och äppelträd* (1933, tr. *Women and Apple Trees*, 1985), portrayed the lives of working-class **women**. In its sequel, *Sallys söner* (1934; Sally's Sons), she offers frank depictions of female desire, pregnancy, and birth. *Rågvakt* (1935; Rye Watch) portrays the hard life of agricultural laborers. The frank presentation of female eroticism is continued in *Drottning Grågyllen* (1937; Queen Greygolden), which uses **fairy tales** and **folklore** legends in the creation of a woman character who returns to her childhood haunts as an old woman, the mythic Queen Greygolden. Supposedly "shameful" aspects of female sexuality also inform Martinson's only poetry collection, *Motsols* (1937; Counterclockwise).

Also in the 1930s Martinson wrote an autobiographical trilogy consisting of *Mor gifter sig* (1936; tr. *My Mother Gets Married*, 1988), *Kyrkbröllop* (1938; Church Wedding), and *Kungens rosor* (1939; The King's Roses), the protagonist of which is a very strong and capable woman similar to Martinson herself. One of its great contributions to Swedish literature was its depiction of working-class life from a woman's perspective. Another autobiographical series of novels was published in the 1940s and 1950s. Consisting of the volumes *Den osynlige älskaren* (1943; The Invisible Lover), *Du är den enda* (1952; You Are the Only One), *Klockor vid sidenvägen* (1957; Bells along the Silk Road), and *Hemligheten* (1959; The Secret), this series made use of Martinson's experiences during the early years of her first marriage.

Martinson's "Östergötland Epic" uses characters from *Drottning Grågyllen* and *Kvinnor och äppelträd*, It comprises three novels in which she tells about life in her home district: *Vägen under stjärnorna* (1940; The Road beneath the Stars), *Brandliljor* (1941; Fire Lilies), and *Livets fest* (1949; The Celebration of Life). This trilogy is also a family saga, as it tells about several generations of people from the same farm. Other novels that make use of Martinson's own life experience are *Armén vid horisonten* (1942; The Army at the Horizon), *Bakom svenskvallen* (1944; Behind Swedish Fortifications), and *Kärlek mellan krigen* (1947; Love between the Wars).

MARXISM. Marxism, particularly as practiced in the Soviet Union, first became influential in Scandinavian literature following World War I, when it was often paired with **Freudianism** as a means of social and economic analysis. One of the best examples is **Hans Kirk**'s collective novel *Fiskerne* (1928; tr. *The Fishermen*, 1999), which tells the story of a group of Danish fishermen who migrate from the Jutland coast to the relatively sheltered Limfjord area. **Sigurd Hoel**'s novels from the 1920s and 1930s also show evidence of Marxist thinking, as do the works of **Martin Andersen Nexø**, in which the history of the Danish labor movement figures prominently. The Swede **Karin Boye** strongly expressed her reservations concerning Marxist totalitarianism in her dystopian novel *Kallocain* (1940; tr. 1966).

In the 1960s and 1970s Marxism again became a major force in the literature of Scandinavia, but at that time the inspiration came chiefly from China and to a lesser extent Albania; the latter was particularly attractive to the Norwegian novelist **Espen Haavardsholm**. The Swede **Jan Myrdal** reported on Mao Zedong's revolution in China, and the Norwegian writers **Edvard Hoem**, **Tor Obrestad**, and **Dag Solstad** wrote novels in which the Maoist variety of Marxist-Leninism was held up as an ideal; Solstad's *Arild Asnes, 1970*

(1971) is perhaps the best example of this type of literature. *See also* ABELL, KJELD; GYLLENSTEN, LARS; LUNDKVIST, ARTUR; SØRENSEN, VILLY.

MICHAEL, IB (1945–). A Danish novelist, poet, and dramatist, Michael is one of Denmark's best-known writers of the late 20th century. While studying Central American indigenous languages and culture at the University of Copenhagen, he traveled extensively among the Mayans, and his first two novels were strongly informed by those experiences. *En hidtil uset drøm om skibe* (1970; A Previously Unseen Dream of Ships) and *Den flyvende kalkundræber* (1971; The Flying Turkey Hunter) are both highly experimental and challenging texts that violate most of the conventions of traditional linear narrative.

After taking his degree in 1972, Michael embarked on a career as a writer of literary texts without giving up his connection with the world of Maya scholarship. He translated the *Popol Vuh*, the Mayan sacred texts of myths and history, into Danish (1975) and wrote a travelogue, *Mayalandet* (1973; The Land of the Maya), in which he argues that European-style ethnography is in reality an imperialist tool. His novel *Hjortefod* (1974; Stag's Hoof) recounts Mexican history with an emphasis on the abuses of the European colonialists.

In his books about Central America, Michael is powerfully inspired by the area's mythology. He relies on myth in his novel *Rejsen tilbage* (1977; The Journey Back), in which he created the myth of the immortal soldier, a figure related to the Wandering Jew. The immortal soldier has been cursed by a Native American medicine man, who has deprived him of the ability to die and to learn from his experiences; the curse is essentially that of a permanent stasis. The same mythic figure returns in *Keiserfortællingen* (1981; The Emperor's Tale), a nonlinear narrative that covers thousands of years and takes place in a variety of locales. In the novel *Kilroy, Kilroy* (1989), it is stated that the immortal soldier was created at the time of the Big Bang and consequently is as old as the universe.

The novel *Troubadurens lærling* (1984; The Minstrel's Apprentice) is set in Europe during the time of the plagues of the 14th century. Its protagonist is a wandering minstrel who experiences the contrast between the elite culture of the church and the lower cultural forms of the people. This mixture of high and low is one of the defining characteristics of **postmodern** fiction, of which *Troubadurens lærling* is a good example. During the 1980s Michael also produced two collections of poetry. The first, *Himmelbegravelse: Digte fra Tibet* (1986; Sky Burial: Poems from Tibet) is the result of several visits to Tibet and shows a great deal of sympathy with Tibetan culture. The second, *Vinden i metroen* (1990; The Wind in the Metro), is the result of Michael's encounter with Rome.

In the first half of the 1990s Michael wrote a trilogy that is largely about family relationships, and in which he confronts some of his own childhood memories. Consisting of the volumes *Vanillepigen* (1991; The Vanilla Girl), *Den tolvte rytter* (1993; The Twelfth Knight), and *Brev til månen* (1995; Letter to the Moon), the trilogy is recognized as a significant artistic achievement.

Most of Michael's works depart from the conventions of **realist** fiction. The novel *Prins* (1997; tr. *Prince*, 1999) goes further than most of the others, however, in that its narrator is a ghost. *Atkinsons biograf: En vandrehistorie* (1998; Atkinson's Biographer: A Traveling Story) contains nine short stories that have many of the characters in common. Michael had long been interested in the magic realism of Latin American literature, and *Kejserens atlas* (2001; The Emperor's Atlas), drawing on a Japanese legend, may well be regarded as a magic realist text. The story takes place on three different temporal levels—past, present, and future—but the levels are interconnected and events on one level depend for their resolution on what happens on the other two. *Paven af Indien* (2003; The Pope of India) makes extensive use of the *Inca Chronicle*, written by Guaman Pomas in 1610 and addressed to the king of Spain for the purpose of bringing about reforms in Spanish colonial rule in the Andean region. Michael's novel tells the story of both the manuscript itself and its historical background. Michael appears to have made a turn in the direction of traditional realist narrative in his novel *Grill* (2005), in which he criticizes Denmark's involvement in the **war** in Iraq.

MICHAËLIS, KARIN (1872–1950). A Danish novelist, short story writer, and journalist, Michaëlis was, like her contemporary **Thit Jensen**, involved in a number of causes, primarily pacifism and animal rights; her early opposition to vivisection is notable. A highly productive writer throughout her life, she had her debut with a collection of short stories, *Højt Spil* (1898; Risky Game), a rather immature work that was not well received. She did much better with the diary novel *Barnet* (1902; The Child), in which her female protagonist goes through puberty. *Lillemor* (1902) is an epistolary novel. Michaëlis found that the diary and epistolary forms were useful for portraying the mental life of her protagonist within a realistic frame.

The novel *Den farlige Alder* (1910; tr. *The Dangerous Age*, 1912) and its sequel *Elsie Lindtner* (1912) discuss postmenopausal female eroticism. Michaëlis also shows how difficult it is for a middle-aged woman to go through a divorce, for men tend to seek younger partners, and a nontraditional relationship between a younger man and an older woman is a threat to the male ego. *Atter det skilte* (1918; Again, the Divorced) deals with similar themes. Michaëlis perfected interior monologue as a narrative technique in the novels *Syv Søstre sad* (1923; Seven Sisters Sat) and *Hjertets Vagabond* (1931; The Vagabond of the Heart).

Michaëlis was well informed about American intellectual life and spent World **War** II as a refugee from the Nazis in the United States, where she worked as a journalist. She was concerned about reforming education for girls—she appears to have learned from John Dewey—and discussed this topic in her four-volume autobiographical novel *Træet paa godt og ondt* (1924–1930; The Tree, for Good and Evil). She also wrote books for young **women**.

MISS JULIE. See *FRÖKEN JULIE*.

MOBERG, VILHELM (1898–1973). A Swedish novelist and dramatist, Moberg hailed from the district of Småland, the folk culture of which he memorialized, however critically, in his first novel, *Raskens* (1927; The Rask Family). He was one of several writers from working-class backgrounds who came to the fore in the 1930s, and he is one of the great storytellers in Swedish literature, as well as one of its most relentless radicals. Moberg's criticism of the rural culture in which he grew up is also voiced in the novels *Långt från landsvägen* (1929; Far from the Highway) and *De knutna händerna* (1930; The Clenched Fists), as well as in the love story *Mans kvinna* (1933; Man's Woman).

Moberg's ambivalent attitude toward the rural culture of Småland is further expressed in an autobiographical trilogy consisting of *Sänkt sedebetyg* (1935; tr. *Memory of Youth*, 1937), *Sömnlös* (1937; tr. *Sleepless Nights*, 1940), and *Giv oss jorden!* (1939; tr. *The Earth Is Ours*, 1940). A later autobiographical novel, *Soldat med brutet gevär* (1944; tr. *When I Was a Child*, 1956), is also set in Småland, to which Moberg found himself unable to return in person. Småland in the 17th century is the setting for a powerful attack on oppression and control, the novel *Rid i natt!* (1941; tr. *Ride This Night!*, 1943), which served as encouragement to resistance fighters everywhere during World War II. Moberg would return to 17th-century Småland with the novel *Förrädarland* (1968; Land of Traitors).

Småland is a district with poor soil, where it has traditionally been hard to eke out a living. For this reason it also became the source of numerous emigrants to America, starting in the middle of the 19th century. Moberg's greatest literary achievement is a tetralogy that tells the story of the vanguard of these emigrants. Consisting of the volumes **Utvandrarna** (1949; tr. *The Emigrants*, 1951), *Invandrarna* (1952; tr. *Unto a Good Land*, 1954), *Nybyggarna* (1956; tr. *The Settlers*, 1961), and *Sista brevet till Sverige* (1959; tr. *The Last Letter Home*, 1961), the tetralogy explains the social and economic reasons for the emigration, describes both the journey across the ocean to the new land and the immigrants' travels in the United States, the process of homesteading, and their lives as more or less successful American citizens. Perhaps influenced by **Ole E. Rølvaag**'s novel *Giants in the Earth* (1924–1925), Moberg portrayed his male protagonist, Karl Oskar Nilsson, as a man who relishes the hard physical labor associated with homesteading, while his wife Kristina never gets over her homesickness for the old country. Other unforgettable characters are the parish harlot Ulrika, who in America becomes the wife of a Baptist minister, and the dreamer Arvid, Karl Oskar's younger brother, who loses his health and eventually dies because of his attraction to the California gold rush. Jan Troell's two films based on Moberg's novels are classics in their genre.

Moberg studied the Swedish-Americans of his own generation in *Din stund på jorden* (1963; tr. *A Time on Earth*, 1965), in which his protagonist discovers that he is unable to feel at home back in Sweden because the country has changed too much in his absence. His at times critical attitude toward the United States is expressed in the essay collection *Den okände släkten* (1950; tr. *The Unknown Swedes*, 1988). Moberg also wrote a large number of plays, many of them folk comedies but some with more serious intentions. *Vår ofödde son* (1945; Our Unborn Son) discusses abortion, and a rather bitter drama about legally administered injustice, *Domaren* (1957; The Judge), is similar to dramas written by the Norwegian playwright **Jens Bjørneboe** a few years later.

MODERN BREAKTHROUGH. The period 1870–1890 is generally referred to as the Modern Breakthrough in Scandinavian literature. Its beginning is associated with a series of lectures given in Copenhagen by **Georg Brandes** in 1871, in which he argued that the purpose of modern literature was to debate current issues. The period of the Modern Breakthrough largely coincides with the periods of **realism** and **naturalism** in Scandinavia. *See also* JACOBSEN, JENS PETER.

MODERNISM. Literary modernism is usually defined in contradistinction to **realism** and **naturalism**, and especially in opposition to the scientific worldview on which they rest. One of the great early European modernists was **Knut Hamsun**, whose novel *Sult* (1890; tr. *Hunger*, 1899) offers a textbook example of modernism's emphasis on a distinctive imagination and attention to peculiar psychological states. *Sult* tells about its narrator's mental experiments as he periodically starves himself so as to observe the effects of starvation on his mind.

The decade of the 1930s was the time when modernism had its definitive breakthrough in Scandinavian literature. While such poets as the Finland-Swedish writers **Edith Södergran** and **Elmer Diktonius** had presented modernist poetry in Scandinavia quite early, the Swede **Pär Lagerkvist** wrote both modernist poetry and prose and became one of modernism's great champions in Scandinavian literature. Modernist poetry became increasingly significant in Scandinavian literature both before and after World War II, and a number of modernist prose writers were also active. In addition to Lagerkvist, the Dane **Tom Kristensen** published his important modernist novel

Hærværk (1930; tr. *Havoc*, 1968), and the Norwegian **Cora Sandel** published her Alberte trilogy, consisting of *Alberte og Jakob* (1926; tr. *Alberta and Jacob*, 1962), *Alberte og friheten* (1931; tr. *Alberta and Freedom*, 1963), and *Bare Alberte* (1939; tr. *Alberta Alone*, 1965). Other modernists of the interwar period are the Finland-Swedish novelist **Hagar Olsson** and the Swede **Moa Martinson**. See also BLICHER, STEEN STEENSEN; BRANNER, HANS CHRISTIAN; CLAUSSEN, SOPHUS; DITLEVSEN, TOVE; EKELÖF, GUNNAR; ENCKELL, RABBE; JOHNSON, EYVIND; LIDMAN, SARA; LUNDKVIST, ARTUR; MARTINSON, HARRY; NORÉN, LARS; RIFBJERG, KLAUS; SANDEMOSE, AKSEL; SEEBERG, PETER; SOLSTAD, DAG; VESAAS, TARJEI.

MØLLER, POUL MARTIN (1794–1838). A Danish novelist and poet, Møller took a degree in theology but was deeply interested in classical literature. Strongly influenced by German idealism, he taught philosophy, first at the University of Christiania (now Oslo) and later at the University of Copenhagen, where his teaching influenced **Søren Kierkegaard**. In Danish literary history, Møller is remembered chiefly for his unfinished novel *En dansk Students Eventyr* (1824; The Adventures of a Danish Student), which is notable both for its psychological portrayal of the characters and its satirical attitude toward some of the excesses of the **romantics**. It is a precursor for the poetic **realism** of the 1840s. Møller's poems were published as *Scener i Rosenborg Have* (1820–1821; published 1855; Scenes from Rosenborg Garden) and are marked by their psychological insight.

MONRAD, MARCUS JACOB (1816–1897). A Norwegian philosopher and **critic**, Monrad was strongly influenced by Hegelianism but was also one of the first serious readers of **Søren Kierkegaard** in Norway. A man with a distinctly conservative bent, Monrad was the primary spokesperson for the right in the cultural and political struggle in Norway during the **Modern Breakthrough**. A prolific contributor to the literary debates in the **Scandinavian literary journals** and newspapers, he wanted to harmonize **romanticism** and **realism**; the Hegelian synthesis of these to opposites was referred to as poetic realism. His most important philosophical work is *Tankeretninger i* *den nyere Tid: Et kritisk Rundskue* (1874; Directions of Thought in Recent Times: A Critical Survey).

MUNK, KAJ (1898–1944). A Danish playwright, Munk was raised in a religious home and took a degree in theology, after which he served as a minister in the Lutheran Danish People's Church for the rest of his life. He was also a very productive writer and wrote more than 50 plays. These dramas are traditional in form, but their content is sui generis; Munk was very much the individualist and his work reflects that fact.

Munk's first drama to be performed was *En Idealist* (1928; tr. *Herod the King*, 1953), but it was a failure. Although his hero worship at times included admiration for Adolf Hitler and Benito Mussolini, Munk's play *Sejren* (1936; The Victory) is nevertheless critical of Italy's actions in Ethiopia. In *Han sidder ved Smeltediglen* (1938; tr. *He Sits at the Melting Pot*, 1953), the protagonist discovers that Jesus was a Jew and not an Aryan, as his government masters would like him to conclude. Although Munk admired Hitler, he was not in agreement with the Nazi treatment of the Jews. In *Før Cannae* (1943; tr. *Before Cannae*, 1953), Munk favors the Churchill figure in the play at the expense of the Hitler figure.

Munk's most successful drama is *Ordet* (1932; tr. *The Word*, 1953), which, like the Norwegian dramatist **Bjørnstjerne Bjørnson**'s play *Over ævne I* (1883; tr. *Pastor Sang*, 1893), discusses the possibility of miracles. Munk, in contrast to Bjørnson, shows a miracle on stage as he contrasts the attitudes of boundless faith with those of more common Christian belief.

During World **War** II Munk became the spiritual leader of the resistance in Denmark. When he was arrested and executed by the Gestapo, he became a martyr to the cause. His dramas have withstood the test of time rather poorly, however. *See also* THEATER.

MYKLE, AGNAR (1915–1994). A Norwegian novelist and short story writer, Mykle is remembered chiefly for testing Norwegian obscenity legislation in the 1950s. His literary debut was the short story collection *Taustigen* (1948; The Rope Ladder), in which he focused on the conflict between expectations and quotidian reality. The novel *Tyven, tyven skal du hete* (1951; tr. *The Hotel Room*, 1963) inveighs against puritanism and defends people's right to sexual freedom. The same concerns animate a book of short stories, *Jeg er like glad, sa gutten* (1952; I Couldn't Care Less, Said the Boy).

Mykle's major works are the two novels *Lasso rundt fru Luna* (1954; tr. *Lasso Round the Moon*, 1960) and *Sangen om den røde rubin* (1956; tr. *The Song of the Red Ruby*, 1961), which present the character Ask Burlefot and his various erotic escapades. Set in the towns of Trondheim and Bergen, the two books offer interesting portraits of the respective social environments but are marred by the similarity of many of their characters to models that were easily recognized by Mykle's contemporary audience. Mykle was accused of pornography but was acquitted by Norway's Supreme Court. While in the middle of the trial, Mykle published a collection of old and new short stories, *Kors på halsen* (1958; Cross My Heart).

The protagonist in the novel *Rubicon* (1965; tr. 1966) is similar to Ask Burlefot, but he is portrayed more humorously. Mykle's focus on sexuality continues in a collection of short stories, *Largo* (1967). The three volumes of *Brev og annen prosa* (1997–1999; Letters and Other Prose), selected from thousands of pages of manuscript materials, were edited by Gordon Hølmebakk and published after Mykle's death. Arne B. Mykle edited *Kjære lille Moff: Reisebrev fra Amerika* (2001; Dear Little Moff: Letters from Travels in America). Several biographies of Mykle were published in the 1990s, and many younger Norwegian writers have found inspiration in his work.

MYRDAL, JAN (1927–). A Swedish novelist, journalist, and dramatist, Myrdal has been a controversial figure in the cultural life of his country—and in the Western world—since the 1960s. Always the radical, and often perceived as being on the extreme left, he has been a clear-eyed observer and a relentless critic of cultural and political forces. His output as a writer is truly voluminous. His books have been widely translated, and he has collected his articles and occasional pieces into 18 volumes of *Skriftställning* (1968–1998; Writings).

Myrdal's greatest significance is as a travel writer who combined the study of an area's geography, history, and economics with extended personal residence and close contact with the common people, whose views he accorded great weight. He became internationally known for his *Rapport från kinesisk by* (1963; tr. *Report from a Chinese Village*, 1965), the first of several books about China. It was illustrated with photographs taken by his wife, Gun Kessle. Other books about China include *Chinese Journey* (1965), originally published in English, *Kina: Revolutionen går vidare* (1970; tr. *China: The Revolution Continued*, 1970), *Kinesiska frågor från Liu Ling* (1976; Chinese Questions from Liu Ling), and *Kinesisk by 20 år senare: Rapport med frågetecken* (1983; tr. *Return to a Chinese Village*, 1984). All of these books have a focus on politics, and particularly on the revolution of Mao Zedong and its aftermath, which Myrdal admired. *Sidenvägen* (1977; tr. *The Silk Road*, 1979) is a more traditional account of a journey.

Other travel books include two volumes about visits to Afghanistan, *Kulturens korsväg: En bok om Afghanistan* (1960; The Crossroad of Culture: A Book about Afghanistan) and *Bortom berg och öknar: Afghanistan, ett framtidsland* (1962; Beyond Mountains and Deserts: Afghanistan, Land of the Future). A similar volume is *Turkmenistan: En revolutions övergångsår* (1966; Turkmenistan: The Transitional Year of a Revolution). Myrdal also wrote about Albania, another poster-boy of **Marxist**-Leninism, in *Albansk utmaning* (1970; tr. *Albania Defiant*, 1976). His inability to perceive the horrors of Enver Hoxha's regime attests to both his idealism and his penchant for viewing the world through ideological glasses, and it was shared by other Scandinavian writers such as the Norwegian **Espen Haavardsholm**. Myrdal has also written about Cambodia and the Soviet Union. India is presented in *Indien väntar* (1980; tr. *India Waits*, 1984), in which Myrdal attributes the significance of Indian religion to the country's poverty. In *Mexico: Dröm och längtan* (1996; Mexico: Dream and Longing), he speaks less favorably about revolutionary change and seems more inclined to allow the forces of democratic capitalism to do their work.

Myrdal is also significant as a confessional and autobiographical writer. The child of two Nobel Prize winners, the economist Gunnar Myrdal and the diplomat Alva Myrdal, he has been critical of the influence of the class of intellectuals to which his parents belonged, members of which, in his observation, tended to place career considerations ahead of the idealism that had originally served as the impetus for their intellectual achievements. His most significant effort in this vein is *Confessions of a Disloyal European* (1968), his own translation and revision of two earlier versions of the book in Swedish. Memoirs of his childhood are found in *Barndom* (1982; tr. *Childhood*, 1991), *En annan värld* (1984; tr. *Another World*, 1994), and *Tolv på det trettonde* (1989; tr. *12 Going on 13*, 1995). The story is continued in *När mongondagarna sjöng: Från glömda år: En berättelse* (1994; When Tomorrow Was Singing: A Tale from Forgotten Years), in which Myrdal's protagonist has reached the age of 17. The book *Maj: En kärlek* (1998; Maj: A Love Story) tells about Myrdal's relationship with his second wife. A sixth volume of autobiography is *Gubbsjuka* (2002; Old Man's Sickness).

Myrdal has written a number of novels, which are thoroughly informed by his commitments and his worldview. Some of his early efforts are the satire *Jubelvår* (1955; Spring of Jubilee); *Att bli och vara* (1956; Becoming and Being), which tells about the young protagonist's problems with work, love, and family; and *Baderumskranen* (1957; The Bathroom Faucet), which satirizes the Swedish welfare state. A later satire, directed at the Swedish social democrats, is the novel *Karriär* (1975; Career). Myrdal's dramatic works include a number of radio plays as well as the screenplay for the television movie *Myglaren* (1966; The Broker).

– N –

NATIONAL ROMANTICISM. Many Scandinavian writers were greatly influenced by the ideas of the German thinker Johann Gottfried von Herder (1744–1803), who emphasized the role of the nation as well as language and its connection to the divine spirit that could be found in **nature**. Starting with the Dane **Adam Oehlenschläger**, national romanticism became a major force in Scandinavia. Oehlenschläger's poem "Guldhornene" (1802; The Golden Horns), for example, features a young man who finds a golden horn with a runic inscription on it while plowing his field. Another characteristic example of national romantic literature is a short story by the Norwegian writer **Maurits Hansen** entitled "Luren" (1819; The Shepherd's Horn), in which the narrator tells about a visit to a Norwegian farm family in the interior of the country. As in Oehlenschläger's poem, there is an emphasis on the continuity between the present and the nation's past, the connection between the people and the soil, and the role of language.

National romanticism manifested itself throughout the entire Scandinavian cultural area, from Iceland in the west to Finland in the east. In Iceland, the work of the poet **Jónas Hallgrímsson** emphasized both the past of the nation and the significance of its language. In Sweden, **Esaias Tegnér** and **Per Daniel Amadeus Atterbom** exemplify the movement. Atterbom was a core member of the group Auraraförbundet (The **Aurora Society**), which published the journal *Phosphorus*, an important voice for **romanticism** in Sweden. Tegnér's best-known work is *Frithiofs saga* (1825; tr. 1833), which expands a brief Old Norse story into a Swedish national epic consisting of 24 songs. In Finland, the **folklore** collections of **Elias Lönnrot** (1802–1884) are emblematic of the later stage of national romanticism, while the work of **Johan Ludvig Runeberg**, particularly his play *Kung Fjalar* (1844; tr. *King Fjalar*, 1904), is a classic example of the movement's antiquarian side.

The greatest and most enduring significance of national romanticism in Scandinavia, however, is found in its attitude toward the oral literature of the people, as their ballads, folk tales, and legends were collected and analyzed, after which they began to influence the work of educated writers. In Denmark, for example, the stories of **Steen Steensen Blicher** show influence from folk literature in terms of both their subject matter and the language in which they are presented. In Norway, the self-taught linguist **Ivar Aasen** single-handedly created a separate written form of Norwegian called **Landsmaal** (country language), based on the dialects spoken in western Norway, as an alternative to the Danish-influenced language that was standard at the time. *See also* BJØRNSON, BJØRNSTJERNE; GEIJER, ERIK GUSTAV; IBSEN, HENRIK; VINJE, AASMUND OLAFSSON.

NATURALISM. A further development of **realism**, naturalism is the use of scientific determinism in literature. According to this doctrine, human beings have no real agency but act according to their biological inheritance and the influence of their social milieu. For the naturalists, truth was to be found in **nature** rather than, as for the

romantics, in some kind of transcendental reality, and the task of the writer was to imitate the scientist as far as possible.

These theoretical concerns had certain consequences for both the style of the naturalist literary work and the author's choice of subject matter. The story would be told in great detail, as in the short story by the Norwegian writer **Amalie Skram** entitled "Karens jul" (1885; Karen's Christmas), in which an unwed teenage mother and her baby freeze to death in Christiania (now Oslo) a couple of days before Christmas. **Arne Garborg** similarly offers numerous details in his naturalist works, for example, the novel *Hjaa ho Mor* (1890; Living with Mama), which is partly based on the life of his wife, Hulda.

While many of the realists discussed the position of **women** in the family and in society, the naturalists went further by examining the sexual roles of men and women, showing that people of both sexes were biologically unable to control their sexual urges. In **August Strindberg**'s play *Fröken Julie* (1888; tr. *Miss Julie*, 1912), for example, the two major characters are powerless when faced with a combination of temptation and opportunity.

The naturalists were particularly interested in demonstrating that prostitution was a necessary counterpart to middle-class marriage and held that the daughters of the middle class were raised to become sexually dysfunctional, thus more or less compelling their future husbands to seek the company of prostitutes. Illness was also a favorite topic, and the naturalists' concern with illness ranged from portraying the ravages of pulmonary tuberculosis to discussing the etiology of syphilis, as **Henrik Ibsen** did in his play *Gengangere* (1881; *Ghosts*, 1885). Yet another favorite topic was crime, as in **Jonas Lie**'s novel *Livsslaven* (1883; tr. *One of Life's Slaves*, 1895). This theme was attractive because a determinist outlook on life is not logically consistent with the idea that people should be held morally and legally responsible for their actions. *See also* HEIDENSTAM, VERNER VON; JACOBSEN, JENS PETER; LAGERLÖF, SELMA; PONTOPPIDAN, HENRIK.

NATURE. Both **romanticism** in general and **national romanticism** show a strong preoccupation with nature, which in the latter manifests itself as worship of the nature of one's homeland. The Swedish poet **Erik Gustav Geijer** exemplifies romanticism's concern with nature, while the Dane **Adam Oehlenschläger** and the Norwegians **Johan Sebastian Welhaven** and **Henrik Wergeland** regard nature as closely connected with the nation. **Karl August Tavaststjerna** celebrated Finnish nature, while **Olav Duun, Arne Garborg**, and **Jonas Lie** offered descriptions of Norwegian nature in their works. The conflict between nature and culture is a pervasive motif in Scandinavian literature, as shown by the works of such writers as **Benny Andersen, Peter Høeg, Leena Krohn, Artur Lundkvist**, and **Jacob Paludan**. Some Scandinavian writers urge a return to or oneness with nature, such as **Eeva Joenpelto, Eyvind Johnson, Erik Axel Karlfeldt**, and **Tarjei Vesaas**. *See also* BJØRNVIG, THORKILD; CLAUSSEN, SOPHUS; EKMAN, KERSTIN; HAMSUN, KNUT; HEIBERG, JOHAN LUDVIG; HJARTARSON, SNORRI; LEINO, EINO; MARTINSON, HARRY; VON SCHOULTZ, SOLVEIG.

NEOROMANTICISM. A reaction against **realism** in the Scandinavian literature of the 19th century, neoromanticism was a form of the **symbolist** movement that originated in France. *See also* ROMANTICISM.

NEXØ, MARTIN ANDERSEN (1869–1954). A Danish novelist, short story writer, poet, and essayist, Nexø was born into the family of a poor laborer in Copenhagen but grew up on the Danish island of Bornholm in the Baltic, where his father worked as a stonecutter. Nexø did agricultural labor and was a shoemaker's apprentice before attending the Askov folk high school, after which he found work as a teacher. His literary achievement is to have chronicled the history of the Danish proletariat, to which he gave life in the unforgettable figures of Pelle and Ditte.

After getting an education and finding work as a teacher, it is likely that Nexø's experience with grueling physical work as a young man became somewhat distant for him. His early novel *Dryss* (1902; Waste) indicates that he had bought into the essentially middle-class concerns of the literature of the 1890s. With a diagnosis of tuberculosis, however, he traveled to Italy and Spain to get well, and there he came into close contact with labor organizations. His sympathies were at times with the most radical of these, anarchists and syndicalists, and at other times with the more moderate social democrats. *Soldage* (1903; tr. *Days in the Sun*, 1929) tells about the radicalizing experiences Nexø had in Spain, after which he returned to Denmark ready to devote his life to the cause of socialism.

After writing some short stories where political themes occur from time to time, Nexø allowed his anger at the injustice visited on the working class to give life to his greatest artistic achievement, the epic multivolume novel **Pelle Erobreren** (1906–1910; tr. *Pelle the Conqueror*, 1930). Pelle grows up in Bornholm, then goes to the factories and slums of Copenhagen, and finally becomes a leader in the cooperative movement, which was conceived of as a just alternative to capitalist exploitation. But Pelle is not without flaws; he has not understood that justice for proletarian men is not sufficient and that there must be justice for **women** too. *Pelle the Conqueror* has been immensely popular for a long time, and its reputation was enhanced when a film version received the Academy Award for best foreign film in 1989.

Nexø's second great literary work, *Ditte Menneskebarn* (1917–1921; tr. *Ditte*, 1931), is a five-volume series of novels. Born in the countryside, Ditte, like Pelle, is brought to the city by the process of industrialization, but as a woman she has challenges that Pelle avoids. She has a baby out of wedlock and becomes a seamstress to support herself and her child, and as a seamstress she is ruthlessly taken advantage of. Also, she shows compassion to whoever needs it, and the brutal world of exploitative capitalism does not allow her to generate the surplus resources that she would need to help others without harming herself. She is dying at the end of the novel, and her child has just been killed by a train while scavenging for lumps of coal.

A third series of novels had been contemplated by Nexø. This series bears the title *Morten hin Røde* (1945–1957; Morten the Red) but was left unfinished; the last volume was published posthumously. While Pelle is a reformist socialist and Ditte is just a kind and rather apolitical human being, Morten is a revolutionary **Marxist** who also appears in *Pelle the Conqueror*, where he is critical of the direction Pelle is taking the labor movement. *Morten hin Røde* is less successful artistically than *Pelle* and *Ditte*. It is too much of a record of the infighting in the Danish labor movement and lacking in the mythic dimension that is present in the two former series.

Nexø wrote other novels, but they are of less significance than *Pelle* and *Ditte*. The novel *Familien Frank* (1901; The Frank Family) displays a kind of direct **realism** that points toward some of the depictions of proletarian life in Nexø's later books. In the novel *Midt i en Jærntid* (1929; tr. *In God's Land*, 1933), Nexø assigns blame for the great financial crash of 1929; greedy and corrupt farmers are singled out for special treatment. Some of Nexø's short fiction, including a number of stories set in Bornholm, was collected in the three volumes of *Muldskud* (1900–1926; From the Soil). His memoirs, *Erindringer* (1932–1939; Recollections), offer many details about his early life. Nexø also wrote poetry, published a play, wrote numerous articles, and published a book about his travels in the Soviet Union. Disappointed with the political direction taken by Denmark's social democrats, he elected to spend his later years in communist East Germany, where he died.

NOBEL PRIZE IN LITERATURE. One of several prizes established through the will of Alfred Nobel (1833–1896), the Nobel Prize in literature is awarded by the Swedish Academy, a self-perpetuating body of 18 Swedish men and women of letters elected for life and first established by King **Gustav III**. Since Nobel's will specified that the prize was to be awarded to a writer from any country who had produced "the most outstanding work of an idealistic tendency," there has been some debate about what "idealistic" was intended to mean. Such social critics as, for example, **Henrik Ibsen** and **August Strindberg** did not receive the prize. Since its inception in 1901, the following Scandinavian writers have been selected as recipients: **Bjørnstjerne Bjørnson** (1903), **Selma Lagerlöf** (1909), **Verner von Heidenstam** (1916), Karl Gjellerup (1917; shared prize), **Henrik Pontoppidan** (1917; shared prize), **Knut Hamsun** (1920), **Sigrid Undset** (1928), **Erik Axel Karlfeldt** (1931), **Frans Eemil Sillanpää** (1939), **Johannes V. Jensen** (1944), **Pär Lagerkvist** (1951), **Halldór Kiljan Laxness** (1955), **Eyvind Johnson** (1974; shared prize), and **Harry Martinson** (1974; shared prize). More men than women have historically received the prize, and more Scandinavian writers than non-Scandinavians, given the size of the populations of the Scandinavian countries relative to the rest of the world.

NORDBRANDT, HENRIK (1945–). A Danish poet and essayist, Nordbrandt is generally recognized as one of the truly outstanding poets of his homeland, not only in his generation but in the 20th century as a whole. His first book was entitled simply *Digte* (1966; Poems), after which he published a long series of poetry collections, among which are *Syvsoverne* (1969; The Late Sleepers), *Ode til blæksprutten og andre kærlighedsdigte* (1975; Ode to the Squid and Other Love Poems), *Glas* (1976; Glass), *Guds hus* (1977; tr. *God's House*, 1979), and *Armenia* (1982). His poetic vision has been remarkably consistent throughout his career. While Nordbrandt has a **modernist** sensibility and at times may be read as a **postmodernist**, he does not despair at the inability of human beings to get language to hook onto the world. Rather, it is the gap between word and thing, the world and language, which enables Nordbrandt's poetic vision. Any despair at finding that meaning is a myth is compensated for by the opportunity for poetic creation that the absence of meaning affords him.

A similar dynamic is present in Nordbrandt's love poetry, which constitutes a major portion of his oeuvre. As is the case with the absence of meaning in the world, it is the absence of the beloved that stimulates him to speak of her, and the images that are a part of those speech acts serve as consolation for the speaker. This is shown particularly clearly in the volume *Glemmesteder* (1991; Places of Forgetting), in which Nordbrandt mourns the loss of his companion Ingrid. While dealing with what is arguably the greatest sorrow that life can inflict on a human being, Nordbrandt responded to the pain by composing some of his finest poetry, as shown also by his next collection, *Ormene ved himlens port* (1995; The Worms at the Gate of Heaven). The pain associated with the speaker's childhood is similarly transformed in the volume *Drømmebroer* (1998; Dream Bridges). Nordbrandt returns to investigating the incommensurability of word and thing in the collection *Pjaltefisk* (2004; Rag Fish).

Nordbrandt has also produced crime fiction and essays. *Døden fra Lübeck* (2002; The Death from Lübeck) is a book about his childhood.

NORDENFLYCHT, HEDVIG CHARLOTTA (1718–1762). A Swedish poet, Nordenflycht is the most significant Enlightenment woman writer in Sweden. Born into a noble family and widowed in her early 20s, she lived on the island of Lidingö near Stockholm. In addition to writing occasional poetry and lyric expressions of her own situation in life, she advocated for improved education of women in her *Qvinligt Tankespel af en Herdinna i Norden* (1744; Womanly Thought Play by a Shepherdess in the North). She was also a central figure in the group Tankebyggarorden (The Order of Thought Builders), which worked to promote Swedish literary and intellectual life.

NORDIC LITERARY PRIZE. The Nordic Literary Prize, in the amount of 350,000 Danish kroner, is awarded by the Nordic Council each year for a literary work written in one of the languages of the Scandinavian countries. The work may be a novel, a drama, or a collection of poetry, short stories, or essays. The Nordic Council is an organization consisting of members of parliament from each of the Scandinavian countries, including the Faroes and Greenland.

Among the recipients are **Johan Borgen**, **Bo Carpelan**, **Lars Saabye Christensen**, **Sven Delblanc**, **Gunnar Ekelöf**, **Kerstin Ekman**, **Per Olov Enquist**, **Kjartan Fløgstad**, **Thorkild Hansen**, **William Heinesen**, **Snorri Hjartarson**, **Eyvind Johnson**, **Jan Kjærstad**, **Sara Lidman**, **Väinö Linna**, **Ivar Lo-Johansson**, **Henrik Nordbrandt**, **Klaus Rifbjerg**, **Peter Seeberg**, **Dag Solstad**, **Per Olof Sundman**, **Villy Sørensen**, **Pia Tafdrup**, **Tomas Tranströmer**, **Göran Tunström**, **Nils-Aslak Valkeapää**, **Tarjei Vesaas**, **Thor Vilhjálmsson**, **Herbjørg Wassmo**, and **Dorrit Willumsen**.

While it took 18 years before the prize was first awarded to a **woman**, approximately one-third of the prize winners in recent years have been women. The prize winners are fairly equally distributed among the five Scandinavian countries.

NORÉN, LARS (1944–). A Swedish poet, playwright, novelist, and scriptwriter, Norén is an extremely prolific writer and has a dominant place in Swedish drama. He started out as a poet, however, and had his debut with the collection *Syrener, snö* (1963; Lilacs, Snow), which received a very negative reception. His second volume, *De verbala resterna av en bildprakt som förgår* (1964; The Verbal Remnants of a Vanishing Pictorial Splendor), contained echoes of **mod-**

ernism and surrealism. But Norén, who had suffered a psychotic episode as a young man, created very disturbing images that conveyed a vision of the world as being completely without order and meaning. In several additional volumes of poetry, most notably *Encyclopedi* (1966; Encyclopedia) and *Stupor* (1968; Stupor), his extremely personal poetry of schizophrenia was sufficiently structured to be meaningful to readers.

In the early 1970s Norén published two novels, *Biskötarna* (1970; The Beekepers) and *I den underjordiska himlen: Biskötarna II* (1972; In the Subterranean Heaven: The Beekeepers II), which tell about experiences of a writer modeled on Norén, particularly the effects of his father's death, and offer depictions of dysfunctional family life. His poetry at this time also adhered more fully to conventional principles of mimesis. The collection *Viltspeglar* (1972; Game Reflectors) includes poems that have the form of letters to home written by a soldier during the Thirty Years War. Other volumes, such as *Kung Mej och andra dikter* (1973; King Me and Other Poems) and *Dagliga och nattliga dikter* (1974; Poems of Night and Day), show that Norén was still trying to work through his psychic conflicts, but in a more systematic and organized manner than before. This project continued in a large number of poetry collections throughout the 1970s.

While working hard to maintain his psychic health, Norén also wrote a number of dramas. His dramatic debut was the television piece *Amala, Kamala: Punkter för televisjon* (Amala, Kamala: Points for Television, produced in 1971). The first work to be staged was *Fursteslickaren* (The Prince Licker, produced at the Royal Dramatic Theater, Stockholm, in 1973). Set in Europe during the 16th century, it is an investigation of the relationship between sadomasochism, power, and art. Plays written during the late 1970s exhibit a higher degree of realism in their form, and this is especially the case after Norén sought formal psychotherapy subsequent to the death of his father.

Norén is currently the central figure in Swedish drama and **theater**. Since 1980 he has written several dozen plays. Many of them deal with family relations, especially with difficulties in communication. A paradigmatic example is a play written about Eugene O'Neill, *Och ge oss skuggorna* (1991; And Give Us the Shadows), which deals with O'Neill's family life and uses *Long Day's Journey into Night* (1956) as an intertext.

NYNORSK. A successor to **Ivar Aasen**'s **Landsmaal**, nynorsk (New Norwegian) is a less old-fashioned alternative to the earlier Danish-influenced form of written Norwegian.

– O –

OBRESTAD, TOR (1938–). A Norwegian novelist, short story writer, and poet, Obrestad was one of the most active members of the Norwegian *Profil* group. He started out as a rather traditional late **modernist**, publishing both a collection of poetry, *Kollisjon* (1966; Collision), and a volume of short stories, *Vind* (1966; Wind). Writing in **nynorsk**, Obrestad showed that he had learned from **Arne Garborg** and **Tarjei Vesaas**. With the poetry collections *Vårt daglige brød* (1968; Our Daily Bread) and *Den norske løve* (1970; The Norwegian Lion), as well as the novel *Marionettar* (1969; Marionettes), he showed that he had made the transition to **Marxist**-Leninism that his colleague **Dag Solstad** celebrated in *Arild Asnes, 1970*. Obrestad's revolutionary fervor is on display in his documentary novel *Sauda! Streik!* (1972; Sauda! Strike!), which tells the story of a strike in the industrial community in western Norway that **Kjartan Fløgstad** has memorialized as Lovra. Other volumes in praise of revolution are the poetry collections *Sauda og Shanghai* (1973; Sauda and Shanghai) and *Stå saman* (1974; Stand Together), the short story collection *Tolken* (1975; The Interpreter), and the novel *Stå på!* (1976; Hang In There!).

Like many other writers of his generation, Obrestad became less strident in the 1980s. A love story is an important component of the novel *Ein gong må du seie adjø* (1981; Someday You Must Say Good-Bye), and a volume of stories and other prose texts entitled *Sjå Jæren, gamle Jæren* (1982; Look at Jæren, Old Jæren) is in many ways a declaration of love for this district in southwestern Norway. The poetry collection *Misteltein* (1988; Mistletoe) was followed by the novel *Seks netter, seks dagar* (1989; Six Nights, Six Days) and the short story collection *Forsøk på å halda fast tida* (1993; Attempting to Make Time Stay Put) as well as a volume of poetry entitled *Mimosa Myosotis Rosmarin* (1994; Mimosa, Myosotis, Rosemary). *Jæren: eld og blått* (1997; Jæren: Fire and Blue) contains poems in praise of Obrestad's home district, while the novel *Bernhards mor* (1998; Bernhard's Mother) focuses on questions of identity and marriage. *Kvinnene i Casablanca* (2002; The Women of Casablanca) is a collection of 14 stories set in Europe, North Africa, and China. Obrestad has also written **children's books**, published many volumes of literature in translation, and produced biographies of such canonical Norwegian writers as Arne Garborg and **Alexander Kielland**.

OEHLENSCHLÄGER, ADAM (1779–1850). A Danish poet and dramatist, Oehlenschläger was the central figure in Danish **romanticism**. With the exception of **Johannes Ewald**, who was active as a poet around the time of Oehlenschläger's birth, Oehlenschläger gets the credit for having advanced Danish literature from the neoclassicism of the mid to late 1700s and introduced the ideas and literary practice of romanticism not only to Denmark but to the rest of Scandinavia as well. While receptive to the ideas of German universal romanticism, Oehlenschläger soon transcended its limited aesthetics and adopted a **national romanticism** that emphasized both Danish **nature** and Scandinavia's glorious past. While Oehlenschläger wrote most of his groundbreaking works during approximately one decade, he was an active presence on the Scandinavian literary scene for half a century.

Oehlenschläger's first significant literary work was his *Digte* (1803; Poems), which includes an epic section, a lyrical one, containing the poem "Guldhornene" (The Golden Horns)—a poem about two golden horns from 400 CE that were found by a farm boy and then stolen and probably melted down—and a dramatic section, consisting of the drama "Sanct Hansaften-Spil" (Saint John's Eve Play). This mixing of genres was an essential element among the German romantics. While spending four years abroad, Oehlenschläger next published his two-volume *Poetiske Skrifter* (1805; Poetic Writings). The first volume contains nature poetry in the two poetry cycles *Langelands-Reise* (Langeland Journey) and *Jesu Christi gientagne*

Liv i den aarlige Natur (The Life of Jesus Christ Restored in the Annual Cycle of Nature). The second volume contains *Vaulundurs Saga* (Volund's Saga), which takes its theme from an Eddaic poem, and the five-act drama *Aladdin* (tr. 1857, 1968), in which good and evil are contrasted and where Aladdin, the representative of the forces of goodness, can triumph only after having been chastened and tested in adversity.

Nordiske Digte (1807; Nordic Poems) represented a further turn toward national themes. The ancient Scandinavian gods Thor, Baldur, and Loki figure prominently, as do ancient heroes, for example, in *Hakon Jarl* (tr. 1857, 1874, 1905). Characters set in Danish history appear in *Axel og Valborg* (1810; tr. *Axel and Valborg*, 1851, 1873, 1874, 1906), a tragic love story.

Oehlenschläger was later criticized for being overly sentimental by both **Jens Baggesen** and **Johan Ludvig Heiberg**. This criticism was deserved, for Oehlenschläger tended to shy away from presenting dramatic conflicts without any hope of resolution. Oehlenschläger's later works are simply not of the same high quality as his earlier ones. One exception is *Helge* (1814), in which wrongdoing destroys a family line until the misdeeds have been completely atoned for. A couple of plays from the 1840s also show that Oehlenschläger eventually caught on to the need to provide a more nuanced psychological portrayal of his characters.

OLSSON, HAGAR (1893–1978). A Finland-Swedish **critic**, novelist, short story writer, essayist, and dramatist, Olsson grew up in the Åland Islands and Karelia, after which she went to Helsinki to attend the university. She quickly embarked on a career in journalism and became a literary critic in Helsinki's Swedish-language press, in which capacity she became very helpful to the young poet **Edith Södergran**.

Olsson's earliest novels are apprentice pieces. However, important themes emerge as early as in her literary debut, *Lars Thorman och döden* (1916; Lars Thorman and Death), in which both fear of death and an interest in mysticism are evident. The second theme is strongly present in her third novel, *Kvinnan och nåden* (1919; The Woman and Grace), in which the story of the biblical Hannah and her son, the prophet Samuel, is retold. Other novels, such as *Mr. Jere-*

mias söker en illusion (1926; Mr. Jeremiah Seeks an Illusion), *På Kanaanexpressen* (1929; On the Canaan Express), and *Det blåser upp till storm* (1930; A Storm Is Brewing), show that Olsson had not yet found herself as a novelist. The partly autobiographical novel *Chitambo* (1933), on the other hand, which depicts the development of a young woman, introduced a figure that from then on was to be a strong presence in Olsson's fiction. *Träsnidaren och döden* (1940; tr. *The Woodcarver and Death*, 1965) pays homage to Karelia, much of which had just been taken by Russia. Her shorter prose work *Kinesisk utflykt* (1950; Chinese Excursion), as well as the tales in *Hemkomst: Tre berättelser* (1961; Homecoming: Three Tales), *Drömmar* (1966; Dreams), and *Ridturen och andra berättelser* (1968; On Horseback and Other Stories), feature young women as protagonists.

Olsson also wrote drama. *Hjärtats pantomim* (1927; The Pantomime of the Heart) shows influence from German **expressionism**. In *S.O.S.* (1928) the inventor of a superpowerful poison gas is accused of being unpatriotic when he destroys the gas's chemical formula, while *Det blå underet* (1931; The Blue Wonder) dramatizes the conflict between different political positions—liberalism, communism, and fascism—within a single family. In *Rövaren och jungfrun* (1944; The Robber and the Maiden) there is yet another young woman who embodies the hope for the future, while *Kärlekens död* (1952; Love's Death) shows that the malaise of the time was caused by human selfishness.

ØRSTAVIK, HANNE (1969–). A Norwegian novelist, Ørstavik is considered one of the most interesting and promising writers of her generation, and she is one of several Norwegian writers who provided extensive discussions of family relations in their works from the 1990s. She had her debut with a collection of brief fragments entitled *Hakk* (1994; Pecks), and followed it up with a psychological thriller, *Entropi* (1995; Entropy), in which it is difficult to grasp the distinction between what happens in reality and in the protagonist's mind. The apparently simple story concerns a woman who refuses to go to work and stays home for an undetermined period of time; there is no way of telling how long, and no resolution to her conflict is offered. *Kjærlighet* (1997; Love), a minimalist story about a single mother who lets her son freeze to death because she is too busy with her interesting work and trying to find a man, is a poignant examination of the mother role in Norway toward the end of the 20th century. In *Like sant som jeg er virkelig* (1999; As If I Were Real) the story concerns the relationship between a mother and her adult daughter, a student of psychology who one day wakes up and discovers that she has been accidentally locked into her room. While waiting for her mother to return home, she reviews the various conflicts in her life through interior monologue.

Tiden det tar (2000; The Time It Takes) portrays family dynamics at their worst. The protagonist, Signe, appears on two narrative levels, as a 13-year-old girl and as a 30-year-old mother of a small child. Life in Signe's family of origin is characterized by dissimulation, manipulation, and violence, and Signe's challenge is to not perpetuate these traditions in her relationship with her own child. In *Uke 43* (2002; Week 43) a young literary scholar tries to find meaning in life by cultivating a relationship with an older colleague but finds herself without any kind of center to her personality. *Presten* (2004; The Minister) tells the story of a woman who has been appointed the new state church minister in a small coastal town in Finnmark, the northernmost county in Norway. She has to provide comfort for suffering parishoners and try to come to terms with the lingering oppression of the Sámi people by the area's ethnic Norwegians. *Presten* also has an interesting historical dimension, as Ørstavik weaves the story of a Sámi rebellion in the 1840s into her narrative.

– P –

PALUDAN, JACOB (1896–1975). A Danish novelist and essayist, Paludan was a conservative voice in Danish literature during the interwar period. The son of a literary historian, he was educated as a pharmacist, and he traveled to the United States and Ecuador in 1920–1921. While in the United States he developed a strong dislike for the American emphasis on success and the role of materialism in American culture. This criticism was first voiced in the novel *De vestlige veje* (1922; The Western Roads), in which a disillusioned emigrant offers his satirical view of the hollowness of American life in general and urban life in particular. Paludan's next novel, *Søgelys* (1923; Searchlight), deals with similar themes but is set in Copenhagen. In the novel *En vinter lang* (1924; Winter Long) Paludan drew on his own experience and offered a psychological analysis of the figure of the outsider. His next book, *Fugle omkring fyret* (1925; tr. *Birds around the Light*, 1928), has as its setting the economic bubble during World **War** I, which led to decline among many older moneyed families but created a great deal of new wealth. Paludan's novel describes a hubristic construction project, a new port, which the ocean rises up and washes away, thus demonstrating the superiority of **nature** over culture. The novel *Markerne modnes* (1927; The Fields Are Ripening) likewise expresses Paludan's cultural pessimism.

Paludan's finest novel is the two-volume family saga *Jørgen Stein* (1932–1933; tr. 1966), which covers the history of the Stein family, starting before World War I and ending around 1930. Jørgen's father, a government official, is most likely modeled on the father of Paludan's close friend Eric C. Eberlin (1899–1943), who provided Paludan with much of the material for his novels. In *Jørgen Stein* the father experiences financial ruin and the disintegration of his system of values, while Jørgen's brother Otto becomes a speculator and eventually commits suicide. Jørgen himself knows that he cannot go back to the life of his father and refuses to accept the values of his brother; in the end, he marries and becomes a chicken farmer.

Jørgen Stein was Paluden's last novel. He then turned to the essay, of which he became a master, eventually publishing numerous volumes on the subjects of nature and literature. He also wrote several volumes of memoirs.

PALUDAN-MÜLLER, FREDERIK (1809–1876). A Danish poet and dramatist, Paludan-Müller had a literary career that illustrates the Danish philosopher **Søren Kierkgaard**'s aesthetic and ethical stages of existence. While a law student at the University of Copenhagen, Paludan-Müller sought the favor of the city's lovers of literature with his two volumes of *Poesier* (1836–1838; Poems) and the epic *Danserinden* (1833; The Dancer); the latter tells about the unsuccessful love relationship between a nobleman and a woman of low rank. Classical mythology gave him material for the dramas *Amor og Psy-*

che (1834; Cupid and Psyche) and *Venus* (1841), as well as for the dramatic poem *Tithon* (1844), which draws on the legends about Troy. Paludan-Müller's work was well received, and he became a much celebrated literary figure in Copenhagen.

Paludan-Müller's turn toward ethical seriousness came as a consequence of a potentially fatal illness and resulted in one of the great works of Danish literature, the epic *Adam Homo* (1842–1849; tr. 1981), which has a religious as well as an ethical dimension. Adam is an everyman whose path through life is that of a scoundrel and sinner; when he dies and enters the afterlife, he is saved from damnation only because of the prayers and pure love of a woman named Alma. The similarities to the Norwegian dramatist **Henrik Ibsen**'s *Peer Gynt* (1867) are fairly obvious. Other parallels are that both Adam and Peer experience great financial and social success, which contributes to their downfall, and like Paludan-Müller's younger self, both are Kierkegaardian aesthetes. Paludan-Müller also wrote an ethical counterpart to *Adam Homo*, the trilogy *Ivar Lykkes Historie* (1866–1873; The Story of Ivar Lykke), in which Ivar's stature as a human being increases as he suffers material adversity and defeat.

PANDURO, LEIF (1923–1977). A Danish novelist, short story writer, and radio and television dramatist, Panduro was a dentist as well as a resistance fighter who took a bullet on the last day of the German occupation of Denmark during World **War** II. With an insane mother and a father who was on the opposite side during the war, it is perhaps no wonder that Panduro underwent formal psychotherapy and wrote in order to maintain his sanity.

Panduro's literary debut, the novel *Av, min guldtand* (1957; Ouch, My Gold Tooth), and its successor, *Rend mig i traditionerne* (1958; tr. *Kick Me in the Traditions*, 1961), are light and humorous narratives. Most of Panduro's novels, however, deal with characters who have lost their way in the world. This is the case with a young person in *De uanstændige* (1960; The Indecent Ones), but the later novels feature older protagonists who are becoming set in their confusion and lack of a sense of belonging. *Fejltagelsen* (1964; The Mistake), *Den gale mand* (1965; The Crazy Man), *Fern fra Danmark* (1963; Fern from Denmark), *Daniels anden verden* (1970; Daniel's Other World), and *Vinduerne*, 1971; The Windows) are all in this vein. Two characters from *De uanstændige* return as a middle-aged couple in *Amatørerne* (1972; The Amateurs), and it is no surprise that their problems have not diminished. *Den ubetænksomme elsker* (1973; The Thoughtless Lover) is, quite literally, full of insanity, while *Høfeber* (1975; Hay Fever) is a novel about love and jealousy that questions the boundaries of what is considered normal.

Panduro wrote radio plays as well as 12 television dramas, in which characters are portrayed realistically in the context of stories that emphasize social issues. *Farvel Thomas* (1968; Goodbye, Thomas) shows how getting divorced causes a middle-aged man to fall apart psychologically. *Et godt liv* (1971; A Good Life) tells about a man who learns that he has heart trouble just as he is about to embark on the kind of life that he has always dreamt of. There are no easy answers and no easy way to get through life in Panduro's world.

PELLE EROBREREN. An epic multivolume novel by the Dane **Martin Andersen Nexø**, *Pelle Erobreren* (1906–1910; tr. *Pelle the Conqueror*, 1930) expresses Nexø's anger at injustice suffered by the working class. Its reputation was enhanced when a film version received the Academy Award for best foreign film in 1989.

PELLE THE CONQUEROR. See PELLE EROBREREN.

PLEIJEL, AGNETA (1940–). A Swedish poet, playwright, and novelist, Pleijel writes mostly about the experience of creative **women** in an unsupportive patriarchal society. While her early work had a strong socialist tenor, she later came to focus more on problems associated with individual creativity. After a significant career as a newspaper and academic literary **critic**, Pleijel turned to playwriting. She had her debut with the play *Ordning härskar i Berlin* (1970; Order Reigns in Berlin), written with Ronny Ambjörnsson, about the trial of the murderers of the socialist Rosa Luxemburg in Weimar Germany. The drama *Kollontay* (1979), based on the life of the Russian revolutionary Alexandra Kollontay, and on which she collaborated with the director Alf Sjöberg, became her definitive breakthrough. The Russian mathematician Sonja Kovalevsky was the subject of the film *Berget på månens baksida* (1983; The Mountain on the Dark Side of the Moon), for which Pleijel wrote the screenplay. Kovalevsky is portrayed caught in a classic conflict between her intellectual commitments and the man she loves. Pleijel has also written the screenplay for *Undanflykten* (1986; The Escape).

Pleijel's poetry further discusses questions associated with frustrated creativity. The collection *Änglar, dvärgar* (1981; Angles, Dwarves) uses the tension between a **fairy tale** princess and a dwarf to give a mythical expression to the conflict between the creative and the mundane. *Ögon ur en dröm* (1984; tr. *Eyes from a Dream*, 1991) presents the autobiographical impulse as essentially creative.

There is a strong autobiographical component in Pleijel's first novel, *Vindspejare* (1987; Wind-Watcher), which has Java as its setting and tells about the life of Pleijel's maternal grandfather. The novel *Hundstjärnan* (1989; tr. *The Dog Star*, 1991), on the other hand, approaches the question of identity from the perspective of a girl who has to find a sense of identity while faced with going through puberty and also while having to deal with the presence of incest in her family. *Fungi* (1993) speaks in favor of holism by emphasizing the connectedness between humans and other elements of the world, while *En vinter i Stockholm* (1997; A Winter in Stockholm) returns to the problems of **women** who have to balance their intellectual needs with their desire for love. *Lord Nevermore* (2000) examines norms of masculinity prior to World **War** I by telling the story of two Polish friends who travel to Australia.

Pleijel returned to drama with *Standard Selection* in 2000. Named for a brand of cheap Swedish whiskey, it is a critique of life in Sweden in the 1970s and was published in 2003 together with a companion piece in *Vid floden: Två pjäser* (At the River: Two Plays). *Vid floden* features two old siblings—a brother and sister—who share conflicting memories of their mother. The theme of remembered relatives is continued in the poetry collection *Mostrarna* (2004; The Aunts), which features memories of Pleijel's own family and childhood. *See also* THEATER.

PONTOPPIDAN, HENRIK (1857–1943). A Danish novelist and short story writer, Pontoppidan came from a staunchly Lutheran background, against which he rebelled with gusto. After studying engineering and teaching at a folk high school, he published the short story collection *Stækkede Vinger* (1881; Clipped Wings), the stories in which are marked by the pessimism and determinist leanings of the literary movement called **naturalism**. Two other short story collections, *Landsbybilleder* (1883; Village Sketches) and *Fra Hytterne* (1887; From the Cottages), offer naturalistic depictions of Danish rural life. *Mimoser* (1886; tr. *The Apothecary's Daughter*, 1890) is the work of a great ironist.

The core of Pontoppidan's oeuvre is three major novels. *Det forjættede Land* (1891–1895; tr. *The Promised Land*, 1896) is a bitter satire on the educational movement inaugurated by **N. S. F. Grundtvig**, the Danish folk high schools. The young minister who is the protagonist of the novel seeks a sufficiently strong faith to sustain him in an idealistic project. He fails and descends into madness. In *Lykke-Per* (1898–1904; Lucky Per) the protagonist defies the will of his religious father. Although he is met with outward success, he also experiences an inward failure. *De Dødes Rige* (1912–1916; The Kingdom of the Dead) tells about a group of characters who pessimistically conclude that their lives are metaphysically scripted, and that free will is an illusion. With a mind-set like that, death equals deliverance.

Pontoppidan received the **Nobel Prize** for literature in 1917. He wrote some additional shorter novels as well as a memoir in four volumes (1933–1940).

POSTMODERNISM. Sometimes used so as to include metafiction, fabulation, and literary self-reference, postmodernism is a manifestation of a broader tendency against **realism**. Unencumbered by the dreams of dialectical harmony, postmodernism celebrates the contradictions of existence and mixes old and new, high and low forms of literary expression. The mystery story, a "low" genre, for example, is mixed with more traditional "high" narrative in the Swede **Kerstin Ekman**'s *Händelser vid vatten* (1993; tr. *Blackwater*, 1997). A similar mixture can be found in some of the work of the Finland-Swedish novelist **Kjell Westö**, whose books *Drakarna över Helsingfors* (1996, Kites above Helsinki) and *Lang* (2002) exemplify some of the literary techniques of postmodernism as well as its focus on cultural analysis. These techniques are also found in the work of the Danish novelists **Peter Høeg** and **Ib Michael**. The former's novel *Frøken Smillas fornemmelse for sne* (1992; tr. *Smilla's Sense of Snow*, 1993), for example, contains a strong admixture of elements from the thriller.

Two contemporary Norwegian writers, **Kjartan Fløgstad** and **Jan Kjærstad**, exemplify postmodernism in Norway. Fløgstad has written a long series of novels in which anti-realist techniques figure prominently, starting with *Dalen Portland* (1977; tr. *Dollar Road*, 1989), while Kjærstad's novel *Forføreren* (1993; tr. *The Seducer*, 2003) is the first volume in a trilogy about a television personality. *See also* BURMAN, CARINA; GAARDER, JOSTEIN; HOEM, EDVARD; KYRKLUND, WILLY; LUGN, KIRSTINA; SOLSTAD, DAG; SVENDSEN, HANNE MARIE; WASSMO, HERBJØRG.

***PROFIL* GROUP.** *Profil* (Profile) was an inexpensively produced periodical published by a group of literature students at the University of Oslo between 1966 and the early 1970s. At first this group of young writers favored **modernism**, but a number of them turned away from middle-class aesthetics altogether and adopted a **Marxist** perspective on literature, finding their ideals in Mao Zedong's China. *See also* OBRESTAD, TOR; SOLSTAD, DAG.

PUBLISHERS IN SCANDINAVIA. Publishers are vital to the health of the literary institution—the network of writers, publishing houses, **critics**, bookstores, academic literature departments, and so forth—through which books are produced, promoted, read, and studied. The first Scandinavian publishers were bookstore owners who arranged to have books printed; before that, writers often published their own works. **Ludvig Holberg**, for example, had his books privately printed and sold them from his home.

Most publishing houses were traditionally located in the capital cities. Copenhagen, in particular, was the center of literary activity not only in Denmark but in Norway and Iceland as well. The most prestigious publisher in Denmark was Gyldendalske Boghandel, Nordisk Forlag (Gyldendal Bookstore, a Nordic Publisher), which under the leadership of Fredrik Hegel published the works of **Henrik Ibsen** and many other significant writers. When Gyldendal Norsk Forlag (Gyldendal Norwegian Publishers) was formed in Oslo in 1925, it purchased and thus brought home the publication rights to books by Norwegian writers held by its Danish parent company. Another significant Danish publisher of the late 19th century was P. G. Philipsens Forlag, which through 1895 published such writers as **Henrik Pontoppidan** and **Arne Garborg**. In Sweden Albert Bonnier's Publishing House had a position similar to that of Gyldendal in Copenhagen.

The activities of commercial publishers have long been supplemented by the work of various literary societies. The Finnish Literature Society, for example, was founded in 1831, and the Swedish Literary Society in Finland came into being in 1885, while Det Norske Samlaget (The Norwegian Common Publishing Society) was established in 1868 for the purpose of promoting literature written in **nynorsk** (New Norwegian). In Iceland, Mál og Menning (Language and Culture) was formed as a book club in 1937 and has developed into a diversified modern publishing house. In Denmark, Gyldendal is still the major publisher, while Munksgaard and Museum Tusculanums Forlag are of great significance to literature and literary studies. In Finland, Schildt's Publishing House has an important place in Finland-Swedish literary life, as does Söderström's Publishers. Ten different Finnish-language publishers publish approximately 80 percent of all Finnish-language books produced in Finland, including older and new literature. Gyldendal Norsk Forlag remains the largest publishing house in Norway, while Ascheoug, Cappelen, Pax, and Samlaget are its major competitors. In Sweden Bonnier remains the most prestigious publishing house. In general, book publishing in Scandinavia is subject to market forces that have tended to reduce the number of independent publishers in favor of increasingly larger and more powerful entities.

– R –

REALISM. Inspired by the French writers Honoré de Balzac (1799–1850) and Gustave Flaubert (1821–1880), the literary style called realism was a major force in Scandinavian letters from around 1840 through the 1880s, but particularly in the 1870s. The term denotes an attempt to describe life as it is, without idealization or the subjectivity of the **romantics**, against whom the realists reacted. The best early example of realism in Scandinavian literature is arguably the novel *Det går an* (1839; tr. *Sara Videbeck*, 1919; *Why Not?*, 1994) by the Swedish writer **Carl Jonas Love Almqvist** (1793–1866), which discusses the position of **women** in the family and in society, one of the major topics of the realists. In Norway **Camilla Collett** treated a similar theme in her seminal novel *Amtmandens Døttre* (1854–1855; tr. *The District Governor's Daughters*, 1992). Also in Norway, the peasant stories of **Bjørnstjerne Bjørnson** (1832–1910) anticipated the prose writings of the 1870s through their use of everyday language.

Realism coexisted with late romantic idealism in Scandinavian literature throughout the 1840s, 1850s, and 1860s, but in 1871 the Danish **critic Georg Brandes** (1842–1927) decisively called for a literary practice that would use literature to debate modern problems and issues. Most progressive writers in Scandinavia took up this challenge. Brandes's countryman **Jens Peter Jacobsen** produced two realist novels that adhered to the new program, *Fru Marie Grubbe* (1876; tr. *Marie Grubbe*, 1917) and *Niels Lyhne* (1880; tr. 1919, 1990), while the Swedish writer **August Strindberg** (1849–1912) wrote a great novel, *Röda rummet* (1879; tr. *The Red Room*, 1967), which offers a panoramic view of life in Stockholm.

Brandes's influence was at least as great in Norwegian literature. Many of the plays of **Henrik Ibsen** (1828–1906) from the 1870s and early 1880s come to mind, for example, *Samfundets støtter* (1877; tr. *The Pillars of Society*, 1888) and *Et dukkehjem* (1879; tr. *A Doll's House*, 1880), which deal with such favorite realist topics as corruption, the role of women, and outmoded ideas. Bjørnstjerne Bjørnson vigorously advocated for Brandes's view of the purpose of literature and practiced it in his plays *En fallit* (1875; tr. *The Bankrupt*, 1914), *Redaktøren* (1875; tr. *The Editor*, 1914), and *Kongen* (1877; tr. *The King*, 1914). The novelist **Jonas Lie** wrote *Tremasteren "Fremtiden"* (1872; tr. *The Barque"Future,"* 1879), Norway's first novel about business matters, and later *Familjen paa Gilje* (1883; tr. *The Family at Gilje*, 1920), which is set in the 1840s and debates the right of women to make their own life choices.

Elements of realism have persisted in Scandinavian literature up to the 21st century. *See also* AHO, JUHANI; BREGENDAHL, MARIE; BLICHER, STEEN STEENSEN; BRANNER, HANS CHRISTIAN; EKMAN, KERSTIN; FALDBAKKEN, KNUT;

HEINESEN, WILLIAM; HØEG, PETER; HOEL, SIGURD; HOEM, EDVARD; JÆGER, FRANK; JAKOBSDÓTTIR, SVAVA; KYRKLUND, WILLY; LAGERKVIST, PÄR; LEHTONEN, JOEL; MADSEN, SVEND ÅGE; MØLLER, POUL MARTIN; NEXØ, MARTIN ANDERSEN; NORÉN, LARS; SOLSTAD, DAG; STANGERUP, HENRIK; SVENDSEN, HANNE MARIE; THORUP, KIRSTEN; UNDSET, SIGRID; VESAAS, TARJEI; WINTHER, CHRISTIAN.

RIFBJERG, KLAUS (1931–). A Danish novelist, poet, dramatist, critic, and journalist, Rifbjerg is motivated both by a desire to understand himself as a human being and by a wish to create an alternative vision that counteracts **modernism**'s sense of meaninglessness. An extremely prolific writer, Rifbjerg publishes constantly, and some of his work is of greater value than the rest. His best poetry is better than his best novels, but he is known to many people mostly as a novelist. His literary debut was the poetry collection *Under vejr med mig selv: En utidig selvbiografi* (1956; Getting Wind of Myself: An Untimely Autobiography), in which he introduces himself to the world as a poet. It was followed by his first novel, *Den kroniske uskyld* (1958; Chronic Innocence), which tells the story of two friends, Janus and Tore, who are both in love with Helle. Helle commits suicide and Tore ends up in a mental hospital.

The poem *Camouflage* (1961) tries to strip away the layers of acculturation that cover up the true identity of a person. The poetry collection *Mytologi* (1970; Mythology) begins with a rather disrespectful poem about Prometheus, which sets the tone for the rest of the volume. *Amagerdigte* (1965; Amager Poems) offers poetic snapshots from Rifbjerg's childhood. In the collection *Fædrelandssange* (1967; Patriotic Songs), Rifbjerg tries to remove the layers of myth with which the true image of Denmark has been covered over.

In his youth Rifbjerg spent a year as a student at Princeton University, in the United States, and the novel *Leif den lykkelige jun.* (1971; Lucky Leif Jr.), the title of which is a pun on the name of Leif Ericsson, the Old Norse voyager to America, tells about his experiences in a humorous manner. His novel *Arkivet* (1967; The Archive) has Denmark in the 1950s as its setting and describes the lives of perfectly ordinary people in a realistic manner. The diary novel *Opera-*

elskeren (1966; The Opera Lover) is the story of a man who is unable to integrate his anima and who therefore is unable to relate productively to the woman in his life. *Brevet til Gerda* (1972; The Letter to Gerda) also portrays a man's failure to communicate. One of Rifbjerg's most successful novels is *Anna (jeg) Anna* (1969; tr. *Anna (I) Anna*, 1982), a tale of mental illness and its cure. Anna lives in Pakistan and travels back to Denmark to get help for her urge to kill her daughter. While en route she helps a young man escape from the policeman who is guarding him, after which the two of them go on a crime spree across Europe. After much violence and several deaths Anna gets to Copenhagen, where she is cured largely due to the **symbolic** significance of the harrowing experiences she has just been through.

Rifbjerg's outspokenness has often made him the target of criticism, to which he has responded in several novels with characters who can be recognized as real people, thinly disguised. He satirizes the confessional autobiography in the novel *Dobbeltgænger eller den korte, inderlige men fuldstændig sande beretning om Klaus Rifbjergs liv* (1978; The Double, or, The Short and Heartfelt but Completely True Account of the Life of Klaus Rifbjerg), the long title of which seems to undermine the book's claim to both brevity and authenticity.

During the 1970s, 1980s, and 1990s, Rifbjerg continued to be highly productive. Some of his more important novels from this period are *Dilettanterne* (1973; The Dilettantes), which is set in Spain and takes social responsibility as its theme, telling the story of a scientist whose discoveries are wanted for evil purposes by a dictatorial government. Similarly, *En omvej til klostret* (1983; A Detour to the Convent) concerns a scientist's political involvement. *De hellige aber* (1981; tr. *Witness to the Future*, 1987) is a political fantasy novel; the Danish title, which means "The Sacred Monkeys," refers to people's inability to perceive evil.

Many additional novels by Rifbjerg explore the lives of ordinary men and women, especially the relationship between the sexes. The novel *Falsk forår* (1984; False Spring) investigates the emotional consequences of adoption. In *Karakterbogen: Et virrehoveds bekendelser* (1992; The Grade Report: The Confessions of a Bobble-Head), *Synderegistret: En angivers betragtninger* (1994; The Rap

Sheet: An Informer's Reflections), *Facitlisten: En gammel snyders papirer* (1995; The Answer Sheet: The Papers of an Old Cheater), and *Tidsmaskinen: En rutsjebaneførers bekendelser* (2002; The Time Machine: The Confessions of a Roller-Coaster Driver) Rifbjerg offers commentary on both public and private events. *Divertimento i Mol* (1996; Divertimento in Minor) is a meditation on the role of the narrator in fictional communication.

Rifbjerg has also written numerous scripts for stage, television, and radio, as well as screenplays and a large number of essays. He received the **Nordic Literary Prize** in 1970.

RIKSMAAL. The Danish-influenced written form of Norwegian, Riksmaal (later known as bokmål, or book language) was the standard until the dialect-based **Landsmaal** was created as an alternative in the 19th century.

RØLVAAG, OLE EDEVART (1876–1931). A Norwegian novelist, short story writer, and essayist, Rølvaag was a native of Norway who lived in the United States while writing in Norwegian. The argument can thus be made that he belongs to both Norwegian and American literature. Born on one of the outlying islands in the Helgeland district of northern Norway, he worked as a fisherman for many years before emigrating to South Dakota. After attending Augustana Academy and St. Olaf College, he did graduate work at the University of Oslo, and then returned to St. Olaf as a teacher of Norwegian.

As an immigrant himself, Rølvaag was in a unique position to understand and interpret the experience of his fellow Norwegians in America. His first work, published under the pseudonym Paal Mørck, was an epistolary novel, *Amerikabreve* (1912; tr. *The Third Life of Per Smevik*, 1971), which introduces one of his major literary themes, the psychological and emotional cost of emigration. It was followed by another novel, *Paa glemte veie* (1914; On Forgotten Roads) and *To tullinger* (1920; tr. *Pure Gold*, 1930), a novel about an immigrant couple's irrational pursuit of wealth. *Længselens baat* (1921; tr. *The Boat of Longing*, 1933) deals with the emotional ties that bind emigrants from Norway to family and friends back home.

The year 1925 was the centenary of organized emigration from Norway to America. Aided by a leave of absence from St. Olaf, Rølvaag holed up in the North Woods of Minnesota and produced the first volume of the work that was to make him famous in the United States. Entitled *I de dage* (1924; In Those Days), it was followed by *Riket grundlægges* (1925; The Kingdom Is Founded); the two volumes were translated by Lincoln Colcord and published as ***Giants in the Earth: A Saga of the Prairie*** (1927). Telling the story of a handful of emigrants from Rølvaag's home district of Helgeland on the prairie of the Dakota Territory, Rølvaag created a tale of hard work and heroism, but also of the awful emotional consequences of emigration, especially as experienced by Beret, the wife of the group's leader, Per Hansa.

Rølvaag had intended to write three more volumes in the series, but he died before the third one could be completed. *Peder Seier* (1928; tr. *Peder Victorious*, 1929) and *Den signede dag* (1931; tr. *Their Fathers' God*, 1931) tell the story of Peder Seier, Per Hansa's son, including his unhappy marriage to an Irish Catholic woman. The story is a tragedy not only on the personal level, for Rølvaag details how the pressure to assimilate leads the Norwegian immigrants and their posterity to forget most of the culture and values of the old country. Rølvaag also wrote short stories as well as a book of essays that argued for cultural preservation, *Omkring fædrearven* (1922; tr. *Concerning Our Heritage*, 1998).

ROMANTICISM. The romantic movement arose as a reaction against the neoclassicism of the 18th century. Its philosophical ideas, shaped partly by the ideas of the German philosophers Johann Gottlieb Fichte (1762–1814) and Friedrich Schelling (1775–1854), emphasized the unity of the object and human perception as well as the unity of spirit and **nature**. God, the highest manifestation of spirit, could thus be found in nature, and the romantic genius was thought to be able to apprehend the divine and thus have a prophetic function. Romantic writers consequently emphasized the central role of the individual, the faculty of the imagination, and the relationship between truth, beauty, and goodness.

The early stirrings of the romantic movement can be observed in the poetry of the Dane **Johannes Ewald** and the Swede **Johan Henric Kellgren**, who were active in the 1770s and 1780s, respectively. The movement found its first full expression in the work of the Dane

Adam Oehlenschläger, while the poetic drama *Lycksalighetens ö* (1824–1827; The Isle of Bliss) by the Swede **Per Daniel Amadeus Atterbom** is recognized as its greatest Swedish manifestation. Under the influence of the thought of Johann Gottfried von Herder (1744–1803), however, romanticism in Scandinavia soon developed into **national romanticism**. *See also* GEIJER, ERIK GUSTAV; GRUNDTVIG, NIKOLAJ FREDERIK SEVERIN; STAGNELIUS, ERIK JOHAN; TEGNÉR, ESAIAS.

RUNEBERG, JOHAN LUDVIG (1804–1877). A Finland-Swedish poet, short story writer, and playwright, Runeberg has traditionally been regarded as the most important writer in Finnish literary history. His significance for the Finnish nation-building project of the 19th century cannot be overestimated, and the image of Finland found in his works continues to inform the self-image of his people. After studies in Åbo and Helsinki, Runeberg spent some time as a tutor in the interior of Finland and became well acquainted with its Finnish-speaking peasant population. Later he worked as a newspaper **critic** in Helsinki. His literary debut was the poetry collection *Dikter* (1830; Poems), which was followed by two more volumes of poetry, *Dikter: Andra häftet* (1833; Poems: Second Issue) and *Dikter:Tredje häftet* (Poems: Third Issue). These volumes contain some of his best-known lyric poetry as well as poems that strongly express his nationalistic ideals.

Runeberg is even better known for his epic poetry. *Elgskyttarne* (1832; The Moose Hunters) draws on his stay in the interior of Finland and depicts the sturdiness of its people in hexameters. Other epic poems are *Hanna* (1836) and *Julqvällen* (1841; Christmas Eve); the latter celebrates the self-sufficiency and courage in the face of adversity of an old soldier. In *Kung Fjalar* (1844; tr. *King Fjalar*, 1904) Runeberg taps into the common Old Norse heritage of Scandinavia and further expresses his **national romanticism**. Fjalar tries to stay the hand of fate but discovers that fate has already anticipated his futile attempt, thereby foiling it. Man's strength, however, is measured by his willingness to stand up to overwhelming forces.

The two-volume *Fänrik Ståls sägner* (1848–1860; tr. *The Tales by Ensign Stål*, 1925) probably contains Runeberg's greatest literary legacy. A collection of long ballads, the work tells about events associated with the **war** of 1808–1809, through which Finland was lost by Sweden and became a Russian grand duchy. The patriotic feeling of these songs is unsurpassed, and the introductory ballad has long been Finland's national anthem. Runeberg is not a great dramatist. One play bears mention, however. *Kungarne på Salamis* (1863; The Kings of Salamis) is set in Greek antiquity and is, like *Kung Fjalar*, a story about man's opposition to his fate.

RYDBERG, VIKTOR (1828–1895). A Swedish novelist and poet, Rydberg wrote historical novels in which he expressed his own ideas about contemporary issues. Writing about the past satisfied the **romantic** in him, and as a journalist working in a liberal newspaper, he was very aware of the issues of the day. His first successful novel was *Fribytaren på Östersjön* (1857; tr. *The Freebooter of the Baltic*, 1891), set during the 17th century. This was a time of witch trials and other atrocities, which Rydberg compares to the fanaticism of his own age. The novel *Singoalla* (1857; tr. 1903), set during the Middle Ages, features a love story involving a Christian knight and a young Rom (Gypsy) woman.

Den siste atenaren (1859; tr. *The Last Athenian*, 1869) expresses Rydberg's humanism and love of classical culture. Its protagonist is the fourth-century Roman emperor Julian the Apostate, who unsuccessfully tried to reestablish paganism as the state religion. Influenced by the dialectical theory of history of Georg Wilhelm Friedrich Hegel (1770–1831), Rydberg hoped for a synthesis of classical humanism and Christianity and viewed Julian as a kindred spirit. The Norwegian dramatist **Henrik Ibsen** deals with the same subject matter in his play *Kejser og Galilæer* (1873; tr. *Emperor and Galilean*, 1876).

Rydberg's novel *Vapensmeden* (1891; The Armorer) is set during the time of the Swedish Reformation and portrays the conflict between Catholicism and Lutheranism. Open-mindedness and tolerance are shown in their age-old conflict with fanaticism and hunger for power. Rydberg overtly criticized Christianity in a pamphlet, *Bibelns lära om Kristus* (1862; Biblical Teachings about Christ), in which he argued that the Bible offered no support for the doctrine of the Trinity and that there was no basis for the dogma that Jesus was both god and a human being. Like that of his romantic predecessors, Rydberg's poetry combined his interest in classical culture with his concern about **folklore** and the national past. He published two volumes of poetry, *Dikter* (1882; Poems) and *Dikter, andra samlingen* (1891; Poems, Second Collection). Rydberg's poems from the 1880s are distinguished by their concern for social justice and his abhorrence of narrow-mindedness and bigotry of all kinds.

– S –

SANDEL, CORA (1880–1974). A Norwegian novelist and short story writer, Sandel was born Sara Fabricius and was one of Norway's most significant writers during the middle decades of the 20th century. Next to **Sigrid Undset**, she is arguably Norway's most important woman writer. Traditionally regarded as a neorealist, she has come to be viewed as one of the most interesting representatives of **modernism** in Norwegian literature; this holds true both for her five novels and her numerous short stories.

Sandel began her career as a writer of short stories, which she published pseudonomously in various magazines while she was studying painting. Encouraged to write a novel by the head of Gyldendal, Norway's most prestigeous **publishing** house, she wrote *Alberte og Jakob* (1926; tr. *Alberta and Jakob*, 1962) about her own experiences growing up in the family of a civil servant in Tromsø, in northern Norway. Sandel has placed a profoundly alienated and thus typically modernist character within the framework of a realistic narrative as she describes a claustrophobic milieu where young **women** are expected to renounce any kind of personal ambition as they prepare to be married.

Conceived as the first volume in a trilogy, *Alberte og Jakob* was followed by *Alberte og friheten* (1931; tr. *Alberta and Freedom*, 1963) and *Bare Alberte* (1939; tr. *Alberta Alone*, 1965). The action in *Alberte og friheten* takes place in Paris, where the lonely Alberte is studying painting while eking out a living as a model and occasional correspondent of Norwegian newspapers. She also falls in love, but the relationship goes nowhere and she ends up pregnant by a fellow artist, Sivert. *Bare Alberte* tells about the experience of World **War I**. Alberte is not comfortable in her role as the mother of a five-year-old boy, and her relationship with Sivert is deteriorating. At the end of the book Alberte has finished the manuscript of her first novel and sets out on her own, leaving her son with Sivert.

Sandel took a long time to finish each of the volumes of the Alberte trilogy, and she continued to write short stories in order to generate some income. These stories vary considerably in theme, setting, and quality, but the best of them are among the very best short stories in Norwegian literature. Most of her stories were collected or first published in the following volumes: *En blå sofa og andre noveller* (1927; A Blue Sofa and Other Stories), *Carmen og Maja og andre noveller* (1932; Carmen and Maja and Other Stories), *Mange takk, doktor* (1935; Many Thanks, Doctor), *Figurer på mørk bunn* (1949; Figures on a Dark Background), and *Vårt vanskelige liv* (1960; Our Difficult Life). Among her best stories are "Amors veie" (Amor's Ways), which shows that there is no significant relationship between physical beauty and success in love; "Lort-Katrine" (Crap-Katrine), a portrait of an aging prostitute in a Norwegian port city; and "Kunsten å myrde" (The Art of Murder), a tale of greed and heartlessness in France during the years after the end of World War I.

Two novels combine dramatic features with narrative. The action of *Kranes konditori* (1945; tr. *Krane's Café*, 1968) takes place in one day's time and concerns a small-town seamstress who leaves her work behind and spends the day sitting in a local café, much to the consternation of her waiting customers. *Kjøp ikke Dondi* (1958; tr. *The Leech*, 1960) features a protagonist who, in her self-centeredness and egotism, is difficult for readers to identify with. Sandel also wrote a volume of autobiographical stories about animals, *Dyr jeg har kjent* (1945; Animals I Have Known).

SANDEMOSE, AKSEL (1899–1965). A Norwegian novelist, Sandemose was born in Denmark and had six books to his credit before he decided to become a Norwegian writer. For several decades he was considered one of Norway's most important literary artists. Most of his early books have little enduring value, but one of them, the novel *Ross Dane* (1928; tr. 1989), which tells about Danish immigrants in

Alberta, Canada, established him as more than a writer of entertainment fiction.

After he moved to Norway, Sandemose quickly published *En sjømann går i land* (1931; A Sailor Goes Ashore), in which he introduces the character Espen Arnakke. Drawing on his own time as a sailor and as a lumberjack in Canada, Sandemose vividly depicts Espen's experiences, which culminate in a murder. The story about Espen continues in *En flyktning krysser sitt spor* (1933; tr. *A Fugitive Crosses His Tracks*, 1936), in which Espen, now age 34, reflects on his actions as a 17-year-old murderer and searches his soul in order to understand the various forces that shaped him. Drawing on Alfred Adler's brand of psychoanalysis, Sandemose depicts Espen's labor as a kind of self-analysis that is presented in a disjointed and fragmentary form similar to that of a clinical narrative. Sandemose thus became both one of the foremost exponents of **modernism** in Norwegian literature and one of its first writers to use psychoanalysis as a significant thematic component. His analysis of Espen's life in the fictional Danish town Jante also made a lasting contribution to the Norwegian language; "Jante" has come to signify any small town, and the "Law of Jante," a set of unspoken rules for social control, has come to mean the kind of norms that are designed to make an individual limit his or her aspirations for fear of offending a community that values mediocrity. Two other but less significant novels about Espen are *Der stod en benk i haven* (1937; A Bench Stood in the Garden), which tells about his puberty, and *Brudulje* (1938; Upset).

Rivalry and jealousy, important motifs in the Espen Arnakke novels, return in *Vi pynter oss med horn* (1936; tr. *Horns for our Adornment*, 1938), which portrays the dynamics among six men on board a ship bound for Newfoundland. Similar themes govern a novel first published in Swedish while Sandemose was in exile during World **War** II, *Det svundne er en drøm* (1944; The Past Is a Dream), which is also strongly influenced by the German occupation of Norway. Its narrator is the Norwegian-American John Torson, who, while trying to come to terms with past wrongdoing, discovers that evil resides within him and is still a threat to himself and others. Sandemose's next novel, *Tjærehandleren* (1945; The Tar Merchant), offers a portrait of a charlatan who preys on older and wealthy women, while

Alice Atkinson og hennes elskere (1949; Alice Atkinson and Her Lovers) again discusses the relationship between jealousy and murder, again prominently featuring the experience of World War II. Nazism and wartime collaboration are central themes in the novel *Varulven* (1958; tr. *The Werewolf*, 1965), which centers on the murder of Felicia Venhaug, the female member of an erotic triangle that also consists of her husband Jan and the narrator of *Varulven*, the writer Erling Vik. The novel is an attempt at understanding both the nature of sexual passion and the desire for revenge. *Felicias bryllup* (1961; Felicia's Wedding) adds additional background information to the story told in *Varulven*.

Some of Sandemose's most productive years were spent at a small farm named Kjørkelvik, where he published a magazine for which he wrote all of the content, *Årstidene* (1951–1955; The Seasons). Some of this material was later published in book form. Sandemose also wrote a book of personal essays, *Murene rundt Jeriko* (1960; The Walls of Jericho).

SCANDINAVIAN LITERARY JOURNALS. Literary and more general journals have been important in all of the Scandinavian countries, starting with **Olof von Dalin**'s *Then Swänska Argus* (1732–1734; The Swedish Argus), which was in the style of Joseph Addison and Richard Steele's *The Tatler* (1709–1711) and *The Spectator* (1711–1714). Most general cultural journals have given some space to both literary contributions and essays about literature, and writers have traditionally had a great deal of influence in Scandinavian society and politics. An important Swedish journal of the **romantic** era was *Phosphorus* (1810–1813), with which **Per Daniel Amadeus Atterbom** was associated. In 1835 the Icelander **Jónas Hallgrímsson** and some of his friends founded the annual *Fjölnir* (1835–1839), which published Hallgrímsson's poems and short stories, as well as articles about Iceland's natural history.

Some of the most important journals of the **Modern Breakthrough** were *For Idé og Virkelighed* (1869–1873; For Idea and Reality), founded by the **critic** Clemens Petersen and the philosopher Rasmus Nielsen, who argued in favor of idealism as opposed to **realism** and **naturalism**. One of its contributors was the Norwegian writer **Bjørnstjerne Bjørnson**. Vilhelm Møller's *Nyt dansk*

Maanedskrift (1870–1874; New Danish Monthly Journal), on the other hand, was published in opposition to Petersen and Nielsen. Together with his brother Edvard, the critic **Georg Brandes** published the *Det Nittende Aarhundrede* (1874–1877; The Nineteenth Century), the chief forum for his radical realist and naturalist critique of literature and culture. In Norway the historian Johan Ernst Sars published the progressive journals *Nyt norsk Tidsskrift* (1877–1878; New Norwegian Journal) and *Nyt Tidsskrift* (1882–1887; Norwegian Journal), which opposed the ideas expressed in such conservative periodicals as Ditmar Mejdell's *Norsk Maanedskrift* (1884–1885; Norwegian Monthly).

As **neoromanticism** appeared on the horizon, the Danish journal *Tilskueren* (1884–1939; The Spectator) became a forum for such writers as **Johannes Jørgensen**, who later published the periodical *Taarnet* (1893–1894; The Tower), through which he championed the **symbolism** of the 1890s in opposition to the naturalists. After World **War** I the Norwegian Erling Falk founded *Mot Dag* (1921–1939; Toward Daybreak), an important forum for **Marxist** ideas with which **Sigurd Hoel** was associated. After World War II the Norwegian writer **Aksel Sandemose** published a magazine for which he wrote all of the content, *Årstidene* (1951–1955; The Seasons). Also subsequent to World War II, the Danish journal *Heretica* (1948–1953) programmatically avoided all forms of dogmatism and attracted contributions from such writers as **Martin A. Hansen**. **Marxism** was, by contrast, represented by the journals *Athenæum* (1945–1950) and *Dialog* (1950–1962), edited by Erik Knudsen and Sven Møller Kristensen. *Vindrosen* (1954–1974; The Compass Card), on the other hand, was more specifically literary under the leadership of **Tage Skou-Hansen, Klaus Rifbjerg**, and **Villy Sørensen**. It became an important voice for both **modernism** and the radicalism of the 1960s and 1970s. In Norway the *Profil* group, among them the writers **Espen Haavardsholm, Tor Obrestad**, and **Dag Solstad**, used the journal *Profil* as a forum for both modernism and Marxism.

Currently the Scandinavian countries have a number of high-quality literary journals. The Danish journal *Hvedekorn* (est. 1920; Grains of Wheat) has received contributions from such writers as **Tom Kristensen** and **Tove Ditlevsen**. *Kritik* (est. 1967; Criticism) emphasizes textual analysis. *Finsk Tidskrift* (est. 1876; Finnish Journal), which is published in Swedish, is the chief cultural voice of Finland's Swedish-speaking population, while *Parnasso* (est. 1951; Parnassus) is a Finnish-language literary magazine. The Icelandic journals *Skírnir* (est. 1827; named for the messenger of the Old Norse god Freyr) and *Tímarit Máls og menningar* (est. 1940; Journal of Language and Culture) publish work of the country's best-known writers. The Norwegian journal *Edda* (est. 1914) publishes academic literary criticism, while the literary magazine *Vinduet* (est. 1947; The Window) focuses on contemporary Norwegian literature and has been edited by a succession of important writers and scholars, among them **Johan Borgen** and **Jan Kjærstad**. The Swedish journal *Ord och bild* (est. 1892; Word and Image) covers a variety of literary and cultural topics.

SCHACK, HANS EGEDE (1820–1859). A Danish novelist, Schack studied law and got involved in liberal politics. He completed a single novel, *Phantasterne* (1857; The Fantasts), which is an important precursor to the **realism** of the 1870s, not only in Danish literature but in Scandinavian literature as a whole. *Phantasterne* tells about three boys, Conrad, the book's narrator, Christian, and Thomas. Conrad and Christian are given to daydreaming about all the great things they are going to do in the future, but Thomas is a skeptic. Christian never develops past the daydreaming stage and ends up in a mental hospital, but Conrad manages to develop a healthy balance between reality and dream. *Phantasterne* is thus a critique of romantic idealism and a defense of political liberalism in contrast to the older forms of social organization that the boys had dwelled on in their fantasies. Shack's death cut short his work on a second novel, *Sandhed med Modification* (Truth with Modification).

SCHERFIG, HANS (1905–1979). A Danish novelist, Scherfig came from an upper-middle-class home but rebelled against his origins and became a communist. Full of contempt for the middle class, he skewered its representatives in his novels. Scherfig's literary debut was the novel *Den døde Mand* (1937; The Dead Man), a detective story set among artists. In his next book, *Den forsvundne Fuldmegtig* (1938; tr. *The Missing Bureaucrat*, 1989), the protagonist stages a suicide in order to get away from his boring existence, including his wife.

When he finds that he cannot stand his newfound freedom, however, he manages to become imprisoned for a murder he did not commit. The novel *Det forsømte Foraar* (1940; tr. *Stolen Spring*, 1986) is a satire on Danish education. The characters, young people who have a great deal of promise, become suited only to middle-class life. Some of them return in Scherfig's later novels.

During the German occupation of Denmark in World **War** II, Scherfig was interned for a while, and he was very bitter about the war experience. *Idealister* (1945; tr. *The Idealists*, 1949) describes how supposedly decent people take advantage of others and allow themselves to be seduced into accepting Nazi ideas. Scherfig had completed the manuscript by 1941, but it was **censored** as he was arrested. *Skorpionen* (1953; The Scorpion) is a fictionalization of a famous Danish court case involving corruption, black market trade, and collusion between criminals and members of the social elite; it draws on some of Scherfig's newspaper articles written while the case was before the courts. *Frydenholm* (1962) tells about how Scherfig and other communists were treated during the war, when, in violation of the Danish constitution, their political rights were retroactively revoked and they were arrested. Scherfig also wrote a number of travel books in which he extols the virtues of communist societies.

SCHILDT, RUNAR (1888–1925). A Finland-Swedish short story writer and dramatist, Schildt had family ties both to the nobility and to the rural parts of Swedish-speaking Finland. He belonged to a group of artists and intellectuals referred to as the "idlers" of Finland-Swedish literature; this upper-class group cultivated a style of disillusionment, skepticism, and irony coupled with a pessimistic outlook. Schildt is considered the outstanding writer in this group, as well as one of the greatest writers in Finland-Swedish literature.

Schildt produced novellas and short stories for a scant eight years, from 1912 to 1920. The stories in his first two collections, *Den segrande Eros* (1912; Victorious Eros) and *Asmodeus och de tretton själarna* (1915; Asmodeus and the 13 Souls), are informed by the general outlook on life common among the "idlers." For example, in the latter collection, the devil Asmodeus has made a bet that he can bag 13 souls during a three-day visit to Helsinki; this structural device allows Schildt to provide a cross-section of life in Finland's capital. The stories in *Regnbågen* (1916; The Rainbow) and *Rönnbruden och Pröfningens dag* (1917; The Bride of the Mountain Ash and Testing Day) are set in the Finnish countryside. In "Rönnbruden" (The Bride of the Mountain Ash) a young woman has been married to a tree through a curse.

The volume *Perdita och andra noveller* (1918; Perdita and Other Stories) contains Schildt's finest short story, "Den svagare" (The Weaker One), which details a man's reaction when he discovers that his wife has committed adultery. He would like to leave her but is too weak, and he rationalizes his behavior by concluding that his life would be worthless without her. Other prose works are the short story collection *Hemkomsten* (1918; The Homecoming) and the novella *Armas Fager* (1920), which offers a portrait of an older man in both physical and social decline. In one of the stories in Schildt's final short story collection, *Häxskogen* (1920; The Witch Forest), the protagonist is a novelist who, terrified by the fact that he has lost his creativity, finds that a disappointment in love brings it back to him so that he is able to finish the book he is writing.

Schildt also wrote the short drama *Galgmannen: En midvintersaga* (1922; tr. *The Gallows Man: A Midwinter Tale*) and the full-length play *Den stora rollen* (1923; The Great Role), both of which did very well on stage. The play *Lyckoriddaren* (1923; The Fortune Hunter), however, was rather unsuccessful. Schildt committed suicide in 1925. *See also* THEATER.

SCHOULTZ, SOLVEIG VON (1907–1996). A Finland-Swedish poet, short story writer, and novelist, von Schoultz wrote about family relationships, human relationships in general, and **nature**. Her work is in many ways an extension of that of the great Finland-Swedish **modernists Edith Södergran** and **Elmer Diktonius**, but von Schoultz early found her own distinctive voice and became one of the great poets writing in Swedish, not only in Finland but in Sweden as well. She had her literary debut with a book written for young **women**, *Petra och silverapan* (1932; Petra and the Silver Monkey). Her only novel, *December* (1937), contains clearly autobiographical elements. The stories in *De sju dagarna: Två barn skapar sin värld* (1942; The Seven Days: Two Children Create Their World) were inspired by the first seven days in the lives of her two daughters, born in 1934 and 1936.

Throughout her career von Schoultz wrote more than 50 stories, some of which were published as *Ingen dag förgäves* (1984; No Day in Vain) and *Nästa dag* (1991; The Next Day). Many of von Schoultz's stories deal with the experience of women. The stories in *Ingenting ovanligt* (1947; Nothing Unusual) have as protagonists women who embody three different possibilities for women's lives: an insecure young married woman, a woman whose love has been betrayed by her husband, and a **war** widow. Similar themes are found in *Närmare nogon* (1951; Closer to Somebody), where some of von Schoultz's protagonists are the lover of a married man, an older woman whose husband is close to death, and an unmarried woman who is dealing with her niece. Other collections of stories are *Den blomstertid* (1958; That Time of Flowers), *Även dina kamelar* (1965; Your Camels Too), and *Rymdbruden* (1970; The Space Bride). Many of the short stories in *Somliga mornar* (1976; Certain Mornings) and *Kolteckning, ofullbordad* (1983; Unfinished Charcoal Drawing) are notable for their depiction of the aging process and the changes in attitude that sometimes accompany that part of life.

It was as a poet, however, that von Schoultz had her greatest impact on Finland-Swedish literature. Starting with *Min timme* (1940; My Hour), von Schoultz regularly published poetry right up to the end of her life, her final collection being *Molnskuggan* (1996; The Shadow of the Cloud). Together with its predecessor, *Samtal med en Fjäril* (1994; Conversations with a Butterfly), it contains reflections on the process of aging. Generally not formally experimental, von Schoultz's poetry mostly uses free verse and deals with personal experience, particularly with **nature**. Her breakthrough as a poet came with *Nattlig äng* (1949; Nocturnal Meadow), and some of her other collections are *Nätet* (1956; The Net), *Terrassen* (1959; The Terrace), *De fyra flöjtspelarna* (1975; The Four Flautists), and *Ett sätt att räkna tiden* (1989; A Way to Count Time). A selection of her poetry bears the title *Alla träd väntar fåglar* (1989; All Trees Wait for Birds).

Working many years as a teacher, von Schoultz also wrote a number of **children's books**. *Porträtt av Hanna* (1978; Portrait of Hanna) is a psychologically penetrating book about her mother, the painter

Hanna Segerstråle, and *Längs vattenbrynet* (1992; Along the Water's Edge) is a memoir that emphasizes the early part of her life.

SEEBERG, PETER (1925–1999). A Danish novelist, short story writer, and essayist, Seeberg came of age during the heyday of **modernism** in Denmark, and his work is marked by modernist concerns. His literary debut was the novel *Bipersonerne* (1956; The Secondary Characters), which takes place in a youth labor camp in Berlin in the middle of World **War** II. Young people from several countries have been brought together in order to produce a film in which they will serve as extras, but they are also secondary characters with regard to the events of the war, as well as minor characters in their own lives, which are marked by emptiness and meaninglessness. Such existential themes become central in Seeberg's next book, the novel *Fugls føde* (1957; tr. *The Impostor*, 1990), in which the author Tom suffers from a major case of writer's block. Offered a large sum of money to simply write something real, he struggles to make the existential choices that would put him in touch with reality.

The absurd and fantastic short stories in *Eftersøgningen* (1962; The Search) also deal with themes of identity and people's connection to the real world. In "Patienten" (The Patient) a man has gone through a series of transplants that have replaced all his organs and limbs, including his head. His identity stays the same, however, as recognized by his wife. Thus Seeberg states that people can maintain a sense of identity by allowing themselves to be embedded in a social fabric. Also, meaning is found in the process of searching for meaning. This is likewise the message of the novel *Hyrder* (1970; Shepherds), in which the human community is shown to provide a sense of meaningful existence for its members.

At the core of Seeberg's oeuvre are three volumes that contain a variety of prose texts, ranging from the **realist** short story to the fantastic tale. *Dinosaurusens sene eftermiddag* (1974; The Late Afternoon of the Dinosaur) was followed by *Argumenter for benådning* (1976; Arguments for a Pardon) and *Om fjorten dage* (1981; In Fourteen Days), which garnered Seeberg the **Nordic Literary Prize** in 1983.

The novel *Ved havet* (1978; By the Sea) tells about the different reactions people have to the ocean during a Sunday at the beach. The three novels *Uden et navn* (1985; Without a Name), *Den sovende dreng* (1988; The Sleeping Boy), and *Frosten hjelper* (1989; The Frost Helps) were all written for teenage readers. Seeberg's short story collections include *Rejsen til Ribe* (1990; The Journey to Ribe), *Erindringer fra hundrede år* (1992; Recollections of a Hundred Years), *Halvdelen af natten* (1997; Half the Night), and the posthumously published *En enkelt afbrydelse* (2001; A Single Interruption). He also published the play *Ferai* (1970) and *På selve dagen* (1978; On the Day Itself), the memoirs *Hovedrengjøring: Stumper af erindring* (1979; Thorough Cleaning: Fragments of Recollection), the essay collection *Slå fritiden ihjel* (1986; Kill Your Spare Time), and a number of **children's books**.

SEITSEMÄN VELJESTÄ. A novel by the Finn **Aleksis Kivi**, *Seitsemän veljestä* (1870; tr. *Seven Brothers*, 1929, 1973, 1991) is both the first and the best-known novel in Finnish. It has been translated into a number of languages.

SEVEN BROTHERS. See *SEITSEMÄN VELJESTÄ*.

SILLANPÄÄ, FRANS EEMIL (1888–1964). A Finnish novelist and short story writer, Sillanpää is a great **modernist** writer and is generally recognized as Finland's finest writer during the interwar period, and perhaps during the entire 20th century. His works have been translated into many languages, and he received the **Nobel Prize** for literature in 1939, the only Finnish writer thus honored so far. Born into a farm family, Sillanpää stayed true to his rural background in his choice of subject matter, writing about the peasants and hired hands around whom he grew up. He had his literary debut with the romance *Elämä ja aurinko* (1916; Life and the Sun), which tells about a young man's involvement with two women of different social status. It was followed by a volume of short stories, *Ihmislapsia elämän saatossa* (1917; The Procession of Life).

Sillanpää became internationally known for *Hurskas kurjuus* (1919; tr. *Meek Heritage*, 1938), set during Finland's bitter civil **war**. The protagonist is the poor tenant farmer Juha Toivola, who is of quite limited intelligence and ends up on the losing side in the war. Accused of a murder he did not commit, he is executed by the victorious White Army, which, backed by Germany, defeated the leftist Reds in the war. Through flashbacks Sillanpää presents Juha's entire life and shows that the circumstances surrounding his death are really of a piece with the rest of his miserable life.

After publishing several volumes of short stories—among them *Maan tasalta* (1924; On the Ground Level) and *Töllinmäki* (1925; Cabin Hill)—Sillanpää wrote his second international success, *Nuorena nukkunut* (1931; tr. *The Maid Silja*, 1933). It, too, is set during the civil war, with Silja and her father as the representatives of a generation in decline. After the loss of the family farm, Silja has to work for other people, and she eventually dies from tuberculosis. She is resigned to her fate, however, which is almost the saddest part of her story.

Sillanpää's main concern is to depict the interior lives of his characters, which he does with psychological subtlety. The novel *Miehen tie* (1932; A Man's Road) portrays sex in a manner that borders on vitalism. Its protagonist, the young farmer Paavo, marries an older widow in order to get possession of her farm, but his life is unhappy until he returns to the love of his youth, subsequent to his first wife's death. The novel *Ihmiset suviyössä* (1934; tr. *People in the Summer Night*, 1966) depicts—almost in the form of sketches—the events of a single summer night and their effect on a whole gallery of characters, who are largely driven by instinct. It is generally considered Sillanpää's most artistically composed work.

SJÁLFSTÆTT FÓLK. A novel by the Icelandic **Halldór Kiljan Laxness**, *Sjálfstætt fólk* (1934–1935; tr. *Independent People*, 1945–1946) depicts the hard life of an Icelandic sheep farmer.

SKALLAGRÍMSSON, EGIL (ca. 910–990). An Icelandic poet, Egil is the central figure in *Egils saga*, one of the major Icelandic family sagas. Egil is both the greatest poet in pre-Christian Scandinavia and an exemplary Viking warrior, a man who worshiped the Old Norse god Odin and exemplifies two of Odin's major characteristics, as he was the primary god for both poetry and war in the ancient Scandinavian pantheon. *Egils saga* tells the story of Egil's life in the context of the culture and political events of his times. Although most of the events reported in it have clear historical foundations, there are many mythological and supernatural details. Three of Egil's poems are included in their entirety, "Höfuðlausn" (The Head Ransom), "Sonatorrek" (The Loss of the Son), and "Arinbjarnarkviða" (The Lay of Arinbjörn). "Höfuðlausn" was composed in praise of King Eirik Bloodaxe, an enemy of Egil who had him in his power; after Egil performed his poem before King Eirik and his men, the king could not kill him without injuring his own honor. "Sonatorrek" and "Arinbjarnarkviða" were both composed by Egil upon the accidental deaths of his two sons. Some scholars have suggested that *Egils saga* was written by the great Icelandic historian **Snorri Sturluson**, but there is no firm evidence.

SKOU-HANSEN, TAGE (1925–). A Danish novelist, Skou-Hansen was born in Jutland but studied comparative literature and spent his early career as an editor and teacher. He is known for two great series of novels, one that deals with the character Holger Mikkelsen and offers an extended commentary on Danish postwar society, and one that is referred to as "Stories from the Round Table."

The first Holger Mikkelsen novel, *De nøgne træer* (1957; tr. *The Naked Trees*, 1959), is set during the German occupation of Denmark in World **War** II and tells about the activities of a group of resistance fighters. Its sequel, *Dagstjernen* (1962; Day Star), deals with the ethics of liquidating informers during wartime. *På den anden side* (1965; On the Other Side) deals with issues of communication in marriage. *Hjemkomst* (1969; Homecoming) deals with Danish development work in India. *Tredje halvleg* (1971; Third Half), which is narrated by Mikkelsen, is centered on sport, while *Medløberen* (1973; The Fellow Traveler) is focused on soccer. *Den hårde frugt* (1977; The Hard Fruit) presents the disintegration of Mikkelsen's marriage. Mikkelsen is perhaps not quite the Danish everyman in *Over stregen* (1980; Over the Line), in which as a lawyer he has to defend the terrorist daughter of one of his former girlfriends. Mikkelsen returns in *På sidelinjen* (1996; On the Sideline), in which he loses an important lawsuit, and he appears again in *Frit løb* (2000; Free Run), in which he is an old man and looks back at his life, which is also life in postwar Denmark.

The Round Table novels are centered on a character named Axel, who joined the Germans during World War II and died fighting on the

Eastern Front. Consisting of the novels *Springet* (1986; The Leap), *Krukken og stenen* (1987; The Pitcher and the Stone), *Det andet slag* (1989; The Second Beat), and *Siste sommer* (1991; Last Summer), the series is a significant artistic achievement.

SKRAM, AMALIE (1846–1905). A Norwegian novelist, short story writer, and dramatist, Skram stands, together with **Camilla Collett**, as one of the first practitioners of **women**'s literature in Norway. Raised in the lower-middle-class family of a shopkeeper with unfulfilled social ambitions, she knew disappointment firsthand from an early age. At the age of 18 she was married to a ship captain named Müller who was nine years her senior. Like many young women of her class and generation, she entered marriage without any clear sense of its conjugal dimension, and her reaction to married life was shock, anger, and disgust. These emotions subsequently fueled the creation of her many mistreated and unhappy woman characters.

After accompanying her husband on many of his voyages and bearing two children, she realized that there was no future in their relationship and wanted a divorce. Her husband did not agree, and she had a nervous breakdown, followed by some months at a mental hospital. When she was discharged, she stayed with her brother for a while, and her marriage to Müller was dissolved in 1882.

Associated with a group of journalists in Bergen, Skram had already written some articles about literature. Her first fiction effort was a short story, "Madam Høiers lejefolk" (1882; Mrs. Høier's Renters). After her 1884 marriage to the Danish writer Erik Skram, who encouraged her to embark on a longer work, she wrote the novel *Constance Ring* (1885; tr. 1988), which tells the story of an unhappy woman's marriage with—from the perspective of the time—great openness and excruciating detail. The same year she published her second short story, "Karens jul" (1885; Karen's Christmas), about an unwed teenage mother and her baby, both of whom freeze to death a couple of days before Christmas.

Three more novels and a play deal with unhappily married women. The novel *Lucie* (1888) explores the match between a former streetwalker and a lawyer, criticizing society's double standard in a manner similar to that of the **Christiania bohemians**. Inspired by some of the author's experiences during her years of sailing with her husband, *Fru Inés* (1891) tells the tragic story about a Spanish woman who is unable to fully express her eroticism. In the novel *Forraadt* (1892; tr. *Betrayed*) Skram pairs an innocent young woman with an older man; the mismatch leads to tragedy for both of them. The eponymous protagonist of *Agnete* (1893), Skram's best dramatic effort, believes that love has the potential to purify, but she is as disappointed as Skram's other married women characters.

The pessimism of Skram's works may seem connected with the aesthetics of **naturalism**, which denied the freedom of the will and saw biological inheritance and social environment as determining factors in human life. Naturalism is even more strongly present in her greatest work, the tetralogy *Hellemyrsfolket* (1887–1898; The People of Hellemyren), which consists of the novels *Sjur Gabriel* (1887), *To venner* (1887; Two Friends), *S. G. Myre* (1890), and *Afkom* (1898; Offspring). It is a great family saga about four generations plagued by poverty, alcoholism, and dishonesty.

Skram's frantic pace of work led to another breakdown, and she was hospitalized in 1894. Two novels, *Professor Hieronimus* (1895) and *Paa St. Jørgen* (1895; tr. with *Professor Hieronimus* as *Under Observation*, 1992), tell about her unhappy experience with the medical authorities of her day. While earlier regarded as inferior to her better-known works, these two novels have come to be recognized as an important personal statement.

SÖDERBERG, HJALMAR (1869–1941). A Swedish short story writer, novelist, playwright, and polemicist, Söderberg is both a superb prose stylist and an example of the aesthetic concerns of fin-de-siècle Swedish literature. His literary debut came with the novel *Förvillelser* (1895; Getting Lost), which tells about an unreflective young man named Tomas Weber and his struggle with his biological urges, which bring him into confusing relationships with several women. The eponymous protagonist in *Martin Bircks ungdom* (1901; tr. *Martin Birck's Youth*, 1930) errs on the opposite end of the spectrum, as he is a hyperreflective dreamer who cannot find contentment in a world that refuses to live up to his ideals. His poetic ambitions founder on his idealism as that idealism impels him to seek a truth he realizes is not to be found.

Söderberg's best book is the diary novel *Doktor Glas* (1905; tr.

Doctor Glas, 1970). Its title character and diarist is a 30-year-old Stockholm physician who confesses to being completely unacquainted with women; a youthful love interest who could have become the love of his life died in a swimming accident shortly after he met her. Glas is approached by Helga Gregorius, the second and much younger wife of a local clergyman, who seeks his aid in deflecting the amorous advances of her 57-year-old husband. The relatively young and aesthetically sensitive Glas is struck by the ugliness of having an old man impose his love on a young wife who, as it turns out, has fallen in love with someone else, and Glas demonizes the pastor, whom he describes as extremely ugly in both body and spirit. He then uses his position as their family doctor to murder the clergyman, with the idea that Helga, with whom Glas is infatuated, will now be free to marry her lover. But the lover marries someone else for money, and in the end Helga and Glas are both lonelier than before, as well as forever separated by Glas's monstrous crime.

Den allvarsamma leken (1912; The Serious Game), Söderberg's final novel, takes up themes from his earlier oeuvre, such as how the sex drive causes people to act in ways that are not in accord with their true interests. A couple, Lydia and Arvid, find themselves caught in a game that has rules they do not comprehend. Like *Doktor Glas*, *Den allvarsamma leken* brings back some of the characters from Söderberg's earlier novels, which heightens the verisimilitude of the author's total narrative fabric.

Söderberg is also known for his short stories. Published in five collections from 1898 to 1929, they deal with themes similar to those treated in his novels. "Pälsen" (The Fur Coat), in which the protagonist, Doctor Henck, loses both his social position and his wife, is a masterpiece of dramatic irony. "En herrelös hund" (A Dog without a Master) is a parable of humankind's existential situation in a world without God or a sense of meaning.

As a dramatist, Söderberg is best known for his plays *Gertrud* (1906), *Aftonstjärnan* (1912; The Evening Star), and *Ödestimman* (1922; The Fateful Hour). *Gertrud* is thematically related to *Den allvarsamma leken*, but the action is viewed from Gertrud's perspective, not that of the men in her life (and in the dramas), with whose work and other interests she finds herself competing for attention.

Söderberg eventually quit writing fiction in favor of nonfiction prose. In a series of books, *Hjärtats oro* (1909; The Unrest of the Heart), *Jahves eld* (1918; Jahve's Fire), *Jesus Barabbas* (1928), and *Den förvandlade Messias* (1932; The Transformed Messiah), he focuses on undermining Christian myths. *See also* THEATER.

SÖDERGRAN, EDITH (1892–1923). A Finland-Swedish poet, Södergran had a short life that is exceptional not only for its events, but largely because those events provided her with experiences that were expressed with remarkable emotional intensity in her poetry. Her life is also remarkable for its impact not only on Finland-Swedish poetry but on Scandinavian literature as a whole, for Södergran introduced literary **modernism** to the Nordic countries.

Born into a well-to-do middle-class family in St. Petersburg, Russia, Södergran spoke a somewhat idiosyncratic Swedish at home but German and Russian around town and at school. Provided with an excellent education on account of her mother's inherited wealth, she had many cultural opportunities. Södergran stayed in St. Petersburg for the school year, but during the summer the family lived in the little Karelian town of Raivola. Her father died from tuberculosis in 1907, and about a year later Södergran was sent to a sanatorium not far from Helsinki for treatment. This was the first time in her life that she lived in a regular Swedish-speaking environment. Later she went to Davos, Switzerland, for treatment and also traveled in Italy. During her stays abroad Södergran became familiar with contemporary European literature, including that of the avant-garde.

Södergran wrote her earliest poetry in German, a few poems in Swedish, and one in Russian. She later switched to exclusively Swedish, however, and that is the language of her first volume of poetry, *Dikter* (1916; tr. *Poems*, 1980). The reception was mixed, for Södergran wrote in free verse with no significant attention to rhythm and rhyme. Her Swedish was also marked by the linguistic idiosyncrasies of her family's dialect background as well as by her multilingual upbringing. Her next collection, *Septemberlyran* (1918; tr. *September Lyre*, 1980), was more self-assured and deviated further from what was expected of poetry at the time. It was alternately ridiculed and hailed as something entirely new in both Finland-Swedish and Swedish poetry. It attracted the favorable attention of such important literary figures as **Hagar Olsson** and **Runar Schildt**.

Septemberlyran shows the influence of the German thinker Friedrich Nietzsche (1844–1900), and that influence is increasingly evident in her next volume of poetry, *Rosenaltaret* (1919; tr. *The Rose Altar*, 1980). A small volume of aphorisms, *Brokiga iakttagelser* (1919; tr. *Motley Observations*, 1984), expresses her admiration for strong men. The poetry in *Framtidens skugga* (1920; tr. *The Shadow of the Future*, 1980) is even more emotionally intense.

The Russian Revolution had reduced Södergran and her mother to abject poverty, which is perhaps part of the reason she published nothing more—Södergran's literary activity was not a source of any significant income—and most certainly a contributing factor in the decline of her health. After the sale of their Raivola villa, mother and daughter lived in an uncomfortable summer house, where the Finland-Swedish poet **Elmer Diktonius** visited Södergran approximately a year before her death. Diktonius later took charge of her papers and arranged for the posthumously published collection *Landet som icke är* (1925; tr. *The Land Which Is Not*, 1980).

SOLSTAD, DAG (1941–). A Norwegian novelist, short story writer, and essayist, Solstad is recognized as one of the foremost Norwegian writers of his generation. A chronicler of life in the Norwegian welfare state, he started out as an exponent of literary **modernism** but soon turned to a kind of socialist **realism** that was intended to help bring about a **Marxist** revolution in Norway. When the failures of that literary program became impossible to ignore, Solstad's writing style changed to a rather traditional psychological realism, albeit with significant **postmodernist** elements. Solstad had his literary debut with the short story collection *Spiraler* (1965; Spirals) and then published *Svingstol* (1967; Swivel Chair), a volume of prose texts of varying lengths. Taken together, these stories and texts portray the meaninglessness and rootlessness of modern society. This is also the general theme of the novel *Irr! Grønt!* (1968; Patina! Green!), a book about role-playing as both a cause and a consequence of a person's sense of meaninglessness and absurdity.

While a student at the University of Oslo, Solstad associated with the *Profil* group, young intellectuals who published the student journal *Profil* (Profile). Around the time of the student revolt of 1968, many members of this group, including Solstad, **Tor Obrestad**, and

Espen Haavardsholm, affiliated with the Socialist Youth Alliance, the youth organization of the Socialist People's Party. In 1973 the Socialist Youth Alliance became part of the Maoist-inspired, **Marxist**-Leninist Workers Communist Party, which became Solstad's ideological home for the rest of the decade. Solstad's transition from late modernist to committed Marxist is chronicled in his second novel, *Arild Asnes, 1970* (1971), at the end of which the first-person protagonist goes door to door to sell the socialist newspaper *Klassekampen* (The Class Struggle). His next book, the novel *25. septemberplassen* (1974; The 25th of September Square), explicates social democracy in postwar Norway from a thoroughgoing Marxist perspective, arguing that the Norwegian working class was betrayed by the leaders of the Labor Party, who collaborated with American capitalism and steered Norway toward membership in the North Atlantic Treaty Organization (NATO).

A similar perspective governs the play *Kamerat Stalin eller familien Nordby* (1975; Comrade Stalin, or the Nordby Family), which defends Stalin's political vision, and a trilogy consisting of *Svik: Førkrigsår* (1977; Betrayal: Prewar Years), *Krig: 1940* (1978; War: 1940), and *Brød og våpen* (1980; Bread and Weapons). A realistic story about working-class life, the trilogy is set against the background of political events in the late 1930s and during World War II. Again Solstad wants to show that social democracy is incompatible with the needs of the workers.

By 1980 it became increasingly difficult to maintain any hope for a Marxist revolution in Norway, and the shining example of Mao Zedong's China had also lost some of its luster. Solstad began a process of self-examination with the novel *Gymnaslærer Pedersens beretning om den store politiske vekkelsen som har hjemsøkt vårt land* (1982; High School Teacher Pedersen's Account of the Great Political Revival That Has Visited Our Country). Commonly referred to as *Gymnaslærer Pedersen*, this tragicomic novel is the story of a young idealistic intellectual who takes a working-class job in order to become one with the people. There is more pessimism in *Forsøk på å beskrive det ugjennomtrengelige* (1984; An Attempt to Describe the Impenetrable), in which Norwegian society is depicted as materially affluent but spiritually shallow.

The protagonist in *Roman 1987* (1987; Novel 1987), for which

Solstad was awarded the **Nordic Literary Prize** in 1989, is similar to the high school teacher Pedersen in that he abandons a promising career as a university teacher and researcher in order to take a job at a cardboard factory. He achieves no real unity with the people but still believes that the experience was worth the effort. Disillusionment and pessimism return in *Ellevte roman, bok atten* (1992; The Eleventh Novel, Book Eighteen), in which the protagonist is a failure in every role he plays, and *Genanse og verdighet* (1994; Shyness and Dignity), in which another high school teacher experiences his lack of significance. *Professor Andersens natt* (1996; Professor Andersen's Night) features a literature professor who finds his life to be so empty of meaning that he fails to report a murder he has witnessed because keeping it a secret gives him something to live for.

T. Singer (1999) offers yet another portrait of life in Norway's welfare state, which in Solstad's eyes continues to be characterized by material affluence coupled with spiritual and emotional poverty. The book *16.07.41* (2002; 16 July 1941), the title of which may be read as gesturing at Solstad's own birthday, appears to be a first-person account of the author's life, including his relationship with his father, who died when Solstad was 11. Solstad has insisted that the book is a novel, but it is difficult to distinguish between the author and the narrator-protagonist. Highly self-reflective about its genre and narrative form, it is one of the most interesting examples of postmodernism in Norwegian literature. Solstad has also published several volumes of essays, talks, and articles.

SØNDERBY, KNUD (1909–1966). A Danish novelist, playwright, and essayist, Sønderby came of age in the period between the two world **wars,** a time marked by great economic instability. His literary debut, the novel *Midt i en Jazztid* (1931; In the Middle of a Jazz Age), depicts the self-absorption and lack of cultural direction of Danish youth in the 1920s. The main character, the law student Peter— Sønderby took a law degree in 1935—is caught between two women of very different social backgrounds. Neither relationship endures, and Peter is left to just dream of happiness.

Sønderby's next novel, *To Mennersker mødes* (1932; Two People Meet), is a continuation of his investigation of love between members of different social classes. His point is that the liberation of modern men and **women** may or may not be strong enough to overcome class differences. Class is also at the center of *En Kvinde er overflødig* (1936; A Woman Is Superfluous), in which the matriarch of an upper-middle-class family attempts to direct the lives of her two grown children. Rather pessimistically, the woman, Mrs. Tang, must die before her children are allowed to develop into autonomous human beings. But Sønderby also appreciates the sincerity of Mrs. Tang's devotion to them; nevertheless, her love is misdirected.

A stay at Greenland in 1935 resulted in two books. The first one was the novel *De kolde Flammer* (1940; The Cold Flames), in which a young couple learns to temper their romantic expectations of each other against the backdrop of Greenland's natural beauty. The second book is a volume of prose narratives, *Grønlandsk Sommer* (1941; Greenlandic Summer). Sønderby dramatized his novel *En Kvinde er overflødig* for performance at the Royal Theater in 1942; the drama appeared in English as *A Woman Too Many* (1955). It was a great success, as was a play based on Aristophanes's *Lysistrata, Kvindernes oprør* (1955; The Women's Rebellion), which addressed itself to conditions during the Cold War. Sønderby also wrote several volumes of essays and some one-act plays. *See also* THEATER.

SONNEVI, GÖRAN (1939–). One of Sweden's most famous modern poets, Sonnevi became known throughout Sweden in 1965, when he published his poem "Om kriget i Vietnam" (About the War in Vietnam), included in *Ingrepp-modeller* (1965; Intervention Models). His literary debut was four years earlier, however, with the collection *Outfört* (1961; Unaccomplished), which was followed by *Abstrakta dikter* (1963; Abstract Poems). The poems in these volumes are characterized by his reliance on the **modernist** tradition in Swedish literature. The collections *och nu!* (1967; And Now!) and *Det måste gå* (1970; It Must Work) argue in favor of democratic socialism and anti-imperialism and promote an activist stance on the part of common men and women.

Det oavslutade språket (1972; The Unfinished Language) marks the beginning of a period in Sonnevi's oeuvre when he focused on writing long poems. Other volumes in this vein include *Det omöjliga* (1975; The Impossible) and *Språk; Verktyg; Eld* (1979; Language; Tools; Fire). While Sonnevi continued to speak in favor of socialism,

Språk; Verktyg; Eld also recognized that socialism was no longer a viable option for most people. *Små klanger, en röst* (1981; Small Tones, a Voice) is a collection of unrhymed sonnets. *Oavslutade dikter* (1987; Unfinished Poems) and *Trädet* (1991; The Tree) deal with current events. Other works are *Mozarts terdje hjärna* (1996; Mozart's Third Brain) and *Klangarnes bok* (1998; The Book of Tones). In 2005 he received the **Nordic Prize** of the Swedish Academy for his lifetime poetic achievement.

SØRENSEN, VILLY (1929–2001). A Danish short story writer and essayist, Sørensen held a philosophical position between the two strong influences on him: the Danish philosopher **Søren Kierkegaard** and the German Karl **Marx** (1818–1883), who theorized about the problems of individuality and of society, respectively. His literary debut was the short story collection *Sære historier* (1953; tr. *Strange Stories*, 1956), in which he offers an absurd and humorous vision of modern life. *Ufarlige historier* (1955; tr. *Harmless Tales*, 1991) gives evidence of increased political awareness, but he still appeals mostly to psychology, not politics, in his search for an explanation of the phenomena on which he comments. This approach to cultural critique is discussed, in essay form, in *Digtere og dæmoner* (1959; Poets and Demons).

Hverken-eller (1961; Neither-Nor) is also a book of essays, the title of which is a play on Kierkegaard's famous ***Enten-Eller*** (1843; tr. *Either/Or*, 1944). Sørensen wants to avoid the extremes of both Soviet-style communism and Western capitalism, and he argues for a third way, which may be understood as the kind of welfare state preferred by the Scandinavian countries. Some of these ideas can also be found in *Formynderfortællinger* (1964; tr. *Tutelary Tales*, 1988).

The 1970s were a period of left-wing political radicalism among many Scandinavian artists and intellectuals. Sørensen, however, hewed closely to the middle, for example, in the essays in *Uden mål- og med: Moralske tanker* (1973; With and Without Goals: Moral Thoughts). As the Marxist enthusiasm was receding, he advocated his middle way in *Seneca: Humanisten ved Neros hof* (1976; tr. *Seneca: The Humanist at the Court of Nero*, 1984) and in *Oprør fra midten* (1978; tr. *Revolt from the Center*, 1981), written with K. Helveg

Petersen and Niels I. Meyer, in which he tried to establish general principles for social organization. The essays in *Den gyldne middelvej* (1979; The Golden Mean) and *Demokratiet og kunsten* (1988; Democracy and Art) again argue that human life can best flourish at some distance from both socialism and capitalism.

During the 1980s Sørensen also published *Vejrdage* (1980; Weather Days), which contained verse and prose drawn from his journals, as well as *De enkelte og andre småhistorier* (1986; tr. *Another Metamorphosis and Other Fictions*, 1990), a collection of fictional prose. *Ragnarok: En gudefortælling* (1982; tr. *The Downfall of the Gods*, 1989) is a retelling of Old Norse myths in the context of the work of the Danish writer **Adam Oehlenschläger**. In *Den berømte Odysseus* (1988; The Famous Odysseus) Homer's story is retold from the perspective of Odysseus's son, Telemachus. Sørensen has also published three volumes of his journals, as well as retellings of the myths of Odysseus and Apollo. He received the **Nordic Literary Prize** in 1974.

STAGNELIUS, ERIK JOHAN (1793–1823). A Swedish poet, Stagnelius may be regarded as the epitome of **romanticism** in his country. Although he lived only until the age of 30, he left a strong imprint on Swedish romantic poetry. He was born into a clerical family and educated at the universities of Lund and Uppsala, after which he had a minor governmental position in Stockholm. He was preoccupied with gnosticism and other forms of mysticism. His first published poem, *Vladimir den store* (1817; Vladimir the Great), is written in hexameter and tells about Saint Vladimir (956–1015), the first Russian ruler to embrace Christianity. The poetry collection *Liljor i Saron* (1821; Lilies in Sharon) expresses Stagnelius's mystical worldview. Its third edition also contained two poetic dramas, *Martyrerna* (1821; The Martyrs) and *Bacchanterna eller Fanatismen* (1822; The Bacchantes, or Fanaticism). These works drew heavily on classical themes and attest to his affinity with neoclassicism.

Much of Stagnelius's poetry concerns itself with erotic longing and its renunciation rather than its satisfaction. Some of his poems are addressed to a woman named Amanda, who serves as the speaker's muse. She is beyond his reach, for it is necessary to abstain from earthly love in order to achieve a purification of soul.

STANGERUP, HENRIK (1937–1998). A Danish novelist, filmmaker, and cultural journalist, Stangerup is the grandson of the Swedish writer **Hjalmar Söderberg**. After studying theology, but without taking a degree, he worked as a journalist, specializing in movie **criticism**. He also made three motion pictures; the last of them, a film version of **Ludvig Holberg**'s play *Erasmus Montanus* (1731; tr. 1915), was panned by the critics. Stangerup's work as a journalist gave him material for his first novel, the polemical *Slangen i brystet* (1969; tr. *Snake in the Heart*, 1996), a story of progressive psychic disintegration set in Paris and an example of the Danish neorealism of the 1960s.

Stangerup's next novel, *Løgn over løgn* (1971; Lie upon Lie), investigates the Danish tendency to feel shame and guilt. It is also critical of the ruling leftist faction that, in Stangerup's opinion, held an unhealthily dominant position in Danish cultural life. His critique of the Danish social democratic government is intensified in *Manden der ville være skyldig* (1973; tr. *The Man Who Wanted to Be Guilty*, 1982), in which Stangerup argues that people are simply not allowed to take responsibility for their actions. The autobiographical novel *Fjenden i forkøbet* (1978; Preempting the Enemy) discusses such problems in Stangerup's life as his divorce, the death of his father, and the questionable reputation that his father acquired during World **War** II.

A great admirer of the thought of **Søren Kierkegaard**, Stangerup illustrated the Kierkegaardian theory about the aesthetic, ethical, and religious stages of development, or spheres of existence, in a trilogy written during the 1970s. The ethical stage is illustrated by *Vejen til Lagoa Santa* (1981; tr. *The Road to Lagoa Santa*, 1984) and tells the story of Kierkegaard's brother-in-law, the natural scientist P. W. Lund, a pioneer in paleontology who lived in Brazil for years. The second volume, which presents the aesthetic sphere, bears the title *Det er svært at dø i Dieppe* (1985; tr. *The Seducer: It Is Hard to Die in Dieppe*, 1990) and recounts the story of the literary critic P. L. Møller, another contemporary of Kierkegaard. The final volume, *Broder Jacob* (1991; tr. *Brother Jacob*, 1993), describes the life and times of a Franciscan monk and illustrates Kierkegaard's thought about the religious sphere.

Stangerup's last book, *Datter af: Scener om en mor* (1995; Daughter of: Scenes about a Mother), has his mother Betty Söderberg as its subject. He also published several collections of essays, in which the best of his journalistic output has been preserved.

STEINARR, STEINN (1908–1958). An Icelandic poet, Steinarr is perhaps his country's most significant poet in the 20th century. Raised an orphan in a rural area, he became both an urban dweller and a cosmopolitan who introduced **modernist** lyrics to Iceland. After moving to Reykjavík, Steinarr came into contact with a communist group and was a communist for a while. Both his political radicalism and his abject poverty informed the poems in his first collection, *Rauður loginn brann* (1934; The Red Flame Was Burning), where he mocks the norms of the middle class and despairs at the human condition in general. The best poems in his second collection, *Ljóð* (1938; Poems), have more striking imagery, and the hope for the future that was implicit in his politically radical stance gives way to increasing pessimism.

The volume *Spor í sandi* (1940; Tracks in the Sand) contains both satirical poetry and poems about love, but the speaker in the love poems expresses a deep sense of hopelessness. *Ferð án fyrirheits* (1942; Aimless Journey) is even more strongly given to love poetry, but it is mixed with Steinarr's previous philosophical themes in such a way that the reader is left with a deep sense of existential angst. Steinarr's final poetry collection, *Tíminn og vatnið* (1948; Time and Water), shows that he used language not to convey a specific meaning but to create a linguistic structure that in itself constitutes the meaning of the poem. He was the first Icelandic poet to accomplish this, and it took a poor and uneducated orphan from a peripheral rural community to do it.

STORY OF GÖSTA BERLING, THE. See *GÖSTA BERLINGS SAGA.*

STRINDBERG, AUGUST (1849–1912). A Swedish dramatist, novelist, short story writer, and poet, Strindberg is Sweden's best-known man of letters. Although he is known internationally chiefly for his dramas, he was an early practitioner of the modern psychological novel as well as a great literary artist whose career reflects most of the intellectual currents of his day. Together with **Henrik Ibsen** he stands as a father of modern drama, but he was a man of controversy his entire life. Strindberg's career got its start with two historical plays, *Hermione* (1869) and *Den fredlöse* (1871; tr. *The Outlaw*, 1969), which were performed at the Royal Dramatic Theater in Stockholm. Strindberg's next play, the prose version of *Mäster Olof* (1872; tr. *Master Olof*, 1915), was rejected, however. Strindberg was no doubt too critical of his subject, the Lutheran reformer Olaus Petri, a religious icon in Sweden, and this bit of adversity caused Strindberg to turn away from drama for a time.

For several years Strindberg made a living as a journalist and assistant at Stockholm's Royal Library. After marrying Siri von Essen, he had his breakthrough as a writer of fiction with the novel *Röda rummet* (1879; tr. *The Red Room*, 1967), a panoramic novel about life among artists, intellectuals, and government employees in Stockholm. He then moved with his family to France, from which he returned briefly in 1884 in order to stand trial on the charge of blasphemy. He had published a volume of short stories about the relationship between the sexes entitled *Giftas* (1884; tr., with a second volume, as *Married*, 1913; also as *Getting Married*, 1972), and one of these stories had attracted the attention of the authorities. He was acquitted, and a second volume of *Giftas* stories was published in 1886.

At this time he also published the first two volumes of a somewhat fictionalized autobiography, *Tjänstekvinnans son: En själs utvecklingshistoria* (1886–1909; tr. *The Son of a Servant: The Story of the Evolution of a Human Being*, 1966). The title reflected the fact that Strindberg's mother had been a servant before she became his father's second wife. Strindberg could not claim to have come from the lower classes, however, as his father was reasonably well to do and solidly middle class.

Returning to Scandinavia in 1887, Strindberg published his most popular novel, *Hemsöborna* (1887; tr. *The Natives of Hemsö*, 1965), which is set in the Stockholm archipelago. But his main reason for coming back was that he had gotten back to writing plays, and his first modern drama, *Fadren* (1887; tr. *The Father*, 1899), was to be staged in Copenhagen. Ideologically, *Fadren* is both a descendant of the traditional bourgeois tragedy (*Trauerspiel*) and influenced by the radical **naturalistic** ideas of Emile Zola (1840–1902). Strindberg wants to show that there is a perpetual war between men and women, and the female protagonist, Laura, is ruthless in her drive to destroy her husband by causing him to be declared insane. Her chief weapon is to get him to doubt that he is the biological father of their child, and the resulting "psychic murder," as Strindberg calls it, is truly a tragedy because he is a highly gifted man, much more so than his wife, who will henceforth be able to raise their child as she alone sees fit.

The following year Strindberg published the naturalistic drama *Fröken Julie* (1888; tr. *Miss Julie*, 1912), which adheres closely to Zola's ideas. Julie, a young noblewoman, is seduced by her father's valet Jean, who is more fit for survival than she. Julie consequently commits suicide at the end of the drama. Another play, *Fordringsägare* (1888; tr. *Creditors*, 1914), follows Zola's naturalism even more closely.

After starting a short-lived experimental theater, Strindberg focused on fiction writing for a few years. His marriage to Siri von Essen was deteriorating, and he had written a novel about it in French, *Le plaidoyer d'un fou* (1888; tr. *The Confessions of a Fool*, 1912). He also wrote several more prose works, the most important of which is the novel *I havsbandet* (1890; tr. *By the Open Sea*, 1913 and 1984), in which he paid homage to the idea of the superman promulgated by Friedrich Nietzsche (1844–1900). The protagonist in *I havsbandet* deteriorates mentally to the point that he commits suicide, and this slide into depression and psychosis is carefully charted by the narrator.

Strindberg's marriage to Siri von Essen was dissolved in 1891. He met the Austrian Frida Uhl in 1893, and they were married the next year. They soon separated, however, and Strindberg went to live in Paris again, with the ambition of becoming a scientist. He carried out chemical and alchemical experiments, looking for a way to make gold from baser elements, but he suffered from a case of painful psoriasis that was probably aggravated by the chemicals he touched. He was also psychically unstable; he believed that some of his enemies were out to get him, and that they were somehow reaching him with electric currents. He interpreted everyday occurrences as signs from higher powers, and believed that these powers (*maktarna*) were deliberately tormenting him. Strindberg had by now departed from the science-based worldview of the 1880s and had adopted a very personal form of spirituality. Aided by the writings of the Swedish mystic **Emanuel Swedenborg**, he had a religious breakthrough that he termed his personal Inferno, which he regarded as an expiation of and cleansing from his earlier way of life.

The immediate artistic result of these experiences was the autobiographical novel *Inferno* (1897; tr. 1968) and the narratives *Legender* (1898; tr. *Legends*, 1912) and *Jakob brottas* (1899; tr, *Jacob Wrestles*). *Inferno* detailed his very difficult life while in Paris, and it is hard to determine if he was truly psychotic or if he was in part playing with his ideas and moods in order to have material for his art. It is quite clear, however, that he was not entirely well, and that he suffered both physically and mentally. Strindberg's new outlook on life manifested itself in such plays as the conversion trilogy *Till Damaskus* (1898–1904; tr. *To Damascus*, 1913), *Dödsdansen* (1901; tr. *The Dance of Death*, 1912), and *Ett drömspel* (1902; tr. *A Dream Play*, 1929). In *Ett drömspel*, Indra's daughter comes to earth as a human being in order to experience the joys and pains of the human condition. This is a far cry from Strindberg's naturalism in *Fröken Julie*.

Strindberg's literary productivity increased dramatically after the Inferno crisis, and he published almost half of his literary works during the years 1897–1909. Some of these were such chamber plays as *Oväder* (1906; tr. *Storm Weather*, 1962), *Spöksonaten* (1907; tr. *The Ghost Sonata*, 1962), and *Pelikanen* (1908; tr. *The Pelican*). Others were *Kronbruden* (1902; tr. *The Crown Bride*), which drew on Swedish **folklore**, and such history plays as *Gustav Vasa* (1899; tr. 1959) and *Erik XIV* (1899; tr. 1959), two of his approximately 20 historical plays.

Prose narratives were also produced during these years. *Götiska rummen* (1904; The Gothic Rooms) was thought of as a counterpart to his early novel *Röda rummet*. The satirical novel *Svarta fanor* (1907; tr. *Black Banners*, 1981) was a thinly veiled attack on his Swedish contemporaries. This book was a manifestation of his strident nature, which was probably one reason Strindberg never received the **Nobel Prize** in literature. When in 1910 a suggestion was made that he should be given an equivalent sum of money by the Swedish people, a series of newspaper articles set off the final conflict in his life, the "Strindberg Feud." He died from stomach cancer on 14 May 1912. *See also* THEATER.

STURLUSON, SNORRI (1178–1241). An Icelandic historian, Snorri is the greatest man of letters in medieval Iceland. Having been educated in a literary tradition that combined medieval European scholarship with native Icelandic learning, he was well equipped to undertake the two projects on which his reputation rests. The first was to preserve the knowledge of the composition and interpretation of ancient Scandinavian court poetry. This tradition, known as the skaldic tradition, had arisen in Norway but had more or less become the monopoly of Icelandic skalds. Snorri composed a handbook for young poets, which came to be known as *The Prose Edda* (also known as *The Younger Edda* and *Snorra-Edda*), in which he surveyed the ancient myths that had served as a source material for the poetic imagery and diction of the court poets of the past. He also quoted about 350 stanzas by 60 different poets, thus helping to preserve a significant corpus of work that up to this point had been known mostly in oral tradition. Finally, he included a long poem that he had composed as a model for those who would study his handbook.

Snorri's second project was to provide a reasonably critical history of Scandinavian kings. Having first compiled a history of the Norwegian king Saint Olaf, he added shorter histories, or sagas, that deal with the preceding rulers, going back to mythological times. Sagas of the kings who succeeded Olaf were also added, up to the year 1177, when the reign of King Sverre Sigurdsson began, for Sverre had already arranged for the history of his reign to be written during his lifetime. Snorri's great historical work came to be known as *Heimskringla*, after the first two words of his text, "kringla heimsins" (the round disc of the world).

It has been hypothesized that Snorri is also the writer of the well-known *Egils saga*, which tells about the life and times of **Egil Skallagrímsson**, but no firm evidence has yet come to light.

SULT. A novel by the Norwegian **Knut Hamsun**, *Sult* (1890; tr. *Hunger*, 1899) is set in Christiania (now Oslo) and tells about its narrator's mental self-experiments as he periodically starves himself in order to observe the effects of starvation on his mind. Hamsun's breakthrough novel, *Sult* is an early example of literary **modernism**.

SUNDMAN, PER OLOF (1922–1992). A Swedish novelist and short story writer, Sundman was influenced by the French New Novel, and his oeuvre is a paradigmatic example of the literary documentarism of the 1960s. He is an adherent of a strong philosophical skepticism, so he believes that it is impossible for a writer to know the minds of his characters. Therefore, a writer should not engage in imaginative investigations of their mental life but should be content with describing their observable behavior. Since it is equally impossible to truly know objects in the world, a writer should not offer constructions of meaning but should instead describe the surface of reality as it is available to the senses. Sundman's work is strongly marked by these epistemological and narratological concerns.

Sundman lived for many years in the district of Jämtland, near the Norwegian border in northern Sweden, and many of his narratives are set there. The short story collection *Jägarna* (1957; The Hunters) contain stories about the search for understanding. This theme is continued in the novel *Undersökningen* (1958; The Investigation), in which a government official investigates possible criminal activity by a person who temporarily lives within his jurisdiction. The information he gathers is conflicting, and that is precisely Sundman's point: objective truth is an illusion, and we cannot comprehend other minds. The novel *Skytten* (1960; The Hunter) makes the same point, as a hunting accident is investigated without any conclusive result.

One of Sundman's best-known novels, *Expeditionen* (1962; tr. *The Expedition*, 1967), is set in Africa and tells the story of the travels in the Congo by Henry Morton Stanley (1841–1904). The story is told from two perspectives, that of a military officer and that of an Asian man who understands both European and native African ways of looking at the world. The use of two narrators is a very effective tool for showing that truth is neither something given nor something easily constructed from sense observation. In the novel *Två dagar, två nätter* (1965; tr. *Two Days, Two Nights*, 1969) Sundman returns to the hunting theme in the form of the story of a manhunt. Two men succeed in capturing a young criminal out in the wilderness. Although such a story could be told with all kinds of embellishments of plot and character, Sundman offers a strictly minimalist account devoid of rhetorical flourish, but his attention to detail makes it possible for readers to create their own structures of meaning.

The novel *Ingeniör Andrées luftfärd* (1967; tr. *The Flight of the Eagle*, 1970) offers an eponymous protagonist similar to the Stanley character in *Expeditionen*, in that he is arrogant, vainglorious, and nationalistic. It tells the story of a Swedish balloon journey to the North Pole in 1897 that ends in disaster and the death of the three participants. The novel was filmed by the director Jan Troell in 1982.

Sundman's style shows influences from the Icelandic sagas, and *Berättelsen om Såm* (1977; The Story about Såm) is a retelling of one of the shorter saga texts, *Hrafnkels saga*. Sundman's reinterpretation of his intertext focuses on the political dimension of the story, particularly the role of power.

SVENDSEN, HANNE MARIE (1933–). A Danish novelist, short story writer, and dramatist, Svendsen grew up at Skagen, the northern tip of the Jutland Peninsula, and early acquired a love of the sea, which is present in many of her works. Her books also give evidence of her interest in **postmodern** theories of literature, especially magic realism, as the everyday and the fantastic exist side by side in them. Her first literary work was the short novel *Mathildes drømmebog* (1977; Mathilda's Dream Book), in which the protagonist's reality is juxtaposed with her dream world. Her definitive breakthrough came with the novel *Guldkuglen: Fortælling om en ø* (1985; tr. *The Gold Ball*, 1989), in which she weaves together both reality and the fantastic, both past and present, into a kaleidoscopic narrative in which an island functions as a microcosm of the world.

The novel *Karantæne* (1995; Quarantine) tells about modern alienation with great psychological insight, while *Rejsen med Emma* (1996; The Journey with Emma) mixes high and popular literary forms into an internationally flavored account of the conditions of both liberty and creativity. *Ingen genvej til Paradis* (1999; No Back Road to Paradise) emphasizes the role of **women** in the story of a multigenerational family. In *Unn fra Stjernestene* (2003; Unn from Stjernestene), a novel set in medieval Greenland, Svendsen provides much historical information as a backdrop to the story of a young woman's process of maturation.

Svendsen has written two collections of short stories, *Samtale med Gud og med Fandens oldemor* (1982; A Conversation with God and with the Devil's Dam) and *Kristines ting og andre historier om genfærd* (1992; Kristine's Things and Other Stories about Ghosts), in which her magic realism is in full force. She has also written several well-received **children's books** and a number of dramas for **theater**, television, and radio, including *Drømmen om byen* (2000; The Dream of the City).

SWEDENBORG, EMANUEL (1688–1772). A Swedish Enlightenment philosopher and theologian, Swedenborg is notable for his influence on such writers as the Swedes **Carl Jonas Love Almqvist** and **August Strindberg**, as well as the American Ralph Waldo Emerson. The son of a Lutheran bishop, Swedenborg studied classical philology at Uppsala University and then spent the next 30 years studying natural science within the Enlightenment framework of his day. A great synthesizer of the research of other scientists, he made significant contributions to geology and metallurgy. Through the study of physiology he attempted to solve the mysteries of the human soul.

A series of mystical experiences, including visions and dreams, led him to claim contact with the divine. Influenced by the ideas of neoplatonism, he developed a religious system that emphasized the existence of a spiritual reality that is reflected in the visible world. He described his visions with scientific exactness in *De coelo et de inferno* (1758, tr. *Heaven and Hell*, 1852), as well as in other works where conditions in heaven and hell are detailed, and which exist in multiple editions in English translation.

SYMBOLISM. A literary movement that had its origins in France in the second half of the 19th century, symbolism represents a **romantic** reaction against **realism** and is often referred to as **neoromanticism** in Scandinavian literary history. It lays stress on the personal and emotional response to events in the life of a writer or a character, as observed in such literary works as **August Strindberg**'s novel *I havsbandet* (1890; tr. *By the Open Sea*, 1913 and 1984) and **Arne Garborg**'s *Trætte Mænd* (1891; tr. *Weary Men*, 1999); the latter offered a careful articulation of the difference between the scientific worldview of the 1880s, represented by the character Georg Jonathan, and the religious striving of its narrator-protagonist, Gabriel Gram. But the most clear-cut example of the new subjectivist literature was **Knut Hamsun**'s novel *Sult* (1890; tr. *Hunger*, 1899), which tells about its narrator's experimentation with his own mind. In drama, the female psyche was probed by **Henrik Ibsen** in the plays *Fruen fra havet* (1888; tr. *The Lady from the Sea*, 1890) and *Hedda Gabler* (1890; tr. 1891), while the male mind was similarly examined in *Bygmester Solness* (1892; *The Master Builder*, 1893). In Denmark **Johannes Jørgensen** championed the literary ideas of the 1890s in opposition to the **naturalists** through his editorship of the literary magazine *Taarnet* (1893–1894; The Tower). *See also* EKELÖF, GUNNAR; HOEL, SIGURD; KALLAS, AINO JULIA MARIA; LAGERLÖF, SELMA; LEHTONEN, JOEL; VESAAS, TARJEI.

– T –

TAFDRUP, PIA (1952–). A Danish poet, dramatist, and novelist, Tafdrup offers a poetic vision that spans human existence from the strength and beauty of youth to the finality of death. By focusing that vision particularly on **women**'s experience, Tafdrup's poetry in the 1980s came to be seen as quite different from that of her more overtly **feminist** contemporaries. She had her debut with the collection *Når det går hul på en engel* (1981; When an Angel Starts Speaking) and followed it up with *Intetfang* (1982; No Hold), both of which celebrate the experiences of young women, such as falling in love and motherhood.

In *Den inderste zone* (1983; The Innermost Zone) the body is regarded as a representation of the core of the individual, which the poet is able to touch through her words and images that, on the surface, refer only to the body. *Springflod* (1985; tr. *Spring Tide*, 1989), which adhered to this development in Tafdrup's theory of poetry, became a critical success.

The next collection, *Sekundernes bro* (1988; The Bridge of Seconds), reflects Tafdrup's position as a recognized poet, and she subsequently explained her poetics in some detail in *Over vandet går jeg: Skitse til en poetik* (1991; Walking over the Water: A Sketch of a Poetics). In *Krystalskoven* (1992; The Crystal Forest) she puts her ideas into practice, striving hard for poetic perfection, while *Territorialsang: En Jerusalemkomposition* (1994; Territorial Song: A Jerusalem Composition) reflects a journey to Israel. A second stay in Israel resulted in *Dronningporten* (1998; tr. *Queen's Gate*, 2001), for which she received the **Nordic Literary Prize** in 1999. She has also published the poetry collections *Tusindfødt* (1999; Born of a Thousand) and *Hvalerne i Paris* (2002; The Whales of Paris).

Tafdrup's novel *Hengivelsen* (2004; The Surrender) describes a young woman's first experience with love. She has also written two plays, *Døden i bjergene* (1988; Death in the Mountains) and *Jorden er blå* (1991; The Earth Is Blue).

TAVASTSTJERNA, KARL AUGUST (1860–1898). A Finland-Swedish poet, novelist, and short story writer, Tavaststjerna came from an upper-class background and became interested in literature while a student in Helsinki. He had his literary debut with a collection of poetry, *För morgonbris* (1883; With the Morning Breeze), which was followed by *Nya vers* (1885; New Verses), poems written in a rather old form inherited from his great predecessor **Johan Ludvig Runeberg**. His novel *Barndomsvänner* (1886; Childhood Friends) offers a partly **naturalistic** account of the lives of weary dreamers in Helsinki, and the short stories in *En inföding* (1887; An Aboriginee) and *I förbindelser* (1888; In Connections) provide his comments on Finland's cultural and political dependency. *Marin och genre* (1890; Marine and Genre Paintings), a volume of stories and sketches, celebrates Finnish **nature**.

Some of the poetry in *Dikter i väntan* (1890; Poems While Waiting) is patriotic, while other poems are intensely personal. The novel *Hårda tider* (1891; Hard Times) is a depressing tale of poverty, trickery, and eventually murder, while *Kvinnoregemente* (1894; Rule by Women) satirizes the romantic attitude some city-bred Finnish intellectuals had toward the peasantry. The growing decadence of European literature of the 1890s is visible in the novel *I förbund med döden* (1893; In League with Death). *En patriot utan fosterland* (1896; A Patriot without a Homeland) takes aim at internationalism. Tavaststjerna's final prose work was an autobiographical narrative, *Lille Karl* (1897; Little Karl).

TEGNÉR, ESAIAS (1782–1846). A Swedish poet, Tegnér was born into a clerical family of modest means but was raised by a well-to-do foster father after his own father's death. He distinguished himself as a brilliant student at Lund University, where he became a professor of Greek; later he became a bishop in the Swedish Lutheran state church. He was well read not only in classical languages but also in philosophy, and he was influenced by the German **romantics**. But Tegnér was less sanguine in his romanticism than, for example, **Per Daniel Amadeus Atterbom**. Tegnér appreciated classicism's emphasis on the unity of clear thought and balance and moderation of expression. Although he, like other **national romantics**, found inspiration in the deeds of the ancient men of the north, he was also inspired by the literature and mythology of the classical world, to which he referred liberally in his many poems written for celebrations of various kinds.

In 1811 Tegnér wrote a prize-winning poem, "Svea" (Sweden), the first of a number of individual poems that added to his luster as a poet and all-round cultural personality. Tegnér is also well known for his long verse narratives. *Nattvardsbarnen* (1820; The Child Communicants), a narrative in hexameter, was much admired, for example, by the American poet Henry Wadsworth Longfellow, who translated it into English. Other narrative poems are *Kronbruden* (1841; The Crown Bride) and *Axel* (1822), which takes place during the war with Russia under King Karl XII. Tegnér is best remembered, however, for *Frithiofs saga* (1825; tr. 1833), which takes a minor Old Norse saga and spins it into a Swedish national epic consisting of 24 songs. Set in the Viking Age, it is a story about romantic love and its resulting conflict between men, but also about forgiveness and reconciliation.

The romantics believed that the poetic genius had a unique understanding of transcendental realities, and Tegnér shared this view. Some of his lyric poetry spoke of his own troubles, which he was struggling to understand. His mental health failed him in his later years, but he left a strong and lasting impression on the literature and culture of his people.

THEATER. During the Middle Ages, Scandinavian theater followed practices common in Europe at the time, with mystery and morality plays being performed in churchyards and marketplaces, and in connection with religious festivals. After the Reformation, school dramas took the place of the earlier performances, and classical tragedies and comedies provided patterns for vernacular plays. The purpose of the school dramas was to teach good manners and morals, and although the players were students and their teacher the director, the audience was often townspeople. The scripts used were both translations and native dramas, often with Old Testament subjects.

The next stage in the development of Scandinavian theater was performances at the courts of the kings Frederik II (r. 1559–1588), Christian IV (r. 1588–1648), and Frederik III (r. 1648–1670) of Denmark, and Queen Christina of Sweden (r. 1632–1654). These performances consisted of regal processions and *ballets de cour*, in which their royal sponsors were celebrated in music, recitation, theatrical sketches, and a closing dance. Prevalent were also courtly masquerades in which the participants moved about in pastoral surroundings while dressed as shepherds, shepherdesses, soldiers, and other characters of the time. Such forms of theater continued under both Christian V of Denmark (r. 1670–1699) and Charles XI of Sweden (r. 1660–1697).

Traveling theater companies from England, France, Germany, and Holland also strongly influenced the development of the native Scandinavian theater. Charles XII of Sweden (r. 1697–1718) engaged a permanent French company for his court, as did Frederik IV of Denmark (r. 1699–1730). Frederik IV was also an enthusiastic supporter of Scandinavia's first permanent playhouse, located in Lille Grønnegade in Copenhagen. This was the theater, established in 1722, for which **Ludvig Holberg** wrote his comedies, and which produced 15 of his plays during the first 18 months of its existence.

Holberg is Scandinavia's first major playwright, and his comedies are staples of the repertoire, particularly in Denmark and Norway. Some representative plays are *Den Politiske Kandestøber* (tr. *The Political Tinker*, 1915), which satirizes common people who want to get involved in political life; *Jeppe paa Bierget* (1722; tr. *Jeppe of the Hill*, 1915), which presents the miserable life of a drunken peasant; and *Erasmus Montanus* (1731, tr. 1915), a satire on learning for its own sake. Although mostly types, Holberg's characters are anchored in a realistically portrayed social and economic environment.

The first permanent Swedish stage was established in 1737, and the Danish Royal Theater, located on Kongens Nytorv in Copenhagen, opened in 1748, after the death of the pietistic King Christian VI in 1746. The Swedish queen Lovisa Ulrika, the mother of **Gustav III**, made the summer castle Drottningholm a theatrical center. After the first theater located there burned, a new and larger one was built on the castle grounds by the architect Carl Frederik Adelcrantz. This playhouse opened in 1766 and has been restored to its original appearance, including the original stage machinery.

During the reign of Gustav III, Sweden experienced a great cultural flowering centered in Stockholm. The king collaborated with **Johan Henric Kellgren** on several librettos and wrote other scripts. After the assassination of Gustav III in 1792, Copenhagen assumed the leadership in Scandinavian theater.

One of the best-known plays in Danish from this period was a parody of French tragedy entitled *Kierlighed uden Strømper* (1772; Love without Stockings), written by the Norwegian **Johan Herman Wessel**. Adhering closely to the unities of time, place, and action, Wessel's play exhibits the formal perfection of neoclassical tragedy, but there is a complete mismatch between the drama's high style and its utterly quotidian reality. A far more productive dramatist was **Johannes Ewald**, whose dramatic debut was a play about the Fall entitled *Adam og Ewa eller Den ulykkelige Prøve* (1769; Adam and Eve, or, The Unlucky Test). It was followed by *Rolf Krage* (1770), an action drama with the subject taken from the Danish history written by the 13th-century historian Saxo Grammaticus; *Balders Død* (1774; tr. *The Death of Balder*, 1889), which inspired **Adam Oehlenschläger**; and *Fiskerne* (1779; The Fishermen), the story of a dramatic rescue at sea. Oehlenschläger was primarily a poet and is remembered as a dramatist chiefly for his five-act drama *Aladdin* (tr. 1857, 1968), in which good and evil are contrasted and where Aladdin, the representative of the forces of goodness, can triumph only after having been chastened and tested in adversity. As the **romantic** era came to an end in Denmark, **Johan Ludvig Heiberg** introduced the vaudeville, the first one being *Kong Salomon og Jørgen Hattemager* (1825; King Salomon and George Hatter). Heiberg also wrote more traditional dramas, for example, the romantic **folklore** plays *Elverhøi* (1828; The Elves' Hill) and *Alferne* (1835; The Elves), in which the elves are portrayed as being superior to the skeptics and materialists of Heiberg's own time.

Although a group of enthusiastic amateurs had established the Comedy House in Bergen as early as the year 1800, theater came into its own in Norway with the founding of Christiania Theater in 1827, for which the poet **Henrik Wergeland** wrote a number of now largely forgotten plays. A new building was erected at Bankplassen in Christiania in 1837. **Henrik Ibsen** was briefly associated with Christiania Theater in the 1850s, but he was to acquire his expertise in stagecraft at the violinist Ole Bull's Norwegian Theater in Bergen, which was founded in 1849 and operated at the old Comedy House. Closing in 1863, this theater reopened as the National Stage in 1876.

Ibsen's significance to both Scandinavian and world theater cannot be overemphasized. Although his earliest plays have been largely forgotten, such dramas as the historical tragedy *Fru Inger til Østeraad* (1855; tr. *Lady Inger of Østråt*, 1890) and *Hærmændene paa Helgeland* (1858; tr. *The Vikings at Helgeland*, 1890) deserve to be remembered. *Peer Gynt* (1867) is considered Norway's national drama. Ibsen's place in world drama, however, was secured by such titles as *Samfundets støtter* (1877; tr. *The Pillars of Society*, 1888), which concludes that the spirit of truth and freedom are the real pillars of society, and **Et dukkehjem** (1879; tr. *A Doll's House*, 1880), which explores the role of **women** in the home and in society. *Gengangere* (1881; *Ghosts*, 1885) scandalized theatergoers because Ibsen discussed such delicate matters as syphilis and euthanasia. *En folkefiende* (1882; tr. *An Enemy of the People*, 1888) dramatizes the conflict between an exceptional intellect and the community in which he lives, while *Vildanden* (1884; tr. *The Wild Duck*, 1890) radically questions the correspondence between illusion and truth. *Rosmersholm* (1886; tr. 1891) and *Fruen fra havet* (1888; tr. *The Lady from the Sea*, 1890) probe relationships between men and women, while the eponymous protagonist in *Hedda Gabler* (1890; tr. 1891) quite dramatically bores herself to death. The demands of art are discussed in *Bygmester Solness* (1892; *The Master Builder*, 1893), while *Lille Eyolf* (1894; tr. *Little Eyolf*, 1895) presents a man who has used his work as an excuse for neglecting his wife. *John Gabriel Borkman* (1896; tr. 1897) is another example of what can happen when work consumes life, while *Når vi døde vågner* (1899; tr. *When We Dead*

Awaken, 1900) shows that an excessive commitment to art can be equally destructive.

Ibsen's Norwegian contemporary **Bjørnstjerne Bjørnson** contributed historical dramas such as *Halte-Hulda* (1858), *Kong Sverre* (1861; King Sverre), and *Sigurd Slembe* (1862; tr. 1888), and modern plays such as *De Nygifte* (1865; tr. *A Lesson in Marriage*, 1911), *En fallit* (1875; tr. *The Bankrupt*, 1914), *Redaktøren* (1875; tr. *The Editor*, 1914), and *Kongen* (1877; tr. *The King*, 1914). *En handske* (1883; tr. *A Gauntlet*, 1886) was central to the morality debate of the **Modern Breakthrough**, while Bjørnson's dramatic masterpiece *Over ævne I* (1883; tr. *Pastor Sang*, 1893) probes the psychology of faith.

Next to Ibsen the greatest innovator in Scandinavian drama is the Swede August Strindberg, who established the famed Intimate Theater in Stockholm (1907–1910), at which his chamber plays were performed. Strindberg's career got its start with two historical plays, however, *Hermione* (1869) and *Den fredlöse* (1871; tr. *The Outlaw*, 1969), which were performed at the Royal Dramatic Theater in Stockholm. His first modern dramas were the **realist** *Fadren* (1887; tr. *The Father*, 1899) and the **naturalist** play *Fröken Julie* (1888; tr. *Miss Julie*, 1912). His most experimental works were *Till Damaskus* (1898–1904; tr. *To Damascus*, 1913), *Dödsdansen* (1901; tr. *The Dance of Death*, 1912), and *Ett drömspel* (1902; tr. *A Dream Play*, 1929), as well as such chamber plays as *Oväder* (1906; tr. *Storm Weather*, 1962), *Spöksonaten* (1907; tr. *The Ghost Sonata*, 1962), and *Pelikanen* (1908; tr. *The Pelican*).

Most Scandinavian playwrights of the 20th century have lacked the international stature of Ibsen and Strindberg but have influenced their respective national traditions. In Denmark **Kjeld Abell**'s first play, *Melodien der blev væk* (1935; tr. *The Melody That Got Lost*, 1939), criticized Danish middle-class life in the 1930s, while *Anna Sophie Hedvig* (1939; tr. 1944) warned against the threat of Nazism. *Dronningen gaar igen* (1943, but published 1955; tr. *The Queen on Tour*, 1955), written during World **War** II, contained a hidden call to resistance against the Germans. In *Han sidder ved Smeltediglen* (1938; tr. *He Sits at the Melting Pot*, 1953) **Kaj Munk** criticized Nazi ideology. The Swede **Pär Lagerkvist** argued in favor of **expressionism** in drama in his essay *Modern teater* (1918; tr. *Modern Theatre*,

1961) and wrote a series of plays in which he attempted to put his ideas into practice: *Sista människan* (1917; tr. *The Last Man*, 1988), *Den svåra stunden* (1918; tr. *The Difficult Hour*, 1961) and *Himlens hemlighet* (1919; tr. *The Secret of Heaven*, 1966). **Stig Dagerman** wrote six dramas, among them *Den dödsdömde* (1947; tr. *The Condemned*, 1951), *Ingen går fri* (1949; Nobody Goes Free), and *Den yttersta dagen* (1952; The Day of Judgment). In Finland **Walentin Chorell** wrote such plays as *Systrarna* (1955; tr. *The Sisters*, 1971) and *Kattorna* (1963; tr. *The Cats*, 1978). The National Theater of Iceland was founded in 1950, and among those who have written for the stage in Iceland is **Halldór Kiljan Laxness**. Influenced by the ideas of Bertolt Brecht, the Norwegian novelist and dramatist **Jens Bjørneboe** made a valiant attempt to overcome Ibsen's influence on Norwegian drama through such plays as *Til lykke med dagen* (1965; Many Happy Returns) and *Fugleelskerne* (1966; tr. *The Bird Lovers*, 1993), his greatest dramatic success. *Semmelweis* (1968; tr. 1996) and *Amputasjon* (1971; tr. *Amputation*, 2003) are both strongly antiauthoritarian.

The foremost contemporary Scandinavian dramatist is arguably **Jon Fosse**, who has published a large number of plays, starting with *Og aldri skal vi skiljast* (1994; And Never Shall We Be Separated), which focuses on the limitations of language. Communication is also the theme of *Namnet* (1995; tr. *The Name* 2002) and *Nokon kjem til å komme* (1996; tr. *Someone Is Going to Come*, 2002), in which a marriage breaks down after the arrival of a third person. The failure to communicate returns in *Natta syng sine songar* (1998; tr. *Nightsongs*, 2002), *Ein sommars dag* (1998; A Day in Summer), *Draum om hausten* (1999; Autumn Dream), *Besøk* (2000; Visit), *Vinter* (2000; Winter), and *Ettermiddag* (2000; Afternoon). *Dødsvariasjonar* (2002; Variations on Death) discusses suicide, while *Suzannah* (2004) is a dramatic presentation of the life of Suzannah Thoresen, the wife of Henrik Ibsen. The Swede **Lars Norén** is also well known internationally. His first play to be staged was *Fursteslickaren* (The Prince Licker, produced at the Royal Dramatic Theater, Stockholm, in 1973). Norén's dramas written during the late 1970s exhibit a higher degree of realism in their form, and since 1980 he has written several dozen plays. Like his Norwegian colleague Jon Fosse, he often writes about difficulties in communication. A paradigmatic example is a play about Eugene O'Neill, *Och ge oss skuggorna* (1991; And Give Us the Shadows), which deals with O'Neill's family life and uses *Long Day's Journey into Night* (1956) as intertext. *See also* AASEN, IVAR; AHLIN, LARS; ALMQVIST, CARL JONAS LOVE; ANDERSEN, BENNY; ANDERSEN, HANS CHRISTIAN; ATTERBOM, PER DANIEL AMADEUS; BANG, HERMAN; BERGMAN, HJALMAR; BORGEN, JOHAN; BRANNER, HANS CHRISTIAN; BRØGGER, SUZANNE; CANTH, MINNA; CHRISTENSEN, LARS SAABYE; DELBLANC, SVEN; ENCKELL, RABBE; ENQUIST, PER OLOV; FALDBAKKEN, KNUT; FORSSELL, LARS; FROSTENSON, KATARINA; GARBORG, ARNE; GRESS, ELSA; GRIEG, NORDAHL; GUNNARSSON, GUNNAR; HAMSUN, KNUT; HEIBERG, GUNNAR; HENNINGSEN, AGNES; HOEM, EDVARD; JAKOBSDÓTTIR, SVAVA; JAKOBSSON, JÖKULL; JENSEN, THIT; KALLAS, AINO JULIA MARIA; KIELLAND, ALEXANDER; KIVI, ALEKSIS; KJÆR, NILS; KROG, HELGE; KYRKLUND, WILLY; LEINO, EINO; LIDMAN, SARA; LUGN, KRISTINA; LØVEID, CECILIE; MADSEN, SVEND ÅGE; MANNER, EEVA-LIISA; MARTINSON, HARRY; MICHAEL, IB; MOBERG, VILHELM; MYRDAL, JAN; PALUDAN-MÜLLER, FREDERIK; PLEIJEL, AGNETA; OLSSON, HAGAR; PANDURO, LEIF; RIFBJERG, KLAUS; RUNEBERG, JOHAN LUDVIG; SCHILDT, RUNAR; SKRAM, AMALIE; SÖDERBERG, HJALMAR; SOLSTAD, DAG; SØNDERBY, KNUD; SVENDSEN, HANNE MARIE; TAFDRUP, PIA; THORUP, KIRSTEN; TOPELIUS, ZACHARIAS; VESAAS, TARJEI; VIK, BJØRG; WALTARI, MIKA TOIMI; WASSMO, HERBJØRG; WILLUMSEN, DORRIT.

THORUP, KIRSTEN (1942–). A Danish poet, novelist, and dramatist, Thorup started out as a **modernist** who wrote about alienation, fragmentation of one's worldview, meaninglessness, and schizoid states of mind. Her literary debut was a volume of poetry entitled *Indeniudenfor* (1967; Inside-Outside), which was followed by a small collection of short stories, *I dagens anledning* (1968; In Honor of the Occasion). Other early volumes of poetry are *Love from Trieste* (1969; tr. 1980) and *Idag er det Daisy* (1971; Today It's Daisy).

Thorup was born into a working-class family and has a sense of identification with outsiders of various kinds. The characters in her first novel and literary breakthrough, *Baby* (1973; tr. 1980), live on the margins of society. Although *Baby* has some experimental features, her story and plot are complicated and show that Thorup has a flair for traditional narrative. This is even more pronounced in her next two novels, *Lille Jonna* (1977; Little Jonna) and *Den lange sommer* (1979; The Long Summer), which are works of psychological **realism**. They are thematically similar to *Baby* in that the lower-middle-class characters find themselves sinking socially. There are autobiographical elements in both books, and especially in *Den lange sommer*, in which a working-class girl suffers the alienating effect of receiving an education.

The psychological realism and convoluted plots continue in *Himmel og helvede* (1982; Heaven and Hell) and *Den yderste grænse* (1987; The Outermost Border). While Thorup's characters experience all manner of vicissitudes, they nevertheless manage to hold on to such fundamental values as their family relationships. Thorup also discusses issues concerning one's sense of identity in the two novels *Elskede ukendte* (1994; Beloved Unknown) and *Bonsai* (2000); the latter also offers a critique of an overly aesthetic approach to life. *Ingenmandsland* (2004; No Man's Land) tells the story of a man who suffers from senile dementia and wants to escape from the rest home in which he is living so that he can put a flower on his wife's grave. Its social criticism is severe. Thorup has also written plays for the **theater**, television, and radio.

TIKKANEN MÄRTA (1935–). A Finland-Swedish novelist, Tikkanen came from a well-connected Finland-Swedish family and trained to become a teacher of Swedish. While working as a summer intern at a Swedish-language newspaper in Helsinki, she met and later married the writer Henrik Tikkanen, and their relationship has provided the bulk of the material for her creative work. Tikkanen's first novels were apprentice pieces. *Nu imorron* (1970; Now Tomorrow) and *Ingenmansland* (1972; No Man's Land) deal with a couple, modeled on the Tikkanens, and their stormy relationship, including the social conditions that enable such marriages. *Vem bryr sej om Doris Mihailov?* (1974; Who Cares about Doris Mihailov?) further examines the relationship between private tragedies and the social apparatus that exists in order to prevent them.

The novel that made Tikkanen's reputation bears the provocative title *Män kan inte våldtas* (1975; tr. *Manrape*, 1978) and tells the story of a rape victim who stalks her rapist, eventually succeeding in raping him as an act of revenge. This book was hotly debated, and it was clear that Tikkanen had developed into a writer of stature. Her reputation was further strengthened by *Århundradets kärlekssaga* (1978; tr. *The Love Story of the Century*, 1984), which was widely translated. Written in a lyrical prose verging on the prose poem, it was a response to Henrik Tikkanen's presentation of their marriage in his own work, essentially refuting his views of it. But Tikkanen also admits that she has a share of the blame for their marital problems, and this admission lifts the book above the level of most confessions of this type.

The Tikkanens had a daughter who suffered from Attention Deficit Hyperactivity Disorder (referred to as Minimal Brain Dysfunction in Finland), and in her next book, *Mörkret som ger glädjen djup* (1981; The Darkness That Gives Joy Its Depth), Tikkanen fused her story with that of a Finland-Swedish writer, Josef Julius Wecksell, who spent the last 40 years of his life in a mental hospital. In *Sofias egen bok* (1982; Sofia's Own Book) and *Önskans träd* (1987; Tree of Wishes) Tikkanen further discusses her daughter's diagnosis and treatment in such a manner as to be of help to other parents in the same situation. A later book about the topic was *Sofia vuxen med sitt MBD* (1998; Sofia as an Adult with Her Minimal Brain Dysfunction).

The novel *Rödluvan* (1986; Little Red Riding Hood) uses the **fairy tale** about Little Red Riding Hood as a background for an analysis of Tikkanen's own childhood. In Tikkanen's version of the story, the girl runs away from a loving and secure home in order to pursue the wolf erotically; she essentially moves in with him. After the novel *Storfångaren* (1989; The Great Hunter), which is set in Greenland, Tikkanen found a detail in Greek myth that she used as a framework for the novel *Arnaía kastad i havet* (1992; Arnaía Thrown into the Sea), in which she rewrote the story of the patient Penelope, the wife of Odysseus.

Tikkanen's *Personliga angelägenheter* (1996; Private Matters) uses traditional narrative rather than the prose poem form employed in her other recent novels. *Två—Scener ur ett konstnärsäktenskap* (2004; Two—Scenes from a Marriage of Artists) is Tikkanen's most recent analysis of her life with Henrik Tikkanen.

TOPELIUS, ZACHARIAS (1818–1898). A Finland-Swedish poet, novelist, journalist, and dramatist, Topelius is one of the truly classic figures in the literature of his people. Born into a family with literary and historical interests, he attended Helsinki University and eventually received a doctorate. His broad interests suited him to cultural journalism, however, and his first significant publication was a series of fictive letters, *Leopoldinerbrev* (1843–1854; Leopoldine Letters), in which he offered witty reports about life in Helsinki, reports that had been first published in the paper where he worked, *Helsingfors Tidningar* (Helsinki News). There he also first published his copious poetic efforts, which were later collected as *Ljungblommar* (1844, 1850, and 1854; Heather Blossoms), and then *Nya blad* (1870; New Leaves) and *Ljung* (1889; Heather). The paper also published his historical tales, many of them collected as *Fältskärns berättelser* (1853–1857; tr. *The Surgeon's Stories*, 1883–1884).

Topelius's favorite genre was the novella, and he often wrote cycles of stories. Some of them had contemporary settings, for example, *Gamla baron på Rautakylä* (1849; The Old Baron at Rautakylä) and *Vincent Vågbrytare* (1860; Vincent Breakwater), both of which are set in milieus that Topelius knew by personal experience. Others were set in the past, such as *Hertiginnan av Finland* (1850; The Duchess of Finland). A large collection of these kinds of tales bears the title *Winterkvällar* (1880–1897; Winter Evenings).

Having served as a professor of history at Helsinki University for some years, Topelius next wrote historical narratives with the common title *Planeternas skyddslingar* (1886–1889; Those Protected by the Planets), which he later renamed *Stjänornas kungabarn* (The Royal Children of the Stars), in which he offers an imaginative survey of Finland's history. *Ljungars saga* (1896; The Saga of Ljungar) was set in Finland around the year 1500.

Aware that Finland had no native dramatic tradition, Topelius turned his energies to the **theater**, offering dramatizations of two of his tales, and he wrote the librettos for two early Finnish operas. Topelius also wrote didactic **children's books**.

TRANSTRÖMER, TOMAS (1931–). A Swedish poet of international renown, Tranströmer is the foremost poet of his generation and has been extensively translated into English. He had his debut at the age of 23 with *17 dikter* (1954; Seventeen Poems), which made it clear that he was going to be a literary force to be reckoned with. His second collection, *Hemligheter på vägen* (1958; Secrets on the Way), was the result of several years of education and travel. At the start of his career Tranströmer was an observer who created bold metaphors that, combined with traditional **modernist** form, provided both a sense of tradition and a startling newness of vision.

Den halvfärdiga himlen (1962; The Half-Finished Heaven) marks a transition from objective observation to a more personal expression, signaled by more frequent use of the first-person pronoun. *Klanger och spår* (1966; Resonances and Tracks) shows increased concern with matters of society and politics; the Tranströmer family had left Stockholm in 1960, and the poet was holding down a day job as a psychologist at a reform school for boys. Tranströmer was, however, criticized by younger Swedish poets for not having gone far enough; the **war** in Vietnam and exploitative behavior by multinational corporations had radicalized many Swedish artists and intellectuals, and the student revolt of 1968 was right around the corner.

The volume *Mörkerseende* (1970; tr. *Night Vision*, 1971) acknowledged the ideological distance that separated Tranströmer from his younger colleagues, and it also included poems that were influenced by his work experience and some that stemmed from his family life, including experience with illness and death. The long poem *Östersjöar* (1974; tr. *Baltics*, 1975) is even more personal, as it is filled with recollections of his maternal grandfather and summers in the Stockholm archipelago, but it also reflects the political realities of the time. In the collection *Sanningsbarriären* (1978; tr. *Truth Barriers*, 1980) the erstwhile observer of life has become an active participant who writes about his intimate involvement in the lives of other human beings.

Tranströmer has cultivated a variety of verse forms. *Det vilda torget* (1983; tr. *The Wild Market Place*, 1985) and *För levande och döda* (1989; tr. *For the Living and the Dead*, 1994) are notable for their prose poems. The latter garnered Tranströmer the **Nordic Literary Prize** in 1990. After partly recovering from a stroke, Tranströmer published a memoir, *Minnena ser mig* (1993; The Memories Look at Me). The collection *Sorgegondolen* (1996; Grief Gondola), the title of which refers to two piano pieces by Franz Liszt (1811–1886), contains poems informed by his illness, but they also attest to his courage. *Den stora gåtan* (2004; The Great Riddle) consists of five relatively short poems followed by a section of haikus.

TROTZIG, BIRGITTA (1929–). A major Swedish poet, novelist, and essayist, Trotzig writes about such fundamental issues as the nature of good and evil and the presence of the divine in human life. While living in Paris in the 1960s she converted to Roman Catholicism, and her religious engagement can be felt throughout her work.

Trotzig debuted with a story about three women entitled *Ur de älskandes liv* (1951; From the Life of Lovers). Her second book, *Bilder* (1954; Images), is a collection of prose poems with strong visual power. Her artistic breakthrough came with *De utsatta* (1957; The Exposed), which was a retelling of the biblical story of Job. Set in 17th-century Skåne, in southern Sweden, it tells of a man who suffers rejection and poverty through no fault of his own, and who tries to maintain his religious faith throughout his seemingly endless tribulations. *En berättelse från kusten* (1961; A Tale from the Coast) is also set in Skåne and in the past.

Three rather brief narratives constitute *Levande och döda* (1964; Living and Dead), which gives examples of the significance of family dynamics in human development. Trotzig's next two novels deal with similar themes. *Sveket* (1966; The Betrayal) tells about a father who fails to understand the difference between true parental love and control and manipulation in his relationship with his daughter. *Sjukdomen* (1972; The Illness) features a protagonist who is capable of appropriate love for his son but is unable to communicate that love.

I kejsarens tid (1975; In the Time of the Emperor) is a collection of stories that emphasize the presence of negative forces as a necessary complement to the positive in human life. But even though human beings are captives of dark forces, there are also many reasons to hope for transcendence and, ultimately, renewal. A similarly dark vision is present in the novel *Dykungens dotter* (1985; The Mud King's Daughter), which, set in the 1920s, details the fate of some of society's losers.

Trotzig produced several volumes of prose poems in addition to the early *Bilder*. *Ordgränser* (1968; Word Limits) shows how words alone are incapable of expressing profound suffering. *Anima* (1982) takes as its theme such dualisms as those between body and soul and light and darkness. *Sammanhang: Material* (1996; Connection: Material) suggests that melancholia and the inability to communicate, which for Trotzig is a kind of autism, can be overcome. Similar themes are at the core of *Dubbelheten: Tre sagor* (1998; Doubleness: Three Tales).

TUNSTRÖM, GÖRAN (1937–2000). A Swedish poet, novelist, and short story writer, Tunström was born in Sunne, a town in the province of Värmland in southwestern Sweden; Sunne is frequently used as the setting for Tunström's books. Tunström began his career as a poet with the volume *Inringning* (1958; Ringing In/Encircling) and followed it up with two more collections, *Två vindar* (1960; Two Winds) and *Nymålat* (1962; Newly Painted). The poet, who had spent some time at a mental hospital as a young man, regarded these works as therapy. Additional volumes of poetry were *Om förtröstan* (1965; About Comfort), the main theme of which is love, and *De andra de til hälften synliga* (1966; The Others, the Half Visible), which manifests his empathy with unfortunate people everywhere. *Samtal med marken* (1969; Conversations with the Ground) expresses similar concerns. *Svartsjukens sånger* (1975; Songs of Jealousy) and *Sandro Botticellis dikter* (1976; The Poems of Sandro Botticelli) both deal with interpersonal relationships, while *Sorgesånger* (1980; Songs of Sorrow) takes a broad spectrum of mourning as its theme.

Although Tunström was a very prolific poet, he had greater success with his novels. The first one, *Karantän* (1961; Quarantine), tells of a marriage that fails because the protagonist in unable to trust in his wife's love for him. *Maskrosbollen* (1962; The Dandelion Head) is the story of a young man in his relationship to his girlfriend and his older brother. *Familjeliv: En berättelse från Tobobac* (1964: Family Life: A Story from Tobobac), which was published the year Tunström married the painter Lena Cronquist, depicts some of the absurdities of life, while *Hallonfallet* (1967; Raspberry Falls) is a rather traditional mystery story.

Tunström secured his position in Swedish literature with three novels that were informed by his brush with mental illness and the experience of his wife, who had suffered a breakdown after the birth of their child. These volumes, *De heliga geograferna* (1973; The Holy Geographers), *Guddöttrarna* (1975; The Goddaughters), and *Prästungen* (1976; The Pastor's Kid), are all set in his hometown, Sunne, and use material from the history of his family. A fourth novel also set in Sunne is *Juloratoriet* (1983; tr. *The Christmas Oratorio*, 1995). The title refers to the attempt by a group of local people to produce a choral work by Johann Sebastian Bach (1685–1750) in a church in Sunne. The structure of the novel resembles the musical structure of the oratorio, and like Bach's work, the story is one of how to overcome grief. The novel earned Tunström the **Nordic Literary Prize** in 1984.

The novel *Tjuven* (1986; The Thief), on the other hand, is far less optimistic. Its protagonist has an elaborate plan to steal the famed Codex Argentus, written in Gothic, in order to have the financial resources necessary to help his ill cousin. As becoming a famous scholar of Gothic is part of his plan, however, his focus gradually shifts from his concern for his cousin to satisfying his own ambitions. *Tjuven* thus becomes a poignant story of ambition and betrayal.

After a long hiatus Tunström published a short story collection, *Det sanna livet* (1987; The True Life), and the novel *Chang Eng* (1987), which tells the story of the original Siamese twins exhibited in the circus of P. T. Barnum. Chang and Eng Bunker (1811–1874) later married two sisters, Sarah and Adelaide Yates, and had a large number of children. In *Chang Eng* Tunström cleverly uses forms of address in order to cause readers to examine their understanding of what a human being is.

Ill with cancer for several years, Tunström next published a memoir, *Under tiden* (1993; Meanwhile) and the novel *Skimmer* (1996; Shimmering Light), which has Iceland as its setting and deals with the relationship between a son and his father. The author's final work, *Berömda män som varit i Sunne* (1998; Famous Men Who Have Been to Sunne), recycles a minor figure from *Tjuven* and offers a large number of interesting characters. It is thus emblematic of and a fitting conclusion to Tunström's oeuvre.

– U –

UNDSET, SIGRID (1882–1949). A Norwegian novelist and short story writer, Undset was the third Norwegian writer to be awarded the **Nobel Prize** (after **Bjørnstjerne Bjørnson** and **Knut Hamsun**). Her worldwide reputation rests primarily on her trilogy *Kristin Lavransdatter* (1920–1922), which has been translated into more than 70 languages. The daughter of an archeologist, Undset early developed a love for the Middle Ages, but on the advice of the editor who rejected her first work of fiction, a story with a medieval setting, her earliest published works are set in her own time. Great examples of the neorealism of the early 20th century, these books deal with social issues and the existential situation of their protagonists, particularly their love relationships. Undset's first novel, *Fru Marta Oulie* (1907; Mrs. Marta Oulie), recounts the story of the narrator-protagonist's marriage and adultery. *Den lykkelige alder* (1908; The Happy Age) is a collection of short stories. Both of these volumes were well received, and Undset next published a short novel with a medieval setting, *Fortællingen om Viga-Ljot og Vigdis* (1909; tr. *Gunnar's Daughter*, 1936), in which love and revenge are major themes.

Undset's literary breakthrough came with the novel *Jenny* (1911; tr. 1920), the story of a young painter who first falls in love with a man of her own generation, then becomes pregnant by his father, is raped by the son, and commits suicide. Although starkly realistic, it differs from many other novels about **women** and love in that Jenny sees her flaw as being too impatient to wait for the man who is to be her lord and master, and Undset was criticized for not sufficiently emphasizing Jenny's need for freedom and independence. Undset continued to speak openly about matters of sex in her next book, a collection of stories entitled *Fattige skjebner* (1912; Poor Fates).

The tone of Undset's literary works at this time was clearly at variance with the **feminism** of her age. For example, her novel *Vaaren* (1914; Spring) has as its protagonist a married woman who sacrifices to hold her family together during a crisis. The two stories in *Splinten av troldspeilet* (1917; The Splinter of the Troll Mirror) offer radically different solutions to problems in marriage, but Undset is clearly on the side of the character who gives up her lover in order to keep her husband. *De kloge jomfruer* (1918; The Wise Virgins) contains stories about growth through suffering. Undset's views on the relationship between the sexes was presented in expository form in a collection of articles entitled *Et kvindesynspunkt* (1919; A Woman's Point of View).

Undset's interest in religion led to her conversion to Roman Catholicism in 1924, and the trilogy *Kristin Lavransdatter*, her literary masterpiece, should be seen against the background of her developing religious commitment. Consisting of the volumes *Kransen* (1920; tr. *The Bridal Wreath*, 1923), *Husfrue* (1922; tr. *The Mistress of Husaby*, 1925), and *Korset* (1922; tr. *The Cross*, 1927), it tells the story of Kristin's stormy relationship with her husband, the knight Erlend Nikulausson. Having rejected the likable and honorable man chosen for her by her father, Kristin suffers greatly during her marriage to Erlend, who lacks both a sense of responsibility and good judgment; Kristin even has to beg for his life because he has gotten involved in a plot against the king. After Erlend's violent death, Kristin chooses to become a nun; she learns to acknowledge God's hand in her life as she succumbs to the Black Death while caring for some of its victims.

Staying with the Middle Ages, Undset next wrote a two-part epic, *Olav Audunssøn i Hestviken* (1925; tr. *The Axe* and *The Snake Pit*, 1928–1929) and *Olav Audunssøn og hans børn* (1927; tr. *In the Wilderness* and *The Son Avenger*, 1929–1930). A story about guilt and redemption, it is theologically complex and is considered less interesting than *Kristin*.

Conversion to Catholicism is the overt theme of *Gymnadenia* (1929; tr. *The Wild Orchid*, 1929) and its sequel, *Den brænnende busk* (1930; tr. *The Burning Bush*), in which a young man overcomes agnosticism while experiencing a difficult marriage. The novels *Ida Elisabeth* (1932; tr. 1933) and *Den trofaste hustru* (1936; tr. *The Faithful Wife*, 1937) also have a contemporary setting and are focused on a woman's relationship with children and husband. These novels have strong religious overtones as well.

Madame Dorthea (1939; tr. 1940), set in the late 1700s, was intended as the first volume of a series of novels, but this project was interrupted by the onset of World **War** II. Undset spent the war in the United States as an unofficial cultural ambassador for Norway. She published no more works of fiction. She did, however, write articles, speeches, memoirs, and saints lives.

UTVANDRARNA. The first volume in a tetralogy by the Swede Vilhelm Moberg, *Utvandrarna* (1949; tr. *The Emigrants*, 1951) was followed by *Invandrarna* (1952; tr. *Unto a Good Land*, 1954), *Nybyggarna* (1956; tr. *The Settlers*, 1961), and *Sista brevet till Sverige* (1959; tr. *The Last Letter Home*, 1961). The novels explain the social and economic reasons for emigration from Sweden to the United States and describe both the journey across the sea, the process of homesteading, and the lives of the immigrants as more or less successful American citizens.

– V –

VALKEAPÄÄ, NILS-ASLAK (1943–2001). A Sámi poet who wrote in both Sámi and Finnish, Valkeapää is as yet the only Sámi awarded the **Nordic Literary Prize**. Valkeapää had his literary debut with a book of essays in Finnish, *Terveisiä Lapista* (1971; tr. *Greetings from Lappland*, 1984). A book in Sámi bears the title *Ruoktu váimmus* (1985; tr. *Trekways of the Wind*, 1994). The volume for which he received the Nordic Literary Prize in 1991, *Beaivi, áhcázan* (1991; tr. *The Sun, My Father*, 1997), contains poems and photographs and refers to a Sámi myth that holds people to be the children of the sun. Valkeapää's last book was *Eanni, Eannazan* (2001; The Earth, Our Mother). Valkeapää was also recognized as a composer, musician, sculptor, painter, and actor.

VESAAS, TARJEI (1897–1970). A Norwegian novelist, short story writer, poet, and playwright, Vesaas is one of the great innovators in Norwegian **modernism**. He started out writing books that offer a mixture of traditional psychological **realism**, **symbolism**, and stylized narration. Two of the more notable early novels are *Dei svarte hestane* (1928; The Black Horses), which is characterized by psychologically complex characters, and *Det store spelet* (1934; tr. *The Great Cycle*, 1967), a vitalistic portrait of farm life set in a rural community in his native Telemark; this novel gave Vesaas his breakthrough as a writer.

The first example of Vesaas's mature work came after he had published two collections of short stories and 13 novels. The novel *Kimen* (1940; tr. *The Seed*, 1964) combines realistic narrative with allegorical structures of meaning, presenting them in a terse, almost minimalist style. It tells about an island to which an unbalanced man comes and then experiences an incident that triggers his latent madness so that he kills a young girl. His fit of insanity is then replicated in the community as the locals hunt him down and kill him in a collective frenzy, after which they realize that they have, at least temporarily, lost their claim to civilization. As they try to work through what has happened to them, they renew their commitment not to allow irrational forces to take over their lives. *Kimen* can easily be read as an allegory of World **War** II, including the dangers involved in fighting evil with evil.

Vesaas wrote *Huset i mørkret* (1945; tr. *The House in the Dark*, 1976) during the war, and his novel can be read not just as an allegory of the German occupation of Norway but of occupation or totalitarianism in general. The protagonist, Stig, is the leader of a resistance group, and even though he is murdered by the occupiers, there is greater hope for freedom at the end of the novel than at the beginning. Symbolism is also central to Vesaas's next novel, *Bleikeplassen* (1946; tr. *The Bleaching Yard*, 1981), as well as *Tårnet* (1948; The Tower), *Signalet* (1950; The Signal), and *Brannen* (1961; The Fire); allegory and symbolism are so pervasive in these novels that their narrative coherence suffers at times. There is both realistic action and psychological drama in the short novel *Vårnatt* (1954; tr. *Spring Night*, 1964).

Vesaas published his first volume of poetry, *Kjeldene* (1946; The Springs), shortly after the end of the war. Most of these poems are in traditional form, but that changed in the next collection, *Leiken og lynet* (1947; The Game and the Lightning), which was entirely in free verse. Vesaas's poetic modernism continued in *Lykka for ferdesmenn* (1949; Happiness for Travelers), *Løynde eldars land* (1953; tr. *Land of Hidden Fires*, 1973), and *Ver ny, vår draum* (1956; Be New, Our Dream).

Vindane (1952; The Winds), his third collection of short stories, is considered excellent, as are some of the stories in *Ein vakker dag* (1959; A Beautiful Day). The title character in one of the stories from *Vindane*, "Tusten," became the protagonist in one of Vesaas's most successful novels, *Fuglane* (1957; tr. *The Birds*, 1968). Mattis, nicknamed Tusten, is a developmentally delayed man who lives in close harmony with **nature** and has many characteristics of the artist. There is no place for him in the world of practical men, however, and he seeks death in the end of the book.

Death is also an important theme in the novel *Is-slottet* (1963; tr. *The Ice Palace*, 1966), for which Vesaas received the **Nordic Literary Prize** in 1964. It tells about two 11-year-old girls, Siss and Unn, and their friendship. Siss is outgoing and friendly, while Unn is an introvert. On the realistic level the ice palace is a huge frozen waterfall; Unn gets lost and freezes to death while exploring it, so it seems to symbolize those things in life that are attractive but dangerous. Human relationships, illuminated through symbolism, are also at the core of the novel *Bruene* (1966; tr. *The Bridges*, 1969), in which a young couple becomes a threesome after the harrowing experience of finding a dead baby in the woods and wondering what to do about its mother.

In the poetry collection *Båten om kvelden* (1968; tr. *The Boat in the Evening*, 1971) an old man looks back at his life. Another volume of poetry, *Liv ved straumen* (1970; Life by the River), was published posthumously.

VIK, BJØRG (1935–). A Norwegian novelist, short story writer, and dramatist, Vik is one of the foremost **feminist** writers in Norway and has published numerous collections of short stories, several novels, and a large number of plays. Most of her early stories deal with complications brought about by erotic encounters, marital infidelity, gender roles, and the position of **women** in patriarchal society. The short story collections *Søndag ettermiddag* (1963; Sunday Afternoon), *Nødrop fra en myk sofa* (1966; Cries of Distress from a Soft Sofa), *Det grådige hjerte* (1968; The Greedy Heart), *Kvinneakvariet* (1972; tr. *An Aquarium of Women*, 1987), and *Fortellinger om frihet* (1975; Stories of Freedom), as well as the novel *Gråt, elskede mann* (1970; Cry, Beloved Man), won Vik a devoted readership.

Later volumes of short stories evidence the author's concern for the situation of women who are at or beyond middle age. Many of the stories in *En håndfull lengsel* (1979; tr. *Out of Season and Other Stories*, 1983), *Snart er det høst* (1982; Soon It Will Be Fall), and *En gjenglemt petunia* (1985; A Forgotten Petunia) are love stories marked by melancholy or nostalgia. Vik's preoccupation with love in the lives of women is continued in *Den lange reisen til et annet menneske* (1993; The Long Journey to Another Person) and *Forholdene tatt i betraktning* (2002; The Relationships Taken into Consideration), in which the situation of widows is depicted with great tenderness and humor.

Vik's most important contribution to the Norwegian novel is an autobiographical trilogy, *Små nøkler, store rom* (1988; Small Keys, Big Rooms), *Poplene på St. Hanshaugen* (1991; The Poplars at St. Hanshaugen), and *Elsi Lund* (1994). Through the protagonist Elsi, Vik offers a detailed depiction of Norwegian life in the 1940s and 1950s, including young women's struggle for autonomy. Her later novel *Roser i et sprukket krus* (1998; Roses in a Cracked Mug) tells about a widow who, soon after her husband's death, finds a new love and has to deal with the reactions of her children.

Vik has written for the stage, TV, and radio. Her first play was *To akter for fem kvinner* (1974; partly tr. as *Two Acts for Five Women*, 1995), in which five women who went to school together discuss their experiences with life and love. *Hurra, det ble en pike!* (1974; Hurrah, It's a Girl!) is more overtly feminist, while *Sorgenfri: Fem bilder om kjærlighet* (1978; Sans Souci: Five Images of Love) depicts love relationships as well as issues related to age. *Døtre* (tr. *Daughters*, 1989), the most important of five radio plays published as *Det trassige håp* (1981; The Defiant Hope), is a study in isolation and generation gaps as three women of different generations offer their perspectives on life. *Vinterhagen* (1990; The Winter Garden) and *Reisen til Venezia* (1991; The Trip to Venice) depict challenges of life associated with middle age and beyond. *Alt kvinner tilgir* (1999; Everything Women Forgive), in which a man is confronted by his three ex-wives, asks whether women are too forgiving of men, thus enabling their bad behavior. *Salong Saratustra* (2001; Salon Zarathustra) features the hairdresser Sara and her conversations about life and love with her customers. Vik has also published **children's books** and a volume of miscellaneous writings, *Gatens magi: Kåserier, dikt* *og spredte tanker* (1996; The Magic of the Street: Causeries, poems, and Scattered Reflections).

VILHJÁLMSSON, THOR (1925–). An Icelandic novelist and essayist, Vilhjálmsson is recognized as one of Iceland's most innovative writers. After travel and studies abroad, including stays in England and France, he became a librarian at the National Library in Reykjavík. Vilhjálmsson's first book was a collection of short prose entitled *Maðurinn er alltaf einn* (1950; Man Is Always Alone). It was followed by the short story collections *Dagar mannsins* (1954; The Days of Man) and *Andlit í spegli dropans* (1957; tr. *Faces Reflected in a Drop*, 1966), which deal with existential themes. Several travel books and collections of essays came next, and then came the important first novel *Fljótt fljótt sagði fuglinn* (1968; tr. *Quick Quick Said the Bird*, 1987), which is set in Italy and deals with alienation. It was followed by *Óp bjöllunnar* (1970; The Cry of the Beetle) and *Mánasigð* (1976; Moonsickle).

After several more novels and essay collections, Vilhjálmsson published his most important book, *Grámosinn glóir* (1986; tr. *Justice Undone*, 1995), for which he received the **Nordic Literary Prize** in 1988. Drawing on an actual criminal case, it is a narrative in which it is difficult to determine where reality ends and pure fantasy takes over. Vilhjálmsson has also written additional essays as well as two volumes of autobiography. The novel *Náttvíg* (1989; Night Killing) is a crime story that take place in Reykjavík's underworld, while *Tvílysi: Myndir á syningu* (1994; Twilight: Pictures at an Exhibition) deals with such central themes as love and death. The novel *Morgunþula í stráum* (1998; A Morning Rhyme in the Grass) has a medieval setting and recounts a pilgrimage to Rome.

VINJE, AASMUND OLAFSSON (1818–1870). A Norwegian poet and journalist, Vinje was born on a farm at Vinje in Telemark County. He adhered to many of the ideas of **national romanticism**, particularly that Norway, independent from Denmark since 1814 and since then in a union with Sweden, should develop a written language based on popular dialects rather than the Danish-inspired written norm that had emerged in the course of the 400-year union with Denmark. But Vinje did not share **Ivar Aasen**'s love of archaic grammar and vocabulary, and instead he based his form of **Landsmaal** (later renamed **nynorsk**) on the dialect of his native district. Although educated in Dano-Norwegian, Vinje used his own form of Landsmaal when in 1858 he started the newspaper *Dølen* (The Dalesman), in which he commented on the social, political, and cultural issues of his day.

In addition to being a talented journalist, Vinje was also a gifted poet. His best works are *Ferdaminni fraa Sumaren 1860* (1861; Travel Memories from the Summer of 1860), in which he tells about a journey from Christiania (now Oslo) to Trondheim, and which includes many of his best-known poems, and the epic cycle *Storegut* (1866; Big Boy). A travelogue written in English and entitled *A Norseman's View of Britain and the British* (1863), although a perceptive analysis of the British national character, found few readers and did not appear in Norwegian until after Vinje's death. Many of Vinje's poems remain popular, especially through the musical settings by Edvard Grieg (1843–1907).

– W –

WÄGNER, ELIN (1882–1949). A Swedish novelist, short story writer, and journalist, Wägner was a prominent voice in favor of equal rights for **women** and one of the most important writers of her generation. After working as a journalist from the age of 18, she had her literary debut with *Från det jordiska museet* (1907; From the Earthly Museum), a collection of short stories and vignettes. Her first novel, *Norrtullsligan: Elisabeths krönika* (1908; tr. *Men and Other Misfortunes* in *Stockholm Stories*, 2002), tells about the lives of four young women, office workers who share living quarters. Like its successor, *Pennskaftet* (1910; The Penholder), it is a realistic narrative of a new class of woman in clerical jobs at the beginning of the 20th century. *Pennskaftet*, however, advocates very strongly for women's suffrage and is a major work of **feminist** writing.

In *Släkten Jerneploogs framgång* (1916; The Success of the Jerneploog Family) Wägner likewise advocates for women's rights, but she also expresses awareness of the entrenched nature of patriarchal power, particularly as it manifests itself in everyday language. It is thus not a particularly optimistic story. *Åsa-Hanna* (1918), generally considered Wägner's best work, is more hopeful, as it offers a detailed portrait of a strong woman character. Set against the backdrop of World War I, *Kvarteret Oron: En stockholmshistoria* (1919; tr. *Stormy Corner* in *Stockholm Stories*, 2002), is the story of the upper-class widow Brita, who tries to sell a cellar-full of alcohol on the black market. But Brita, who has to leave her country estate and move to a tiny apartment in Stockholm, also learns to identify with her new proletarian friends and works to get out the vote once Sweden has extended the franchise to women in 1919. Other books from this period are *Den befriade kärleken* (1919; Liberated Love), *Den förödda vingården* (1920; The Ruined Vineyard), *Nyckelknippan* (1921; The Key Ring), and *Den namnlösa* (1922; The Nameless Woman), all of which express the author's feminist and anti-militarist leanings through narratives that are given a variety of settings. The same general sentiments are expressed in *Från Seine, Rehn och Ruhr* (1923; From Seine, Rhine, and Ruhr), *Silverforsen* (1924; Silver Falls), and *Natten til söndag* (1926; The Night before Sunday).

The allegorical novel *De fem pärlorna* (1927; The Five Pearls) was not well received. A novel set in Wägner's home district of Småland, *Svalorna flyga högt* (1929; The Swallows Are Flying High), was more successful. The story of a schoolteacher who has been abandoned by the father of her child, it offers a convincing portrayal of the many difficulties society has placed in the paths of women. In *Dialogen fortsätter* (1932; The Dialogue Continues) Wägner shows that hope for the future lies in giving mothers more power than what is enjoyed by the proponents of militarism.

Wägner's two autobiographical novels, *Genomskådad* (1937; Found Out) and *Hemlighetsfull* (1938; Secretive), offer a review of her work on behalf of women's rights and peace. In the book *Väckarklocka* (1941; Alarm Clock) she combined these concerns with an awareness of the need for sustainable agricultural practices. Wägner's last novel, *Vinden vände bladen* (1947; The Wind Turned the Leaves), spans nearly a thousand years of Värmland history and offers matriarchy as a remedy for the social ills created by men.

WALTARI, MIKA TOIMI (1908–1979). A Finnish novelist, short story writer, and playwright, Waltari grew up in Helsinki and received a degree in philosophy from Helsinki University. Having published three books by the time he was 20 years old, he had his literary breakthrough with the novel *Suuri illusioni* (1928; The Great Illusion), which deals with the lives of young people in Helsinki. Waltari's first significant work, which may have foretold what was to come later in his career, was the trilogy *Mies ja haave* (1933; A Man and a Dream), *Sielu ja liekki* (1934; The Soul and the Flame), and *Palava nuoruus* (1935; Burning Youth); all three volumes were later published in one volume as *Isästä poikaan* (1942; From Father to Son). The trilogy gives an overview of the growth of Helsinki from 1870 to 1935.

Waltari's strength can be observed most readily in two subgenres: the very short novel or novella, and the long historical novel. Thirteen of the former were published in one volume entitled *Pienoisromaanit* (1966; Miniature Novels), which includes two that were written earlier and that have been translated into English, *Ei koskaan huomispäivää!* (1942; tr. *Never a Tomorrow*, 1965) and *Fine van Brooklyn* (1939; tr. *Fine van Brooklyn*, 1965). All together, 10 miniature novels have been published in English: five in *Moonscape and Other Stories* (1953) and five more in *The Tree of Dreams and Other Stories* (1965), which includes both *Never a Tomorrow* and *Five van Brooklyn*.

The long historical novel was Waltari's genre of choice, and he became internationally known for many of these works. *Kaarina Maunustytär* (1942; Karin Månsdotter) tells about the life of the wife of Sweden's King Erik XIV. *Sinuhe, egyptiläinen* (1945; tr. *Sinuhe the Egyptian*, 1949) takes place in the 14th century BCE. *Mikael Karvajalka* (1948; tr. *Michael the Finn*, 1950) and its sequel, *Mikael Hakim* (1949; tr. *The Sultan's Renegade*, 1951), are set in the 16th century and relate a story of high adventure. *Johannes Angelos* (1952; tr. *The Dark Angel*, 1953) is a diary novel set in 1453 and tells about the fall of Constantinople to the Turks. *Turms, kuolematon* (1955; tr. *The Etruscan*, 1956) is set in Etruria in Italy and elsewhere. The early period in the history of Christianity is the subject of the two novels *Valtakunnan salaisuus* (1959; tr. *The Secret of the Kingdom*, 1960) and *Ihmiskunnan viholliset* (1964; tr. *The Roman*, 1966). Religion is also the subject of a contemporary novel, *Feliks onnellinen* (1958; tr. *The Tongue of Fire*, 1959).

Waltari published many other novels and stories, as well as mystery novels, travel books, film scripts, and 24 plays for stage and radio. His plays are not of the same quality as his fiction.

WAR. The ancient Scandinavian Vikings had a well-deserved reputation for being a warlike people, as shown by *Egils saga*, a story of the life of **Egil Skallagrímsson**. War remains a significant theme in Scandinavian literature, from **Thomas Kingo**'s glorification of the Danish campaign against Sweden during the years 1675–1679, to **Ib Michael**'s opposition in 2004 to the war in Iraq. In *Fänrik Ståls sägner* (1848–1860; tr. *The Tales by Ensign Stål*, 1925), **Johan Ludvig Runeberg** memorialized the war between Sweden and Russia in 1808–1809, through which Finland was lost by Sweden and became a Russian grand duchy. The war between Denmark and Prussia, in which Denmark lost a great deal of territory, shows up in novels by the Danes **Herman Bang** and **Jens Peter Jacobsen**, as well as in a novel by the Norwegian **Herbjørg Wassmo**, *Lykkens sønn* (1992; tr. *Dina's Son*).

Although the Scandinavian countries were neutral during World War I, the experience of that war changed long-standing social customs and structures of economic power, as depicted in **Johan Borgen**'s *Lillelord* trilogy (1955–1957) and **Jacob Paludan**'s two-volume family saga *Jørgen Stein* (1932–1933; tr. 1966). Finland, however, experienced a brutal civil war in 1918, which deeply affected Finnish literature, for example, the work of **Elmer Diktonius** and **Frans Eemil Sillanpää**. The latter produced two internationally successful novels related to the war, *Hurskas kurjuus* (1919; tr. *Meek Heritage*, 1938) and *Nuorena nukkunut* (1931; tr. *The Maid Silja*, 1933). Another great Finnish war novel is **Väinö Linna**'s *Tuntematon Sotilas* (1954; tr. *The Unknown Soldier*, 1957), set during Finland's Continuation War (1941–1944).

Both Denmark and Norway were attacked by Germany on 9 April 1940 and remained occupied for the next five years. Sweden remained neutral, while Iceland was used by American and British troops as a base. Postwar Scandinavian literature was deeply affected by the war experience. In Denmark, **Kaj Munk** lost his life because of his resistance to the Nazis. The Danish resistance was described by **Tage Skou-Hansen** in *De nøgne træer* (1957; tr. *The Naked*

Trees, 1959) and *Dagstjernen* (1962; Day Star). In Norway **Jens Bjørneboe** discussed the government's treatment of wartime collaborators in *Under en hårdere himmel* (1957; Under a Harder Sky), while **Sigurd Hoel**, **Aksel Sandemose**, and **Tarjei Vesaas** probed the psychology of those who turned to Nazism. **Knut Hamsun**, Norway's greatest writer at the time, sided with the Nazis. In Sweden **Pär Lagerkvist** published his novel *Dvärgen* (1944; tr. *The Dwarf*, 1945), an exploration of the Nazi personality. The Swede **Eyvind Johnson** (1900–1976) explored the problem of evil in his novel *Drömmar om rosor och eld* (1949; tr. *Dreams of Roses and Fire*, 1984) and of war itself in his *Krilon* trilogy (1941–1943). The Icelander **Guðmundur Gíslason Hagalín** described the effects of the war on Icelandic society in *Módir Ísland* (1945; Mother Iceland).

The 1950s brought the Cold War and widespread concern about nuclear destruction. The worry about nuclear war can be observed in the work of **Bo Carpelan**, **Sophus Claussen**, **Per Christian Jersild**, and **Svava Jakobsdóttir**. The Vietnam War was bitterly opposed by many Scandinavian writers, particularly the Swedes **Sara Lidman**, **Lars Forssell**, **Göran Sonnevi**, and **Tomas Tranströmer**. *See also* ABELL, KJELD; AHO, JUHA; ANDERSEN, BENNY; BLIXEN, KAREN; BRANNER, HANS CHRISTIAN; BRANTENBERG, GERD; DAGERMAN, STIG; EKELÖF, GUNNAR; ENQUIST, PER OLOV; FLØGSTAD, KJARTAN; GRESS, ELSA; HAUGE, ALFRED; HANSEN, MARTIN A.; HEINESEN, WILLIAM; KALLIFATIDES, THEODOR; KÁRASON, EINAR; LAGERLÖF, SELMA; LEINO, EINO; LØVEID, CECILIE; LUNDKVIST, ARTUR; MARTINSON, HARRY; MICHAËLIS, KARIN; MOBERG, VILHELM; PANDURO, LEIF; SANDEL, CORA; SCHERFIG, HANS; SEEBERG, PETER; SOLSTAD, DAG; TEGNÉR, ESAIAS; UNDSET, SIGRID; WÄGNER, ELIN.

WASSMO, HERBJØRG (1942–). A Norwegian novelist, poet, and playwright, the best-selling author Wassmo started out as a poet with the collection *Vingeslag* (1976; Beating Wings), which was followed by *Flotid* (1977; High Tide), neither of which made much of an impression on the public. Many years later, however, came *Lite bilde i stor blå ramme* (1991; A Small Picture in a Big Blue Frame), which was well received and won her a prize. By then she was already one of Norway's foremost writers of her generation.

The foundation for Wassmo's reputation is a trilogy about a girl named Tora who, fathered by a soldier of the German occupation force during World War II, is ostracized in her little island community in northern Norway. Tora's mother is married to the alcoholic Henrik, who sexually abuses Tora. In the trilogy's first novel, *Huset med den blinde glassveranda* (1981; tr. *The House with the Blind Glass Windows*, 1987), Henrik rapes Tora but is finally jailed for arson. In the second book, *Det stumme rommet* (1983; The Mute Room), Tora has left home to attend school but discovers that she is pregnant with Henrik's baby. The baby is stillborn and Tora buries it, thus keeping her secret. In the third volume, *Hudløs himmel* (1986; Sensitive Sky), Tora finally reveals the rape but breaks down mentally. *Hudløs himmel* garnered Wassmo the **Nordic Literary Prize** in 1987.

Wassmo next embarked on another trilogy set in northern Norway, but a hundred years earlier. Its central character is a strong-willed and talented **woman** named Dina, who as a child caused the accident that took her mother's life. Rejected by her father, Dina finds it very difficult to relate to the men in her life, two of whom she murders. *Dinas bok* (1989; tr. *Dina's Book*, 1994) was followed by *Lykkens sønn* (1992; tr. *Dina's Son*), the nominal protagonist of which is Dina's son Benjamin, who as a child watches his mother kill her Russian lover. Benjamin studies medicine in Copenhagen and helps defend Denmark against Prussia in the **war** of 1864. He also fathers a child by a prostitute who dies in childbirth. The child, Karna, becomes the title character in the third novel, *Karnas arv* (1997; Karna's Inheritance), in which Dina burns to death after confessing her crimes.

In *Det sjuende møte* (2000; The Seventh Meeting), which has a contemporary setting, the narrative perspective alternates between a male and a female protagonist, Gorm and Rut. Starting in childhood, they meet seven times. *Flukten fra Frank* (2003; The Flight from Frank), another story of love and betrayal, tells about the female protagonist's journey through Europe, which is also a kind of journey through her own past.

Wassmo has also written a nonfiction book, *Veien å gå* (1984; The

Road to Take), about a Norwegian family that fled to Sweden during World War II, as well as two radio plays. Some critics regard her as a practitioner of the realistic-psychological tradition in Norwegian literature; others find notable **postmodern** elements in her works.

WELHAVEN, JOHAN SEBASTIAN CAMMERMEYER (1807–1873). A Norwegian poet, Welhaven is one of his country's most significant poets of the **national romantic** era. Born and raised in Bergen, he went to Christiania (now Oslo) in 1825 to study theology, but he did not find the subject to his liking. He read aesthetics and literature, however, and paid particular attention of the activities of his Danish second cousin, the critic **Johan Ludvig Heiberg**. In 1830 he became well known for his attack on the work of **Henrik Wergeland**, whose poetry he found undisciplined and formless. A cycle of sonnets, *Norges Dæmring* (1834; Norway's Dawn), argued in favor of maintaining Norway's cultural ties with Denmark, which Wergeland's followers wanted to deemphasize in favor of a focus on the culture of the Norwegian rural population.

Welhaven's collection *Digte* (1838; Poems) shows that personal memories were important as poetic inspiration for him; this is even more evident in poetry collections published in 1844 and 1847. There is evidence of the pain associated with a romance with Henrik Wergeland's sister Camilla (later known as the writer **Camilla Collett**), and even more so of his grief at the death, in 1840, of his fianceé Ida Kierulf, who inspired two of his best-known poems, "Det omvendte Bæger" (The Upturned Cup) and "Den Salige" (The Blessed One). In the former, a knight refuses a magic potion that would have caused him to forget his sorrows, while in the latter, the poet receives a spiritual visit from his departed beloved. Other well-known poems by Welhaven include the long **folklore** poem "Asgaardsreien" (The Ride of the Dead) and the lyrical "Lokkende Toner" (Enticing Tones), the best example of **romantic** longing in Norwegian literature. Welhaven's poem "Digtets Aand" (The Spirit of the Poem) is a forthright statement of his theory of literary communication.

Welhaven was appointed lecturer in philosophy at the University of Oslo in 1840 and became a professor in 1843, after which he married a Danish woman, Josephine Bidoulac, in 1845. He did not have much impact on his academic subject, but he was celebrated for his **nature** descriptions and his folklore poetry, and later for such religous poems as "En Sangers Bøn" (The Prayer of a Singer). He also made significant contributions to the budding literary historiography of the time, publishing works about **Ludvig Holberg** (1854) and **Petter Dass** (1860), as well as a substantial book about the Danish poet **Johannes Ewald**, *Ewald og de norske Digtere* (1863; Ewald and the Norwegian Poets).

WERGELAND, HENRIK ARNOLD (1808–1845). A Norwegian poet, prose writer, and dramatist, Wergeland is recognized as the greatest poet of his country. Raised in Kristiansand and Eidsvoll, he attended Christiania (now Oslo) Cathedral School and the University of Oslo, from which he received a degree in theology in 1829. But Wergeland's personal life was too undisciplined and disorderly for him to be given a living, and he was plagued by financial problems. He nevertheless stood at the center of Norway's public discourse for most of his short life.

To many of Wergeland's contemporaries, his lack of discipline marked both his politics and his art. What Wergeland saw as personal liberty could also be seen as a lack of restraint, and his favoring increased personal freedom was regarded as inimical to a sense of civic duty and social order. What he perceived as his personal genius, for which he claimed complete sovereignty within his personal artistic precincts, his enemies saw as evidence of both bad taste and lack of responsibility. The debate between Wergeland's friends and his opponents became particularly bitter both because it took place within a relatively young nation (the Norwegian constitution dates back only to 1814) and because Christiania was a rather small town where events, however minor, could be quickly blown out of proportion.

At issue were the related questions of whether political power in Norway should rest with the upper middle class, consisting mostly of government servants, large land owners, and merchants, or if it should be shared with farmers and other previously disenfranchised groups. A related issue was the cultural question of whether the new nation should emphasize the creative potential of the indigenous population, particularly the farmers, or foster continuity with the literary culture of Denmark, the political union which had been severed in

1814. A subissue of the latter was the extent to which Norway should accept the political leadership of Sweden in the recently established union with that country. In all these matters, Wergeland and other progressives were bitterly opposed by the traditionalists.

In his early youth Wergeland wrote poetry that celebrated Norway's potential for social and political change, including the significance of its recently established constitution, and that expressed his own grappling with such central personal questions as beauty and love. The imagery in these poems is exceptionally rich and testifies to the greatness of Wergeland's genius, but their form is, mildly stated, unorthodox, and that was very offensive to those who, like his contemporary **Johan Sebastian Welhaven**, prized the classical qualities of balance, organization, and adherence to established form. When Welhaven attacked Henrik Wergeland for violating the dictates of reason, his father Nicolai Wergeland came to his aid, and a bitter and lasting feud ensued. Wergeland's political radicalism joins his disdain for conventional poetics in his major work, a world-historical poem entitled *Skabelsen, Mennesket og Messias* (1830; Creation, Man, and the Messiah), which offers a ringing defense for the ideas of the Enlightenment and, heavily influenced by the philosophy of Plotinus, establishes a cosmic context for human life.

Wergeland was extremely productive, and his marriage to Amalie Sofie Bekkevold in 1839 brought increased order into his life. He was strongly committed to popular education and produced great quantities of educational materials for the common people, many of them published in his paper *For Arbeidsklassen* (1840–1845; For the Working Class). He polemicized against his political opponents in a long series of plays, some of which were lighthearted and others bitingly satirical. But he also produced the imaginative and lyrical *Jan van Huysums Blomsterstykke* (1840; tr. *Jan van Huysum's Flower Piece*, 1960), a great poetic cycle about the nature of art and the connection between art and life.

Wergeland's concern with justice manifests itself in his dislike of the fact that the Norwegian constitution prevented Jews from entering Norway, and when the Norwegian parliament debated the issue in 1842 and 1844, he published two collections of poetry designed to influence public opinion, *Jøden* (1842; The Jew) and *Jødinden* (1844; The Jewess). Another major work is the poetry cycle *Den eng-*

elske Lods (1844; The English Pilot), which despite its melodramatic tone also contains superb **nature** poetry. Ill with consumption, he revised *Skabelsen, Mennesket og Messias* for publication with the title *Mennesket* (1845; Man). While on his deathbed, he produced many of his best-loved poems.

WESSEL, JOHAN HERMAN (1746–1785). A Norwegian poet and playwright, Wessel was a gifted satirist who, although born in Norway, spent most of his adult life in Copenhagen, where he was the leading figure in a group of Norwegian expatriates known as *Det norske Selskab* (The Norwegian Society). Eking out a living as a writer and tutor in French and English, he published a weekly paper, *Votre Servietur Otiosis* (1784–1785), but his reputation rests on his satirical poetry as well as on a parody of French tragedy, *Kierlighed uden Strømper* (1772; Love without Stockings). Adhering closely to the unities of time, place, and action, Wessel's play exhibits the formal perfection of classicist tragedy, but there is a complete mismatch between the drama's high style and its utterly quotidian reality. The hero lacks a suitable pair of stockings for his wedding and obtains them by theft; the consequences are such that all of the main characters stab themselves to death in the final scene. The comedy of the piece rests not only on the incongruity between action and style, however, for Wessel's superb alexandrines, which are considered the best in both Danish and Norwegian literature, add much to the play's comic tenor.

Clever versification and a sharp eye for human folly are also hallmarks of Wessel's many poems. "Smeden og Bageren" (The Blacksmith and the Baker), in which one of the two bakers in a village is condemned to death for a murder committed by the village's only blacksmith solely because the village cannot afford to lose its only smith, has given rise to a proverb in Danish and Norwegian, "killing the baker instead of the smith." In "Hundemordet" (The Murder of the Dog) a man kills another man's dog with an ax when attacked by the dog; he defends his action saying that he was justified in using the sharp part of the ax because he was attacked by the dog's sharp teeth rather than by its tail. Wessel's poetry is hardly ever serious, and it almost always tries pretty hard to be humorous. *See also* THEATER.

WESTÖ, KJELL (1961–). A Finland-Swedish poet, short story writer, and novelist, Westö started out with three poetry collections: *Tango Orange* (1986), *Epitaph över Mr. Nacht* (1988; Epitaph for Mr. Nacht), and *Avig-Bön* (1989; Avig Prayer). He continued with the short story collections *Utslag och andra noveller* (1989; Shot and Other Stories) and *Fallet Bruus* (1992; The Bruus Case), in which he offered detailed portraits of life in Helsinki in the 1980s, depicting linguistic environments where Swedish is very much in the minority, the world of popular music, journalism, the Finland-Swedish family, and erotic conflicts. Westö's novels are written against the background of Anglo-American culture, of which Helsinki is a representative on the eastern edge of Europe.

Combining high and low culture, the textual background for *Drakarna över Helsingfors* (1996, Kites above Helsinki) is, in the fashion of **postmodernism**, both the cartoon character Donald Duck and Karl **Marx** and Friedrich Engels's *Communist Manifesto* (1848). The novel is a record of the development of capitalism in Finland, which, because of the country's marginal status, took place over a briefer period of time than was the case in the centers of capital. Hence, the nature and function of capitalism can be illuminated with particular clarity in such a setting, as Westö does admirably.

In Westö's next novel, *Vådan av att vara Skrake* (2000, The Curse of Being Skrake), the title character bumbles through a series of endeavors, starting with having a collision while driving a Coca-Cola truck in Helsinki during the 1952 Olympics. A potent symbol of American cultural and economic imperialism, Coca-Cola first arrived in Finland in 1952, which is part of the small stories that Westö tells in order to evoke the grander narratives of historical forces. The novel *Lang* (2002) takes its title from the main character, the twice-divorced former Finland-Swedish television talk-show host and author Christian Lang, who in this thriller gets involved with a young Finnish woman named Sarita. Lang's main problem is that, on account of the cult of youth inherent in the contemporary advertising-driven culture, he is unable to accept that he has aged; his deterioration of body and mind has simply gone too far for him to be able to regain the vigor of his youth. As such, he may be a fitting symbol for an economic system that is perhaps close to singing its swan song.

The criminal behavior of Sarita's former lover is another symptom of a system that can no longer be controlled.

WILLUMSEN, DORRIT (1940–). A Danish short story writer, novelist, and dramatist, Willumsen was abandoned by her parents and grew up with her grandparents, who were kind and loving people. The emotional scars resulting from the abandonment show up as early as in her first book, the short story collection *Knagen* (1965; The Hook), where the personal sense of loss is combined with a portrayal of the loss of social stability that resulted from Denmark's rapid process of modernization after World **War** II. While the novel *Stranden* (1967; The Shore) tells about a young man who feels like a failure after running away from his wife, Willumsen returns to the theme of social change in the novel *Da* (1968; Then), which draws on her experiences growing up while living with her grandparents in Copenhagen in the 1940s.

One of the persistent motifs in her early work is the doll metaphor, which in Jungian thought represents the child archetype and gestures at the presence of unresolved childhood experiences. Willumsen uses the doll imagery as an indication of narcissism in the lives of some of her female characters, who do not have a clear sense of where the boundary lies between themselves and other people, or between themselves and the world. The result is inevitably both a feeling of grandiosity and a sense of powerlessness, which are destructive to these characters and to the people around them.

Psychic disintegration is also a main theme in the novels *The, krydderi, acryl, salær, græshopper* (1970; Tea, Spices, Acrylic, Fee, Grasshopper) and *Neonhaven* (1976; The Neon Garden), in which male fantasies are the agents of destruction. The short story collections *Modellen Coppelia* (1973; The Model Coppelia) and *Hvis det virkelig var en film* (1978; tr. *If It Really Were a Film*, 1982) likewise contain many portraits of precarious mental life in modern society.

In the novel *Manden som påskud* (1980; The Man as Pretext), Willumsen attempts to show how **women** and men actually relate to each other in modernity. By being evenhanded in her treatment of the subject and refraining from assigning blame, she succeeds in providing a different perspective on an age-old debate. The novel *Programmeret til kærlighed* (1981; Programmed for Love) features a female robot, created by a woman scientist, that is supposed to be the perfect partner for a man. Willumsen has written several historical novels. *Marie: En roman om Madame Tussauds liv* (1983; tr. *Marie: A Novel about the Life of Madame Tussaud*, 1986) surveys the life of the woman who created the famous wax museum. *Suk hjerte* (1986; Sigh Heart) covers 50 years of life in a working-class neighborhood in Copenhagen. The life of the Empress Theodora, wife of Justinian, is the subject of *Klædt i purpur* (1990; Dressed in Purple). The biography of the Danish writer **Herman Bang** (1857–1912) is fictionalized in the novel *Bang* (1996).

Willumsen returned to contemporary life in *Koras stemme* (2000; Cora's Voice), a soap-opera tale about life in **postmodernity**, in which a woman believes that she has gotten pregnant by watching a certain pop star on TV. The novel offers a vivid portrait of both personal and social confusion and fragmentation at the beginning of the new millennium.

De kattens feriedage (1997; Cat Vacation) is a short novel told from a cat's point of view. In *Tøs: Et hundeliv* (2001; Tøs: A Dog's Life), the animal lover Willumsen writes a sort of biography about her dog. Willumsen has also written the drama *Caroline* (1985) as well as a number of radio plays. She was awarded the **Nordic Literary Prize** in 1997.

WINTHER, CHRISTIAN (1796–1876). A Danish poet and short story writer, Winther belongs to the late **romantic** period in Denmark and points toward the coming **realism**. He had his literary debut with the collection *Digte* (1828; Poems), which contains mostly self-reflective love poetry; it was followed by *Nogle Digte* (1835; A Few Poems), in which the love poetry became a bit too passionate for Winther's audience. *Flugten til Amerika* (1835; tr. *The Flight to America*, 1976), however, is marked by resignation. There is a greater sense of harmony between earthly and heavenly love in the poetry collection *Digtninger* (1843; Poetic Works), though, and the epic *Hjortens Flugt* (1855; The Flight of the Hart), written after Winther's marriage, shows that the poet's emotional turbulence has distilled into a state of relative harmony. The short stories in *Fire Noveller* (1843; Four Stories) have disappointed love as their theme, while the longer tale *Episode af et Familieliv* (1853; Episode from the Life of a Family) is a psychologically well-crafted study of psychic and moral disintegration.

WOMEN. Women played an important role in traditional Scandinavian rural society, where their labor power was urgently needed and where, for example, being the mistress of a farm was a position of authority and respect. The worlds of politics, commerce, and education, and especially higher education, were largely male preserves in all of Scandinavia up to the beginning of the 20th century, however. This situation was criticized by both male and female writers; one of the earliest was the Swede **Carl Jonas Love Almqvist**, whose novel *Det går an* (1839; tr. *Sara Videbeck*, 1919; *Why Not?*, 1994) depicted the situation of a talented woman glazier. Among the women who early discussed what soon became known as the women's question are the Dane **Mathilde Fibiger**, whose novel *Clara Raphael: Tolv Breve* (1850; Clara Raphael: Twelve Letters) describes the effort of a young governess to create independence for herself; the Norwegian **Camilla Collett**, who in *Amtmandens Døttre* (1854–1855; tr. *The District Governor's Daughters*, 1992) argued that women should be free to choose their own husbands; and **Fredrika Bermer**, whose final novel, *Hertha, eller en själs historia* (1856; tr. *Hertha*, 1856), was quite radical in its demands for reform and has since been recognized as one of Scandinavia's earliest and most interesting **feminist** novels.

The situation of women in the home and in society became one of the most important topics for debate during the period of the **Modern Breakthrough**, or approximately the years 1870–1890, when most progressive writers offered portraits of women's lives as part of a plea for greater social justice. In Norway, **Arne Garborg**, through the assistance of his wife Hulda Bergersen Garborg (1862–1934), produced a novel of development entitled *Hjaa ho Mor* (1890; Living with Mama), which was partly based on Hulda's life and told the story of the childhood and youth of a woman who consents to marrying a man more than twice her age. **Henrik Ibsen** portrayed the situation of contemporary women in several plays, most notably *Et dukkehjem* (1879; tr. *A Doll's House*, 1880), *Gengangere* (1881; *Ghosts*, 1885), *Fruen fra havet* (1888; tr. *The Lady from the Sea*,

1890), and *Hedda Gabler* (1890; tr. 1891). Garborg's and Ibsen's contemporary, **Alexander Lange Kielland**, discussed the situation of women in several works, among them the novels *Garman og Worse* (1880; tr. *Garman and Worse*, 1885), *Else* (1881; tr. *Elsie: A Christmas Story*, 1894), and *Skipper Worse* (1882; tr. 1885). The most eloquent literary testimony, however, was given by **Amalie Skram** in such novels as *Constance Ring* (1885; tr. 1988), *Professor Hieronimus* (1895), *Paa St. Jørgen* (1895; tr. with *Professor Hieronimus* as *Under Observation*, 1992), and many others. Skram had suffered both the kind of unhappy marriage portrayed in *Constance Ring* and the male-dominated psychiatry of *Professor Hieronimus* and *Paa St. Jørgen*.

The Swede **Victoria Benedictsson**'s novel *Pengar* (1885; Money) combined the theme of financial independence for women with that of the woman who marries an older man. In Finland, **Minna Canth** spoke up against married women's inability to control their own property in *Työmiehen vaimo* (1885; A Worker's Wife), and her play *Sylvi* (1893) shows strong influence from Ibsen's *Et dukkehjem*. Of the major writers of the Modern Breakthrough it was only the Swede **August Strindberg** who seriously questioned the need for the advancement of women. In his drama *Fadren* (1887; tr. *The Father*, 1899) he created one of the most distasteful female characters in world literature, and his own deteriorating marriage gave him the material for a novel, written in French, *Le plaidoyer d'un fou* (1888; tr. *The Confessions of a Fool*, 1912), in which he paints an unflattering portrait of his first wife, Siri von Essen. The same year Strindberg was guided by the ideology of **naturalism** as he investigated women's lives in his play **Fröken Julie** (1888; tr. *Miss Julie*, 1912). In the 1890s **Selma Lagerlöf** created her unforgettable character Margareta Celsing, the mistress of Ekeby Manor, in her novel *Gösta Berlings saga* (1891; tr. *The Story of Gösta Berling*, 1898).

Scandinavian literature of the first half of the 20th century has a large number of outstanding women writers, most of whom portray some aspect of women's lives in their works. One of the best known is the Dane **Karen Blixen**, who told about her years in Kenya in *Den afrikanske Farm* (1937; tr. *Out of Africa*, 1937), and whose stories contain a number of fascinating women characters. **Karin Michaëlis** discussed women's lives in general and such taboo subjects as female eroticism in the novel *Den farlige alder* (1910; tr. *The Dangerous Age*, 1912). In Finland, **Aino Julia Maria Kallas** treated similar themes in *Sudenmorsian* (1928; tr. *The Wolf's Bride*, 1930, 1975), in which a woman in search of erotic fulfillment becomes a werewolf. **Hagar Olsson** discussed women's experience in her biblical novel *Kvinnan och nåden* (1919; The Woman and Grace) and in her autobiographical novel *Chitambo* (1933), the story of a young woman's development. The poetry of **Edith Södergran** is strongly influenced by her experience as a woman.

In Norway, **Sigrid Undset** achieved world renown with her trilogy *Kristin Lavransdatter* (1920–1922), but she also wrote a number of novels with contemporary settings and women protagonists, among them *Jenny* (1911; tr. 1920) and *Vaaren* (1914; Spring). While Undset tended to focus on religious and ethical themes, her colleague **Cora Sandel** wrote her well-known *Alberte* (1926–1939) trilogy about a woman who tries to balance her role as an artist against the roles of wife and mother. In Sweden, **Elin Wägner**'s novels *Norrtullsligan: Elisabeths krönika* (1908; tr. *Men and Other Misfortunes* in *Stockholm Stories*, 2002) and *Pennskaftet* (1910; The Penholder) tell about the lives of young women who are office workers in Stockholm. Also in Sweden, **Karin Boye** touched on lesbian themes in her novel *Kris* (1934; Crisis).

The second half of the 20th century witnessed a great flowering of literature written by women in all of Scandinavia. Among them are the Danes **Suzanne Brøgger**, the author of a number of books that take as their theme various aspects of love; **Tove Ditlevsen**, whose novel *Ansigterne* (1968; tr. *The Faces*, 1991) discusses the threat to female creativity posed by men; and **Dorrit Willumsen**, whose novel *Manden som påskud* (1980; The Man as Pretext) presents her ideas about how women and men relate to each other. The Finns **Leena Krohn** and **Monika Fagerholm** write fiction about women in **postmodernity**, while their countrywoman **Solveig von Schoultz** produced poetry and prose that reflect many facets of women's experience. The Icelandic writer and politician **Svava Jakobsdóttir** wrote poetry, prose, and drama that exemplify postmodernism's interest in the fantastic.

In Norway, **Bjørg Vik** has spent a lifetime depicting the lives of women in plays, short stories, and novels, including a trilogy about the autobiographical character Elsie Lund (1988–1994), which shows what it was like for girls and young women to grow up in postwar Norway. **Herbjørg Wassmo** has covered much of the same literary territory but has also written about the lives of women in northern Norway in the 1800s and has won an unusually large audience for her works. **Cecilie Løveid**, one of Scandinavia's most significant dramatists during the second half of the 20th century, has written plays dealing with the situation of contemporary woman as well as such historical figures as Hildegard von Bingen and Maria Quisling. Among the youngest generation of Norwegian writers, **Hanne Ørstavik** stands out for her portrayal of women both in the family and in such roles as that of a parish priest, the latter in the novel *Presten* (2004; The Minister).

Recent Swedish literature written by women shows particular strength in documentary and historical fiction. **Sara Lidman** pioneered documentarism in Scandinavian literature and has also written the highly acclaimed *Jernbaneepos* (1977–1985; Railway Epic), a series of historical novels about the building of the railway in northern Sweden. Other Swedish women writers of historical fiction are **Carina Burman**, **Kerstin Ekman**, **Ulla Isaksson**, and **Birgitta Trotzig**. The works of Burman and Ekman have a distinct postmodern slant. *See also* BRANTENBERG, GERD; BREGENDAHL, MARIE; CANTH, MINNA; CHRISTENSEN, INGER; FROSTENSON, KATARINA; GRESS, ELSA; GRIPE, MARIA; GYLLEMBOURG, THOMASINE; HENNINGSEN, AGNES; JANSSON, TOVE; JENSEN, THIT; JOENPELTO, EEVA; KRUSENSTJERNA, AGNES VON; LENNGREN, ANNA MARIA; LEONORA CHRISTINA; LINDGREN, ASTRID; LUGN, KRISTINA; MANNER, EEVA-LIISA; MARTINSON, MOA; NORDENFLYCHT, HEDVIG CHARLOTTA; PLEIJEL, AGNETA; SVENDSEN, HANNE MARIE; TAFDRUP, PIA; THORUP, KIRSTEN; TIKKANEN, MÄRTA.

Bibliography

Scandinavian literature is, of course, studied in the Scandinavian countries, where the literatures of the respective languages are taught on all educational levels. However, readers and scholars in each Scandinavian country do not necessarily pay much attention to literature that is published in the other Scandinavian countries. Although Danish, Norwegian, and Swedish are mutually intelligible, most Scandinavians read the literature of their neighbors translated into their own national languages. Literary scholars and critics in one Scandinavian country will often pay less attention to the literature of the other Scandinavian countries than they will to literature written in the major world languages.

Research and scholarship on the literature of one of the Scandinavian countries, when done and published in that country, is therefore usually written in the language of the country and is not intended to reach an international audience, except for other scholars across the world who know how to read the Scandinavian language in question. Criticism written in English is usually either produced in North America or Great Britain, or written by Scandinavians who publish in English-language journals. By far most of the material available in English has been written by scholars residing in the United States, where there are centers of teaching and research in Scandinavian literature at such universities as the University of Minnesota, the University of Wisconsin, the University of Washington, the University of Oregon, the University of California at Berkeley, the University of California at Los Angeles, and others. All of these universities have helpful collections of library materials. There are also excellent library resources at the Harvard College Library, Cambridge, Massachusetts, and at St. Olaf College in Northfield, Minnesota.

Academic journals in which English-language Scandinavian literary criticism is published are located mostly in North America and Europe. *Scandinavian Studies*, the journal of the Society for the Advancement of Scandinavian Study in the United States, is published quarterly and contains articles about Scandinavian literature and other fields of study related to Scandinavia. *Scandinavica*, a British journal, is published two times per year and is devoted exclusively to Scandinavian literature. The Norwegian quarterly *Edda* publishes criticism written both in the Scandinavian languages and in English. There are also journals focused on Scandinavian literature in Germany and the Netherlands, and some of their articles are in English.

Journals devoted to other areas of literary studies also sometimes have articles about Scandinavian literature. The journals *Books from Finland* and *Swedish Book Review* have as their mission to inform speakers of English about Finnish and Swedish literature, respectively.

Many publishers in the United States and Great Britain will publish books about Scandinavian literature if the books are about major writers, such as Henrik Ibsen, August Strindberg, or Søren Kierkegaard, but often only specialized publishers will publish books on relatively unknown subjects. In the 1970s and 1980s Twayne's World Authors Series included a number of books devoted to Scandinavian writers, and these books are still very useful. Unless the writer has a worldwide reputation, however, most current information available in English will be in the form of articles. For those who need only brief factual information about a writer, the Internet is a useful resource.

The quality of the literary criticism published in the standard scholarly journals is uniformly high. Fortunately some excellent literary histories of the Scandinavian countries are available. Edited by Sven Rossel (Denmark), George Schoolfield (Finland), Harald Naess (Norway), and Lars Warme (Sweden), these literary histories were published by the University of Nebraska Press in the 1990s and have individual chapters written by the foremost specialists in the field. The volume for Iceland is scheduled to appear in 2006. Somewhat different from the literary histories, but no less useful, are several volumes devoted to Scandinavia in the series *Dictionary of Literary Biography*. Consisting of essays written by specialists mostly from the Scandinavian countries and the United States, volumes concerning Denmark (edited by Marianne Stecher-Hansen), Iceland (edited by Patrick J. Stevens), Norway (edited by Tanya Thresher), and Sweden (edited by Ann-Charlotte Gavel Adams) have thus far appeared. Another excellent resource is Virpi Zuck, Niels Ingwersen, and Harald S. Naess, eds., *Dictionary of Scandinavian Literature* (Westport, Conn.: Greenwood Press, 1990). This volume is not entirely current, but it is nevertheless a very helpful resource for those who need brief and factual information rather than extensive background essays.

The present bibliography is organized into six sections. The first section, "General Scandinavian Literary History and Criticism," is relatively brief and lists books and articles that address more than one or two Scandinavian countries. This general section is followed by a section for each Scandinavian country: Denmark, Finland, Iceland, Norway, and Sweden. Each of these is divided into "Bibliographic Resources," "Literary History and Criticism," the titles in which address the literature of the specific country, and "Select Bibliography for Specific Writers," in which writers from the country in question are listed alphabetically with information about books and articles that discuss them. Most of the references are to works published during the past two or three decades.

For those who wish a brief but thorough overview of classical Scandinavian literature, Sven Rossel, *A History of Scandinavian Literature, 1870–1980* (Minneapolis: University of Minnesota Press, 1982), has much to recommend it. Although well over twenty years old, it offers a useful overview of the field and can be supplemented by the national literary histories (see below). Another highly useful, although specialized, volume is Ellen Rees, *On the Margins: Nordic Women Modernists of the 1930s* (Norwich, U.K.: Norvik Press, 2005), which offers groundbreaking studies of the works of Scandinavian women modernists.

As indicated above, the best starting point for the study of a national literature is the country's volume in a series of literary histories published by the University of Nebraska Press under the general editorship of Sven Rossel, who also edited the Danish volume in the series, *A History of Danish Literature* (Lincoln: University of Nebraska Press, 1992). When supplemented with two volumes edited by Marianne Stecher-Hansen, *Danish Writers from the Reformation to Decadence, 1550–1900* (Boston: Gale, 2004) and *Twentieth-Century Danish Writers* (Boston: Gale, 1999), a substantial amount of reliable and well-presented information is available. Those who have an interest in the work of Søren Kierkegaard may want to make note of two excellent recent biographies, Joakim Garff, *Søren Kierkegaard: A Biography* (Princeton, N.J.: Princeton University Press, 2005), and Alastair Hannay, *Kierkegaard: A Biography* (Cambridge: Cambridge University Press, 2001). Those with an interest in Karen Blixen, aka Isak Dinesen, will benefit greatly from Susan Brantly's *Understanding Isak Dinesen* (Columbia: University of South Carolina Press, 2002).

Those with a particular interest in the literature of Finland will want to familiarize themselves with George C. Schoolfield, ed., *A History of Finland's Literature* (Lincoln: University of Nebraska Press, 1998), which discusses both the Finland-Swedish literature of Finland and the literature that is written in Finnish. Two very talented younger scholars currently working in Finnish studies in the United States are Thomas A. DuBois and Andrew Nestingen. The former has contributed to the study of the *Kalevala* as well as to that of the Finnish novel; his essays about Aino Kallas and Ilmari Kianto are of particular interest. Nestingen's article "Timely Subjects: Leena Krohn between Universal and Particular" is a major statement about an important current writer. As recognized by all who know the field, the grand old man of Finnish studies is the aforementioned George C. Schoolfield, whose books and articles are listed throughout the Finnish portion of the bibliography.

Iceland has the smallest population of the Scandinavian countries, but its literature is arguably the oldest. Little emphasis is placed on medieval literature in this volume, however. Those interested in modern Icelandic literature will want to consult Patrick J. Stevens, ed., *Icelandic Writers* (Boston: Gale, 2004), which offers excellent essays on a substantial number of older and recent authors from Iceland.

Norwegian literature can be studied in Harald S. Naess, ed., *A History of Norwegian Literature* (Lincoln: University of Nebraska Press, 1993), which can profitably be supplemented with Tanya Thresher, ed., *Twentieth-Century Norwegian Writers* (New York: Gale, 2004); this volume contains essays on many recent and current Norwegian writers. Those with an interest in the rhetorical dimension of literary texts may wish to consult Jan Sjåvik, *Reading for the Truth: Rhetorical Construc-*

tions in Norwegian Fiction (Christchurch, New Zealand: Cybereditions, 2004), in which chapters on a number of canonical Norwegian literary texts will be found.

The literature of Sweden is presented by Lars Warme, the editor of *A History of Swedish Literature* (Lincoln: University of Nebraska Press, 1996). The essays in two volumes edited by Ann-Charlotte Gavel Adams, *Twentieth-Century Swedish Writers before World War II* (Boston: Gale, 2002) and *Twentieth-Century Swedish Writers after World War II* (Boston: Gale, 2002), are very informative.

In addition to the college and university libraries listed above, excellent collections of Scandinavian literature and Scandinavian literary criticism are found at the Library of Congress. In general, most colleges and universities that offer instruction in Scandinavian studies will have helpful library collections. Internet resources will also be useful to many, although they are of varying quality and dependability. The National and University Library of Iceland can be found at www.bok.hi.is, while the Reykjavík Municipal Library is located at borgarboksafn.is. The Internet address for the journal *Books from Finland* is www.finlit.fi/booksfromfinland, while the *Swedish Book Review* can be found at www.swedishbookreview.com/default.asp. Norla, a Norwegian agency that offers information about Norwegian literature abroad, has a stie at www.norla.no/. Much helpful information about Danish literature can be found at www.litteratursiden.dk/.

GENERAL SCANDINAVIAN LITERARY HISTORY AND CRITICISM

Bernd, Clifford A. *Poetic Realism in Scandinavia and Central Europe, 1820–1895.* Columbia, S.C.: Camden House, 1995.

Bisztray, George. "Documentarism and the Modern Scandinavian Novel." *Scandinavian Studies* 48 (1976): 71–83.

Bredsdorff, Elias. "Moralists *versus* Immoralists: The Great Battle in Scandinavian Literature in the 1880s." *Scandinavica* 8 (1969): 91–111.

Budd, John, compiler. *Eight Scandinavian Novelists: Criticism and Reviews in English.* Westport, Conn.: Greenwood Press, 1981.

Carlson, Marvin. "Renaissance Theatre in Scandinavia." *Theatre Survey: The American Journal of Theatre History* 14, no. 1 (1973): 22–54.

Castrén, Gunnar. "Scandinavia's International Baroque Theatre." *Educational Theatre Journal* 28 (1976): 5–34.

Colbert, David W. *The Birth of the Ballad: The Scandinavian Medieval Genre.* Stockholm: Svensk Visarkiv, 1989.

Friese, Wilhelm. "Scandinavian Baroque Literature: A Synthetic View." *Scandinavica* 4 (1965): 89–105.

Gustafson, Alrik. *Six Scandinavian Novelists: Lie, Jacobsen, Heidenstam, Selma Lagerlöf, Hamsun, Sigrid Undset.* Princeton, N.J.: Princeton University Press, 1940.

Höskuldsson, Sveinn Skorri, ed. *Ideas and Ideologies in Scandinavian Literature since the First World War: Proceedings from the Tenth Study Conference of the International Association for Scandinavian Studies*. Reykjavík: University of Iceland, 1975.

Marker, Frederick J., and Lise-Lone Marker. *A History of Scandinavian Theatre*. Cambridge: Cambridge University Press, 1996.

———. *The Scandinavian Theatre*. Oxford: Blackwell, 1975.

Mawby, Janet. *Writers and Politics in Modern Scandinavia*. London: Hodder and Stoughton, 1978.

Nolin, Bertil, and Peter Forsgren, eds. *The Modern Breakthrough in Scandinavian Literature: Proceedings of the Sixteenth Study Conference of the International Association for Scandinavian Studies*. Gothenburg: University of Gothenburg, 1988.

Rees, Ellen. *On the Margins: Nordic Women Modernists of the 1930s*. Norwich, U.K.: Norvik Press, 2005.

Rossel, Sven H. *A History of Scandinavian Literature, 1870–1980*. Minneapolis: University of Minnesota Press, 1982.

Schoolfield, George. "Recent Nordic Lyrics." *World Literature Today* 59 (1985): 212–19.

Steenstrup, Johannes C. H. R. *The Medieval Popular Ballad*. Seattle: University of Washington Press, 1968.

Zuck, Virpi, Niels Ingwersen, and Harald S. Naess, eds. *Dictionary of Scandinavian Literature*. Westport, Conn.: Greenwood Press, 1990.

DENMARK

Bibliographic Resources

Bredsdorff, Elias. *Danish Literature in English*. Westport, Conn.: Greenwood Press, 1973.

Dania Polyglotta: Literature on Denmark in Languages Other than Danish. Copenhagen: Royal Library, 1946–2005.

Mitchell, P. M. *A Bibliographical Guide to Danish Literature*. Copenhagen: Munksgaard, 1951.

Schroeder, Carol L. *A Bibliography of Danish Literature in English Translation 1950–1980*. Copenhagen: Det danske Selskab, 1982.

Literary History and Criticism

Albertsen, Leif L. *On the Threshold of a Golden Age: Denmark around 1800*. Copenhagen: Ministry of Foreign Affairs, 1979.

Allan, R. "Fiction and Fact in the Faroese Novel." *Bradford Occasional Papers* 6 (1984): 72–87.

Andersen, Lise Præstgaard. "The Development of the Genres: The Danish Ballad." *Sumlen* (1981): 25–35.

Bernd, Clifford A. "The Anticipation of German Poetic Realism in Danish 'Poetisk Realisme.'" *Modern Language Notes* 97 (1982): 573–89.

Borum, Poul. *Danish Literature: A Short Critical Survey.* Copenhagen: Det danske Selskab, 1979.

Brønner, Hedin. "The Short Story in the Faroe Isles." *Scandinavian Studies* 49 (1977): 155–79.

Brostrøm, Torben, ed. *Denmarkings: Danish Literature Today.* Copenhagen: Ministry of Foreign Affairs, 1982.

Byram, Michael. "From 'l'art pour l'art' to 'Tendens': Art and Society in Denmark of the 1920s." *Scandinavica* 19 (1980): 151–63.

Claudi, Jørgen. *Contemporary Danish Authors.* Copenhagen: Det danske Selskab, 1952.

Eaton, J. W. *The German Influence in Danish Literature in the Eighteenth Century.* Cambridge: Cambridge University Press, 1929.

Egebak, Jørgen. "Changes in the Concept of Truth in Danish Literature during the Last Part of the Nineteenth Century." *Scandinavica* 24 (1985): 5–15.

———. "The Early Discussion of Nietzsche in Denmark." *Scandinavica* 24 (1985): 143–59.

Engelberg, Karsten, ed. *The Romantic Heritage.* Copenhagen: University of Copenhagen, 1984.

Greene-Gantzberg, Vivian Y. "Approaching the Concept of Family in Nineteenth-Century Danish Narrative." *Scandinavica* 18 (1979): 141–48.

Ingwersen, Niels. "A Danish Literary Debate: 1888–89." *Facets of Scandinavian Literature: Germanistische Forschungsketten* 2 (1974): 40–52.

Jones, W. Glyn. *Faroe and Cosmos.* Newcastle upon Tyne: University of Newcastle upon Tyne, 1974.

———. "France and the Danish Symbolists." *Rencontre et courants literaires franco-scandinaves. Actes du 7e Congrès International* (1972): 165–74.

Jørgensen, Aage. *Idyll and Abyss: Essays on Danish Literature and Theater.* Seattle: Mermaid Press, 1992.

Kuhn, Hans. *Defining a Nation in Song: Danish Patriotic Songs.* Copenhagen: C. A. Reitzel, 1990.

Marx, Leonie. "Literary Experimentation in a Time of Transition: The Danish Short Story after 1945." *Scandinavian Studies* 49 (1977): 131–54.

Mickelsen, David J. "Beating Frenchmen into Swords: Symbolism in Denmark." *Comparative Literature Studies* 14 (1977): 328–45.

Mitchell, P. M. *A History of Danish Literature.* 2nd revised ed. New York: Kraus-Thomson, 1971.

Olrik, Axel. *The Heroic Legends of Denmark.* New York: American-Scandinavian Foundation, 1919.

Petersen, Teddy. "The Many Masks of Censorship: Literary-Sociological Notes on Danish Literature around the First World War." *Scandinavica* 21 (1982): 25–73.
Roger-Henrichsen, Gudmund. *A Decade of Danish Literature, 1960–70.* Copenhagen: Ministry of Foreign Affairs, 1972.
Rossel, Sven H., ed. *A History of Danish Literature.* Lincoln: University of Nebraska Press, 1992.
Skovgaard-Petersen, Inge. "Saxo, Historian of the Patria." *Mediaeval Scandinavia* 2 (1969): 54–77.
Stecher-Hansen, Marianne, ed. *Danish Writers from the Reformation to Decadence, 1550–1900.* Boston: Gale, 2004.
———. *Twentieth-Century Danish Writers.* Boston: Gale, 1999.
Wamberg, Bodil, ed. *Out of Denmark: Isak Dinesen/Karen Blixen 1885–1985 and Danish Women Writers Today.* Copenhagen: Danish Cultural Institute, 1985.

Select Bibliography for Specific Writers

Jeppe Aakjær

Westergaard, W. "Jeppe Aakjær." *American-Scandinavian Review* 12 (1924): 665–69.

Kjeld Abell

Hye, Allen E. "Fantasy + Involvement → Thought: Kjeld Abell's Conception of Theater." *Scandinavian Studies* 63 (1991): 30–49.
———. "'Se alting i spejle': The Mirror and the Other Key Symbols in the Theater of Kjeld Abell." *University of Dayton Review* 23, no. 2 (1995): 47–62.
Lingard, John. "Breaking the Frame: Idea and Image in Kjeld Abell's *The Blue Pekinese.*" *Scandinavian-Canadian Studies/Etudes Scandinaves au Canada* 11 (1998): 101–15.
Marker, Frederick J. *Kjeld Abell.* Boston: Twayne, 1976.

Benny Andersen

Marx, Leonie. *Benny Andersen: A Critical Study.* Westport, Conn.: Greenwood Press, 1983.
———, ed. *Selected Stories.* Willimantic, Conn.: Curbstone, 1983.
Taylor, Alexander, trans. *Selected Poems.* Willimantic, Conn.: Curbstone, 1975.

Hans Christian Andersen

Bredsdorff, Elias. *Hans Christian Andersen: The Story of His Life and Work, 1805–75.* New York: Schribner's, 1975.

Conroy, Patricia L., and Sven H. Rossel, eds. *The Diaries of Hans Christian Andersen*. Seattle: University of Washington Press, 1990.

———. *Tales and Stories*. Seattle: University of Washington Press, 1980.

Dahlerup, Pil. " 'The Little Mermaid' Deconstructed." *Scandinavian Studies* 62 (1990): 418–29.

Grønbech, Bo. *Hans Christian Andersen*. Boston: Twayne, 1980.

Heltoft, Kjeld. *Hans Christian Andersen as an Artist*. Copenhagen: Royal Danish Ministry of Foreign Affairs, 1977.

Hugus, Frank. "Opera as Allegory in Hans Christian Andersen's Improvisatoren and Lykke-Peer." *Edda* 99 (1999): 19–30.

Johansen, Jørgen Dines. "Counteracting the Fall: 'Sneedronningen' and 'Iisjomfruen': The Problem of Adult Sexuality in Fairytale and Story." *Scandinavian Studies* 74 (2002): 137–48.

———. "The Merciless Tragedy of Desire: An Interpretation of H. C. Andersen's 'Den lille Havfrue.' " *Scandinavian Studies* 68 (1996): 203–41.

Lederer, Wolfgang. *The Kiss of the Snow Queen: Hans Christian Andersen and Man's Redemption by Woman*. Berkeley: University of California Press, 1986.

Marker, Frederick J. *Hans Christian Andersen and the Romantic Theatre*. Toronto: University of Toronto Press, 1971.

Robbins, Hollis. "The Emperor's New Critique." *New Literary History: A Journal of Theory and Interpretation* 34 (2003): 659–75.

Rossel, Sven H., ed. *Brother, Very Far Away and Other Poems*. Seattle: Mermaid Press, 1991.

Sanders, Karin. "Signatures: Spelling the Father's and Erasing the Mother's in C. J. L. Almqvist's *Ramido Marinesco* and H. C. Andersen's *O. T.*" *Scandinavian Studies* 65 (1993): 153–79.

Spink, Reginald. *Hans Christian Andersen: The Man and His Work*. Copenhagen: Host, 1972.

Stecher-Hansen, Marianne. "H. C. Andersen's 'Historien om en Moder': Allegory and Symbol in the Danish Golden Age." In *H. C. Andersen: Old Problems and New Readings*, ed. Steven Sondrup. Provo, Utah: Brigham Young University Press, 2004.

———. "Science Fiction in the Age of Romanticism: Hans Christian Andersen's Futuristic Tales." *Selecta: Journal of the Pacific Northwest Council on Foreign Languages* 14 (1993): 74–78.

Jens Baggesen

Bredsdorff, Thomas. "The Fox at Ploen." *Orbis Litterarum: International Review of Literary Studies* 22 (1967): 241–51.

Henriksen, Aage. "Baggesen—The European." *Danish Foreign Office Journal* 48 (1964): 17–20.

Thrane, Lotte. "Visual Pleasure and Writerly Delight: On the Longing for Apocalypse in Baggesen's Alpine Journey." *Scandinavica* 41 (2002): 5–20.

Herman Bang

Bjørby, Pål. "Herman Bang's 'Franz Pander': Narcissism, Self, and the Nature of the Unspoken." *Scandinavian Studies* 62 (1990): 449–67.
———. "The Prison House of Sexuality." *Scandinavian Studies* 58 (1986): 223–55.
Cokal, Susann. "Infectious Excitement: Disease, Desire, and Communicability in *Niels Lyhne* and *Ved Vejen*." *Scandinavian Studies* 71 (1999): 167–90.
Eddy, Beverley Driver. "Herman Bang's 'Irene Holm' as a Study of Life and Art." *Scandinavica* 28 (1989): 17–27.
Heede, Dag. "Queering the Queer: Herman Bang and the Pleasures and Dangers of Allegorical Readings." *Scandinavica* 40 (2001): 11–40.
Shepherd-Barr, Kirsten. " 'Le grand metteur en scène': Herman Bang in Paris, 1893–94." *Scandinavian-Canadian Studies/Etudes Scandinaves au Canada* 9 (1996): 73–90.
Simonsen, Sofus E. "Herman Bang: Life and Theme." *Germanic Notes* 3 (1972): 34–37.

Steen Steensen Blicher

Watson, Harry D. "Steen Steensen Blicher and Macpherson's Ossian." *Northern Studies* 17 (1981): 27–35.

Karen Blixen

Aiken, Susan Hardy. *Isak Dinesen and the Engendering of Narrative*. Chicago: University of Chicago Press, 1990.
Brantly, Susan. "Isak Dinesen: The Danish Scheherazade." *Scandinavian Review* 90, no. 2 (2002): 58–66.
———. *Understanding Isak Dinesen*. Columbia: University of South Carolina Press, 2002.
Gubar, Susan. " 'The Blank Page' and the Issues of Female Creativity." *Critical Inquiry* 8 (1981): 243–63.
Hansen, Frantz Leander. *The Aristocratic Universe of Karen Blixen: Destiny and the Denial of Fate*. Brighton, U.K.: Sussex Academic, 2003.
Henriksen, Aage. *Isak Dinesen/Karen Blixen: The Work and Life*. New York: St. Martin's Press, 1988.

Johannesson, Eric O. *The World of Isak Dinesen*. Seattle: University of Washington Press, 1961.
Juhl, Marianne, and Bo Hakon Jørgensen. *Diana's Revenge: Two Lines in Isak Dinesen's Authorship*. Odense: Odense University Press, 1985.
Langbaum, Robert. *Isak Dinesen's Art: The Gayety of Vision*. 2nd ed. Chicago: University of Chicago Press, 1975.
Mussari, Mark. "L'Heure Bleue: Isak Dinesen and the Ascendant Imagination." *Scandinavian Studies* 73 (2001): 43–62.
Pelensky, Olga Anastasia, ed. *Isak Dinesen: Critical Views*. Athens: Ohio University Press, 1993.
———. *Isak Dinesen: The Life and Imagination of a Seducer*. Athens: Ohio University Press, 1991.
Richter, David H. "Covert Plot in Isak Dinesen's 'Sorrow-Acre.' " *Journal of Narrative Technique* 15, no. 1 (1985): 82–90.
Sabo, Anne G. "Revamped Woman and the Untruth of Truth: Unraveling the Antifeminism of Nietzsche and Dinesen." *Lit: Literature Interpretation Theory* 16, no. 1 (2005): 41–73.
Stambaugh, Sara. *The Witch and the Goddess in the Stories of Isak Dinesen: A Feminist Reading*. Ann Arbor: University Microfilms International Research Press, 1988.
Thurman, Judith. *Isak Dinesen: The Life of a Storyteller*. New York: St. Martin's Press, 1982.
Wilkinson, Lynn R. "Hannah Arendt on Isak Dinesen: Between Storytelling and Theory." *Comparative Literature* 56 (2004): 77–98.
———. "Isak Dinesen's 'Sorrow-Acre' and the Ethics of Storytelling." *Edda* 96 (1996): 33–44.

Georg Brandes

Asmundsson, Doris A. *Georg Brandes: Aristocratic Radical*. New York: New York University Press, 1981.
Jones, W. Glyn, ed. *Georg Brandes: Selected Letters*. Norwich, U.K.: Norvik Press, 1991.
Lundtofte, Anne Mette. "Pointing Fingers at Genius: Reading Brandes Reading Kierkegaard." *Tijdschrift voor Skandinavistiek* 21 (2000): 149–63.
Moritzen, Julius, ed. *Georg Brandes in Life and Letters*. Newark, N.J.: D. S. Colyer, 1922.
Naess, Harald. "Georg Brandes and 19th Century Scandinavian Realism." *Neohelicon: Acta Comparationis Litterarum Universarum* 15 (1988): 113–34.
Nolin, Bertil. "A Critic and His Network: Georg Brandes as a Key Figure of the Modern Breakthrough in the Baltic Area States." *Tijdschrift voor Skandinavistiek* 16 (1995): 145–58.

———. "The Critic and His Paradigm: An Analysis of Brandes' Role as a Critic 1870–1900 with Special Reference to the Comparative Aspect." *Orbis Litterarum: International Review of Literary Studies* Supp. 5 (1980): 21–35.

———. *Georg Brandes*. Boston: Twayne, 1976.

Pages, Neil Christian. "On Popularization: Reading Brandes Reading Nietzsche." *Scandinavian Studies* 72 (2000): 163–80.

Romhild, Lars Peter. "Georg Brandes and Comparative Literature." *Orbis Litterarum: International Review of Literary Studies* Supp. 5 (1980): 284–302.

Sprinchorn, Evert. "Brandes and Strindberg." *Orbis Litterarum: International Review of Literary Studies* Supp. 5 (1980): 109–26.

H. C. Branner

Markey, Thomas L. *Hans Christian Branner*. New York: Twayne, 1973.

Mussari, Mark. "H. C. Branner and the Colors of Consciousness." *Scandinavian Studies* 71 (1999): 41–66.

———. "On Branner, On Blixen: The Battle over Rytteren." *Scandinavian Studies* 75 (2003): 527–38.

Suzanne Brøgger

Allemano, Marina. "Figures, True Stories and Literary Patchwork: The Brøggeresque Subject." *Scandinavica* 32 (1993): 203–25.

———. "Suzanne Brøgger and Eros." *Scandinavian-Canadian Studies/Etudes Scandinaves au Canada* 3 (1988): 61–72.

Woods, Gurli Aagaard. "From Postmodern Fragmentation to Rebirth: Suzanne Brøgger's Work from the Early 1990s." *Scandinavian Studies* 76 (2004): 257–78.

Inger Christensen

Nied, Susanna. "Letting Things Be: Inger Christensen's 'Alphabet.' " *Scandinavian Review* 70, no. 4 (1982): 24–26.

Pape, Lis Wedell. "Oscillations: On Subject and Gender in Late Modernism." *Orbis Litterarum: International Review of Literary Studies* 53 (1998): 252–68.

Sophus Claussen

Elbek, Jørgen. "The Nordic Nineties." In *Fin(s) de Siècle in Scandinavian Perspective: Studies in Honor of Harald S. Naess*, ed. Faith Ingwersen and Mary Kay Norseng. Columbia, S.C.: Camden House, 1993.

Phillips, Patrick. "Dethroning the Dictionary." *Perspectives: Studies in Translatology* 9, no. 1 (2001): 23–32.

Tove Ditlevsen

Brantly, Susan C. "The Madwoman in the Spacious Apartment: Tove Ditlevsen's *Ansigterne*." *Edda* 95 (1995): 257–65.
Petersen, Antje C. "Tove Ditlevsen and the Aesthetics of Madness." *Scandinavian Studies* 64 (1992): 243–62.

Johannes Ewald

Greenway, John L. "The Two Worlds of Johannes Ewald." *Scandinavian Studies* 42 (1970): 394–409.

Meïr Aron Goldschmidt

Ober, Kenneth H. " 'Jeg vil . . . leve som Poet og som Oversætter': Meïr Goldschmidt as a Translator." *Scandinavian Studies* 66 (1994): 23–44.
———. " 'Med saadanne følelser skriver man en roman': Origins of Meïr Goldschmidt's *En Jøde*." *Scandinavica* 30 (1991): 25–39.
———. *Meïr Goldschmidt*. Boston: Twayne, 1976.
———. "Meïr Goldschmidt's 'Hebrew Legends': The Writer as Plagiarist." *Scandinavica* 22 (1983): 15–21.
Rainwater van Suntum, Lisa A. "Creating Jewish Identity through Storytelling: The Tragedy of Jacob Bendixen." *Scandinavian Studies* 73 (2001): 375–98.

N. F. S. Grundtvig

Bradley, S. A. J. "Nicolaj Frederik Severin Grundtvig (1783–1872)." *Cambridge Quarterly* 31 (2002): 307–25.
Chase, Martin. "True at Any Time: Grundtvig's Subjective Interpretation of Nordic Myth." *Scandinavian Studies* 73 (2001): 507–34.
Det danske Selskab, ed. *Grundtvig's Ideas in North America: Influences and Parallels*. Copenhagen: Det danske Selskab, 1983.
Hansen, Gregory. "N. F. S. Grundtvig's Idea of Folklore: Resurrecting Folk-Life through the Living Word." *Folklore Historian: Journal of the Folklore and History Section of the American Folklore Society* 12 (1995): 5–13.
Jensen, Niels Lyhne, ed. *A Grundtvig Anthology*. Cambridge: James Clarke, 1984.
Koch, Hal. *Grundtvig*. Antioch, Ohio: Antioch Press, 1952.

Nielsen, Ernest D. *N. S. F. Grundtvig: An American Study.* Rock Island, Ill.: Augustana Press, 1975.

Thomasine Gyllembourg

Larsen, Lis Helmer, and Jannie Roed. "The Art of Womanhood and Wedlock: Thomasine Gyllembourg: A Writer in Spite of Herself." *New Comparison* 4 (1987): 92–104.
Pages, Neil Christian. "Beyond Foreword: Reading Kierkegaard's *A Literary Review.*" *Tijdschrift voor Skandinavistiek* 20 (1999): 5–24.

Martin A. Hansen

Ingwersen, Faith, and Niels Ingwersen. *Martin A. Hansen.* Boston: Twayne, 1978.

Thorkild Hansen

Jalving, Mikael. "Thorkild Hansen and Documentary Fiction: Or, History with a Human Face." In *Documentarism in Scandinavian Literature*, ed. Poul Houe and Sven Hakon Rossel. Amsterdam, Netherlands: Rodopi, 1997.
Liet, Henk van der. "Just Me, Myself, and I: On Thorkild Hansen as Creator and Creation." *Tijdschrift voor Skandinavistiek* 18 (1997): 71–98.
Riegel, Dieter. "Thorkild Hansen's Jens Munk." *Scandinavian-Canadian Studies/ Etudes Scandinaves au Canada* 4 (1991): 141–52.
Stecher-Hansen, Marianne. "Double-Voiced Discourse in Thorkild Hansen's Jens Munk." *Scandinavian Studies* 66 (1994): 533–51.
———. *History Revisited: Fact and Fiction in Thorkild Hansen's Documentary Works.* Columbia, S.C.: Camden House, 1997.
———. "Whose Hamsun? Author and Artifice: Knut Hamsun, Thorkild Hansen and Per Olov Enquist." *Edda* 99 (1999): 245–51.

Johan Ludvig Heiberg

Fenger, Henning. *The Heibergs.* Boston: Twayne, 1971.
Vinten-Johansen, Peter. "Johan Ludvig Heiberg and His Audience in Nineteenth-Century Denmark." *Scandinavian Studies* 54 (1982): 295–306.

William Heinesen

Brønner, Hedin. *Three Faroese Novelists.* New York: Twayne, 1973.
Joensen, Leyvoy. "Atlantis, Bábylon, Tórshavn: The Djurhuus Brothers and Wil-

liam Heinesen in Faroese Literary History." *Scandinavian Studies* 74 (2002): 181–204.
Jones, W. Glyn. "Toward Totality: The Poetry of William Heinesen." *World Literature Today* 62 (1988): 79–82.
———. *William Heinesen*. New York: Twayne, 1974.
Marnersdóttir, Malan. "William Heinesen's *Tårnet ved verdens ende*." *Scandinavica* 34 (1995): 71–95.

Agnes Henningsen

Allemano, Marina. "Somatic Gaps and Embodied Voices in Agnes Henningsen's Memoirs." *Scandinavian Studies* 76 (2004): 155–80.

Peter Høeg

Hees, Annelies van. "Fiction and Reality in *Smilla's Sense of Snow*." *European Studies: A Journal of European Culture, History, and Politics* 18 (2002): 215–26.
Schaffer, Rachel. "Smilla's Sense of Gender Identity." *Clues: A Journal of Detection* 19 (1998): 47–60.
Thomson, Catherine Claire. " 'Vi æder vores eget lort': Scatology and Eschatology in Peter Høeg's *Forestilling om det tyvende århundrede*." *Scandinavica* 41 (2002): 37–59.

Per Højholt

Berntsen, Dorthe. "How Is Modernist Poetry 'Embodied'?" *Metaphor and Symbol* 14 (1999): 101–22.

Ludvig Holberg

Argetsinger, Gerald S. *Ludvig Holberg's Comedies*. Carbondale: Southern Illinois University Press, 1983.
Billeskov Jansen, F. J. *Ludvig Holberg*. New York: Twayne, 1974.
Bredsdorff, Thomas. "Student Power: Holberg's Ideas on Education." *Orbis Litterarum: International Review of Literary Studies* 58, no. 1 (2003): 11–16.
Buus, Stephanie. "A Comedy of Malapropism: Ludvig Holberg's *Erasmus Montanus*." *Edda* 100 (2000): 334–45.
Campbell, Oscar J. *The Comedies of Holberg*. New York: B. Blom, 1968.
Mitchell, P. M. *Selected Essays of Ludvig Holberg*. Westport, Conn.: Greenwood Press, 1976.

Straubhaar, Sandra Ballif. "Holberg's Apology for Zenobia of Palmyra and Catherine I." *Scandinavica* 36 (1997): 169–88.
Törnqvist, Egil. "The Structure of Holberg's *Jeppe paa Bjerget*." *Scandinavica* 26 (1987): 31–42.

Jens Peter Jacobsen

Cokal, Susann. "Infectious Excitement: Disease, Desire, and Communicability in Niels Lyhne and Ved Vejen." *Scandinavian Studies* 71 (1999): 167–90.
Craft, Robert. "Great Dane." *New York Review of Books* 39, no. 17 (1992): 51–55.
Egebak, Jørgen. "Changes in the Concept of Truth in Danish Literature during the Last Part of the 19th Century." *Scandinavica* 24 (1985): 5–15.
Ingwersen, Niels. "Problematic Protagonists: Marie Grubbe and Niels Lyhne." In *The Hero in Scandinavian Literature*, ed. John M. Weinstock and Robert T. Rovinski. Austin: University of Texas Press, 1975.
Jensen, Niels Lyhne. *Jens Peter Jacobsen*. Boston: Twayne, 1984.
Roy, Christian. "J. P. Jacobsen in the Context of the Intellectual History of Europe." *Scandinavian-Canadian Studies/Etudes Scandinaves au Canada* 4 (1991): 123–40.
Woodson, Jon. "Zora Neale Hurston's *Their Eyes Were Watching God* and the Influence of Jens Peter Jacobsen's *Marie Grubbe*." *African American Review* 26 (1992): 619–35.

Jørgen-Frantz Jacobsen

Brønner, Hedin. *Three Faroese Novelists*. New York: Twayne, 1973.
Jones, W. Glyn. "Duality and Dualism: Jørgen-Frantz Jacobsen (1900–1938) Reassessed." *Scandinavica* 27 (1990): 133–51.

Frank Jæger

Hugus, Frank. "Frank Jæger's Defeated Protagonists." *Scandinavian Studies* 54 (1982): 148–59.

Johannes V. Jensen

Christensen, Erik C. "The Beginning and End of Literature: Mythmaking in Jorge Luis Borges and Johannes V. Jensen." *Edda* 98 (1998): 307–17.
Christensen, Peter G. "Johannes V. Jensen's *Den lange Rejse*: A Blochian Approach." *Scandinavian Studies* 68 (1996): 51–75.
Heitmann, Annegret. "Search for the Self: Aesthetics and Sexual Identity in the

Early Works of Johannes V. Jensen and Thit Jensen." *Scandinavica* 24 (1985): 17–34.
Houe, Poul. "Johannes V. Jensen's Long Journey or Postmodernism Under Way." *Scandinavian Studies* 64 (1992): 96–128.
Rossel, Sven H. *Johannes V. Jensen*. Boston: Twayne, 1984.
Veisland, Jørgen Steen. "The Absent Father and the Inauguration of Discourse in Johannes V. Jensen's *Kongens fald*." *Scandinavian Studies* 61 (1989): 55–67.

Thit Jensen

Heitmann, Annegret. "Search for the Self: Aesthetics and Sexual Identity in the Early Works of Johannes V. Jensen and Thit Jensen." *Scandinavica* 24 (1985): 17–34.

Johannes Jørgensen

Egebak, Jørgen. "Changes in the Concept of Truth in Danish Literature during the Last Part of the 19th Century." *Scandinavica* 24 (1985): 5–15.
Jones, W. Glyn. *Johannes Jørgensen*. New York: Twayne, 1969.

Søren Kierkegaard

Bloom, Harold, ed. *Søren Kierkegaard*. New York: Chelsea, 1989.
Garff, Joakim. *Søren Kierkegaard: A Biography*. Princeton, N.J.: Princeton University Press, 2005.
Hannay, Alastair. *Kierkegaard: A Biography*. Cambridge: Cambridge University Press, 2001.
Kirmmse, Bruce H. *Kierkegaard in Golden Age Denmark*. Bloomington: Indiana University Press, 1990.
Lapointe, Francois. *Soren Kierkegaard and His Critics: An International Bibliography of Criticism*. Westport, Conn.: Greenwood Press, 1980.
Poole, Roger. *Kierkegaard: The Indirect Communication*. Charlottesville: University Press of Virginia, 1993.
Stendahl, Britta. *Søren Kierkegaard*. Boston: Twayne, 1976.
Strawser, Michael. *Both/And: Reading Kierkegaard from Irony to Edification*. New York: Fordham University Press, 1997.
Walsh, Sylvia. *Living Poetically: Kierkegaard's Existential Aesthetics*. University Park: Pennsylvania State University Press, 1994.

Tom Kristensen

Byram, Michael. *Tom Kristensen*. Boston: Twayne, 1982.

Leonora Christina

Baldwin, Birgit. "*Jammersminde* Remembered: A New Look at the Status of History and Literature." *Scandinavian Studies* 62 (1990): 266–79.
Lyngstad, Sverre. "The Danish Princess: Leonora Christina." In *Women Writers of the Seventeenth Century*, ed. Katharina M. Wilson and Frank J. Warnke. Athens: University of Georgia Press, 1989.

Svend Åge Madsen

Marx, Leonie. "Literary Experimentation in a Time of Transition: The Danish Short Story after 1945." *Scandinavian Studies* 49 (1977): 131–54.

Karin Michaëlis

Eddy, Beverley Driver. "The Dangerous Age: Karin Michaëlis and the Politics of Menopause." *Women's Studies: An Interdisciplinary Journal* 21 (1992): 491–504.
Eyben, Merete von. *Karin Michaëlis: Incest as Metaphor and the Illusion of Romantic Love*. New York: Peter Lang, 2003.
Lassner, Phyllis. "Women's Midlife and the Crisis of Writing: Karin Michaelis's *The Dangerous Age* and Rose Macaulay's *Dangerous Ages*." *Atlantis: A Women's Studies Journal/Revue d'Etudes sur la Femme* 14, no. 2 (1989): 21–30.

Poul Martin Møller

Jones, W. Glyn. "Søren Kierkegaard and Poul Martin Møller." *Modern Language Review* 60 (1965): 73–82.
Thielst, Peter. "Poul Martin Møller (1794–1838)." *Danish Journal of Philosophy* 13 (1976): 66–83.

Kaj Munk

Arestad, Sverre. "Kaj Munk as a Dramatist." *Scandinavian Studies* 26 (1954): 151–76.

Martin Andersen Nexø

Ingwersen, Faith, and Niels Ingwersen. *Quest for a Promised Land.* Westport, Conn.: Greenwood Press, 1984.
Lebowitz, Naomi. "Magic Socialism and the Ghost of Pelle Erobreren." *Scandinavian Studies* 76 (2004): 341–68.

Henrik Nordbrandt

Christensen, Nadia, and Alexander Taylor, trans. *Selected Poems.* Willimantic, Conn.: Curbstone, 1978.

Adam Oehlenschläger

Bredsdorff, Thomas. "Oehlenschläger's Aesthetics: Allegory and Symbolism in 'The Golden Horns'—And a Note on 20th Century Eulogy of the Allegory." *Edda* 99 (1999): 211–21.
Hanson, Kathryn S. "Adam Oehlenschläger's Romanticism." *Scandinavian-Canadian Studies/Etudes Scandinaves au Canada* 2 (1986): 39–50.
Høyrup, Helene. " 'Som perler paa den historiske Musas Snor': Romantic Self-Representation and Aesthetics in Adam Oehlenschläger's *Ungdomserindringer.*" *Scandinavian Studies* 72 (2000): 431–44.

Jacob Paludan

Fergenson, Laraine. "A Danish Appreciation of Thoreau: Jacob Paludan's Foreword to *Livet i Skovene.*" *Thoreau Society Bulletin* 205 (1993): 1–3.
Heltberg, Niels. "Jacob Paluden." *American-Scandinavian Review* 40 (1952): 142–45.

Leif Panduro

Hugus, Frank. "Three Danish Authors Examine the Danish Welfare State: Finn Søeborg, Leif Panduro, and Anders Bodelsen." *Scandinavian Studies* 62 (1990): 189–213.

Henrik Pontoppidan

Mitchell, P. M. *Henrik Pontoppidan.* Boston: Twayne, 1979.
Petersen-Weiner, Antje. "Aladdin's Shadow: On Henrik Pontoppidan's *Lykke-Per.*" *Scandinavian Studies* 59 (1987): 28–45.

Weissberg, Liliane. "Utopian Visions: Bloch, Lukács, Pontoppidan." *German Quarterly* 67 (1994): 197–210.

Klaus Rifbjerg

Gray, Charlotte Schiander. *Klaus Rifbjerg*. Westport, Conn.: Greenwood Press, 1986.
Tangherlini, Timothy R. "Uncertain Centers/Uncentered Selves: Postmodernism and the (Re)Definition of Feminine in *Anna (jeg) Anna* and *Baby*." *Scandinavian Studies* 67 (1995): 306–29.
Veisland, Jørgen Steen. "Repetition in Klaus Rifbjerg's *Arkivet*." *Edda* 88 (1988): 162–71.

Hans Egede Schack

Jørgensen, Aage. "On 'Phantasterne,' the Novel by Hans Egede Schack." *Scandinavica* 5 (1966): 50–53.
Madsen, Børge Gedsø. "Hans Egede Schack's 'Phantasterne.' " *Scandinavian Studies* 35 (1966): 51–58.

Hans Scherfig

Bredsdorff, Elias. "Hans Scherfig, Social and Political Satirist." *Studies in Contemporary Satire: A Creative and Critical Journal* 10 (1983): 23–25.
Hugus, Frank. "Hans Scherfig's *Det forsømte forår*: Investigating the Genesis of the Novel." *Scandinavica* 33 (1994): 57–88.
———. "Literary Sources of Hans Scherfig's *Den forsvundne Fuldmægtig*." *Scandinavian Studies* 68 (1996): 19–50.
Kristensen, Sven Møller. "How to Castigate Your Public—And Write Best Sellers." *Danish Journal* 76 (1973): 26–29.
Riegel, Dieter K. H. "Society and Crime in the Novels of Hans Scherfig." *Scandinavian-Canadian Studies/Etudes Scandinaves au Canada* 1 (1983): 109–14.

Peter Seeberg

Rossel, Sven H. "The Search for Reality: A Study in Peter Seeberg's Prose Writings." *Proceedings of the Pacific Northwest Council on Foreign Languages* 27 (1976): 126–29.

Villy Sørensen

Rossel, Sven H. "Villy Sørensen: Mythologist, Philosopher, Writer." *World Literature Today* 65 (1991): 41–45.

Testa, Caterina. "Villy Sørensen: 'I det fremmede.' " *Scandinavica* 35 (1996): 53–70.

———. "The Comic Conception of Reality: The Relationship between the Comic, Language, and Cognition in the Works of Villy Sørensen." *Scandinavian Studies* 64 (1992): 228–42.

Henrik Stangerup

Bluestone, Barbara. "In the Shadow of Northern Lights." *Encounter* 63, no. 2 (1984): 73–77.

Monty, Ib. "An Unsentimental Dane." *Danish Journal* 72 (1972): 14–19.

Hanne Marie Svendsen

Allemano, Marina. "Time Is Inside the Box: Magic and Metafiction in Two Novels by Hanne Marie Svendsen." *Scandinavica* 41 (2002): 235–52.

Pia Tafdrup

Kennedy, Thomas E. "Happy Hour(s): Notes on the Translation of Two Poems by Pia Tafdrup." *Literary Review: An International Journal of Contemporary Writing* 45 (2002): 621–25.

Kirsten Thorup

Gray, Charlotte S. "Identity and Narrative Structure in Kirsten Thorup's Novels." *Scandinavian Studies* 63 (1991): 214–20.

Dorrit Willumsen

Wamberg, Bodil. "Dorrit Willumsen: I Am Only Afraid of Pure Angels." *Scandinavian Review* 74, no. 4 (1986): 79–89.

Christian Winther

Larsen, Svend Erik. "The Speech of Silence and the Silence of Speech: Christian Winther's 'Til Een.' " *Scandinavica* 15 (1976): 101–35.

FINLAND

Bibliographic Resources

Screen, J. E. G. *Finland*. World Bibliographical Series 31. Oxford: Clio, 1981.

Literary History and Criticism

Ahokas, Jaakko A. *A History of Finnish Literature*. Bloomington: Indiana University Press, 1973.
Andersson, Claes. "Disillusions: The Problems of Evil in New Finnish Writing." *Books from Finland* (1987): 80–83.
Apo, Satu. "A Singing Scribe or a Nationalist Author? The Making of the *Kalevala* as Described by Elias Lönnrot." *FF Network* 25 (2003): 3–12.
Dana, Kathleen Osgood. "Sámi Literature in the Twentieth Century." *World Literature Today* 71 (1997): 23–28.
DuBois, Thomas A. "From Maria to Marjatta: The Transformation of an Oral Poem in Elias Lönnrot's *Kalevala*." *Oral Tradition* 8 (1993): 247–88.
Hatavara, Mari. "History, the Historical Novel and Nation: The First Finnish Historical Novels as National Narrative." *Neophilologus* 86, no. 1 (January 2002): 1–15.
Huldén, Lars. "Swedish Poetry in Finland on the Threshold of the Eighties." *World Literature Today* 54 (1980): 47–50.
Ingström, Pia. "Boom Time for the Finland-Swedish Novel." *Swedish Book Review* Supplement (1992): 48–53.
Kalevala, 1835–1985: The National Epic of Finland. Helsinki: Helsinki University Library, 1985.
Laitinen, Kai. "The Finnish War Novel." *World Literature Today* 58 (1984): 31–35.
———. *Literature of Finland: An Outline*. Helsinki: Otava, 1994.
Makkonen, Anna. "Postmodernism in Finland." In *International Postmodernism: Theory and Literary Practice*, ed. Hans Bertens, Douwe Fokkema, and Mario J. Valdés. Amsterdam, Netherlands: Benjamins, 1997.
Minninen, Merja, and Päivi Setälä, eds. *The Lady with the Bow: The Story of Finnish Women*. Helsinki: Otava, 1990.
Petherick, Karin. "Four Finland-Swedish Prose Modernists: Aspects of the Work of Hagar Olsson, Henry Parland, Elmer Diktonius and Rabbe Enckell." *Scandinavica* 15 (1976): 45–62.
Rantavaara, Irma. "A Nation in Search of Identity: Finnish Literature, 1830–1917." In *Literature and Western Civilization 5: The Modern World 2: Realities*, ed. David Daiches and Anthony Thorlby. London: Aldus, 1972.
Schoolfield, George C., ed. *A History of Finland's Literature*. Lincoln: University of Nebraska Press, 1998.

———. "The Postwar Novel of Swedish Finland." *Scandinavian Studies* 34 (1962): 85–110.
———. "Some Reflections on Finland's Literature." *Books from Finland* 6, no. 3 (1972): 2–7.
Shavit, Zohar. *Poetics of Children's Literature*. Athens: University of Georgia Press, 1986.
Simonsuuri, Kirsti. "From Orality to Modernity: Aspects of Finnish Poetry in the Twentieth Century." *World Literature Today* 63 (1989): 52–54.
Varpio, Yrjö. *The History of Finnish Literary Criticism, 1828–1918*. Tampere, Finland: Societas Scintiarum Fennica, 1990.
Wrede, Johan. "The Birth of Finland-Swedish Modernism: A Study in the Social Dynamics of Ideas." *Scandinavica* 15 (1976): 73–103.

Select Bibliography for Specific Writers

Juhani Aho

Alanen, Antti. "Aho and Stiller." *Film History: An International Journal* 13, no. 1 (2001): 65–70.

Minna Canth

Lassila, Pertti. "The Power of the Powerless." *Books from Finland* 2 (1994): 105–6.

Bo Carpelan

Westö, Martin. "Fruits of Reading." *Books from Finland* 4 (1998): 272–76.

Walentin Chorell

Salminen, Johannes. "Walentin Chorell: An Appreciation." *American Scandinavian Review* 56 (1968): 136–39.
Warburton, Thomas. "Literary Portraits: Walentin Chorell." *Books from Finland* 3, no. 3 (1969): 11–12.

Elmer Diktonius

Larsson, Jörgen. "Two Poems, Two Kinds of Rhythm, Two Kinds of Wind." *Language and Literature* 21 (1996): 65–94.
Schoolfield, George C. *Elmer Diktonius*. Westport, Conn.: Greenwood, 1985.

Rabbe Enckell

Schoolfield, George C. "Rabbe Enckell's 'Mot Itaka.' " *Germanic Notes* 7 (1976): 17–22, 36–39.

Monika Fagerholm

Dickens, Eric. "Monika Fagerholm." *Swedish Book Review* Supp. (1992): 86–89.
Ekman, Michel. "Going on a Summer Holiday." *Books from Finland* 2 (1995): 92–94.
Hiidenheimo, Silja. "New Worlds." *Books from Finland* 3 (1998): 184–87.
Sundholm, John. "The Non-Place of Identity: On the Poetics of a Minority Culture." In *Beyond Boundaries: Textual Representations of European Identity*, ed. Andy Hollis. Amsterdam, Netherlands: Rodopi, 2000.

Lars Huldén

Thompson, Laurie. "The World According to Lars Huldén." *Swedish Book Review* 1–2 (1992): 34.

Tove Jansson

Bertills, Yvonne. *Beyond Identification: Proper Names in Children's Literature.* Turku, Finland: Åbo Akademi University Press, 2003.
Huse, Nancy. "The Blank Mirror of Death: Protest as Self-Creation in Contemporary Fantasy." *Lion and the Unicorn: A Critical Journal of Children's Literature* 12, no. 2 (1988): 28–43.
———. "Tove Jansson and Her Readers: No One Excluded." *Children's Literature: Annual of the Modern Language Association Division on Children's Literature and the Children's Literature Association* 19 (1991): 149–61.
Jones, W. Glyn. "Moomin Magic." *Swedish Book Review* 2 (2001): 2–4.
———. *Tove Jansson.* Boston: Twayne, 1984.

Eeva Joenpelto

Laitinen, Kai. "Life at the Turning Point: Eeva Joenpelto and Her Lohja Trilogy." *World Literature Today* 54 (1980): 33–37.
Lehtola, Erkka. "Eeva Joenpelto: Portraits of Change." *Books from Finland* 21, no. 1 (1987): 25–28.
Lehtonen, Soila. "The Price of a Free Lunch." *Books from Finland* 4 (1994): 255–57.

Aino Kallas

DuBois, Thomas A. "Writing of Women, Not Nations: The Development of a Feminist Agenda in the Novellas of Aino Kallas." *Scandinavian Studies* 76 (2004): 205–32.
Laitinen, Kai. "Aino Kallas 1878–1956: Ambassador Extraordinary." *Books from Finland* 12 (1978): 159–63.
Makkonen, Anna. " 'My Own Novel, Yes, Really!': The Early Diary of Aino Kallas and Reading for the Plot." *Scandinavian Studies* 71 (1999): 419–52.

Ilmari Kianto

DuBois, Thomas. "A Farmwife's Lot: The Politics of Portrayal in Ilmari Kianto's *Punainen viiva* and *Ryysyrannan Jooseppi*." *Scandinavian Studies* 65 (1993): 521–38.

Christer Kihlman

Zuck, Virpi. "The Finno-Swedish Genre Problem: Sign of a Social Ailment or a Linguistic Handicap?" *Proceedings of the Pacific Northwest Conference on Foreign Languages* 28 (1977): 104–7.

Aleksis Kivi

Laitinen, Kai. "Aleksis Kivi (1834–1872): The Man and His Work." *Books from Finland* 18 (1984): 100–4.
Paddon, Seija. "Aleksis Kivi and the Finnish Georgics." *Scandinavian-Canadian Studies/Etudes Scandinaves au Canada* 5 (1992): 65–79.
Vähämäki, K. Börje. "Aleksis Kivi's Kullervo: A Historical Drama of Ideas." *Scandinavian Studies* 50 (1978): 269–91.

Leena Krohn

Landon, Philip, and Richard Impola. "Leena Krohn." *Review of Contemporary Fiction* 16, no. 2 (1996): 65–78.
Nestingen, Andrew. "Timely Subjects: Leena Krohn between Universal and Particular." *Scandinavian Studies* 76 (2004): 233–56.

Joel Lehtonen

Tarkka, Pekka. "Joel Lehtonen and Putkinotko." *Books from Finland* 11 (1977): 239–45.

Eine Leino

Sarajas, Annamari. "Eino Leino, 1878–1926." *Books from Finland* 12 (1978): 40–46.

Väinö Linna

Moates, Tom. "Master of the Epic Novel." *Scandinavian Review* 89, no. 3 (2002): 16–19.
Rintala, Marvin. "Vaino Linna and the Finnish Condition." *Journal of Baltic Studies* 8 (1977): 223–31.
Varpio, Yrjo. "Vaino Linna: A Classic in His Own Time." *Books from Finland* 11 (1977): 192–97.

Elias Lönnrot

Alphonso-Karkala, John B. "Transformation of Folk Narratives into Epic Composition in Elias Lönnrot's *Kalevala*." *Jahrbuch für Volksliedforschung* 31 (1986): 13–28.
DuBois, Thomas A. *Finnish Folk Poetry and the Kalevala*. New York: Garland Press, 1995.
———. "Narrative Expectations and the Sampo Song." *Scandinavian Studies* 73 (2001): 457–74.
Hämäläinen, Niina. "Elias Lönnrot's First Kullervo Poem and Its Folk-Poem Models." In *The Kalevala and the World's Traditional Epics*, ed. Lauri Honko. Helsinki: Finnish Literature Society, 2002.
Honko, Lauri. "The Five Performances of *Kalevala*." *FF Network*, 24 (2003): 6–17.
Oinas, Felix J. "Vänämöinen's 'Straw Stallion.' " *Journal of Baltic Studies* 11 (1980): 363–66.
Siikala, Anna-Leena. "Elias Lönnrot the Ethnographer." *FF Network* 25 (2003): 12–17.

Eeva-Liisa Manner

Ahokas, Jaakko A. "Eeva-Liisa Manner: Dropping from Reality into Life." *Books Abroad* 47 (1973): 60–65.
Poom, Ritva. "Parallels in Finnish and Finland-Swedish Modernism: Eeva-Liisa Manner and Edith Södergran." In *Two Women Writers from Finland: Edith Södergran (1892–1923) and Hagar Olsson (1893–1978). Papers from the Symposium at Yale Univ., Oct. 21–23, 1993*, ed. George C. Schoolfield, Laurie Thompson, and Michael Schmelzle. Edinburgh: Lockharton, 1995.

Tuohimaa, Sinikka. "The Poetry of Eeva-Liisa Manner: Unveiling Reflections of Life." *World Literature Today* 61 (1987): 37–40.

Hagar Olsson

Rees, Ellen. "Hagar Olsson's *Chitambo* and the Ambiguities of Female Modernism." *Scandinavian Studies* 71 (1999): 191–206.
Schoolfield, George C. "Hagar Olsson's Chitambo: Anniversary Thoughts on Names and Structure." *Scandinavian Studies* 45 (1973): 223–62.
Schoolfield, George C., Laurie Thompson, and Michael Schmelzle, eds. *Two Women Writers from Finland: Edith Södergran (1892–1923) and Hagar Olsson (1893–1978). Papers from the Symposium at Yale Univ., Oct. 21–23, 1993.* Edinburgh: Lockharton, 1995.
Törnqvist, Egil. "Hagar Olsson's First Play." *Scandinavica* 15 (1976): 63–72.
Zuck, Virpi. "In Defense of Human Dignity: Hagar Olsson and *Tidevarvet*." In *Studies in German and Scandinavian Literature after 1500: Festschrift for George C. Schoolfield*, ed. James A. Parente Jr. and Richard Erich Schade. Columbia, S.C.: Camden House, 1993.

Johan Ludvig Runeberg

Schoolfield, George. "Transfigured Moments: Johan Ludvig Runeberg." *Scandinavian Review* 75, no. 1 (1987): 70–85.
Wrede, Johan. "Runeberg's *Fänrik Ståls sägner*: On the Life and Significance of a Patriotic Work." In *Studies in German and Scandinavian Literature after 1500: Festschrift for George C. Schoolfield*, ed. James A. Parente Jr. and Richard Erich Schade. Columbia, S.C.: Camden House, 1993.
Wretö, Tore. *J. L. Runeberg*. Boston: Twayne, 1980.

Runar Schildt

Schoolfield, George C. "Runar Schildt: Life Is an Outsider." *Books from Finland* 22, no. 3 (1988): 154–62.
Westö, Kjell. "The Man Who Saw Helsinki." *Books from Finland* 2 (1997): 127–29.
Zuck, Virpi. "The Finno-Swedish Short Story." *Scandinavian Studies* 49 (1977): 180–87.

Solveig von Schoultz

Born, Anne. "The Undefinitive Translation of Poetry." *Professional Translator and Interpreter* 3 (1991): 13–15.

Schoolfield, George C. "The Narrative of Solveig von Schoultz." *Swedish Book Review* 1 (1989): 19–26.

Frans Eemil Sillanpää

Kinneavy, Gerald. "Sillanpää." *Scandinavica* 20 (1981): 205–12.
Orton, Gavin. "F. E. Sillanpää's *Människor i sommarnatten*: A Musical Suite." *Edda* 92 (1992): 147–58.
Paddon, Seija. "The De-Centred Subject in F. E. Sillanpää's Short Fiction." *Scandinavica* 29 (1990): 207–13.

Edith Södergran

Broomans, Petra, Adriaan van der Hoeven, and Jytte Kronig, eds. *Edith Södergran: A Changing Image: Looking for a New Perspective on the Work of a Finnish Avant-garde Poet. Proc. of the seminar on 27–5–1992 at the Univ. of Groningen (Department of Scandinavian Studies and Department of Fenno-Ugric Studies).* Groningen, Netherlands: Werkgroep Vrouwenstudies, RUG, 1993.
Holm, Birgitta. "Edith Södergran and the Sexual Discourse of the Fin-de-Siècle." *Nordic Journal of Women's Studies* 1, no. 1 (1993): 21–31.
Humpál, Martin. "The God-Motif in Edith Södergran's Poetry." In *Åndelige rum/ Geistige Räume: Festskrift til Wolf Wucherpfennig*, ed. Karin Bang and Uwe Geist. Roskilde, Denmark: Roskilde Universitetscenter, 2002.
Norseng, Mary Kay. "Przybyszewska's Poetry in the Bright Light of Södergran's." In *Studies in German and Scandinavian Literature after 1500: Festschrift for George C. Schoolfield*, ed. James A. Parente Jr. and Richard Erich Schade. Columbia, S.C.: Camden House, 1993.
Schoolfield, George C. *Edith Södergran: Modernist Poet in Finland*. Westport, Conn.: Greenwood Press, 1984.
Schoolfield, George C., Laurie Thompson, and Michael Schmelzle, eds. *Two Women Writers from Finland: Edith Södergran (1892–1923) and Hagar Olsson (1893–1978). Papers from the Symposium at Yale Univ., Oct. 21–23, 1993.* Edinburgh: Lockharton, 1995.

Märta Tikkanen

Garton, Janet. "Little Red Riding Hood Comes of Age: Or, When the Fantastic Becomes the Feminist." In *Papers in European Languages, Literatures and Culture: Essays in Memory of Michael Parkinson and Janine Dakyns*, ed. Christopher Smith and Mike Carr. Norwich, U.K.: School of Modern Langues and European Studies, University of East Anglia, 1996.

Zacharias Topelius

Apo, Satu. "The Two Worlds of the Finnish Fairytale: Observations on the Folk and Literary Fairytale Tradition of the 19th Century." *Arv: Nordic Yearbook of Folklore* 44 (1988): 27–48.
Hatavara, Mari. "History, the Historical Novel and Nation: The First Finnish Historical Novels as National Narrative." *Neophilologus* 86, no. 1 (2002): 1–15.
Schoolfield, George C. "Fairy Tales of a Journalist." *Books from Finland* 18, no. 1 (1984): 9–19.

Nils-Aslak Valkeapää

Dana, Kathleen Osgood. " 'When a Lapp Is out on the High Fells': Literary Voice and Cultural Identity for the Sámi." *Scandinavian Studies* 75 (2003): 201–28.
Gaski, Harald. "The Son of the Sun Is Dead: A Commemoration of Nils-Aslak Valkeapää." *Scandinavian Studies* 75 (2003): 149–52.
Landon, Philip. "Nils-Aslak Valkeapää." *Review of Contemporary Fiction* 16, no. 2 (1996): 140–44.

Mika Waltari

Pyrhönen, Heta. "Five-Finger Exercises: Mika Waltari's Detective Stories." *Orbis Litterarum: International Review of Literary Studies* 59, no. 1 (2004): 23–38.
Syväoja, Hannu. "Against Ideology." *Books from Finland* 4 (1995): 280–81.

Kjell Westö

Dickens, Eric. "Kjell Westö." *Swedish Book Review* Supp. (1992): 90–98.

ICELAND

Bibliographic Resources

Mitchell, P. M., and Kenneth H. Ober. *Bibliography of Modern Icelandic Literature in Translation: Including Works Written by Icelanders in Other Languages.* Ithaca, N.Y.: Cornell University Press, 1975.
Ober, Kenneth H. *Bibliography of Modern Icelandic Literature in Translation: Supplement, 1971–1980.* Ithaca, N.Y.: Cornell University Press, 1990.

Literary History and Criticism

Andersson, Theodore M. "The Emergence of Vernacular Literature in Iceland." *Mosaic: A Journal for the Interdisciplinary Study of Literature* 8, no. 4 (1975): 161–69.

Chapman, Kenneth G. "From Edda to Atom: A Brief Look at Contemporary Icelandic Poetry." *Books Abroad* 38 (1964): 5–10.

Beck, Richard. *History of Icelandic Poets 1800–1940.* Ithaca, N.Y.: Cornell University Press, 1950.

Einarsson, Stefán. "Hexameter in Icelandic Literature." *Modern Language Notes* 68, no. 5 (1953): 351–54.

———. *A History of Icelandic Literature.* New York: Johns Hopkins University Press, 1957.

———. *History of Icelandic Prose Writers, 1800–1940.* Ithaca, N.Y.: Cornell University Press, 1948.

———. "Letter from Iceland." *Books Abroad* 39 (1965): 296–97.

Einarsson, Sveinn. "The Theatre System of Iceland." In *Theatre Worlds in Motion: Structures, Politics and Developments in the Countries of Western Europe*, ed. Hans van Maanen and Steve E. Wilmer. Amsterdam, Netherlands: Rodopi, 1998.

Gislason, Gylfi Th. "Problems of Icelandic Culture." *American Scandinavian Review* 54 (1966): 241–48.

Gudmundsson, Finnbogi. "America in Icelandic Literature: From a Critical Point of View." In *Amerika og Norden*, ed. Lars Ahnebrink. Stockholm: Alvqvist and Wiksell, 1964.

Hughes, Shaun F. D. "The Re-Emergence of Women's Voices in Icelandic Literature, 1500–1800." In *Cold Counsel: Women in Old Norse Literature and Mythology: A Collection of Essays*, ed. Sarah M. Anderson and Karen Swenson. New York: Routledge, 2000.

Magnusson, Sigurdur A. "Icelandic Literature: Preserver of National Culture." *Mosaic: A Journal for the Interdisciplinary Study of Literature* 1, no. 3 (1968): 83–93.

———. "The Modern Icelandic Novel: From Isolation to Political Awareness." *Mosaic: A Journal for the Interdisciplinary Study of Literature* 4, no. 2 (1970): 133–43.

———. "Nature in Icelandic Poetry." *Literary Review: An International Journal of Contemporary Writing* 39 no. 4 (1996): 505–8.

———. "Postwar Literature in Iceland." *World Literature Today* 56 (1982): 18–23.

Senner, W. M. "The Emergence of Literary Criticism and Poetics in Eighteenth-Century Iceland." *Scandinavica* 36 (1997): 189–216.

Simpson, Jacqueline. *Icelandic Folktales and Legends.* Berkeley: University of California Press, 1972.

Steblin-Kamenskij, M. I. "Folklore and Literature in Iceland and the Problem of Literary Progress." *Scandinavica* 11 (1972): 127–36.

Stevens, Patrick J., ed. *Icelandic Writers*. Boston: Gale, 2004.
Tomasson, Richard F. "The Literacy of the Icelanders." *Scandinavian Studies* 47 (1975): 66–93.
Woods, Leigh. "Iceland: The Contemporary Theatre Scene." *Western European Stages* 13, no. 1 (2001): 99–102.
———. "Theater in Iceland: The Quest for National Identity." *Scandinavian Review* 73, no. 3 (1985): 55–63.

Select Bibliography for Specific Writers

Gunnar Gunnarsson

Beck, Richard. "Gunnar Gunnarsson: Some Observations." In *Scandinavian Studies: Essays Presented to Dr. Henry Goddard Leach on the Occasion of His Eighty-Fifth Birthday*, ed. Carl F. Bayerschmidt and Erik J. Friis. Seattle: University of Washington Press, 1965.
Höskuldsson, Sveinn Skorri. "Gunnar Gunnarsson and Icelandic Folktales." In *Úr Dölum til Dala: Guðbrandur Vigfússon Centenary Essays*, ed. Rory McTurk and Andrew Wawn. Leeds, U.K.: Leeds Studies in English, 1989.

Jónas Hallgrímsson

Ringler, Dick. *Bard of Iceland: Jónas Hallgrímsson, Poet and Scientist*. Madison: University of Wisconsin Press, 2002.

Svava Jakobsdóttir

Magnusson, Sigurdur A., and Dennis Auburn Hill. "The Icelandic Short Story." *Scandinavian Studies* 49 (1977): 208–12.

Halldór Kiljan Laxness

Eysteinsson, Ástráður. "Halldór Laxness and the Narrative of the Icelandic Novel." *Scandinavica* 42 (2003): 47–66.
Guðmundsdóttir, Gunnþórunn. "Becoming a Writer: Halldór Laxness and the Memoir." *Scandinavica* 42 (2003): 95–107.
Guðmundsson, Halldór. "In Search of the Most Precious Pearl: On the Life and Works of Halldór Laxness." *Scandinavica* 42 (2003): 29–45.
Hallberg, Peter. *Halldor Laxness*. New York: Twayne, 1971.
———. "Halldór Laxness and the Icelandic Sagas." *Leeds Studies in English* 13 (1982): 1–22.

Hallmundsson, Hallberg. "Halldór Laxness and the Sagas of Modern Iceland." *Georgia Review* 49, no. 1 (1995): 34–45.
Magnusson, Magnus. "The Fish Can Sing: Translation and Reception of Halldór Laxness in the UK and USA." *Scandinavica* 42 (2003): 13–28.
Magnusson, Sigurdur A. "The World of Halldór Laxness." *World Literature Today* 66 (1992): 457–63.
Palsson, Hermann. "Beyond the Atom Station." In *Ideas and Ideologies*, ed. Sveinn Skorri Hoskuldsson. Reykjavík: University of Iceland, 1975.
Talmor, Sascha. "Halldór Kiljan Laxness, the Bell of Iceland." *European Legacy: Toward New Paradigm* 7, no. 5 (2002): 621–40.

Thor Vilhjálmsson

Hallberg, Peter. "The One Who Sees: The Icelandic Writer Thor Vilhjalmsson." *Books Abroad* 47 (1973): 54–59.

NORWAY

Bibliographic Resources

Grønland, Erling. *Norway in English*. Oslo: Norwegian Universities Press, 1961.
Hoberman, John. "Bibliographical Spectrum." *Review of National Literatures* 12 (1983): 185–207.
Næss, Harald. *Norwegian Literary Bibliography 1956–1970*. Oslo: Universitetsforlaget, 1976.
Ng, Maria, and Michael Batts, compilers. *Scandinavian Literature in English Translation*. Vancouver: Canadian Association of University Teachers of German, 1978.
Sather, Leland B. *Norway*. World Bibliographical Series 67. Oxford: Clio Press, 1986.

Literary History and Criticism

Beyer, Harald. *A History of Norwegian Literature*. New York: American-Scandinavian Foundation, 1956.
Contemporary Norwegian Prose Writers. Oslo: Norwegian University Press, 1985.
Garton, Janet. "New Directions in Norwegian Literature." *Review of National Literatures* 12 (1983): 163–84.
———. *Norwegian Woman Writers, 1850–1990*. London: Athlone Press, 1992.
Masat, Andras. "Modernism, Realism, and Some Other Terms: The Conception and

Praxis of the Writer in Norwegian Prose during the Past Twenty Years." *New Comparison* 4 (1987): 151–63.

Mawby, Janet. "The Norwegian Novel Today." *Scandinavica* 14 (1975): 101–13.

McFarlane, James. *Ibsen and the Temper of Norwegian Literature.* London: Oxford University Press, 1960.

Naess, Harald S, ed. *A History of Norwegian Literature.* Lincoln: University of Nebraska Press, 1993.

Rasmussen, Janet. "Dreams and Discontent: The Female Voice in Norwegian Literature." *Review of National Literatures* 12 (1983): 123–40.

———. "Feminist Criticism and Women's Literature in Norway: A Status Report." *Edda* 80 (1980): 45–52.

Sjåvik, Jan. *Reading for the Truth: Rhetorical Constructions in Norwegian Fiction.* Christchurch, New Zealand: Cybereditions, 2004.

Skard, Sigmund. *Classical Tradition in Norway: An Introduction with Bibliography.* Oslo: Universitetsforlaget, 1980.

Thresher, Tanya, ed. *Twentieth-Century Norwegian Writers.* New York: Gale, 2004.

Vold, Karin Beate. "Contemporary Norwegian Writing for Children." *News from the Top of the World* 2 (1989): 40–53.

Ystad, Vigdis. "Recent Trends in Norwegian Literary Criticism." *Scandinavian Studies* 57 (1985): 32–44.

Select Bibliography for Specific Writers

Ivar Aasen

Walton, Stephen. *Farewell the Spirit Craven: Ivar Aasen and National Romanticism.* Oslo: Det Norske Samlaget, 1987.

———. "Ludvig Holberg and Ivar Aasen's *Ervingen.*" *New Comparison: A Journal of Comparative and General Literary Studies* 3 (1987): 52–61.

Jens Bjørneboe

Bisztray, George. "Semmelweis as Literary Hero." *Hungarian Studies Review* 24, nos. 1–2 (1997): 65–71.

Garton, Janet. *Jens Bjørneboe: Prophet without Honor.* Westport, Conn.: Greenwood Press, 1985.

———. " 'A Vision of a Continual Battle': Jens Bjørneboe and the Theatre." *Scandinavica* 23 (1984): 137–60.

Hoberman, John M. "The Political Imagination of Jens Bjørneboe: A Study of *Under en hårdere himmel.*" *Scandinavian Studies* 48 (1976): 52–70.

Longum, Leif. "In the Shadow of Ibsen: His Influence on Norwegian Drama and on Literary Attitudes." *Review of National Literatures* 12 (1983): 78–100.

Martin, Joe. *Keepers of the Protocols: The Works of Jens Bjørneboe in the Crosscurrents of Western Literature.* New York: Peter Lang, 1996.
Mishler, William. "Jens Bjørneboe, Anthroposophy and Hertug Hans." *Edda* 87 (1987): 167–78.
Mussari, Mark. "Color: The Material of Immateriality in Jens Bjørneboe's *Blåmann.*" *Edda* 99 (1999): 340–49.
Schmiesing, Ann. "Nazi Germany and the Holocaust in Norwegian Literature." In *German Studies in the Post-Holocaust Age: The Politics of Memory, Identity, and Ethnicity,* ed. Adrian Del Caro and Janet Ward. Boulder: University Press of Colorado, 2000.

Bjørnstjerne Bjørnson

Andersen, Arlow W. "American Politics in 1880: Norwegian Observations." *Scandinavian Studies* 40 (1968): 233–47.
Bredsdorff, Elias. "Moralists versus Immoralists: The Great Battle in Scandinavian Literature in the 1880's." *Scandinavica* 8 (1969): 91–111.
Larson, Harald. *Bjørnstjerne Bjørnson: A Study in Norwegian Nationalism.* New York: King's Croom Press, 1944.
Modalsli, Tone. "Ibsen, Bjørnson and Bernhard Dunker, 1864–66: New Material in the Manuscript Collection of the National Library of Norway, Oslo Division." *Ibsen Studies* 1, no. 2 (2001): 94–106.
Noreng, Harald. "Bjørnson Research: A Survey." *Scandinavica* 4 (1965): 1–15.
Rottem, Oystein. "The Multifarious Bjørnson." *Scandinavica* 24 (1985): 59–64.
Schmiesing, Ann. "The Christiania Theater and Norwegian Nationalism: Bjørnson's Defense of the 1856 Whistle Concerts in 'Pibernes Program.'" *Scandinavian Studies* 76 (2004): 317–40.
Sehmsdorf, Henning. "Bjørnson's Trond and Popular Tradition." *Scandinavian Studies* 41 (1969): 56–66.
———. "The Self in Isolation: A New Reading of Bjornson's *Arne.*" *Scandinavian Studies* 45 (1973): 310–23.

Johan Borgen

Birn, Randi. "Dream and Reality in Johan Borgen's Short Stories." *Scandinavian Studies* 46 (1974): 59–72.
———. *Johan Borgen.* New York: Twayne, 1974.
———. "The Quest for Authenticity in Three Novels by Johan Borgen." *Mosaic: A Journal for the Interdisciplinary Study of Literature* 4, no. 2 (1970): 91–99.
Mishler, William. "Metaphor and Metonymy in Johan Borgen's *Eksempler.*" *Scandinavica* 16 (1977): 11–21.
Peterson, Ronald E. "Johan Borgen and Dostoevsky: Some Remarks." *Germano-*

Slavica: A Canadian Journal of Germanic and Slavic Comparative Studies 4 (1982): 101–7.

Gerd Brantenberg

Barr, Marleen S. " 'Laughing in a Liberating Defiance': *Egalia's Daughters* and Feminist Tendentious Humor." In *Discontented Discourses: Feminism/Textual Intervention/Psychoanalysis*, ed. Marleen S. Barr and Richard Feldstein. Urbana: University of Illinois Press, 1989.

Moberg, Verne. "A Norwegian Women's Fantasy: Gerd Brantenberg's *Egalias døtre* as *kvinneskelig* Utopia." *Scandinavian Studies* 57 (1985): 325–32.

Camilla Collett

Garton, Janet. "Women and Literature—Camilla Collett: *Amtmandens Døtre* and the Critics." In *Proceedings of the Conference of Scandinavian Studies in Great Britain and Northern Ireland Held at the University of Surrey: April, 1983*, ed. Nigel Reeves. Surrey, U.K.: University of Surrey Press, n.d.

Rasmussen, Janet. "The Byronic Lover in Scandinavian Fiction." *Pacific Northwest Council on Foreign Languages: Proceedings* 29 (1978) and 30 (1979): 119–23.

Ørjasæter, Kristin. "From Muse to Author: Romantic Rhetoric in Camilla Collett's Diary from the 1830s." *Scandinavian Studies* 76 (2004): 121–36.

Olav Duun

Birkeland, Bjarte. "Olav Duun." *Scandinavica* 10 (1971): 112–21.

Naess, Harald. "Olav Duun Abroad." In *Grenzerfahrung-Grenzüberschreitung: Studien zu den Literaturen Skandinaviens und Deutschlands*, ed. Leonie Marx and Herbert Knust. Heidelberg: Carl Winter, 1989.

Vannebo, Einar. "Biblical Motifs in Olev Duun's *The People of Juvik*." *New Comparison: A Journal of Comparative and General Literary Studies* 4 (1987): 121–35.

Voss, James. "Olav Duun's *Menneske og maktene*: Form, Vision, and Contemporary Significance." *Scandinavian Studies* 52 (1980): 361–80.

Knut Faldbakken

Lessing, Doris. "A Tragedy in Sultry Yellow Light." *Norseman* 1991: 85–87.

Norseng, Mary Kay. "The Crippled Children: A Study of the Underlying Myth in Knut Faldbakken's Fiction." *Scandinavica* 22 (1983): 195–209.

Peterson, Ronald E. "Knut Faldbakken: A Norwegian Contemporary." *Scandinavian Review* 73, no. 3 (1985): 80–85.
Schnurbein, Stefanie von. "Failed Seductions: Crises of Masculinity in Knut Hamsun's *Pan* and Knut Faldbakken's *Glahn*." *Scandinavian Studies* 73 (2001): 147–64.

Johan Falkberget

Lybeck, Rick. "Three Structural Levels in Johan Falkberget's *Christianus Sextus*." *Edda* 94 (1994): 58–72.
Schmiesing, Ann. "Showing versus Telling: Johan Falkberget and the Interpretation of Scripture in *Den fjerde nattevakt*." *Scandinavica* 37 (1998): 66–85.

Jon Fosse

Sætre, Lars. "On the Terms of Words: Masks of a Christian Life." *Scandinavica* 40 (2001): 285–99.

Arne Garborg

Hageberg, Otto. "Premodernism and Postmodernism: 'Decadence' Before and Now." In *Fin(s) de Siècle in Scandinavian Perspective: Studies in Honor of Harald S. Naess*, ed. Faith Ingwersen and Mary Kay Norseng. Columbia, S.C.: Camden House, 1993.
Humpál, Martin. "Irony Revisited: Arne Garborg's *Trætte Mænd*." *Brünner Beiträge zur Germanistik und Nordistik* 15 (2001): 165–70.
Isaacson, Lanae Hjortsvang. "*Haugtussa*: Interweaving Traditional Theme, Character, and Motif." *Edda* 82 (1982): 325–39.
———. "The Poetry of the Past: Reminiscence and Recollection in Arne Garborg's Lyric Prose." *Edda* 85 (1985): 49–61.
———. " 'Son et lumière' in Arne Garborg's Poetry and Prose." *Scandinavica* 23 (1984): 39–50.
Massengale, James. *Haugtussa*: From Garborg to Grieg." *Scandinavian Studies* 53 (1981): 131–53.
Rygg, Kristin. "Mystification through Musicalization and Demystification through Music: The Case of *Haugtussa*." In *Cultural Functions of Intermedial Exploration*, ed. Erik Hedling and Ulla-Britta Lagerroth. Amsterdam, Netherlands: Rodopi, 2002.
Sjåvik, Jan. *Arne Garborgs Kristiania-romaner: En beretterteknisk studie*. Oslo: Aschehoug, 1985.

———. "Form and Theme in Garborg's Mannfolk and Hjaa ho Mor." *Selecta: Journal of the Pacific Northwest Council on Foreign Languages* 1 (1980): 87–90.

———. "Hulda Bergersen, Arne Garborg, and the Rhetoric of *Hjaa Ho Mor*." *Scandinavian Studies* 55 (1983): 134–48.

———. "Reading Arne Garborg's Irony: *Bondestudentar, Trætte mænd, Fred*." *Scandinavian Studies* 72 (2000): 63–88.

Espen Haavardsholm

Fristoe, James A. "Espen Haavardsholm's 'Zink' and the Norwegian Literary Class Struggle." *Scandinavian Studies* 57 (1985): 60–71.

Knut Hamsun

Bjørby, Pål. "Eros and Subjectivity: Knut Hamsun's *Pan* and Ragnhild Jølsen's *Rikka Gan*." In *Fin(s) de Siècle in Scandinavian Perspective: Studies in Honor of Harald S. Naess*, ed. Faith Ingwersen and Mary Kay Norseng. Columbia, S.C.: Camden House, 1993.

Buttry, Dolores. "Earth Mother or Femme Fatale? Femininity as Envisioned by Jean-Jacques Rousseau and Knut Hamsun." *Neophilologus* 72 (1988): 481–98.

———. "Knut Hamsun's Supposed Anti-Semitism: A Refutation." *Edda* 86 (1986): 123–33.

———. " 'Secret Suffering': Knut Hamsun's Allegory of the Creative Artist." *Studies in Short Fiction* 19, no. 1 (1982): 1–7.

Cease, Julie K. "Semiotics, City, *Sult*: Hamsun's Text of 'Hunger.' " *Edda* 92 (1992): 136–46.

Hagen, Erik Bjerck. "Truth and Ethics in Hamsun's *Mysteries*." *Edda* 96 (1996): 307–16.

Humpál, Martin. "Editing and Interpreting: Two Editions of Hamsun's *Pan* and the Question of the Fictional Authorship of 'Glahns død.' " *Edda* 98 (1998): 20–29.

———. "The Narrator in Knut Hamsun's *Børn av Tiden*." *Brünner Beiträge zur Germanistik und Nordistik* 12 (1998): 19–25.

———. *The Roots of Modernist Narrative: Knut Hamsun's Novels Hunger, Mysteries, and Pan*. Oslo: Solum, 1998.

Jernsletten, Kikki. "The Sámi in *Growth of the Soil*: Depictions, Desire, Denial." *Nordlit: Arbeidstidsskrift i litteratur* 15, no. 2 (2004): 73–89.

Kittang, Atle. "Knut Hamsun's *Sult*: Psychological Deep Structures and Metapoetic Plot." In *Facets of European Modernism: Essays in Honour of James McFarlane Presented to Him on His 65th Birthday 12 Dec. 1985*, ed. Janet Garton. Norwich, U.K.: University of East Anglia, 1985.

McFarlane, James. "The Whisper of the Blood: A Study of Knut Hamsun's Early Novels." *PMLA* 71 (1956): 563–94.

Næss, Harald. *Knut Hamsun*. Boston: Twayne, 1984.

———. "Knut Hamsun and *Growth of the Soil*." *Scandinavica* 25 (1986): 5–17.

Oxfeldt, Elisabeth. "Orientalism, Decadence and Ekphrasis in Hamsun's 'Dronningen av Saba.' " *Edda* 103 (2003): 181–94.

Popperwell, Ronald. "Knut Hamsun and *Pan*." *Scandinavica* 25 (1986): 19–31.

Sabo, Anne. "Knut Hamsun in *Paa gjengrodde stier*: Joker, *Übermensch*, or Sagacious Madman?" *Scandinavian Studies* 71 (1999): 453–74.

Sandberg, Mark B. "Writing on the Wall: The Language of Advertising in Knut Hamsun's *Sult*." *Scandinavian Studies* 71 (1999): 265–96.

Sehmsdorf, Henning. "Knut Hamsun's *Pan*: Myth and Symbol." *Edda* 74 (1974): 345–403.

Simpson, Allen. "Knut Hamsun's Anti-Semitism." *Edda* 77 (1977): 273–93.

———. "Midt i Forgjængelsens Karneval: *Markens Grøde* in Knut Hamsun's Authorship." *Scandinavian Studies* 56 (1984): 1–35.

Sjåvik, Jan. Lesning som sentral trope i Knut Hamsuns *Pan*." In *Modernismen i Skandinavisk litteratur som historisk fenomen og teoretisk problem*, ed. Asmund Lien. Trondheim, Norway: Universitetet i Trondheim, 1991.

———. "A New Psychological Novel, a New Narrative Technique, and Salvation through Art: Knut Hamsun's *Pan* and the Artist's Quest for Recognition." *Selecta: Journal of the Pacific Northwest Council on Foreign Languages* 4 (1983): 94–100.

———. "Triangular Structures in Knut Hamsun's *Pan*." *Pacific Coast Philology* 27 (1992): 117–23.

Wells, Marie. "A Narratological Analysis of Knut Hamsun's Novel *En Vandrer spiller med Sordin*." *Scandinavica* 42 (2003): 239–54.

Zagar, Monika. "Imagining the Red-Skinned Other: Hamsun's Article 'Fra en Indianerleir.' " *Edda* 101 (2001): 385–95.

———. "Knut Hamsun's Black Man or Lament for Paternalist Society: A Reading of Hamsun's Play *Livet ivold* through *Fra det moderne Amerikas Aandsliv*." *Edda* 97 (1997): 364–79.

———. "The Rhetoric of Defense in Hamsun's *Paa gjengrodde Stier* (*On Overgrown Paths*)." *Edda* 99 (1999): 252–61.

Maurits Hansen

Sjåvik, Jan. "Rhetorical Manipulation in Maurits Hansen's 'Luren.' " *Scandinavian Studies* 66 (1994): 521–32.

———. "A Rhetorical Approach to Three Norwegian Short Stories." *Selecta: Journal of the Pacific Northwest Council on Foreign Languages* 14 (1993): 79–82.

Alfred Hauge

Flatin, Kjetil A. "The Rising Sun and the Lark on the Quilt: Quest and Defiance in Alfred Hauge's Cleng Peerson Trilogy." *Proceedings of the Pacific Northwest Conference on Foreign Languages* 27 (1976): 133–36.

Sjåvik, Jan. "Alfred Hauge's Utstein Monastery Cycle." *World Literature Today* 56 (1982): 54–57.

Sigurd Hoel

Lyngstad, Sverre. "Sigurd Hoel and American Literature." *Edda* 84 (1984): 193–204.

———. *Sigurd Hoel's Fiction: Cultural Criticism and Tragic Vision.* Westport, Conn.: Greenwood Press, 1984.

———. "Sigurd Hoel: The Literary Critic." *Scandinavica* 22 (1983): 141–58.

Henrik Ibsen

Clurman, Harold. *Ibsen.* New York: Macmillan, 1977.

Downs, Brian W. *Ibsen: The Intellectual Background.* New York: Octagon, 1969.

Durbach, Errol. *'Ibsen the Romantic': Analogues of Paradise in the Later Plays.* Athens: University of Georgia Press, 1982.

Goldman, Michael. *Ibsen: The Dramaturgy of Fear.* New York: Columbia University Press, 1999.

Haugen, Einar. *Ibsen's Drama: Author to Audience.* Minneapolis: University of Minnesota Press, 1979.

Koht, Halvdan. *Life of Ibsen.* New York: Blom, 1971.

Lebowitz, Naomi. *Ibsen and the Great World.* Baton Rouge: Louisiana State University Press, 1990.

Lyons, Charles R., ed. *Critical Essays on Henrik Ibsen.* Boston: Hall, 1987.

———. *Henrik Ibsen: The Divided Consciousness.* Carbondale: Southern Illinois University Press, 1972.

McFarlane, James. *Ibsen and Meaning: Studies, Essays and Prefaces 1953–87.* Norwich, U.K.: Norvik Press, 1989.

Meyer, Michael. *Ibsen: A Biography.* Harmondsworth, U.K.: Penguin, 1974.

Northam, John. *Ibsen: A Critical Study.* London: Cambridge University Press, 1973.

———. *Ibsen's Dramatic Method: A Study of the Prose Dramas.* Oslo: Universitetsforlaget, 1971.

Templeton, Joan. *Ibsen's Women.* Cambridge: Cambridge University Press, 1997.

Theoharis, Theoharis Constantine. *Ibsen's Drama: Right Action and Tragic Joy.* New York: St. Martin's Press, 1996.

Young, Robin. *Time's Disinherited Children: Childhood, Regression and Sacrifice in the Plays of Henrik Ibsen*. Norwich, U.K.: Norvik Press, 1989.

Alexander L. Kielland

Sjåvik, Jan. "A Rhetorical Approach to Three Norwegian Short Stories." *Selecta: Journal of the Pacific Northwest Council on Foreign Languages* 14 (1993): 79–82.

Jan Kjærstad

Hageberg, Otto. "Premodernism and Postmodernism: 'Decadence' Before and Now." In *Fin(s) de Siècle in Scandinavian Perspective: Studies in Honor of Harald S. Naess*, ed. Faith Ingwersen and Mary Kay Norseng. Columbia, S.C.: Camden House, 1993.

Jonas Lie

Lyngstad, Sverre. *Jonas Lie*. Boston: Twayne, 1977.
———. "The Vortex and Related Imagery in Jonas Lie's Fiction." *Scandinavian Studies* 51 (1979): 211–48.
Øyslebø, Olaf. "Nonverbal Presentation of Narrative Characters: Two Aspects of the Visualizing Art of Jonas Lie in *The Family at Gilje*." *Livstegn: Journal of the Norwegian Association for Semiotic Studies* 3 (1987): 181–92.

Cecilie Løveid

Thresher, Tanya. "Bringing Ibsen's *Brand* into the Twentieth Century: Cecilie Løveid's *Østerrike*." *Scandinavian Studies* 74 (2002): 47–60.
———. "The Polymorphous Female Subject in Cecilie Løveid's *Barock Friise*." *Edda* 102 (2002): 202–16.

Ole E. Rølvaag

Eddy, Sara. " 'Wheat and Potatoes': Reconstructing Whiteness in O. E. Rølvaag's Immigrant Trilogy." *MELUS: Journal of the Society for the Study of the Multi-Ethnic Literature of the United States* 26 (2001): 129–49.
Haugen, Einar. *Ole Edvart Rölvaag*. Boston: Twayne, 1983.
Kongslien, Ingeborg R. "Emigration: The Dream of Freedom and Land—And an Existential Quest." In *Fin(s) de Siècle in Scandinavian Perspective: Studies in*

Honor of Harald S. Naess, ed. Faith Ingwersen and Mary Kay Norseng. Columbia, S.C.: Camden House, 1993.
Moseley, Ann. *Ole Edvart Rølvaag*. Boise, Idaho: Boise State University Press, 1987.
Paulson, Kristoffer. "What Was Lost: Ole Rølvaag's *The Boat of Longing*." *MELUS: Journal of the Society for the Study of the Multi-Ethnic Literature of the United States* 7, no. 1 (1980): 51–60.
Reigstad, Paul. *Rolvaag: His Life and Art*. Lincoln: University of Nebraska Press, 1972.
Simonson, Harold P. *Prairies Within: The Tragic Trilogy of Ole Rölvaag*. Seattle: University of Washington Press, 1987.
———. "Rolvaag and Kierkegaard." *Scandinavian Studies* 49 (1977): 67–80.
———. "Rølvaag's Beret Revisited: A Rejoinder." *Norwegian-American Studies* 35 (2000): 141–51.
Sjåvik, Jan. "Between Two Worlds: The Emigrant Novels of Ole E. Rølvaag." In *Places Within, Places Beyond: Norwegian Regionalism in Literature*, ed. Wendy Griswold and Fredrik Engelstad. Oslo: Institute for Social Research, 1996.
Quantic, Diane D. "Fairy Castle or Steamer Trunk? Creating Place in O. E. Rølvaag's *Giants in the Earth*." *Great Plains Quarterly* 23 (2003): 245–59.

Cora Sandel

Hunt, Linda. "The Alberta Trilogy: Cora Sandel's Norwegian Künstlerroman and American Feminist Literary Discourse." In *Writing the Woman Artist: Essays on Poetics, Politics, and Portraiture*, ed. Suzanne W. Jones. Philadelphia: University of Pennsylvania Press, 1991.
Rees, Ellen. "Cora Sandel's *Kjøp ikke Dondi*: '... som de snakker, de menneskene.' " *Scandinavica* 34 (1995): 221–35.
———. "Escape from the Novel: Cora Sandel's *Kranes konditori*." *Scandinavian Studies* 72 (2000): 181–98.
———. "The Riddle Solved: Cora Sandel's 'En gåte.' " *Studies in Short Fiction* 31 (1994): 13–21.
———. "A Quiet Renaissance in Cora Sandel Scholarship." *Scandinavian Studies* 75 (2003): 591–600.
Rokkan, Elizabeth. "Cora Sandel and the Second World War." *Scandinavica* 28 (1989): 155–59.
———. "Cora Sandel's War Story: Stort syn og smått syn." *Scandinavica* 26 (1987): 5–12.
Zuck, Virpi. "Cora Sandel: A Norwegian Feminist." *Edda* 81 (1981): 23–33.

Aksel Sandemose

Birn, Randi. *Aksel Sandemose: Exile in Search of a Home*. Westport, Conn.: Greenwood Press, 1984.

Hale, Christopher S. "Aksel Sandemose's Observations on Racial Prejudice in Prairie Canada of the 1920's." *Selecta: Journal of the Pacific Northwest Council on Foreign Languages* 7 (1986): 131–36.

———. "Aksel Sandemose's View of Prairie Canada." *Scandinavian-Canadian Studies/Etudes Scandinaves au Canada* 4 (1991): 61–76.

———. "Ethnic Minorities on the Canadian Prairies in the Writings of Aksel Sandemose and Sven Delblanc." *Scandinavian-Canadian Studies/Etudes Scandinaves au Canada* 8 (1995): 37–55.

Humpál, Martin. "The Fifth Commandment of the Jante Law and the Theme of Self-Knowledge in Sandemose's *En flyktning krysser sitt spor*." *Brünner Beiträge zur Germanistik und Nordistik* 16 (2002): 191–97.

Jensen, Hans J. L. "René Girard and Aksel Sandemose: The Question of Salvation from Mimetic Double-Binds." *Literature and Theology: An International Journal of Theory, Criticism and Culture* 7, no. 1 (1993): 66–77.

Lien, Asmund. "Sandemose's America." In *Americana-Norvegica: Studies in Scandinavian-American Interrelations Dedicated to Einar Haugen*, ed. Harald S. Naess and Sigmund Skard. Oslo: Universitetsforlaget, 1971.

Nielsen, Erling. "Aksel Sandemose: Investigator of the Mystery of Human Nature." *Scandinavica* 8 (1969): 1–18.

Schnurbein, Stefanie von. "Masking the Trauma: Psychoanalysis and Social Criticism in Aksel Sandemose's *En flyktning krysser sitt spor* [*A Fugitive Crosses His Tracks*]." *Edda* 102 (2002): 408–18.

Vaeth, Johannes. "Misery Harbor." *Kriterium* 2, no. 3 (1967): 38–45.

Amalie Skram

Langås, Unni. "The Struggle for the Body: Hysteria and Rebellion in Amalie Skram's Novel *Professor Hieronimus*." *Scandinavian Studies* 75 (2003): 55–88.

Luxembourg, Jan van. "Servants, Genre and Rhetoric: Some Aspects of Amalie Skram's *Constance Ring*." *Edda* 92 (1992): 336–48.

Rasmussen, Janet. "Amalie Skram as Literary Critic." *Edda* 81 (1981): 1–11.

Dag Solstad

Garton, Janet. "Dag Solstad and Profil." In *Facets of European Modernism: Essays in Honour of James McFarlane Presented to Him on His 65th Birthday 12 Dec. 1985*, ed. Janet Garton. Norwich, U.K.: University of East Anglia, 1985.

Heith, Anne. "The Emergence of an Aesthetic Object: Dag Solstad's *The Front Side of the Medal*." In *Documentarism in Scandinavian Literature*, ed. Poul Houe and Sven Hakon Rossel. Amsterdam, Netherlands: Rodopi, 1997.

Kittang, Atle. *Allegory, Intertextuality and Irony in Dag Solstad*. Minneapolis: Center for Nordic Studies, 1989.

Sehmsdorf, Henning K. "From Individualism to Communism: The Political and Esthetic Transformation of Dag Solstad's Authorship." *Proceedings of the Pacific Northwest Conference on Foreign Languages* 27 (1976): 130–32.

Sjåvik, Jan. "Language and Myth in Dag Solstad's *Arild Asnes, 1970.*" *Pacific Coast Philology* 18 (1983): 30–36.

Zagar, Monika. *Ideological Clowns: Dag Solstad—From Modernism to Politics.* Vienna: Praesens, 2002.

———. "Modernism and Aesthetic Dictatorship: Dag Solstad's Journey from the 1960s to the 1970s." *Scandinavian Studies* 72 (2000): 199–230.

Sigrid Undset

Bjørby, Pål. "Recent Trends in Sigrid Undset Criticism." *Scandinavian Studies* 58 (1986): 308–12.

Harbison, Sherrill. "Medieval Aspects of Narcissism in Sigrid Undset's Modern Novels." *Scandinavian Studies* 63 (1991): 464–75.

Maman, Marie. *Sigrid Undset in America: An Annotated Bibliography and Research Guide.* Lanham, Md.: Scarecrow Press, 2000.

McCarthy, Colman. "Sigrid Undset." *Critic* 32 (1974): 58–64.

Rees, Ellen. "Dreaming of the Medieval in *Kristin Lavransdatter* and *Trollsyn.*" *Scandinavian Studies* 75 (2003): 399–416.

Reinert, Otto. "Unfashionable Kristin Lavransdatter." *Scandinavian Studies* 71 (1999): 67–80.

Sæther, Astrid. " 'Dazzling Dreams and Grey Days': On the Antithesis between Ideal and Reality in Sigrid Undset's Contemporary Novels and Short Stories." *Scandinavica* 29 (1990): 193–205.

Whitehouse, J. C. "Religion as Fulfillment in the Novels of Sigrid Undset." *Renascence: Essays on Values in Literature* 38, no. 1 (1985): 2–12.

Winsnes, A. H. *Sigrid Undset.* New York: Sheed and Ward, 1953.

Tarjei Vesaas

Blackwell, Marilyn Johns. "Primary Experience: Mattis and the Role of the Reader in Vesaas' *Fuglane.*" *Edda* 84 (1984): 129–43.

Chapman, Kenneth G. "Basic Themes and Motives in Vesaas' Earliest Writing." *Scandinavian Studies* 41 (1969): 126–37.

Dale, Johannes A. "Tarjei Vesaas." *American Scandinavian Review* 54 (1966): 369–74.

Hermundsgård, Frode. *Child of the Earth: Tarjei Vesaas and Scandinavian Primitivism.* New York: Greenwood Press, 1989.

———. "Depicting Subjectivity in the Film Adaptation of Tarjei Vesaas' Novel *Fuglane (The Birds).*" *Tijdschrift voor Skandinavistiek* 23 (2002): 243–71.

———. "Tarjei Vesaas and German Expressionist Theater." *Scandinavian Studies* 73 (2001): 125–46.
Nylander, Lars. "Omniscience and Phallocentrism in Tarjei Vesaas's *The Bridges*." *Literature and Psychology* 42, nos. 1–2 (1996): 41–64.
Stendahl, Brita K. "Tarjei Vesaas, a Friend." *Books Abroad* 42 (1968): 537–39.
Wilson, Catherine. "Capability and Language in the Novels of Tarjei Vesaas." *Philosophy and Literature* 27, no. 1 (2003): 21–39.

Bjørg Vik

Sjåvik, Jan. "Bjørg Vik's Short Story 'Annekset': A Programmatic Statement from a Woman Writer." In *Literature as Resistance and Counter-Culture: Papers from the 19th Study Conference of the International Association for Scandinavian Studies*, ed. András Masát. Budapest: Hungarian Association for Scandinavian Studies, 1993.
Waal, Carla. "The Norwegian Short Story." *Scandinavian Studies* 49 (1977): 217–23.

Herbjørg Wassmo

Isaacson, Lanae Hjortsvang. "Fantasy, Imagination, and Reality: Herbjørg Wasmo's *Huset med den blinde glassveranda*." *Scandinavica* 25 (1986): 177–89.
Norseng, Mary Kay. "A Child's Liberation of Space: Herbjørg Wassmo's *Huset med den blinde glassveranda*." *Scandinavian Studies* 58 (1986): 48–66.

Johan Sebastian Welhaven

Sjåvik, Jan. "Presence and Absence in J. S. Welhaven, 'Den Salige.' " *Scandinavian Studies* 65 (1993): 196–206.
Solberg, Olav. "The Ballad as an Expression of Norwegian Nationality in the Mid-Nineteenth Century." *Lore and Language* 12 (1994): 227–40.

Henrik Arnold Wergeland

Abrahamsen, Samuel. "Wergeland and Article 2 of the Norwegian Constitution." *Scandinavian Studies* 38 (1966): 102–23.
Myhren, Dagne Groven. "The Lasting Legacy of Norway's National Poet." *Scandinavian Review* 90, no. 3 (2003): 16–21.
Tysdahl, B. J. "Byron, Norway and Ibsen's Peer Gynt." *English Studies: A Journal of English Language and Literature* 56 (1975): 396–402.

SWEDEN

Bibliographic Resources

Holmbäck, Bure. "About Sweden, 1900–1963: A Bibliographical Outline." *Sweden Illustrated* 15 (1968): 5–94.
Josephson, Aksel G. S. *A List of Swedish Books, 1875–1925*. New York: Bonniers, 1927.
Nelson, Walter W. *A Bibliography of Scandinavian Literature between 1760–1820*. Lund, Sweden: n.p., 1988.
Suecana Extranea: Books on Sweden and Swedish Literature in Foreign Languages. Stockholm: Royal Library, 1963–2005.
Ørvig, Mary. *Children's Books in Sweden, 1945–1970: A Survey*. Vienna: Austrian Children's Book Club, 1973.

Literary History and Criticism

Algulin, Ingemar. *A History of Swedish Literature*. Stockholm: Swedish Institute, 1989.
———. *Contemporary Swedish Prose*. Stockholm: Swedish Institute, 1983.
Benson, Adolph B. *The Old Norse Element in Swedish Romanticism*. New York: Columbia University Press, 1914.
Bisztray, George. "Riksteatern: The Swedish National Provincial Theatre." *Educational Theatre Journal* 15 (1963): 39–46.
Borland, Harold. *Nietzsche's Influence on Swedish Literature, with Special Reference to Strindberg, Ola Hansson, Heidenstam, and Fröding*. Göteborg: Wettergren and Kerber, 1956.
Death, Sarah, and Helena Forsås-Scott, eds. *A Century of Swedish Narrative: Essays in Honor of Karin Petherick*. Norwich, U.K.: Norvik Press, 1994.
Englund, Claes, and Leif Janzon. *Theatre in Sweden*. Stockholm: Swedish Institute, 1997.
Florin, Magnus, Marianne Steinsaphir, and Magareta Sörensen. *Literature in Sweden*. Stockholm: Swedish Institute, 1997.
Forsås-Scott, Helena. *Swedish Women's Writing 1850–1995*. London: Athlone Press, 1997.
Gavel Adams, Ann-Charlotte, ed. *Twentieth-Century Swedish Writers after World War II*. Boston: Gale, 2002.
———. *Twentieth-Century Swedish Writers before World War II*. Boston: Gale, 2002.
Graves, Peter. "The Collective Novel in Sweden." *Scandinavica* 12 (1973): 113–27.

Gustafson, Alrik. *A History of Swedish Literature.* Minneapolis: University of Minnesota Press, 1961.
Hilleström, Gustaf. *Swedish Theater during Five Decades.* Stockholm: Swedish Institute, 1963.
Nolin, Bertil. "A Successful Realization of Group Theater in Sweden." *Scandinavian Studies* 43 (1971): 22–34.
Orton, Gavin. "The Swedish Novel Today." *Scandinavica* 15 (1976): 159–70.
Rosengren, Karl Erik. *Sociological Aspects of the Literary System.* Stockholm: Natur and Kultur, 1968.
Warme, Lars G., ed. *A History of Swedish Literature.* Lincoln: University of Nebraska Press, 1996.

Select Bibliography for Specific Writers

Lars Ahlin

Augustsson, Lars Åke. "Lars Ahlin: A Swedish Writer of European Stature." *Cambridge Quarterly* 9 (1979): 1–17.
Lundell, Torborg. *Lars Ahlin.* New York: Twayne, 1977.
———. "Lars Ahlin's Concept of Equality." *Scandinavian Studies* 47 (1975): 339–51.
———. "Lars Ahlin's Concept of the Writer as *Identificator* and *Förbedjare.*" *Scandinavica* 14 (1975): 27–35.
Printz-Påhlson, Göran. "Narrative Strategies in Lars Ahlin: Problems of Self-embedding and Self-reference in *Kvinna kvinna.*" In *A Century of Swedish Narrative: Essays in Honour of Karin Petherick*, ed. Sarah Death and Helena Forsås-Scott. Norwich, U.K.: Norvik Press, 1994.

Carl Jonas Love Almqvist

Blackwell, Marilyn Johns. *C. J. L. Almqvist and Romantic Irony.* Stockholm: Almqvist and Wiksell, 1983.
Hemming-Sjöberg, Axel. *A Poet's Tragedy: The Trial of C. J. L. Almqvist.* London: Allen and Unwin, 1932.
Romberg, Bertil. *Carl Jonas Love Almqvist.* Boston: Twayne, 1977.

Per Daniel Andreas Atterbom

Denman, Henrik. "Political or Cultural Scandinavianism?" *Scandinavica* 14 (1975): 17–26.

Carl Michael Bellman

Boer, Bertil van. "The Collaboration of Joseph Martin Kraus and Carl Michael Bellman." *Scandinavian Studies* 68 (1996): 461–72.
Britten Austin, Paul. *The Life and Songs of Carl Michael Bellman.* New York: American-Scandinavian Foundation, 1967.
Clover, Carol J. "Improvisation in Fredmans Epistlar." *Scandinavian Studies* 44 (1972): 310–35.
Larson, James L. "The Four Pastoral Epistles." *Scandinavian Studies* 44 (1972): 392–409.
Lönnroth, Lars. "Bacchi Tempel and Bellman's 'Poetic Enthusiasm.' " *Scandinavian Studies* 44 (1972): 410–38.
Massengale, James. *The Musical-Poetic Method of Carl Michael Bellman.* Uppsala: Almqvist and Wiksell, 1979.
———. "The Note That Was Worth a Ducat: The Search for the Source Melody to Bellman's Epistel 81." In *Fin(s) de Siècle in Scandinavian Perspective: Studies in Honor of Harald S. Naess,* ed. Faith Ingwersen and Mary Kay Norseng. Columbia, S.C.: Camden House, 1993.

Victoria Benedictsson

Bjørby, Pål. "Myth and Illusion: The Aesthetics of Self in Victoria Benedictsson's *Pengar.*" *Edda* 85 (1985): 209–29.
Borland, Harold. "Ernst Ahlgren, Novelist in Theory and Practice." *Scandinavica* 13 (1974): 97–106.
Moberg, Verne. "Motherhood as Reality for Victoria Benedictsson." *Edda* 84 (1984): 289–300.
———. "Truth against Syphilis: Victoria Benedictsson's Remedy for a Dreaded Disease." *Edda* 83 (1983): 31–44.
Thompson, Birgitta. "Folklore and Myth in Victoria Benedictsson's Story *Den Bergtagna.*" *Trivium* 28 (1993): 139–53.
———. "Three Sisters: Benedictsson's Selma and Marianne, and Strindberg's Miss Julie." *Swedish Book Review* 1–2 (1992): 24–29.
Wichmann, Sonia. "In Search of the Self: Authorship and Identity in Victoria Benedictsson's Diary *Stora boken.*" *Scandinavian Studies* 76 (2004): 137–54.

Hjalmer Bergman

Bock, Sigge. *Lowly Who Prevail: Vistas to the Work of Hjalmar Bergman.* Uppsala: Uppsala University, 1990.
Dahlbäck, Kerstin, and Janet Cole. "A Cacophony and Simple Melodies: Some Reflections on the Composition of Hjalmar Bergman's Novels." In *A Century of*

Swedish Narrative: Essays in Honour of Karin Petherick, ed. Sarah Death and Helena Forsås-Scott. Norwich, U.K.: Norvik Press, 1994.

Linder, Erik Hjalmar. *Hjalmar Bergman*. Boston: Twayne, 1975.

Meidal, Björn, and Frank Gabriel Perry. "Lotten Brenner, Indra's Daughter, Ugly Edith and Esther Borg: A Study of Hjalmar Bergman's novel *Lotten Brenners ferier*." In *A Century of Swedish Narrative: Essays in Honour of Karin Petherick*, ed. Sarah Death and Helena Forsås-Scott. Norwich, U.K.: Norvik Press, 1994.

Mishler, William E. "A Reading of Hjalmar Bergman's Story 'Konstapel William.'" *Scandinavica* 10 (1971): 33–41.

Petherick, Karin. *Hjalmar Bergman: Markurells i Wadköping*. Hull, U.K.: Orton and Holmes, 1976.

Sprinchorn, Evert. "Hjalmar Bergman." *Tulane Drama Review* 6, no. 2 (1961): 117–27.

Stevenson, Sarah. "Comedy and Tragedy in *Markurells i Wadköping*." *Edda* 74 (1974): 191–200.

Karin Boye

Forsås-Scott, Helena. "'Reading and Writing Our Tongue': The Examples of Elin Wägner and Karin Boye." *Women's Studies International Forum* 9, no. 4 (1986): 355–61.

Helgeson, Paulina. "Karin Boye: Posthumous Excuses." *Scandinavica* 40 (2001): 71–95.

Mortensen, Ellen. " 'All That Is Nameless and New:' Exploring Queer Paths in Karin Boye's Poetry." *Scandinavica* 40 (2001): 41–70.

Tegen, Gunhild. "Karin Boye in Memoriam." *American-Scandinavian Review* 30 (1942): 240–43.

Fredrika Bremer

Anderson, Carl L. "Fredrika Bermer's 'Spirit of the New World.' " *New England Quarterly* 38 (1965): 187–201.

Asmundsson, Doris R. "Fredrika Bremer: Sweden's First Feminist." In *Woman as Mediatrix: Essays on Nineteenth-Century Women Writers*, ed. Avriel H. Goldberger and Germaine Brée. Westport, Conn.: Greenwood Press, 1987.

Lofsvold, Laurel Ann. "Blaming the Messenger: Mary Howitt's Translation of Fredrika Bremer's *Hemmen i den Nya verlden*." *Scandinavica* 35 (1996): 213–31.

Lundgreen, Mette Domenic. "Sisters in the Shadow: The Link between Fredrika Bremer and Charlotte Brontë." *Angles on the English Speaking World* 7 (1993): 37–64.

Milow, Frederick, and Emily Nonnen, trans. *Life, Letters, and Posthumous Works of Fredrika Bremer.* New York: American-Scandinavian Foundation, 1976.
Rooth, Signe. *Fredrika Bremer and America: Her Literary Contacts and Social Impressions.* Chicago: University of Chicago Press, 1953.
Ryall, Anka. "Domesticating Geographical Exploration: Fredrika Bremer's American Travel Narrative." *American Studies in Scandinavia* 24, no. 1 (1992): 24–36.
Stendahl, Brita K. *The Education of a Self-Made Woman: Fredrika Bremer, 1801–1865.* Lewiston, N.Y.: Edwin Mellen Press, 1994.

Carina Burman

Death, Sarah. "Carina Burman." *Swedish Book Review* 1 (1998): 2–3.
———. "An Interview with Carina Burman, March 1998." *Swedish Book Review* 1 (1998): 4–6.

Stig Dagerman

Bergmann, S. A. "Blinded by Darkness: A Study of the Novels and Plays of Stig Dagerman." *Delta* 11 (1957): 16–31.
Lagercrantz, Olof. "Stig Dagerman Re-assessed." *Swedish Book Review* Supp. (1984): 8–10.
Thompson, Laurie. *Stig Dagerman.* Boston: Twayne, 1983.
———. *Stig Dagerman: Nattens lekar.* Hull, U.K.: University of Hull, 1975.
———. "Stig Dagerman's *Bränt barn* and *Ingen går fri.*" In *A Century of Swedish Narrative: Essays in Honour of Karin Petherick,* ed. Sarah Death and Helena Forsås-Scott. Norwich, U.K.: Norvik Press, 1994.
Törnqvist, Egil. "Heroes and Hero-Worship: On Stig Dagerman's *The Shadow of Mart.*" *Scandinavica* 32 (1993): 69–78.
———. "Stig Dagerman in the Netherlands." *Tijdschrift voor Skandinavistiek* 15 (1994): 55–59.

Olof von Dalin

Swanson, Alan. "Argus on the Stage: Dalin the Playwright." *Scandinavian Studies* 68 (1996): 401–14.
Massengale, James. "The Songs of Olof von Dalin." *Scandinavian Studies* 68 (1996): 415–60.

Sven Delblanc

Robinson, Michael. *Sven Delblanc: Åminne.* Hull, U.K.: University of Hull, 1981.
Sjöberg, Leif. "Delblanc's *Homunculus:* Some Magical Elements." *Germanic Review* 49 (1974): 105–24.

Vowles, Richard B. "Myth in Sweden: Sven Delblanc's *Homunculus*." *World Literature Today* 48 (1977): 20–25.

Wright, Rochelle. "Delblanc's *Kanaans land* and Moberg's Emigrant Tetralogy: Intertextuality and Transformation." *Scandinavian-Canadian Studies* 5 (1992): 81–93.

Gunnar Ekelöf

Fioretos, Aris. "Now and Absence in the Early Ekelöf." *Scandinavian Studies* 62 (1990): 319–30.

Oxenstierna, Elena V. " 'The Black Image—Framed in Silver Worn to Shreds by Kisses:'A Study of Byzantine Cultural Influences on Gunnar Ekelöf's Later Poetry."*Orbis Litterarum: International Review of Literary Studies* 58 (2003): 271–303.

Pettersson, Anders. "Gunnar Ekelöf, or 'the Night Comes.' " *Yearbook of Comparative and General Literature* 50 (2002–2003): 45–58.

Rossel, Sven Hakon. "Gunnar Ekelöf: Poet, Visionary, and Outsider." *World Literature Today* 64 (1990): 62–64.

Rukeyser, Muriel, and Leif Sjöberg, trans. *Selected Poems*. New York: Twayne, 1967.

Shideler, Ross P. "An Analysis of Gunnar Ekelöf's 'Röster under jorden.' " *Scandinavica* 9 (1970): 95–114.

———. "Rediscovering Ekelöf." *Scandinavian Studies* 66 (1994): 400–12.

———. *Voices under the Ground: Themes and Images in the Early Poetry of Gunnar Ekelöf*. Berkeley: University of California Press, 1973.

Sjöberg, Leif. *A Reader's Guide to Ekelöf's* A Mölna Elegy. New York: Twayne, 1973.

———. "Gunnar Ekelöf's 'Tag och skriv': A Reader's Commentary." *Scandinavian Studies* 35 (1963): 307–20.

———. "Two Quotations in Ekelöf's 'Absentia animi.' " *Germanic Review* 44 (1969): 45–60.

Thygesen, Erik. *Gunnar Ekelöf's Open-Form Poem:* A Mölna Elegy, *Problems of Genesis, Structure, and Influence*. Uppsala: Acta Universitatis Upsaliensis, 1985.

———, trans. *Modus vivendi: Selected Prose*. Norwich, U.K.: Norvik Press, 1996.

Vilhelm Ekelund

Johannesson, Erik O. "Vilhelm Ekelund: Modernism and the Aesthetics of the Aphorism." *Scandinavian Studies* 56 (1984): 213–34.

Kerstin Ekman

Ekman, Kerstin, and Linda Schenck. "On Translation and Being Translated." *World Literature Today* 77 (2003): 34–39.

Rugg, Linda Haverty. "Revenge of the Rats: The Cartesian Body in Kerstin Ekman's *Rövarna i Skuleskogen.*" *Scandinavian Studies* 70 (1998): 425–40.

Wright, Rochelle. "Approaches to History in the Works of Kerstin Ekman." *Scandinavian Studies* 63 (1991): 293–304.

———. "Kerstin Ekman: Voice of the Vulnerable." *World Literature Today* 55 (1981): 204–9.

———. "Kerstin Ekman's Crime Fiction and the 'Crime' of Fiction: *The Devil's Horn.*" *Scriptores rerus Sveciacarum* 2 (1984): 12–21.

———. "Textual Dialogue and the Humanistic Tradition: Kerstin Ekman's *Gör mig levande igen.*" *Scandinavian Studies* 72 (2000): 279–300.

———. "Theme, Imagery, and Narrative Perspective in Kerstin Ekman's *En stad av ljus.* *Scandinavian Studies* 59 (1987): 1–27.

Per Olov Enquist

Blackwell, Marilyn Johns. "Enquist's *Legionärerna:* A Plea for the Necessity of Fiction." *Scandinavica* 22 (1983): 129–40.

———. "Ideology and Specularity in Per Olov Enquist's *Tribadernas natt.*" *Scandinavian Studies* 67 (1995): 196–215.

Christensen, Peter G. "The Treatment of Mesmerism in Per Olov Enquist's *Magnetisörens femte vinter.*" *Scandinavian-Canadian Studies/Etudes Scandinaves au Canada*, 6 (1993): 27–46.

Nylander, Lars. "The Celestial Harp: Voices of Desire and Jouissance in Per Olov Enquist's *Downfall.*" *Literature and Psychology* 46, no. 3 (2000): 14–42.

Shideler, Ross. *Per Olov Enquist: A Critical Study.* Westport, Conn.: Greenwood Press, 1984.

———. "Per Olov Enquist's *Hess.*" *Scandinavica* 22 (1983): 5–14.

———. "Putting Together the Puzzle in Per Olov Enquist's *Sekonden.*" *Scandinavian Studies* 49 (1977): 311–29.

———. "The Swedish Short Story: Per Olov Enquist." *Scandinavian Studies* 49 (1977): 241–48.

Stecher-Hansen, Marianne. "Whose Hamsun? Author and Artifice: Knut Hamsun, Thorkild Hansen and Per Olov Enquist." *Edda* 99 (1999): 245–51.

Törnqvist, Egil. "Translating Docudrama: Per Olov Enquist's *Tribadernas natt* in English and French." *Tijdschrift voor Skandinavistiek* 19 (1998): 128–48.

Per Anders Fogelström

Brantly, Susan. "Testing the Boundary between History and Fiction: Per Anders Fogelström's Stockholm Series." *Scandinavian Studies* 65 (1993): 1–28.

Lars Forsell

Carlson, Harry G., trans. *Five Plays*. San Francisco: Literary Discoveries, 1964.
———. "Lars Forssell: Poet in the Theater." *Scandinavian Studies* 37 (1965): 31–57.
McKnight, Christina S. "Lars Forssell: The Jester as Conscience." *World Literature Today* 55 (1981): 210–15.

Jan Fridegård

Bjork, Robert E. "Medievalism in the Service of the Swedish Proletariat: Jan Fridegård's Viking Trilogy." *Studies in Medievalism* 8 (1996): 86–99.
Graves, Peter. *Jan Fridegård: Lars Hård*. Hull, U.K.: University of Hull, 1977.

Gustaf Fröding

Fleisher, Frederic. "Gustaf Fröding, 1860–1911." *American-Scandinavian Review* 42 (1954): 303–8.
Flygt, Sten G. "Gustaf Fröding's Conception of Eros." *Germanic Review* 25 (1950): 109–23.

Katarina Frostenson

Niewiarowska-Rasmussen, Ewa, and Neil Smith. "The Concept of Boundaries in Modern Swedish Poetry: Katarina Frostenson and Stig Larsson." *Scandinavica* 41 (2002): 61–76.

Jonas Gardell

Smith, Neil. "Jonas Gardell." *Swedish Book Review* 2 (1997): 16–17.

Maria Gripe

Mannheimer, Carin. "Maria Gripe." *Bookbird* 2 (1973): 24–34.

Lars Gustafsson

Dubois, Ia. "In Search on an Identity: The Heroic Quest in Lars Gustafsson's Fiction, 1960–1986." *Scandinaian Studies* 67 (1995): 163–80.

Fulton, Robin, trans. *Selected Poems.* New York: New Rivers, 1972.
Geddes, Tom. "Murder Mystery or Moral Philosophy? Lars Gustafsson's Judge." *Swedish Book Review* 1 (1996): 2–10.
Hertz-Ohmes, Peter. "The Public Lie, the Truth of Fiction, and Herr Gustafsson Himself." *Pacific Coast Philology* 17 (1982): 112–17.
Oscarson, Christopher. "Literary Castlings in Bernard Foys tredje rockad." *Scandinavian Studies* 72 (2000): 301–30.
Sandstroem, Yvonne L. "The Machine Theme in Some Poems by Lars Gustafsson." *Scandinavian Studies* 44 (1972): 210–23.
Weinstein, Arnold. "The Powers and the Self: Strindberg's Inferno and Gustafsson's *Tennisspelarna.*" *Scandinavian Studies* 59 (1987): 46–85.

Lars Gyllensten

Haack, Elizabeth G. "Semantic Detour: A Poststructuralist Study of Lars Gyllensten's Text *Senilia.*" *Proceedings of the Pacific Northwest Conference on Foreign Languages* 30 (1979): 119–21.
Isaksson, Hans. *Lars Gyllensten.* Boston: Twayne, 1978.
Orton, Gavin. "St Anthony in Värmland: Lars Gyllensten's *Grottan i öknen.*" *Scandinavica* 30 (1991): 41–62.
———. "A Swedenborgian Dream-Book: Lars Gyllensten's *Palatset i parken.*" *Scandinavica* 23 (1984): 5–23.
Sjöberg, Leif. "Lars Gyllensten: Scientist Turned Novelist." *World Literature Today* 55 (1981): 221–28.
Warme, Lars G. "Lars Gyllensten's *Diarium Spirituale:* The Creative Process as a Novel." *Scandinavica* 19 (1980): 165–80.

Verner von Heidenstam

Allnutt, A. A., trans. *Five Stories Selected from "The Karolines."* London: Harrap, 1922.
Brantly, Susan. "Heidenstam's *Karolinerna* and the Fin de Siècle." In *Fin(s) de Siècle in Scandinavian Perspective: Studies in Honor of Harald S. Naess,* ed. Faith Ingwersen and Mary Kay Norseng. Columbia, S.C.: Camden House, 1993.
Stork, C. W., trans. *Sweden's Laureate: Selected Poems.* New Haven: Yale University Press, 1919.

Ulla Isaksson

Wilson, Berit, and Sarah Death. "Contemporary Issues and Narrative Techniques in Ulla Isaksson's *Paradistorg.*" In *A Century of Swedish Narrative: Essays in*

Honour of Karin Petherick, ed. Sarah Death and Helena Forsås-Scott. Norwich, U.K.: Norvik Press, 1994.

Per Christian Jersild

Brantly, Susan. "P. C. Jersild's *Geniernas återkomst* and the Conventions of Historical Writing." In *Studies in German and Scandinavian History after 1500: A Festschrift for George C. Schoolfield*, ed. James A. Parente Jr. and Richard E. Schade. Columbia, S.C.: Camden House, 1993.

Shideler, Ross. "The Battle for the Self in P. C. Jersild's *En levande själ*." *Scandinavian Studies* 56 (1984): 256–71.

———. "Dehumanization and the Bureaucracy in Novels by P. C. Jersild." *Scandinavica* 23 (1984): 24–38.

———. "Jersild's Humpty-Dumpty Darwin." *Scandinavian Studies* 72 (2000): 261–78.

———. "P. C. Jersild's *Efter floden* and Human Value(s)." *Scandinavica* 27 (1988): 31–43.

———. "Identity, Vision, and P. C. Jersild." In *The I of the Beholder: A Prolegomenon to the Intercultural Study of Self*, ed. Steven Sondrup and J. Scott Miller. Provo, Utah: International Comparative Literature Association, 2002.

———. "Zola and the Problem of the Objective Narrator in Per Olov Enquist and Per Christian Jersild." In *Documentarism in Scandinavian Literature*, ed. Poul Houe and Sven Hakon Rossel. Amsterdam, Netherlands: Rodopi, 1997.

Eyvind Johnson

Blackwell, Marilyn Johns. "The Redemption of the Past: Narration as Moral Imperative in *Strändernas svall*." *Scandinavica* 25 (1986): 153–76.

Orton, Gavin. *Eyvind Johnson*. New York: Twayne, 1972.

Warme, Lars G. "Eyvind Johnson, Aldous Huxley, and the Devils of Loudon." *Selecta: Journal of the Pacific Northwest Council on Foreign Languages* 2 (1981): 103–6.

———. "Eyvind Johnson's *Några steg mot tystnaden*: An Apologia." *Scandinavian Studies* 49 (1977): 452–63.

Theodor Kallifatides

Norlen, Paul. "Theodor Kallifatides: An Introduction." *Swedish Book Review* 2 (1989): 20–24.

Erik Axel Karlfeldt

Fleisher, Frederic. "The Vagabond in the Life and Poetry of Erik Axel Karlfeldt." *Scandinavian Studies* 26 (1954): 25–27.
Hildeman, Karl-Ivar. "Erik Axel Karlfeldt: An Evaluation." *Scandinavian Studies* 40 (1968): 81–94.
Stork, C. W., trans. *Arcadia Borealis: Selected Poems*. Minneapolis: University of Minnesota Press, 1938.

Agnes von Krusenstjerna

Jones, Llewellyn. "Agnes von Krusenstjerna: A Swedish Poet." *Books Abroad* 23 (1949): 10–14.

Willy Kyrklund

Norlén, Paul. *"Textens villkor": A Study of Willy Kyrklund's Prose Fiction*. Stockholm: Almqvist and Wiksell, 1998.

Pär Lagerkvist

Beijer, Agne. "Two Swedish Dramatists: Pär Lagerkvist and Hjalmar Bergman." *World Theatre* 4 (1955): 14–24.
Benson, A. B. "Pär Lagerkvist: Nobel Laureate." *College English* 13 (1952): 417–24.
Brantly, Susan. "The Stylistic Legacy of Religious Literature in Pär Lagerkvist's Poetry." *Scandinavica* 22 (1983): 47–68.
Buckman, Thomas. "Pär Lagerkvist and the Swedish Theatre." *Tulane Drama Review* 6 (1961): 60–89.
Ellested, Everett M. "Pär Lagerkvist and Cubism: A Study of His Theory and Practice." *Scandinavian Studies* 45 (1973): 37–52.
Johannesson, Eric O. "Pär Lagerkvist and the Art of Rebellion." *Scandinavian Studies* 30 (1958): 19–29.
Linnér, Sven. "Pär Lagerkvist's 'The Eternal Smile' and *The Sybil*." *Scandinavian Studies* 37 (1965): 160–67.
Schwab, Gweneth B. "Herod and Barabbas: Lagerkvist and the Long Search." *Scandinavica* 20 (1981): 75–85.
Scobbie, Irene. *Pär Lagerkvist: Gäst hos verkligheten*. Hull, U.K.: University of Hull, 1974.
———. "The Origins and Development of Lagerkvist's *Barabbas*." *Scandinavian Studies* 55 (1983): 55–66.
Sjöberg, Leif. *Pär Lagerkvist*. New York: Columbia University Press, 1976.

Sondrup, Steven P. "Terms of Divergence: The Vocabularies of Pär Lagerkvist's *Ångest* and Artur Lundkvist's *Glöd*." *Scandinavian Studies* 58 (1986): 25–36.
Spector, Robert Donald. *Pär Lagerkvist*. New York: Twayne, 1973.
Swanson, Roy. "Evil and Love in Lagerkvist's Crucifixion Cycle." *Scandinavian Studies* 38 (1966): 302–17.
———. "Lagerkvist's Dwarf and the Redemption of Evil." *Discourse* 13 (1970): 192–211.
Weiss, Hanna Kalter. " 'Myten om Människorna': The Myth of Modern Man in Pär Lagerkvist's Novels." *Scandinavica* 26 (1987): 13–29.

Selma Lagerlöf

Afzelius, Nils. "The Scandalous Selma Lagerlöf." *Scandinavica* 5 (1966): 91–99.
Berendsohn, Walter. *Selma Lagerlöf: Her Life and Works*. London: Nicholson and Watson, 1931.
Delblanc, Sven. *Selma Lagerlöf*. Stockholm: Swedish Institute, 1986.
Edström, Vivi. *Selma Lagerlöf*. Boston: Twayne, 1984.
Forsås-Scott, Helena. "Beyond the Dead Body: Masculine Representation and the Feminine Project in Selma Lagerlöf's *Herr Arnes penningar*." *Scandinavica* 36 (1997): 217–38.
Graves, Peter. "Narrator, Theme and Covert Plot: A Reading of Selma Lagerlöf's *Löwensköldska ringen*." *Scandinavica* 36 (1997): 7–21.
Lagerroth, Erland. "The Narrative Art of Selma Lagerlöf: Two Problems." *Scandinavian Studies* 33 (1961): 10–17.
———. "Selma Lagerlöf Research 1900–1964: A Survey and an Orientation." *Scandinavian Studies* 37 (1965): 1–30.
Lagerroth, Ulla-Britta. "The Troll in Man: A Lagerlöf Motif." *Scandinavian Studies* 40 (1968): 51–60.
Nordlund, Anna. "Corpses, Curses, and Cannibalism: Containment and Excess in Selma Lagerlöf's *Bannlyst* and Its Reception." *Scandinavian Studies* 76 (2004): 181–204.
Nylander, Lars T. "Psychologism and the Novel: The Case of Selma Lagerlöf's *Gösta Berlings saga*." *Scandinavian Studies* 67 (1995): 407–33.
Setterwall, Monica. "Two Sides to an Ending in 'Herr Arnes penningar.' " *Scandinavian Studies* 55 (1983): 123–33.
Vrieze, F. S. de. *Fact and Fiction in the Autobiographical Works of Selma Lagerlöf*. Stockholm: Almqvist and Wiksell, 1958.

Anna Maria Lenngren

Nelson, Philip K, trans. *Anna Maria Lenngren, 1784–1817*. Stockholm: Imprime, 1984.

Swanson, Alan. "Anna Maria Malmstedt and the Swedish Musical Theatre." *Scandinavica* 36 (1997): 139–67.

Oscar Levertin

Murdock, Elinor E. "Oscar Levertin: Swedish Critic of French Realism." *Contemporary Literature* 5 (1953): 137–50.

Sara Lidman

Borland, Harold. "Sara Lidman, Novelist and Moralist." *Svensk litteraturtidskrift* 36 (1973): 27–34.
———. "Sara Lidman's Progress: A Critical Survey of Six Novels." *Scandinavian Studies* 39 (1967): 97–114.
Brantly, Susan C. "History as Resistance: The Swedish Historical Novel and Regional Identity." In *Literature as Resistance and Counter-Culture: Papers of the Nineteenth Study Conference of the International Association for Scandinavian Studies*, ed. András Masát and Peter Madl. Budapest: Hungarian Association for Scandinavan Studies, 1993.
Forsås-Scott, Helena. "In Defense of People and Forests: Sara Lidman's Recent Novels." *World Literature Today* 58 (1984): 4–9.
———. "Sara Lidman's *Järnkronan*: An Introduction." *Swedish Book Review* 1 (1990): 34–36.
Hale, Frederick. "The South African Immorality Act and Sara Lidman's *Jag och min son?*" *Tijdschrift voor Skandinavistiek* 21 (2000): 55–80.
Tchesnokova, Tatiana. "Sara Lidman and the Art of Narration in *The Tar Valley*." In *Documentarism in Scandinavian Literature*, ed. Poul Houe and Sven Hakon Rossel. Amsterdam, Netherlands: Rodopi, 1997.

Erik Lindegren

Ekner, Reidar. "The Artist as the Eye of a Needle." *Scandinavian Studies* 42 (1970): 1–13.
Volwes, Richard B. "Sweden's Modern Muse: Exploded Sonnets and Panic Poetry." *Kentucky Foreign Language Quarterly* 2 (1955): 132–40.

Astrid Lindgren

Edström, Vivi. *Astrid Lindgren: A Critical Study*. Stockholm: Raben and Sjögren, 2000.

Holmlund, Christine. "Pippi and Her Pals." *Cinema Journal* 42, no. 2 (2003): 3–24.
Huse, Nancy. "The Blank Mirror of Death: Protest as Self-Creation in Contemporary Fantasy." *Lion and the Unicorn: A Critical Journal of Children's Literature* 12 (1988): 28–43.
Lundqvist, Ulla. "The Child of the Century: The Phenomenon of Pippi Longstocking and Its Premises." *Lion and the Unicorn: A Critical Journal of Children's Literature* 13 (1989): 97–102.
Metcalf, Eva-Maria. *Astrid Lindgren*. New York: Twayne, 1995.
———. "Astrid Lindgren's *The Robber's Daughter*: A Twentieth-Century Fairy Tale." *Lion and the Unicorn: A Critical Journal of Children's Literature* 12 (1988): 151–64.
———. "Tall Tale and Spectacle in *Pippi Longstocking*." *Children's Literature Association Quarterly* 15 (1990): 130–35.
Phillips, Mark. "False Identities." *North Dakota Quarterly* 61 (1993): 108–12.
Russell, David L. "Pippi Longstocking and the Subversive Affirmation of Comedy." *Children's Literature in Education* 31 (2000): 167–77.

Torgny Lindgren

Geddes, Tom. "Torgny Lindgren." *Metamorphoses: Journal of the Five-College Seminar on Literary Translation* 8 (2000): 39–48.
Hinchliffe, Ian. "Torgny Lindgren." *Swedish Book Review* Supp. (1985): 5–12.

Ivar Lo-Johansson

Bjork, Robert E. "Ivar Lo-Johansson's *Statarna* and the Aesthetics of Social Consciousness." In *Studies in German and Scandinavian History after 1500: A Festschrift for George C. Schoolfield*, ed. James A. Parente Jr. and Richard E. Schade. Columbia, S.C.: Camden House, 1993.
Graves, Peter. "Ivar Lo-Johansson and the Passions." In *Proceedings of the Conference of Scandinavian Studies in Great Britain and Northern Ireland Held at the University of Surrey: April, 1983*, ed. Nigel Reeves. Surrey, U.K.: University of Surrey Press, 1985.
Wright, Rochelle. "The Author as (Counter)Cultural Advocate: Ivar Lo-Johansson and Working-Class Literature." In *Literature as Resistance and Counter-Culture: Papers of the Nineteenth Study Conference of the International Association for Scandinavian Studies*, ed. András Masát and Peter Madl. Budapest: Hungarian Association for Scandinavan Studies, 1993.
———. "Dream and Dream Imagery in Ivar Lo-Johansson's *Godnatt, jord*." *Scandinavian Studies* 64 (1992): 53–67.

———. "Ivar Lo-Johansson and the Autobiographical Narrative." *Swedish Book Review* Supp. (1991): 15–19.
———. "Meeting Ivar Lo." *Swedish Book Review* Supp. (1991): 5–9.

Kristina Lugn

Moberg, Verne. "On Kristina Lugn." *Metamorphoses: Journal of the Five-College Seminar on Literary Translation* 8 (2000): 71–83.

Artur Lundkvist

Eriksson, Magnus. "The Formation of an Artistic Identity: The Young Artur Lundkvist." *Scandinavian Studies* 66 (1994): 382–99.
Sjöberg, Leif. "An Interview with Artur Lundkvist." *Books Abroad* 50 (1976): 329–36.
Sondrup, Steven P. "Artur Lundkvist and Knowledge for Man's Sake." *World Literature Today* 55 (1981): 233–38.
Vowles, Richard. "From Pan to Panic: The Poetry of Artur Lundkvist." *New Mexico Quarterly* 22 (1952): 288–96.

Harry Martinson

Bergman, S. A. "Harry Martinson and Science." *Scandinavian Proceedings* 88 (1966): 99–120.
Green, Brita. "Foregrounding and Prominence: Finding Patterns in Harry Martinson's Poetry." *Scandinavica* 36 (1997): 43–57.
Johannesson, Eric O. "*Aniara*: Poetry and the Poet in the Modern World." *Scandinavian Studies* 32 (1960): 185–202.
Quist, Robert. "Spatial Forms as Metaphors in Blomdahl's *Aniara*." *Scandinavian Studies* 76 (2004): 71–86.
Steene, Birgitta. "The Role of the Mima: A Note on Martinson's *Aniara*." In *Scandinavian Studies: Essays Presented to Dr. Henry Goddard Leach on the Occasion of His Eighty-fifth Birthday*, ed. Carl F. Bayerschmidt and Erik J. Friis. Seattle: University of Washington Press, 1965.
Swanson, Alan. "*Aniara* as a Libretto." *Tijdschrift voor Skandinavistiek* 17 (1996): 71–82.

Moa Martinson

Wright, Rochelle. "The Martinsons and Literary History." *Scandinavian Studies* 64 (1992): 263–69.

Vilhelm Moberg

Alexis, Gerhard T. "Sweden to Minnesota: Vilhelm Moberg's Fictional Reconstruction." *American Quarterly* 18 (1966): 81–94.
Holmes, Philip. *Vilhelm Moberg*. Boston: Twayne, 1980.
Johnson, Walter. "Moberg's Emigrants and the Naturalistic Tradition." *Scandinavian Studies* 25 (1953): 134–46.
McKnight, Roger. "Hooch and Hymnals: Vilhelm Moberg Looks Twice at American Society." *Swedish-American Historical Quarterly* 39, no. 4 (1988): 101–21.
———. *Moberg's Emigrant Novels and the Journals of Andrew Peterson: A Study of Influence and Parallels*. New York: Arno Press, 1979.
———. "The New Columbus: Vilhelm Moberg Confronts American Society." *Scandinavian Studies* 64 (1992): 356–89.
Winther, Sophus K. "Moberg and a New Genre for the Emigrant Novel." *Scandinavian Studies* 34 (1962): 170–82.

Jan Myrdal

Graves, Peter. "The Myrdals: Parents and Children." *Swedish Book Review* 2 (1993): 17–28.

Hedvig Charlotta Nordenflycht

Pettersson, Isabell. "Interplay of Logos and Pathos in Young's Night Thoughts and Nordenflycht's Mourning Turtle-Dove." *Studies on Voltaire and the Eighteenth Century* 305 (1992): 1446–49.

Lars Norén

Anderman, Gunilla. "At the Crossroads: Narrative Technique in Lars Norén's Novels." In *A Century of Swedish Narrative: Essays in Honour of Karin Petherick*, ed. Sarah Death and Helena Forsås-Scott. Norwich, U.K.: Norvik Press, 1994.
Neuhauser, Lotta. "The Intoxication of Insight: Notes on Lars Norén." *Theater* 22 (1990–91): 89–92.
Nylander, Lars. "Literature in and out of Time: Temporality in Theory, Narrative, and Authorship." *Literature and Psychology* 47, no. 4 (2001): 1–37.
Törnqvist, Egil. "Playwright on Playwright: Per Olov Enquist's Strindberg and Lars Norén's O'Neill." In *Documentarism in Scandinavian Literature*, ed. Poul Houe and Sven Hakon Rossel. Amsterdam, Netherlands: Rodopi, 1997.
———. "Strindberg, O'Neill, Norén: A Swedish-American Triangle." *Eugene O'Neill Review* 15, no. 1 (1991): 64–78.

Agneta Pleijel

Thomson, Laurie. "Introducing Agneta Pleijel." *Swedish Book Review* 8 (1990): 2–4.

Hjalmar Söderberg

Butt, Wolfgang. *Hjalmar Söderberg: Martin Bircks ungdom.* Hull, U.K.: University of Hull, 1976.
Geddes, Tom. *Hjalmar Söderberg: Doktor Glas.* Hull, U.K.: University of Hull, 1975.
Jarvi, Raymond. "Hjalmar Söderberg on August Strindberg: The Perspective of a Theater Critic and the Influence of a Dramatist." *Scandinavian Studies* 68 (1996): 343–55.
Lofmark, Carl. *Hjalmar Söderberg: Historietter.* Hull, U.K.: University of Hull, 1977.
Merrill, Reed. "Ethical Murder and Doctor Glas." *Mosaic: A Journal for the Interdisciplinary Study of Literature* 12 (1979): 47–59.
Stork, C. W., trans. *Selected Short Stories.* Princeton, N.J.: Princeton University Press, 1935.

Göran Sonnevi

Hogue, Cynthia, et al., trans. *Göran Sonnevi: Poetry in Translation.* Göteborg: Swedish Books, 1982.
Lesser, Rika. "Voice; Landscape; Violence: Sonnevi into English in Helsinki." In *Translating Poetry: The Double Labyrinth*, ed. Daniel Weissbort. Iowa City: University of Iowa Press, 1989.

Erik Johan Stagnelius

Toepfer, Karl. "Orfeus and the Maenads: Two Modes of Ecstatic Discourse in Stagnelius's *Bacchanterna*." *Scandinavian Studies* 64 (1992): 26–52.

August Strindberg

Bellquist, John Eric. *Strindberg as a Modern Poet: A Critical and Comparative Study.* Berkeley: University of California Press, 1986.
Blackwell, Marilyn J., ed. *Strutures of Influence: A Comparative Approach to August Strindberg.* Festschrift to Professor Walter Johnson. Chapel Hill: University of North Carolina Press, 1981.

Carlson, Harry G. *Out of Inferno: Strindberg's Reawakening as an Artist.* Seattle: University of Washington Press, 1996.

———. *Strindberg and the Poetry of Myth.* Berkeley: University of California Press, 1982.

Dahlström, Carl. *Strindberg's Dramatic Expressionism.* Ann Arbor: University of Michigan Press, 1930.

Feuk, Douglas. *August Strindberg: Inferno Painting, Pictures of Paradise.* Hellerup, Denmark: Edition Bløndal, 1991.

Grant, Vernon W. *Great Abnormals: The Pathological Genius of Kafka, Van Gogh, Strindberg, and Poe.* New York: Hawthorne, 1968.

Johannesson, Eric O. *The Novels of August Strindberg.* Berkeley: University of California Press, 1963.

Johnson, Walter. *August Strindberg.* Boston: Twayne, 1978.

———. *Strindberg and the Historical Drama.* Seattle: University of Washington Press, 1963.

Kvam, Kela, ed. *Strindberg's Post-Inferno Plays.* Copenhagen: Munksgaard/Rosinante, 1994.

Lagercrantz, Olof. *August Strindberg.* New York: Farrar, Straus and Giroux, 1984.

Lamm, Martin. *August Strindberg.* New York: B. Blom, 1971.

Madsen, Børge Gedsø. *Strindberg's Naturalistic Theatre.* Seattle: University of Washington Press, 1962.

Meyer, Michael. *Strindberg: A Biography.* New York: Random House, 1985.

Robinson, Michael. *Strindberg and Autobiography.* Norwich, U.K.: Norvik Press, 1986.

———. *Studies in Strindberg.* Norwich, U.K.: Norvik Press, 1998.

———, ed. *Strindberg and Genre.* Norwich, U.K.: Norvik Press, 1991.

Robinson, Michael, and Sven H. Rossel, eds. *Strindberg and Expressionism.* Vienna: Praesens, 1999.

Sprinchorn, Evert. *Strindberg as Dramatist.* New Haven: Yale University Press, 1982.

Steene, Birgitta. *August Strindberg: An Introduction to His Major Works.* Stockholm: Almqvist and Wiksell International, 1982.

———, ed. *Strindberg and History.* Stockholm: Almqvist and Wiksell International, 1992.

Stockenström, Göran, ed. *Strindberg's Dramaturgy.* Minneapolis: University of Minnesota Press, 1988.

Törnqvist, Egil. *Strindbergian Drama: Themes and Structure.* Stockholm: Almqvist and Wiksell International, 1982.

Törnqvist, Egil, and Barry Jacobs. *Strindberg's Miss Julie: A Play and Its Transpositions.* Norwich, U.K.: Norvik Press, 1988.

Per Olof Sundman

Hinchcliffe, Ian. *Per Olof Sundman: Ingenjör Andrées luftfärd.* Hull, U.K.: University of Hull, 1982.

Houe, Poul. "Per Olof Sundman's Documentarism: Knowledgeable Representation of Unknowable Man." In *Documentarism in Scandinavian Literature*, ed. Poul Houe and Sven Hakon Rossel. Amsterdam, Netherlands: Rodopi, 1997.
Jenkins, David. "A Rugged Individual." *Sweden Now* 5, no. 5 (1971): 38–43.
McGregor, Rick. *Per Olof Sundman and the Icelandic Sagas: A Study of Narrative Method*. Göteborg: University of Göteborg, 1994.
———. "The Silence of Per Olof Sundman: A Swedish Novelist's Guilty Secret." *Swedish Book Review* 1 (1998): 25–31.
Sjöberg, Leif. "Per Olof Sundman: The Writer as a Reasonably Unbiased Observer." *Books Abroad* 47 (1973): 253–60.
Stendahl, Brita. "Per Olof Sundman on the Expedition of Truthtelling." *World Literature Today* 55 (1981): 250–56.
Warme, Lars G. *Per Olof Sundman, Writer of the North*. Westport, Conn.: Greenwood Press, 1984.
———. "Per Olof Sundman and the French New Novel: Influence or Coincidence?" *Scandinavian Studies* 50 (1978): 403–13.
———. "The Quests in the Works of Per Olof Sudman." *Proceedings of the Pacific Northwest Conference on Foreign Languages*, 28 (1977): 108–11.

Emanuel Swedenborg

Bergquist, Lars. *Emanuel Swedenborg*. Uppsala: Swedish Institute, 1986.
Brock, Erland, ed. *Swedenborg and His Influence*. Bryn Athyn, Pa.: Academy of the New Church, 1988.
Lindrot, Sten. *Emanuel Swedenborg*. Stockholm: Swedish Institute, 1952.

Esaias Tegnér

Bellquist, John Eric. "Tegnér's First Romantic Poem." *Scandinavica* 31 (1992): 5–20.
Böök, Fredrik. "Esaias Tegnér." *American-Scandinavian Review* 14 (1926): 653–59.
Harvey, Anne-Charlotte. "The First Swede in Worcester." *Swedish-American Historical Quarterly* 46, no. 1 (1995): 74–92.

Tomas Tranströmer

Bly, Robert. "Tomas Tranströmer and 'The Memory.'" *World Literature Today* 64 (1990): 570–73.
Bly, Robert, et al. *Selected Poems, 1954–1986*. New York: Ecco Press, 1987.

Fulton, Robin, trans. *Collected Poems.* Newcastle-upon-Tyne: Bloodaxe Books, 1987.
Rönnerstrand, Torsten. " 'The Frontier between Silence and What Can Be Articulated': On the Idea of Language in Tomas Tranströmer's Poetry." *Scandinavica* 29 (1990): 215–32.
Sellin, Eric. "Tomas Tranströmer and the Cosmic Image." *Scandinavian Studies* 43 (1971): 241–50.
Sjöberg, Leif. "The Poetry of Tomas Tranströmer. *American Scandinavian Review* 60 (1972): 37–42.
———. "Tomas Tranströmer, Traffiker in Miracles." *Books Abroad* 46 (1972): 44–48.
Söderberg, Lasse, and Sjöberg, Leif. "The Swedishness of Tomas Tranströmer." *World Literature Today* 64 (1990): 573–76.
Steene, Birgitta. "Vision and Reality in the Poetry of Tomas Tranströmer." *Scandinavian Studies* 37 (1965): 236–44.

Birgitta Trotzig

D'Heurle, Adma. "The Image of Woman in the Fiction of Birgitta Trotzig." *Scandinavian Studies* 55 (1983): 371–82.
———. "To See the Other: The Holy Quest of Birgitta Trotzig." *Cross Currents* 35, nos. 2–3 (1985): 257–73.
Sondrup, Steven P. "Birgitta Trotzig and the Language of Religious and Literary Experience." *Scandinavian Studies* 72 (2000): 331–43.

Göran Tunström

Petherick, Karin. "Göran Tunström." *Swedish Book Review* Supp. (1988): 2–7.
Tate, Joan. "How Would You Put It?" *Swedish Book Review* Supp. (1988): 38–40.

Elin Wägner

Death, Sarah. "The Sleeping Fury: Symbol and Metaphor in Elin Wägner's *Silverforsen.*" *Scandinavica* 24 (1985): 183–95.
Forsås-Scott, Helena. "The Revolution That Never Was: The Example of Elin Wägner." *European Legacy* 1 (1996): 914–19.
———. "The Voice of Elin Wägner: *Kvarteret Oron.*" In *Women's Voice in Literature and Society,* ed. Maggie Allison and Anne White. Bradford, U.K.: University of Bradford, 1992.
Merchant, Carolyn, and Abby Peterson. "Peace with the Earth: Women and the Swedish Environment." In *Earthcare: Women and the Environment,* ed. Carolyn Merchant. New York: Routledge, 1996.

About the Author

Jan Sjåvik (B.A. Brigham Young University; Ph.D. Harvard University) is an associate professor of Scandinavian studies at the University of Washington, Seattle, where he has been a faculty member since 1978. He is the author of *Arne Garborgs Kristiania-romaner: En beretterteknisk studie* (1985; Arne Garborg's Kristiania Novels: A Study in Narrative Technique), *Reading for the Truth: Rhetorical Constructions in Norwegian Fiction* (2004), and a large number of articles on Norwegian and other Scandinavian writers, including Knut Hamsun, Ole E. Rølvaag, Alfred Hauge, Dag Solstad, and Johan Sebastian Welhaven. He has written entries on Scandinavian writers for many reference works and regularly reviews books for *Scandinavian Studies* and *World Literature Today*. He also teaches and writes on critical theory.